THE HISTORY OF GAELIC FOOTBALL

EOGHAN CORRY

Gill & Macmillan

Gill & Macmillan Ltd
Hume Avenue, Park West, Dublin 12
with associated companies throughout the world
www.gillmacmillan.ie

First published in hard cover 2009
First published in paperback 2010
978 07171 4818 9

Index compiled by Cover to Cover
Typography design by Make Communication
Print origination by O'K Graphic Design, Dublin
Printed and bound by ScandBook AB, Sweden

The paper used in this book comes from the wood pulp of managed forests. For every tree felled, at least one tree is planted, thereby renewing natural resources.

A CIP catalogue record for this book is available from the British Library.

5 4 3 2 1

To the next Kildare team to win the All-Ireland
agus
I gcuimhne Aine Uí Chomhraí 1929–2009

CONTENTS

AUTHOR'S NOTE

The absence of a proper history of Gaelic football was one of the things that fascinated and disappointed me from a very early age when my love of reading crossed over with my love of sport. It was something I wanted to redress myself if nobody else did. The ambition to do so sent me to spend many, many hours, almost all the discretionary time I could muster, at the long tables of the National Library in Dublin and the Russell Library in Maynooth, poring over yellowing pages and wondering at the extraordinary descriptions I found there of long-forgotten exploits, scores, matches, disputes, opinions, heroes and villains.

A casual interest became a passion, almost an obsession, and my desire to share, to correct, to challenge, led me to retell some of this material and to muster others to do the same. When I wrote my first Gaelic football book in my teens, the shelf was short and the readership small.

Thankfully all that has changed. The shelf, or shelves, are longer and more treasure-laden, as writers, players, administrators and managers commit their thoughts and anecdotes, observations and analysis to print. As for myself, I continued to feel that the story of football is bigger, more complex and more intriguing than anything I or others had managed to convey. We owe it to the players who left us this legacy to retell the story of their achievements.

I have no doubt that today's Gaelic footballers are faster, fitter, stronger and better prepared than the ones who played in previous generations. In sports that can be measured, athletic performances have improved beyond anything that could have been predicted. Ronnie Delany's gold medal-winning performance in Melbourne in 1956 would not be fast enough to qualify him for the London Olympics in 2012. Maybe the same is true of footballers. Dick Fitzgerald, Paddy Kennedy or even Mick O'Connell might not be good enough to make a Kerry team nowadays, or tactically fitted to face a tough championship match against Tyrone.

But thankfully it doesn't work like that. The greats of many, many years ago remain great, and probably get greater as they pass on. This book is a tribute to all those who made life happy through good times and bad for generations of Irish sports followers.

INTRODUCTION

'The finest players are often sacrificed if they be placed under an incapable leader.'

DICK FITZGERALD, *How to Play Gaelic Football* (1914)

At the time of the GAA centenary in 1984, renowned film-maker Louis Marcus, who was once nominated for an Oscar, was searching for any footage that might help illustrate a documentary about the games he was making. The archive system at documentary-makers Pathé was not as sophisticated as he had hoped. But Louis had a lead; somebody had found a few lengths of footage in a drawer in New Ross.

The transfer process was difficult. Marcus and his team had to find a machine capable of transferring the ancient film on to something more readable. It disintegrated as they did so.

But when he sat back to watch the piece of film he had found, he had a surprise in store. The film was of Gaelic football all right, but it was very old. It had a throw-in instead of a sideline kick. The foggy group of players were kicking the ball along the ground, rather than attempting any fancy catching. A mascot was clearly shouting 'Up Kerry' for the camera. It didn't take long to figure out that this footage was from 1914, the All-Ireland final between Kerry and Wexford, and the oldest film footage in existence. And across the grainy distance of seven decades he was looking into the face of Dick Fitzgerald.

> 'If there are five pieces of advice I would dispense after my long years in management they are these: be your own person, always trust your instincts, take calculated chances, give your players confidence, and never select a player who is carrying an injury, no matter how good he is.'
>
> MICK O'DWYER, *Blessed and Obsessed* (2007)

Dick Fitzgerald wrote the first instructional book on Gaelic football in 1914. Much of his book was spent lauding the changes in the game and defending it against its opponents. Some of the points he made are still valid a hundred years later.

- The defence must be beaten before any score can be registered against them, and the defence is usually beaten by being drawn, as footballers say, or deceived by some ruse or other.
- We feel bound to maintain stoutly that the fielding of the ball should ever be recognised as an essential and most attractive feature of our game, and the rules which secure this attribute of Gaelic football should be allowed to stand in the Gaelic code.
- Gaelic football is what may be called a natural football game. There is no incentive in it towards rough play. One player can hamper or impede another in one way, and only one way, and that by means of the shoulder. Hence it is that severe tackling, rough handling and all forms of tripping are banned.
- True it is that there is a tendency on the part of the greatest exponents of the game to pick up the ball with the foot, transfer to the hands, and get in a long punt. If that excellent feat can be executed with great rapidity, we must admit that it is all that can be desired. But unfortunately there are occasions when a back has not time to stop or stoop to handle the ball. The ball must then be kicked as it runs, or the situation is lost.
- We do not count on the two midfield men for regular and defined combination, for they are supposed to have a roving commission. One bit of advice to the midfield men is not out of place or unnecessary. They should resist the tendency to play amongst their own backs when the latter appear to be sorely pressed. The backs should be allowed to do their own work, and interference with them by any of the eight forwards, the midfield men included, would be rather detrimental to a successful defence. The backs must be permitted to work out their own salvation.
- Occasions will occur when the centre forward, after passing the ball on to either scorer, may expect the latter to re-pass to himself. All this manoeuvring is feasible enough between competent men who know one another's play.
- It would appear desirable to look for good height and a fair amount of weight in the centre one of the three scorers.
- If notwithstanding the centre scorer be rather on the light side, he must have other compensating qualities. The Irish saying applies to this case: the man who is not strong needs to be cunning.
- The referee should be as active on the field as most of the players. He must make the players feel he will tolerate no serious breaches of the rules. At the same time he must not err on the side of severity by keeping his whistle blowing like a foghorn at sea. He must be prepared to temper justice with mercy, and overlook, therefore, accidental infringements of the rules.

- Consequently he should be a youngish man and physically fit to keep going from one end of the ground to the other. Our Irish temperament would appear to be more controllable in the hands of a referee who is familiar with members of the teams.

Dick's advice was not always heeded.

> 'Training must always be undertaken in a spirit of light-heartedness and freedom from worry.'
>
> DR EAMONN O'SULLIVAN

Dick Fitzgerald's slim volume was to serve a generation of footballers. Larry Stanley wrote a fascinating instructional manual for Gaelic footballers in the 1940s, but it was only distributed among Garda members. In effect, little changed between 1914, when Fitzgerald wrote his manual, and the 1950s. Kerry's trainer during those years, presiding over thirteen All-Ireland victories after 1924, was Dr Eamonn O'Sullivan, son of a champion athlete and captain of Kerry's first finalists in 1891, and a fourth placed hurdler in the 1932 Olympics.

The Doctor, as he was affectionately known in Kerry, preached that players should stick rigorously to their field positions, because 'close adherence to positioning by the forwards opens up play and gives more scope to each player for the development of scoring opportunities. What has been described as machine forward play is based entirely on positioning and is incapable of development when indiscriminate wandering to other sectors leads to bunching.'

Seán Murphy recalled the policy. 'Just as if you were driving a car, you're in a tight squeeze, you can't look left or right, you have to drive instinctively and get an instinctive feel for your position,' he told Joe Ó Muircheartaigh in the 2008 history of football in Kerry, *Princes of Pigskin.*

Dr Eamonn elaborated on a whole variety of basic skills: follow the centre line of the ball in catching and kicking; follow through a kick; never hesitate; clasp ball to the chest; pass only when necessary; cover opponent's kicks; hop the ball only to gain time; train on the weak foot. The programme that he introduced at full-time collective training sessions makes intriguing reading today. Evening training was out of the question because of the transport problems of the time, so employers were asked to release players to go into full-time training. It sounded suspiciously professional for an all-amateur game. Some counties adopted the practice for provincial finals. Kerry always waited until the All-Ireland final. (When they went into full-time training for the All-Ireland semi-final replay against Cavan in 1952, they were beaten.)

There they would live under the Dr Eamonn O'Sullivan military-like regime:

8.00 am Arise.
8.30 am All assemble for short walk before breakfast.
9.00 am Breakfast.
9.30 am Complete relaxation.
11.00 am All assemble at training ground for short lecture and field manoeuvre in togs.
1.30 pm Lunch.
3.30 pm Complete rest and relaxation after chief meal.
4.00 pm All assemble at training ground for short lecture and training exercise.
6.00 pm Evening meal.
6.30 pm Complete relaxation.
8.00 pm Walks, recreation etc.
10.30 pm Supper.
11.00 pm Retire.

By 1954 the idea was becoming outdated. Evening training was more viable. On purist, amateur grounds, training was abolished at the 1954 congress, and Kerry, surprisingly, lost the following All-Ireland final to Meath, some say as a result of the move. Four years later, Dr Eamonn produced a book, *The Art and Science of Gaelic Football*, but the game technique he had published was already becoming outdated.

The doctor was so inflexible that he did not believe in switching a left-hand midfielder for a right-side midfielder. When in 1962, one of the last finals in which all six forwards lined up with the midfielders for the throw-in, Kerry snatched a goal in the first minute, everyone in the Kerry backroom team was happy except one. According to the doctor, goalscorer Garry MacMahon should have stayed on his own side and Paudie Sheehy should have been in position to take the chance. When Tom Ashe scored a point for Kerry against Louth in the All-Ireland semi-final of 1953, Dr Eamonn upbraided him for leaving his area to score the point.

Veteran RTÉ commentator Micheál Ó Muircheartaigh recalls how O'Sullivan, a psychiatrist at St Brendan's in Killarney, acted as a sports psychologist before his time. He once congratulated Paudie Sheehy, then suspected of hanging on to the ball a little too long, on a goal he had scored. 'I didn't score it,' Paudie protested. 'But it was your pass that made it,' said the doctor, and went off to leave Paudie thinking about what he had said.

'Dr Eamonn's presence seemed to dominate the footballers,' the 1959 player of the year Seán Murphy recalls. 'He was bigger than the team itself: his demeanour, the way he stood, the confidence he exuded. He immersed the team in a psychological process. You felt he was going to win the match for us.'

Ó Muircheartaigh reflects that the doctor's rigorist positional game was based on the enormous confidence he had in the superiority of Kerry footballers. A truth, universally acknowledged among followers of the game in the south-west, is that a Kerry footballer will always be more skilful than an opponent. Skilful players need space in which to operate. Bunching was to be avoided at all costs. Kerry backs could kick downfield with the knowledge that the Kerry forward would beat his opponent every time if they had enough space. The doctor's theory served Kerry teams well. Lesser football mortals had to find something more flexible.

> 'It is not so very long ago, since the very knowledgeable people were shaking their heads and dishevelling their hair over what they pronounced the corpse of Kerry football. Kerry, they said, had paid the penalty for being too rigid and tradition bound. The game had passed them out. Failure to adapt to new ideas and new methods had found Kerry lagging behind. And while Down and Galway and others were dividing the spoils between them, the funeral of Kerry football was being well attended by those who could hardly catch and only kicked when no alternative appeared.'
>
> Programme article for All-Ireland final,
> possibly by BRENDAN MAC LUA, 1970

Doctor Eamonn's theories saw off many challengers. Kildare, using a hand passing game, were described as technically better than their opponents in several finals in which they were beaten by Kerry. When Antrim came south using a particularly fast version of the hand pass in 1946, Kerry solved that problem by tackling the man before he got the ball. It brought howls of derision and protest from the supporters at the game. They boohed the Kerry man who was sent off after one Antrim player became a victim of an assassination attempt when the ball was not in his vicinity at all. After the game, protests crowded in from people everywhere who loved the spectacle Antrim offered. The letters section of the *Evening Mail* was filled for weeks. 'Like Nuremberg', Joe Keohane described the condemnation. But Kerry had shown that old ways are best, and went on to win the 1946 All-Ireland while Antrim went back into obscurity.

Peter O'Reilly, who learned his football in St Canice's on the North Circular Road and played senior for Dublin before he was 18, tinkered with the traditional 3-3-2-3-3 positioning of players when he coached Dublin teams. In the 1954 Leinster final, full forward Kevin Heffernan strayed out of position, taking the highly reputed Meath full back Paddy O'Brien with him. Dublin scored five goals to put the All-Ireland champions out of the championship, and Heffernan contributed to three of the Dublin goals. Heffernan was not the first 'roving' full forward, but never had a legendary name in football been so completely outfoxed by a wandering forward.

Dublin were tipped to win the All-Ireland. The team that stopped them was Dr Eamonn's Kerry, playing football that was as traditional as ever. Tom Woulfe concluded afterwards: 'If Dublin had won in 1955, Gaelic football would have developed more rapidly.'

O'Reilly's football was fast and open. Mick O'Connell was among those who were impressed: 'It was no accident that some of the best games of the 1950s and early 60s were those in which the Dublin team was involved. Their attractive brand of combination football was almost totally constructive and they were never wont to adopt spoiling tactics to beat the other side. This was probably their undoing in not harvesting more championships, but it was certainly conducive to open, continuous football.' O'Connell ranked the 1959 semi-final between Dublin and Kerry as one of the fastest, most open and best to watch in his entire career.

By 1959 a new Down team, based on the Queen's University team of 1958 that had won the Sigerson Cup, won the Ulster championship in extraordinary style. Their tactic was to bear down on the player in possession and to leave players unmarked everywhere. In 1960 Down won the league and beat a stronger Cavan team in the Ulster final by breaking the ball in midfield rather than attempting to catch it. It involved bunching of the type that would have given Dr Eamonn nightmares. But it worked.

Lennon's 1963 *Coaching Gaelic Football for Champions* was the polar opposite of Doctor O'Sullivan, preaching interchangeability for full backs, speed to back up the forwards for half backs, a block system of midfielders arranging back-up for the breaking ball, a more roving role for midfielders, half forwards who are prepared to back-pass and help out defence, as well as range in on the opposition goal, and speedy full forwards with lots of free movement among the forwards but little or none among the backs. Joe Lennon wrote: 'The position of midfield is probably wrongly blamed more often than any other position on the field. There is a tendency to lay too much stress on the comparative influence of midfield play. Although strength in midfield is often the key to success, it is seldom acknowledged that the amount of good a midfielder does depends to a large extent on the play of the rest of the team.'

Lennon admitted that his ideas, which 'sounded original', were already being practised by the best players, even if subconsciously. He directed the first GAA national coaching course in 1964. Their opponents' response to the fluid Down game was predictable. The referee had to be escorted to the dressing room after both the 1961 and 1966 Ulster finals broke into fist fights, and the free-flowing football degenerated into pulling and dragging.

Kerry blamed their team, not their tactics, when they lost to Down in 1961 and 1968. Joe Lennon's remark in 1968 that Kerry tactics were 'ten years out of date' was a direct reference to Doctor Eamonn's 1958 book.

Ten years further on, Down colleague Seán O'Neill was to say that he 'did not think it was possible for a Gaelic team to arrive as fit as Kerry did for an All-Ireland final. They have brought an entirely new dimension to football.'

'The transformation of Kerry football in 1975 was as profound as anything that has ever happened in the history of the game in the county,' Mick O'Dwyer wrote in his 2007 biography, *Blessed and Obsessed*. 'Our style had changed from catch and kick to a new inclusive game where every player's individual skills were fitted into the pattern rather than the other way round.'

> 'At the very start, Tony O'Brien hit the side netting after a mix-up in the Kerry defence. Ironically it was the nearest Laois came to scoring.'
>
> *The Irish Times* report on Kerry's 6-11 to nil victory over Laois, 4 December 1978

The reintroduction of the hand pass in 1975 reinforced an emphasis on fitness that was to engulf the game in the 1970s. Dublin manager Kevin Heffernan introduced Brian Trimble and John Furlong into his football panel briefly in 1973, not because they could play football, but to set higher standards in the sprints for the squad. When this was achieved, they stopped coming to the sessions.

Coaching methods were being imported from abroad. Mickey Whelan studied sports science in the US. A trickle of players went to Strawberry Hill in London in the 1960s pursuing PE teaching careers, and eventually Thomond College in Limerick opened.

When 1970s Offaly manager Eugene McGee and Richie Connor paid a visit to Highbury in London to watch soccer club Arsenal train in 1976, they were astonished how little physical training was involved. Their physical training had been done in the month before the beginning of the season. During the season they were just tipping the ball around at training, maintaining freshness rather than fitness.

The idea of winter training pre-dated the Kerry and Dublin teams of the late 1970s, but their fitness levels were so far ahead of everyone else that they dominated the championship for two decades. Kerry won their six All-Ireland semi-finals against Connacht and Ulster opposition between 1975 and 1982 by 17, 16, 12, 22, 16 and 10 points. On 2 December 1978 Kerry beat Laois 6-11 to nil in a National League match.

Midfield had been imbued with almost mythic importance by Dr Eamonn and Dick Fitzgerald. Teams had set out to disrupt this with a deep-lying centre half forward, as with Dublin's Bill Casey in 1965, or a spare player, as with Kerry's Seamus Fitzgerald in a league match against Offaly in 1969. The third midfielder, used in November 1970 by Dublin in a National League match against Offaly, was used again by Dublin against Kerry in the 1984 All-Ireland final and became a staple of the 1980s.

By the end of the 1980s there were ladders in training sessions, and the backroom teams of inter-county football teams were growing to include dieticians, psychologists and chemists.

Meath manager Seán Boylan had been a pioneer of new training techniques. When he was suddenly elevated from hurling physio to football manager in 1983, he saw his role as 'getting the players fit to play at top level, realise you can't store fitness, realise it is something that has to be worked at and, if you do get injured, realise the effect that will have on your muscles.'

He brought his squad to the Hill of Tara for uphills and downhills, utilising its spiritual significance as well as its physical attributes. He trained his team on the beach at Bettystown, having learned that athletes can train in water, despite a variety of injuries.

In the spring of 1991, Seán Boylan had the team training in swimming pools at Navan and Gormanston, despite the fact that many of them could not swim, until the week before they played Dublin in what was to become a famous encounter in the first round of the Championship.

'We tried hard to keep everything fairly confidential. Imagine being beaten in the first round of the Championship and then revealing that you had been training in water. We could never face the people of Meath. I'd prefer to be running around a training field, thinking about Dublin, but this is one of those occasions when Seán asked us to trust him. So we thrashed in the water, up to our necks, for an hour', Liam Hayes wrote in his biography, *Out of Our Skins.*

> 'Before parting with the ball the winger should try—after having beaten one man already, let us suppose for possession—to draw another back away from the man to whom he intends passing the ball.'
>
> DICK FITZGERALD, *How to Play Gaelic Football* (1914)

The need for room to practise skills was as great for the players of 2004 as it was for Dick Fitzgerald's men in 1914 or Dr Eamonn's men in 1924. So was the need to speed up the game, a subject of debate in the 1980s as much as it had been at the convention of 1937 or of 1891.

The solution was found in the unlikeliest of places, Australia. Sustaining that improvement was the job left to the rule-makers. The Australian series of 1984 and 1986 showed the GAA it had a pedestrian game compared with its Australian counterpart. Two-thirds of the time the ball was out of play, being retrieved for line balls, frees and kick-outs. A group of football thinkers under former Dublin player Tony Hanahoe was asked to confront this problem during 1988. The breathtakingly simple solution was borrowed straight from the Australian game. Take all kick-outs, frees and sideline balls from the hands instead of from the ground. The hand pass was brought back after its eight-year sojourn under a new definition: 'Pass the ball with one or both hands provided that there is a definite striking action with the hands.' Another proposal allowing players on the run to scoop up the ball with one hand was eventually abandoned, as was the decision to use quarters rather than halves. The tackle remained a grim issue. The committee proposed that a side-to-side tackle should be delivered only by the hip or shoulder to the hip or shoulder. The Australian tackle was rejected because it is a common cause of injury in Australia and is responsible for the majority of frees in the game.

That would mean there were four legal ways to challenge the player in possession of the ball in Gaelic football: from the side with one foot on the ground; flicking the ball with the open hand when it is being bounced or toe-tapped; blocking down an intended kick or pass; and shadowing or shepherding an opponent to force him to stop, turn or move wide. The effect was immediate. The amount of time the ball was in play doubled. The new rules were eighteen months in operation when Dublin and Meath showed them off to their fullest extent in four Leinster Championship meetings in 1991.

Was it seven passes or eleven before the Kevin Foley goal that decided the series? The question reflects exactly what the impact of those Tony Hanahoe rule changes had on the game. You wouldn't know it, but it was two moves. The first had four passes, the second seven. Martin O'Connell to Mick Lyons to Matty McCabe to Liam Harnan to Colm O'Rourke. O'Rourke was fouled. In the old days this would have meant a stoppage of about a minute and a hefty downfield kick. Instead O'Rourke took a quick free to David Beggy, to Kevin Foley, to P. J. Gillic, to Tommy Dowd, to Colm O'Rourke, to Dowd again and to Kevin Foley for the goal.

The second most dramatic goal in Gaelic football history would not have happened under the rules that applied for 104 of the previous 106 years.

> 'We have always made a clear distinction between the man who is fleet of foot and the man, not necessarily over fast, who is ready to do what is to be done.'
>
> DICK FITZGERALD, *How to Play Gaelic Football* (1914)

As the game was speeding up and space was opening on every football field on the island, there were those who schemed to close it down again. The nineties and noughties were defined by matches that defined new limitations as well as the new heights of the game.

Alongside the epoch-making excitement of the 1991 series of matches between Dublin and Meath, something that showed the potential of Gaelic football for immersing itself in Irish popular culture, the 1994 Down v Derry match, which many regarded as the best ever, and the classic purist's All-Ireland final of 1998, were games where the stoppers triumphed, notably Meath's semi-final against Tyrone in 1996 and Tyrone's semi-final against Kerry in 2003.

Meath manager Seán Boylan denies accusations that his team were the originators of the blanket defence. 'It was not blanket defence. It was just being available. You had worked hard enough in winning the ball. There was no point raffling it. The intensity of the Dublin-Meath championship matches was ferocious. If Dublin won, that was fine. If Meath won, that was fine. Once it was over, it was over. It might not have been pretty for some people, but it was still admired by many others and it ultimately brought success.'

> 'Only recently I was talking to an old veteran who saw the first All-Ireland football final and although he witnessed most of the big games in the intervening years, he still holds that the smallest man of the 42 was the greatest player he has witnessed in any code.'
>
> SEAMUS Ó CEALLAIGH, *Limerick Leader*, 11 January 1954

Who was the best? Dick Fitzgerald glares out of that grainy 1914 footage, now safely ensconced on a loop in the GAA museum in Croke Park, and challenges us to answer.

Since Louis Marcus's discovery, more archive footage has come to light. But it is impossible to get a sense of the ability of the great players to impose themselves on games of the 1920s from flickering newsreel taken by a dizzy camera placed behind the Railway end goal.

We see John Joe Sheehy, tall and broad shouldered, leading his 1926 team into battle; Larry Stanley jumping to attention, dropping a shoulder and springing off towards the Canal end; and Paddy McDonnell towering above his O'Tooles team mates, a man without a care in the world. But only a handful of people survive who actually saw them play.

A greatest team of all time would be easiest to pick, but was the Kerry team deprived of five in a row by a late Seamus Darby goal in 1982 superior to the

Kerry team deprived of a five in a row by a late Vincent McGovern goal in 1933?

Memory serves certain players better than others. The middle-aged panels who sat down to pick the team of the century in 1984, and the team of the millennium (*sic*) in 1999, all picked similar types of players, those who had been at their peak when the selection panels were young and impressionable. Just one of the members of either team pre-dated the 1940s, Tommy Murphy from Laois.

Team of the millennium 1999:

	1. Dan O'Keefe (Kerry)	
2. Enda Colleran (Galway)	3. Joe Keohane (Kerry)	4. Seán Flanagan (Mayo)
5. Seán Murphy (Kerry)	6. John Joe O'Reilly (Cavan)	7. Martin O'Connell (Meath)
8. Mick O'Connell (Kerry)		9. Tommy Murphy (Laois)
10. Seán O'Neill (Down)	11. Seán Purcell (Galway)	12. Pat Spillane (Kerry)
13. Mikey Sheehy (Kerry)	14. Tom Langan (Mayo)	15. Kevin Heffernan (Dublin)

It showed just three changes from the team of the century selected in 1984:

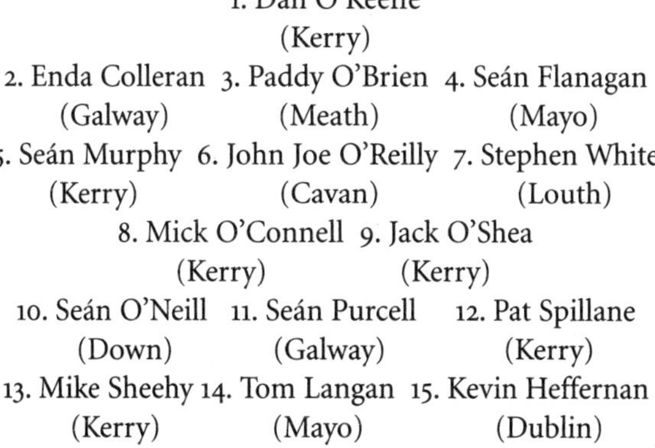

	1. Dan O'Keeffe (Kerry)	
2. Enda Colleran (Galway)	3. Paddy O'Brien (Meath)	4. Seán Flanagan (Mayo)
5. Seán Murphy (Kerry)	6. John Joe O'Reilly (Cavan)	7. Stephen White (Louth)
8. Mick O'Connell (Kerry)		9. Jack O'Shea (Kerry)
10. Seán O'Neill (Down)	11. Seán Purcell (Galway)	12. Pat Spillane (Kerry)
13. Mike Sheehy (Kerry)	14. Tom Langan (Mayo)	15. Kevin Heffernan (Dublin)

Pádraig Puirséil of the *Irish Press* selected the team of his lifetime in 1961. He selected four of the millennium team:

	1. Tom Bourke (Mayo)	
2. Jerome O'Shea (Kerry)	3. Joe Barrett (Kerry)	4. Seán Flanagan (Mayo)
5. Seán Murphy (Kerry)	6. Jack Higgins (Kildare)	7. John Joe O'Reilly (Cavan)
8. Padraig Kennedy (Kildare)		9. Tommy Murphy (Laois)
10. Phelim Murray (Roscommon)	11. Seán Purcell (Galway)	12. Paul Doyle (Kildare)
13. Paddy Moclair (Mayo)	14. Paddy McDonnell (Dublin)	15. Kevin Heffernan (Dublin)

The memory of Paddy Mehigan, known as 'Carbery' or 'Pato' in the various publications he wrote for, extended back to 1900 when he selected his all-time selection in 1945. His is probably the best guide to the great players of the early part of the century, and just two of them made a millennium or century selection, Dan O'Keeffe and John Joe O'Reilly.

	1. Dan O'Keeffe (Kerry)	
2. Maurice McCarthy (Kerry)	3. Joe Barrett (Kerry)	4. Pat Prendergast (Mayo)
5. John Joe O'Reilly (Cavan)	6. Jack Higgins (Kildare)	7. Joe Rafferty (Kildare)
8. Con Brosnan (Kerry)		9. Jack Carvin (Louth)
10. Pat Cocker Daly (Dublin)	11. Paddy Moclair (Mayo)	12. Larry Stanley (Kildare)
13. Bill Mackessy (Cork)	14. Dick Fitzgerald (Kerry)	15. John Joe Sheehy (Kerry)

Some of the stars of the century were overlooked by selectors of provincial teams in their own day. When *High Ball* magazine painstakingly went through the Railway Cup records and picked county teams based on the not exactly infallible basis of whichever player had played most in a particular position with his province, there was no shortage of disputes over the outcome. The chances were never going to be high of players like Malachi O'Brien, hero of the first All-Ireland championship in 1887, getting a fair comparison with Larry Stanley or Tommy Murphy, never mind Pat Spillane or Mick O'Connell.

So we are left with the classic sports follower's dilemma. Who to mention and what to leave out in our attempt to tell the story of Gaelic football.

When someone refers to the sport of 'football', (calcio, piłka nożna, Fútbol, Futebol, Voetbal, Fußball, fotboll, fotball, fotbal, fodbold, fótbolti, jalkapallo, beldroed, nogomet, foci) in most of the world, it is assumed they are referring to the Association game as derived from a meeting in a London public house in 1863.

There are few exceptions, but these are important. In New Zealand and South Africa, it is more usually Rugby Union; in Sydney, Rugby League; in the states of Victoria, Tasmania and Western Australia, it is assumed they mean Australian Rules; and in the United States and Canada it is American and Canadian football.

In Ireland it is Gaelic football, a game played by Irish ex-pats abroad, but still, 125 years after it was codified, rooted almost exclusively in its native place. Football is the game of choice in Ireland, with the largest attendances, the biggest aggregate TV audiences and the largest number of participants at every age group. Its roots in community life, especially in rural areas, may be unique among sports organisations everywhere.

The game, and its place in Irish life, is much mentioned by historians but little understood. Its history touches all the sporting staples, of heroes and mythology, exaggerated deeds and injustices, and the untold and forgotten little stories that made the big ones possible. It also helped shape the way Irish people have looked at the world, and nurtured and defined the ambitions of six generations of Irish sportsmen.

It is a good story.

Let us go back to the days when three large ball games battled for the cherished place of being the 'football' of Irish sporting culture. Let's start, as is the custom with sports fixtures, with the marching band and the pre-match build-up.

Chapter 1 ❧

1873–1903: THE BATTLE OF THE BALLS

Spring 1884. Tipperary v Waterford. No scoreline. No date. Little evidence

'The establishment of football in Ireland may now be reckoned as an established fact, and, so far from their being any sign of it giving way to some other pastime, the very reverse seems to be the case.'

The Irish Times, 24 October 1879

Three myths, three misses. A new way of playing football (we are told) was initiated in 1823 when William Webb Ellis, Tipperary-born son of a British army officer, picked up the ball and ran with it, defying the playground code at Rugby College in England.

Another type of football arrived in Ireland in 1869 when a Belfast merchant, John McAlery, saw Queen's Park playing soccer while on honeymoon in Scotland. He came home, started Cliftonville, and then founded the Irish Football Association.

A third type of football was ushered into being in 1884 at a rough and tumble match between Waterford and Tipperary, when champion athletes Maurice Davin and his brother Tom started a sideline discussion. 'You make rules for hurling, and I'll make them for football' went the conversation.

Foundation myths are important to sportsmen and all three have served their purpose. But they are all being consigned to mythology by recent research. Nowadays the semi-mythical Webb Ellis has rugby's World Cup named in his honour, but even when the story was invented for a dubious centenary in 1923, it had its doubters.

The business of codifying football, transforming a pastime into a sport, started 30 years later. The invention of the pneumatic bladder was still 40 years away.

Ireland's own football story started with the rugby code, when Trinity College rugby club was founded. It still claims to be the second oldest in the world after Guy's Hospital in London. But even then it is clear that these rules, framed in 1654, were not the same as those played at Rugby in England. While football was widely played throughout the country in the 1860s and 70s, it was not always rugby that was played.

By the time the Irish Football Union (after 1880 the IRFU) tried organising the existing clubs in 1873, there were far more clubs on the island than the 40 that were affiliated during the decade. Soccer was also played by at least three clubs before McAlery's honeymoon, which apparently wasn't even a honeymoon. Soccer's foundation myth emerged in the 1920s and was documented by Malcolm Brodie, the *Belfast Telegraph* soccer writer from the 1950s to the 80s. McAlery's contribution to history was in founding the Irish FA, but the impact of the sport he loved was a highly localised affair.

So to Gaelic, whose rules were drawn up, rather incongruously, by a former holder of the world record hammer throw, Maurice Davin, in December 1884 or January 1885, and presented to the third meeting of the fledgling Gaelic Athletic Association. The 'you make the rules for football' conversation was transformed from foundation myth to documented source by another world hammer throw record-holder James Mitchel. He was one of the GAA athletes who went to America with an 1888 fundraising exhibition tour, the 'invasion', and never returned. He became a sportswriter with the *New York Sun* and a source for the 1911 edition of the *Encyclopaedia Britannica*, including the entry on Gaelic games.

As foundation myths go, it has served football well.

24 JANUARY 1763: 'GOLF, HURLING, FOOTBALL AND WENCHING'

> 'A riot happened near Finglas bridge among a parcel of Fellows playing football, in which one of them had his skull fractured and his nose partly cut off.'
>
> *Slater's Public Gazetteer*, 21 April 1759

As recently as the 1980s the pedigree of football in Ireland could be traced along a neat linear storyline, a small and tidy litany of football references in calendar roles, legal cases and newspaper notices.

It has become clear since then that this list is just a tiny snapshot of the evidence that is there for the widespread playing of football on Sundays and holidays. An army of local historians have devoured newspaper files and are producing more newly discovered references with every summer school. Football was a game of the people, in the same sense and possibly across a greater geographical spread, than hurling was.

The first legal reference to football in the calendar rolls came from a legal case in 1308, where a bystander at a football match in *Novum Castrum de*

Leuan (the New Castle of Lyons). John McCorcan was charged with accidentally stabbing a player, William Bernard. A field near Newcastle, Co. Dublin, is still known as the football field.

A Statute of Galway in 1527 prohibited citizens 'at no time to use the hurling of the little ball with hockey sticks or staves but only the great football.'

The newspaper references are all of a similar type, giving notice of a prearranged venue and a time, an editorial of condemnation, an assizes report of an injury or affray (as in Dublin and Athlone in 1850) or a report of disorder or a raid by a military party, but truly useless in giving any indication of rules, winners or heroic performances.

For these we must turn to surviving poetry, of which there is also a considerable body. Séamus Dall Mac Cuarta wrote a football poem, 'Iomáin na Bóinne', about a match in Slane in the early 1700s. Matt Concanon described another on Oxmantown Green in 1720.

Travellers' descriptions are also useful, notably John Dunton's famous premonition of the 1983 All-Ireland final, when he found football in Fingal in 1699, noting that the citizens 'trip and shoulder very handsomely'. Eighty years later another traveller, Coquebert de Montbret from France, found football only in Leinster.

Where football was referred to in poetry or the press, it was assumed that readers needed no introduction to the rudiments of the game. Ideas, we are told in the vortex of constitutional debate in the 1780s, are 'tossed around like footballs'.

'Is there any day of the week that can cope with Sunday for all sorts of revelry throughout the nation' the *Freeman's Journal* asked on 24 January 1763, and then listed some familiar pursuits: 'for goff matches, football matches, hurling matches, wenching matches?' An 1838 proscribed list went 'hurling, communing, football playing, cudgels, wrestling'.

1731 BACHELORS V MARRIED MEN

> 'Birr—Last Monday there was the greatest match of Football that was ever seen in this Kingdom, between the married men and the Bachelors of this town.'
>
> *Pue's Occurrences*, 23 August 1746*

* The principal eighteenth-century references to football occur in *Dublin Courant* 23/7/1745, *Pue's Occurences* 23/8/1746, *Universal Advertiser* 19/3/1754, *Cork Evening Post* 3/7/1754, *Slater's Public Gazetteer* 21/4/1759, *Dublin Gazette* 28/4/1765, *Faulkner's Dublin Journal* 15/4/1765 and 12/2/1779, *Hibernian Journal* 30/4/1774, *The Observer* 26/2/1792.

In Dangan, Co. Meath, in 1731 and in Birr in 1746 the local bachelors played the married men. When the Liffey froze over in 1741, the citizens of Dublin played a football match on the ice. In 1754 a party of soldiers and constables were called to break up a football match in Baggot Street. The sheriff surprised a group of footballers on Oxmantown green later in 1754. The bakers played the brewers of Dublin in a football match on Royal Hospital lands in Kilmainham in April 1765, and another match took place in Milltown the same month. Contemporary newspapers objected to the 'profanity' of players who disregarded the establishment's strongly held views on how the Sabbath should be observed. Their indignant pronouncements were usually accompanied (in what must be admitted was an extremely hostile press) by reports of how the matches degenerated into drunken faction fights. A riot resulted from a match near Finglas bridge in 1759. A 'desperate quarrel' ensued from a match at Three Rock mountain above Rathfarnham in 1779. Soldiers quelled a riotous mob who assembled weekly to play football in Drumcondra in 1774, and eventually in 1792 in Timolin, Co. Kildare, 'A match at football between the villages in this neighbourhood has been attended with effects particularly distressing. The lads met on the green at Ballitore, from whence, when the sport was over, they, with many of the spectators, adjourned to this place in perfect good humour; but the demon of discord, whiskey, soon introduced a battle, in which all were engaged and almost all suffered.'

Wogan Browne of Clongoweswood was a magistrate for three counties when, in 1797, in the words of his friend Valentine Lawless, 'He was some Friday riding past a field where the country people were about to hold a football match. The whole assembly of course recognised and paid their respect. He got off his horse and opened the sports by giving the ball the first kick—a sort of friendly sanction of the amusements of their neighbours which was then not unusual among the gentry in Ireland.'

So far, this is not very different from the references to football that can be found throughout mainland Europe or England in the eighteenth century. What is of significance to us is what patterns emerge that lead us to Davin's game. One is the significance of the county team selection. Kildare played Meath for 'a piece of plate' in the eighteenth century, and Meath played Louth 'for a piece of plate and fifty sovereigns'. Kildare and Meath teams met at Maynooth in 1845.

There are also interesting questions from some researchers that the phrase, Iomáin, as applied to hurling in the romantic and heroic literature, might sometimes refer to football as well as hurling.

All of this gives us a clue as to how football became so widely played throughout the country, despite the vagueness of those 1885 rules. Football was clearly a familiar and widely played game in Ireland before the GAA. But for decades it had been in decline. The playing surface was a problem. Graziers were no longer happy to let footballers trample over their land. The Commons listed in those eighteenth-century newspaper accounts, Oxmantown, Crumlin, Lyons and Saggart, were enclosed one by one by Acts of Parliament in the 1810s and 20s.

It was going to require a greater state of organisation to organise the playing fields for a new generation of footballers. And like canal boats, not one but three football organisations came along at once.

> 'Irish football is a great game and worth going a long way to see when played on a fairly laid out ground and under proper rules. Many old people say just hurling exceeded it as a trial of men. I would not care to see either game now as the rules stand at present. I may say there are no rules and therefore those games are often dangerous.'
>
> MAURICE DAVIN, 13 October 1884

The man who invented football was an astonishing all-rounder, even for an age of sporting all-rounders.

What Irish football was he talking about? The Fenian papers mention allegations that football matches were used as a cover for military recruiting or training. One informer, Pierce Nagle, a teacher in Powerstown close to Clonmel, said he was at four such matches in 1863.

Dublin University's rules of 1854 were possibly the ones in use by the Munster football teams that sprang up in the 1860s and 70s and played against each other. The first newspaper report of a football match in Tipperary is a harvest home affair at Longorchard in the *Freeman's Journal* of 21 November 1856, while goalposts were specially erected at Coolarne, near Athenry, for a football match reported on 22 October 1866.

The first modern football notice advertised a Trinity College match in the *Dublin Daily Express* of 1 December 1855. *The Irish Times* carried its first proper match report, Trinity v Wanderers, in December 1860. Newspaper accounts of the spread of rugby, as in *The Irish Times* of October 1879, decry the lack of progress of the game in Munster. The writer may have been looking in the wrong place.

South Tipperary was, then as now, a stronghold of football in a hurling county. A Fenian informer, Pierce Nagle from Powerstown in Clonmel, said he had attended four football matches on Sunday afternoons after which military instructions were given by a man named Ryan.

The Kilruane Football Club, founded in 1876, recorded matches against Carrigatoher Cricket and Football Club, Killeen Football Club, the 53rd

Regiment of the British Army stationed at Nenagh, and the Nenagh Cricket Club. The club acquired two footballs and a 'Book of Football', so the rules were likely those for rugby. The Carrick-on-Suir Athletic, Cricket and Football club and the Killean Cricket and Football Club both followed in 1879.

Killarney, Valentia, Ballyhar, Firies and Killorglin had clubs. In Dingle, Seán Ó Dúbhda recalled that young people called the form of rugby they played in the 1870s 'the scrummage' and a match played there in 1884 was 'between rugby and Gaelic'. In Killorglin, Pat Begley told the folklore commission that later GAA champion captain J. P. O'Sullivan 'captained the rugby team'. Sullivan, whose son Eamonn was to attain fourth place at the 1932 Olympics and become the most famous team trainer in Kerry football history, started the club (according to Begley) after one rough-and-tumble match 'between Ballymac and Ballyvourney'.

26 APRIL 1874. KILLARNEY 10 COULES, POULNAMUCK 7 COULES, KILLARNEY

> 'Rugby was installed, with soccer on the way coming.'
>
> PAT BEGLEY describes football in Kerry in the 1870s

What rules were used? What shape was the ball? It is hard to tell. Intriguingly, Paddy Foley's book about Kerry football, *Kerry's Football Story*, published in 1944, refers to the fact that Australian football 'is played with the oval ball as was early Gaelic football'. But we get the best picture of immediate pre-GAA football in the Irish tradition from the five matches reported by the *Cork Examiner* in Killarney in April and May 1874 and again in March 1875. The Irish word cúl (goal) is the only type of score mentioned. The match of 26 April 1874 was reported as follows:

> **FOOT BALL AT KILLARNEY, SUNDAY**
>
> This match, which has been the general topic here during the past week, came off today. The Killarney team, not being quite pleased with the finish last Sunday, gave a second channel to Poulnamuck men, and both parties met at the usual place. Seldom have I seen a larger concourse of people meet in any ordinary sport.
>
> Immediately after second Mass crowds of people might be seen weaving their way in the direction of the field. Our Killarney young ladies were not backward in putting on an appearance and their presence on the field, no doubt, tended much to animate the highest efforts of several who took part in the game.
>
> The Poulnamuck men won the toss for points, which was much in their

favour as there was a strong breeze blowing, but it was settled at the outset to change the goals every half hour, so as to give each party a share of the wind.

The ball was thrown up at half past twelve amidst loud cheers. Although it was laid down that there should be no tripping, as on last Sunday, and that all should play fairly, friendly and good humouredly, yet during the first half hour's play there were some heavy spills which called forth cheers from both sides.

The Poulnamuck men succeeded in getting a few cooles whilst they played with the wind, but as soon as the half hour was up, and the Killarney men had the wind at their back, the scale was turned. The townspeople scored ten cooles against seven on the other side.

There was an amount of confusion throughout which made the game unpleasant and uninteresting at times. The field was very badly kept during the play and were it not for the united efforts of a few gentlemen who assisted in keeping the field clear, there would be no sport at all, as it was kept indeed, I cannot boast of the order maintained.

At three o'clock there was a general drop-off on both sides, with a hint to meet again at Muckross next Sunday when it would then be decided which were the better men. As far as this day's proceeding went, the Killarney men came off best.

Correspondent

1 NOVEMBER 1884. SEVEN MEN IN THURLES

'On the Irish side Thompson and St George McCarthy were the only men who played up towards the end, and we very much question if we are mistaken in the latter being the best back in Ireland.'

Freeman's Journal, report of Ireland v Wales, 30 January 1882

Not long before the GAA was founded, a large crowd of people assembled at Glen near Carrick-on-Suir in a field owned by Bob Hurley. It was by all accounts a rough and tumble affair. Davin may well have been there. The Mitchell conversation may have taken place.

With or without the sideline conversation, Davin's were the rules that were to prevail in Ireland and win the affection of the people. Davin attached his name to Michael Cusack's circular of 25 October 1884, calling for a Gaelic Athletic Association 'for the preservation and cultivation of National Pastimes, and to provide rational amusement for the Irish people during their leisure hours'.

The seven men who gathered in Thurles to found the GAA spent most of the meeting talking about athletics and the revival of Aonach Tailteann, but many of them had strong football credentials. Michael Cusack had played rugby with Phoenix. Cusack's past pupil and rugby team mate the Bansha born Police District Inspector Thomas St George McCarthy played rugby for Ireland against Wales in 1882. Journalist John McKay had reportedly played rugby with W. J. Goulding and G. K. Meyer's Cork Football Club. Maurice Davin had been an official and possibly a player with Carrick-on-Suir. It seems reasonable to assume the other founders, John Wyse Power from Waterford, Carrick-born solicitor P. J. O'Ryan and John K. Bracken, a stonemason who played cricket for Templemore, may also have been more familiar with football than hurling.

Gaelic football, as some have termed it after the parent association, has been the sport that has defined Irish sporting culture since, more so than the more heavily mythologised sport of hurling. Hurling remains trapped within a geographical footprint that has not changed over the centuries.

It seems reasonable to assume that the man who invented Gaelic football wasn't much of a footballer. Maurice Davin was one of the most respected sportsmen in the country when the GAA was founded in 1884. He had been on the committee of Carrick-on-Suir Rowing and Football Club, but it was rowing and athletics that grabbed the attention of the eldest of the Davin brothers. In fact, the Carrick-on-Suir Amateur Athletic Cricket and Football Club, which existed between 1879 and 1883, paid little attention to football of any type.

At a time when measuring athletic achievement was a relatively new endeavour, Davin had thrown the hammer further than anyone on the planet, 131 feet 6 inches, just over 40 metres, at Lansdowne Road on 5 June 1876.

It was first reported in 1913 that the seven foot (2.13 m) circle used in the Olympics was based on the threshing ring in Davin's barn in Carrick-on-Suir. English throwers used a nine foot circle until 1908; the GAA standard of seven feet was prevalent in the US after the invasion of 1888.

Davin drew up ten rules for the game which, according to Cusack, were adopted by the GAA on 17 January 1885.

- Teams were to have between 14 and 21 players
- Rules were enforced by two umpires and a referee, whose decision was final
- The ground was to be 120 x 80 yards
- Goalposts were to be 15 feet by 8 feet
- Captains were to toss for choice of ends and players hold hands, standing in two ranks until the ball was thrown
- Pushing, tripping or head-butting were grounds for a straight dismissal

- The match was to be of two halves duration of 30 minutes each
- The number of goals was to decide a game (points are not mentioned)
- If kicked over the sideline or endline by a defending player the ball was to be thrown by an opposition player; if kicked over the end line by an attacking player, a kick-out was to be awarded
- Players were to wear knee breeches and stockings without iron tips on their boots

And that was about it. We have no idea whether football was to be a carrying or a propulsion game, although propulsion is more likely. No mention of team positions was made, although goalkeepers were mentioned in terms of kick-outs. Rugby (or Dublin University) rules did not have goalkeepers. Association, or Scottish rules, did.

W. F. Mandle described the football rules as 'bordering on the farcical'. Davin's biographer Séamus Ó Riain replies that Davin's rules were fully vindicated when the rules were widely adopted in games throughout the country in 1886, and in the following year inter-club competitions and All-Ireland championships in hurling and football were played. 'Looked at from any perspective this was a remarkable achievement for the young association that was starting from a situation where scarcely any rules existed. The progress made in the space of a few years was in striking contrast to the decades required to reach acceptable codes for rugby and association football in England.'

There is no mention of offside, nor do the rules mention how long a player could handle the ball. The rules for hurling, which closely parallel those for football, say the ball may not be lifted off the ground with the hand. Only Rule 6 gives any clue of what was likely to happen when two teams tried to play under these rules. What was not mentioned there was presumably permissible.

Most problematically, the dimensions of a football field (120 x 80 yards) were different from a hurling field (200 x 150), and the length of a hurling match, 80 minutes, as against 60 for football, was also different.

On 6 October 1886 an ad appeared for William Lawrence's sports shop at 5–6 Upper Sackville Street in Dublin offering Association Footballs, Rugby Footballs and Gaelic Footballs. It was the first indication that a ball of a separate size was being used for Gaelic football.

The field size had changed by 1886 to 140 x 84 yards (hurling to 196 x 140), until both were standardised at between 140 x 84 and 196 x 140 in 1889. The soccer-style goals survived for just a year, when point posts were added on either side, and thus the scoring area remained until 1910. The throw-in from the sideline survived until 1946. All players were required to stand in the middle of the field for the throw-in until 1910. After that, the backs and goalkeepers were allowed to stay in position. Until 1965 the eight forwards and midfielders lined up for the throw-in. Teams were reduced to seventeen a side in 1892 and fifteen a side in 1913.

15 FEBRUARY 1885. SEVERAL SCORELESS DRAWS

> 'Next Sunday for the first time for a few years a match of football will be played under GAA rules in Naas, Sallins v Naas.'
>
> *Leinster Leader*, 14 February 1885

As the Suir water lapped by the Davin homestead in Tipperary, so the Liffey waters lapped by the homesteads of Straffan in Kildare. The tiny picturesque village is far enough from Dublin to retain its bucolic charm and close enough to feature in some of the political action of old Ireland. Many of the plots of Regency Ireland were hatched in nearby houses, Bishopscourt, four miles to the south-west and Castletown four miles to the north-east. Just 30 years had passed since the laying of the last of the 1798 Kildare rebels, Luke Doyle, near the rebellion's father figure Wolfe Tone at nearby Bodenstown. Kildare's grandees hunted over the rich plains of the county. Local rebels had stopped the hunt as part of the Land War effort. And in 1880, tiny Straffan had two cricket teams.

But now it had a new sport. Tom Cribben brought a football to the club, the first football in Co. Kildare, he was to claim in a letter written in 1934. The only problem was, there were no rules in February 1885. The game's rules were still in the process of being drafted in Tipperary. The men of Straffan were undeterred by this. They knew how football should be played. And it is reasonable to suppose they had been doing it for at least a generation.

Even before the rules were published, the first matches were played. Kilkenny played Bamford before the new rules were sanctioned, on 14 January. Whitegate played Bayanna on 29 January. Callan played Kilkenny Commercials and two town clubs, St Patrick's and St Canice's, met at St Canice's Park in Kilkenny town on 15 February. That same day the *Leinster Leader*, the newspaper of GAA founder John Wyse Power, advertised a match between Naas and Sallins. Also in Kildare, Straffan played Clane on St Patrick's Day.

While football spread slowly, athletics was the success story of the early GAA. The most famous phrase relating to the Association's early growth was penned by Cusack in his article in *The Nation* of Saturday, 12 October 1889: 'For sixteen months the association spread with the devastating rapidity of a prairie fire.'

Cusack's most astute move in 1884 was not in establishing the GAA (there had been eight previous attempts to set up a controlling body for Irish sport) but in grafting the GAA to the network of 1,200 National League clubs available to him in mid-1885. While much has been written, particularly by William Mandle, on the connections between the Irish Republican Brotherhood (IRB) and the early GAA, derived from a rich treasure trove of RIC files, the importance of the constitutional National League movement to the early GAA has been understated. It gave the Association instant access to a network of local community activists throughout Munster, Leinster and Connacht along a parish system that dated to Daniel O'Connell's time. The link was damaged by events in Tralee in June when the local MP supported the cricket club meet against the GAA rival. But the GAA retained the network until a political split over the leadership of Charles Stewart Parnell in 1891 clove the Association apart.

The appointment of Dr Croke as patron was, according to Cusack, 'with a view to disarming such of our clerical friends as might view with suspicion any movement likely in the remotest degree to violate the sanctity of the Sunday as it has to be observed by Catholics'. Cusack continued: 'His Grace's incomparable influence was calculated to be more than sufficient to suppress any abuses that were likely to arise or to creep in anywhere to the moral injury of the youth of Ireland. In Ireland every sound departure in which the masses of the people are concerned is to some extent necessarily political.' Hence the necessity that existed for the patronage of Mr Parnell and Mr Davitt. Mr William O'Brien's support was secured on 5 October 1884 as soon as the whole scheme had been explained to him.

'Subsequent events led to the infusion into the Association of those disintegrating agencies that burst up the Young Ireland Society in Dublin and whose dreary motto seems to be "rule or ruin". What the Archbishop called the "sinister influence" had been devastating the Gaelic fields of Ireland during the summer and autumn of that year, and it culminated on the 9th of November in Thurles.'

The prairie fire was extinguished by what Cusack's 1889 thoughts described as 'the virulent storm that has left an almost indelible stain on the mightiest athletic association that the world has seen for sixteen centuries.'

While athletics and what Cusack referred as to as the glories of Queen Tailte had been the focus of the GAA during prairie fire time, the action now moved from the track to the playing field.

7 FEBRUARY 1885. ENGLAND 2 TRIES, IRELAND 1 TRY, WHALLEY RANGE, MANCHESTER

> 'From a very loose scrimmage Payne picked up, as it appeared to us, offside, passed to Rotherham, who chucked to Bolton, who, being barely missed by Wheeler, got in close to the touch line.'
>
> *Belfast News Letter*, 9 February 1885

If not inspired by rugby, was Gaelic football a reaction to it? Cusack had been a rugby player and played with Phoenix club. Davin had been an official of Carrick club and likely played. Fellow GAA founder J. St George McCarthy had played for Ireland against Wales in 1882 (when eleven of the original selection unexpectedly cried off) and John McKay played at club level. The evidence is that the GAA founders had dabbled in the game and decided that it was incompatible with the native Irish game.

While Davin was at work, Cusack was at his fiery best, and one of the letters he sent in the direction of former colleagues, such as the three Christian brothers, the Dunlops and the two Dunbar brothers, mentioned that 'my opponents have favoured nothing but what an Englishman can beat an Irishman at. Rugby football has been played on many an international field, but Ireland has never yet scored against England. Therefore of course we are inferior to the English. I have not the smallest doubt but that we could beat them at our game of football, and no man will say that we could not sweep them off the field at a game of hurling.'

On 5 February, Maurice Davin followed with a letter of his own. 'Irish football is a fine manly game, yet it is never played in an international match. Ireland never beat England in an international football match. Rugby Union is the game played. It is practised all over England, and the Englishmen have a great number of players to pick from. In Ireland there are comparatively few players, so we cannot have a representative team at the Rugby game. It is not a game to be encouraged if we are to believe late accounts.' He cited reports of violence at matches in London, a Monkstown-Bective match on 24 January 1885 and an American description of rugby as 'brutal and demoralising'.

J. A. H. Christian replied that Ireland were indeed competitive, and had been beaten by a flukey try in the 1885 international at Manchester.

19 APRIL 1886. ASSOCIATION FOOTBALL AT CLONBYNANE, CASHEL. GOLDEN 2 POINTS, BALLYDINE ROVERS 5 MINOR POINTS, A DRAW

> 'Mr Pluck of Waterford said that if the body that sent him thought there was anything English in the rules of the Munster National Football

Association, it would cut off its hand before having anything to do with it.'

Freeman's Journal, 7 April 1886

Even Cusack was making no extravagant claims for the pedigree of his new game, which looked like adopted soccer to many. In one newspaper article he referred to the 'national game of hurling' and then added 'as well as football according to Gaelic rules'.

In Cork there were suspicions that some rugby clubs had changed their allegiance, but not their playing rules. In April 1885, Cusack declared that under Gaelic rules 'the ball must not be carried'. The rules that were in use in Cork city were branded as 'rugby undisguised' at a GAA meeting in October 1885.

On 26 February 1886 the new rules had been in use for a year without any further clarification, and the first serious signs of dissatisfaction with them were emerging. J. H. Murphy of Cork was removed from the vice presidency of the association because he had 'framed the so-called National Football Rules in opposition to the GAA'. Murphy's laws had a big following in Cork. On 7 March 1886 a meeting in the Foresters' Hall in Cork formed the Munster National Football Association, elected Murphy president and managed to get the allegiance of Lees, John McKay's club. Secretary of the new MNFA Jim Forrest declared: 'Gaelic rules might do very well for country clubs. But they are not suitable for clubs in the city. If a young man behind the counter received a black eye or scratch playing football under GAA rules it would be of more consequence to them than a player not employed in the city. He would be sent playing football for the other six days of the week.'

Almost certainly at Cusack's behest, another Cork group from Blarney, Riverstown and Little Island, met to disagree. Cusack attended and was not in conciliatory mood. These clubs wanted J. F. Murphy to talk to the GAA about the differences in the rules. The MNFA resolved not to play under rugby rules, although it was claimed by GAA personnel that 'opponents of the GAA were present at the meeting in the Foresters' Hall'. Maurice Davin advised the Cork footballers that they could play under the Munster rules and still be recognised by the GAA as athletes.

Cusack resisted. In a February 1886 issue of *United Ireland*, he vilified Murphy and 'the English League' he was running, playing 'the garrison game of rugby, characterised by collaring and carrying'. The GAA continued to claim at their special convention in Thurles in May that 'several clubs in the south are playing football under rugby rules'. Cusack defended his code, saying: 'This was intended to bring out the working man at such times as they were at liberty to go, and leave more respectable people to his colleagues.'

An American emigrant, Fr John Devane, recalled the heady mixture of chaos and brute force that 21-a-side football represented in his native Tralee:

> In those days positional play was not in vogue, as we know it today, except at the goal and point posts. Invariably therefore, Captain Jim Foley's instructions to his men before taking the field were brief and simple: 'Follie the ball, men,' he would say, and 'follie it' they did like Foley's beagles at a fox chase. This form of strategy suited Garrett Landers—the father of the three famous Landers brothers—to a nicety, because his plan of campaign was to throw himself in front of a bunch of players and bring down three or four at a time. Foxy Tom Connor was an adept, too, at bringing down the enemy in a cluster, but Tom, of rugged robust mould, did the execution with his robust shoulders, whereas Garrett was rather slight of build and had to depend more on brain than brawn. Another bone crusher was Denis Kelleher of the Killarney Dr Crokes, who in this fashion rendered great service to his team. In those days it was the practice to play the man oftener than the ball, and the bone crushing style of play was popular with the multitude when the home team was losing. In 1888 we saw Castleisland defeat Tralee in the Tralee Sports Field, but our sorrow was soon turned to joy when we asked one another: 'Did you see Foxy Tom throw three Castleisland fellows in a heap over the ropes with his shoulder?'

AUGUST 1886. WEXFORD GAA COUNTY FINAL: ROSSLARE 3 TRIES, CROSSABEG 2 TRIES

> 'If the people cannot learn how to conduct themselves the annual sports will become a thing of the past as it would be ridiculous to attempt to carry them out in such a bear garden as the spectators converged on yesterday.'
>
> *Freeman's Journal*, 5 August 1886

There was a bigger problem with Davin's rules. Nobody seemed able to score. Six matches at a Gaelic festival in Thurles in April produced just one goal from among them. In May, when Dunleary scored a goal against Grocers' Assistants, it may have been the only one all month.

On 14 June in Dublin, Maurice Davin, the author of the rules, was present at another scoreless hurling match. He suggested that Nenagh should be declared winners against Athenry because they 'had hit the ball over the crossbar, Galway having gained no point'.

There the phrase originated. Scores were soon being counted unofficially as 'overs', and a 4 July meeting suggested that 'going over the end line five times should count as a point'.

That 4 July meeting abolished wrestling, or handigrips, as contemporary reports liked to call it. 'Handigrips have always been much abused,' *Sport* declared. Dan Fraher spoke at a meeting in Waterford four days later complaining that the move was 'subversive to Gaelic rules', and that 'to abolish catching the man below the knee would be more suitable'. A letter to the *Freeman's Journal* on 12 July 1886 by Waterford GAA president W. J. Fisher suggested that the sudden move was a result solely of an ill-tempered match between two Tipperary teams, Kilcash and Moycarkey, and that the game was being made 'what it should never be made, an Anglo-Scotch game', and asked whether the 'Gaelic Athletic Association did not wish to see our national games revived, but that a substitute be provided in the shape of a conglomeration of Rugby, Association and Irish football, and foisted upon the country as a Gaelic sport.' Cusack too was dissatisfied, suggesting that they might as well ban the hand pass as well and 'then we have the Association game'. Kilkenny officials objected but conformed.

In August, the Wexford County Board arranged a county championship with the most remarkable scorelines in Gaelic history. Michael Duggan's Rosslare team beat Edward Pierce's Lady's Island by two tries to nil, William Wall's Ballymore by three tries to one and John McDonald's Crossabeg team by three tries to two after extra time to win the championship. It was not acknowledged in subsequent record books. Wexford's 'tries' were probably the same as the previous month's 'overs', scored by going over the end line.

When six Wexford teams played six Wicklow teams in the GAA's first 'great inter-county contest' on the lawn of the Parnell homestead in Avondale, winning four and drawing one of the matches, it was goals, points and forfeit points that were recorded.

1 OCTOBER 1886. WEXFORD TOWN 3 POINTS, WICKLOW TOWN 1 POINT

> 'This was the first [inter-county] contest under the auspices of the Gaelic Athletic Association, and the manner in which everything went off was a most unqualified success.'
>
> *Freeman's Journal*, 1 November 1886

Some of the distinctive features of the 1886 game still survive: the ball could not be lifted off the ground with the hands, but could be knocked on with the hand or arm, and could not be carried or thrown, but could be caught. A free kick had to be taken from the ground, not dropped from the hands (this appears to have been a major issue in Cork). All games were shortened from the occasional 80-minute match to a uniform one hour long.

The game was still cumbersome. Close rushed ground play with a phalanx of forwards trying to rush the ball in the opposite direction was still the sole tactic. The ball was heavy and not yet quite of spherical shape.

Local variations persisted, like the Australian-sounding game recalled in the 1940s by Sceilg on the Ring of Kerry:

> When one player fielded the ball, he stood back; and no member of the opposing team was permitted to approach beyond the mark thus made until the man in possession had kicked off. One was not allowed to catch from a hop, nor was lifting with the toe, except when it was done without bending the body. When a goal was scored, the teams changed sides. These rules remained in force until the arrival of school-teachers from Drumcondra, where Erin's Hopes team were one of the leading exponents of the newly evolved Gaelic rules in Dublin.

The differences between the GAA and Munster rules were brought down to a minimum. Founder member John McKay was still in an invidious position. In August, McKay resigned as Cork secretary, and in September he resigned from the vice presidency of the Association. By November Lees had re-embraced GAA rules.

On 10 October 1886 the concept of a point was defined further when a rule was made that point posts be erected 21 yards on each side of the goalposts. A trial period until 1 November met with great enthusiasm and the rules were altered for the third time in a six-month period. The trial period was due to end on the day of the most successful football tournament yet organised by the GAA. Wicklow and Wexford county boards got together to hold an inter-county contest, matching six clubs against six others in half-hour games that drew a crowd of 12,000 to Avondale. Parnell himself was in London, but his mother, his brother John and sister Emily attended. Mrs Parnell graciously supplied reporters with enlightened comments such as 'How they do run!'

It was a chaotic affair. The sidelines were so badly roped the crowds burst through them before play had commenced and the end lines were not roped at all, so the crowd filled the goals and end lines, which according to the *Freeman's Journal* 'rendered it difficult to decide in cases of scoring'. But the new rules had succeeded. A goal, fifteen points and three forfeit points were served up by the afternoon's contests. The days of the scoreless draw were over and spectators warmed to the idea of an inter-county contest. 'Previous to the union county contests in hurling were a regular occurrence, even inter-provincial ones occasionally,' Wexford man P. P. Sutton suggested in *Sport*. 'The future of the Association lies in inter-county competition.'

The GAA were happy to enshrine the county system, introduced by the Normans and regularised by King John in 1210. Saxon borders would prevail.

The irony did not go unnoticed and a short-lived newspaper, *The Gaelic Athlete*, called in 1912 for the abolition of the county system, formed by the hated British 'in varied sizes and most irregular and absurd shapes'. But by then the GAA was not going to throw out what had become a winning formula.

24 JULY 1887. LIMERICK 3-2, MEATH 0-2, ELM PARK

> 'I have now an army of athletes that would do honour to any county.'
> DAN H. RYAN, Limerick Commercials executive meeting, February 1885

Malachi O'Brien was 14 when Pat Hartigan, a family friend who worked in the Royal George Hotel in Limerick and had influence in the city, fixed him up with an apprenticeship.

He moved from his native Ballinvinna in Emly to work as a draper's assistant, cutting cloth in one of the best-known stores in the city, Cannock's of George Street. At Cannock's Malachi met fellow Tipperary man Dan H. Ryan and was recruited to his football team, Limerick Commercials. Drapers' hours were long. They worked six days a week, and although Limerick was in 1880 already regarded as a rugby city, the drapers affiliated their football club to the GAA for the opportunity to play football matches on their one free day, Sundays.

Malachi took to the game immediately, showing his kicking skills in challenges against Lees, Kilrush, Kimacduane, Bansha and others. 'A sunny faced, quiet, unassuming youth of medium size, with nothing great in his stature beyond that he is very well proportioned', he was loved by followers of the new sport.

After a match against Bohercrowe in Limerick Junction, where he was cheered off the field, he walked back to his native Ballinvinna, danced all night at a soirée in the family home and returned at daybreak to Cannock's in Limerick for work.

Events elsewhere were about to give Malachi and Limerick Commercials a unique place in history. When the GAA decided on its most ambitious project yet, to organise a championship for its 635 clubs, it needed to dream up a more efficient way of organising it. Emboldened by the success of the Wexford-Wicklow affair at Avondale, it decided to set up a network of county committees to put some order on its championship, delegating the locals to run local fixtures. It was to be the most important decision in GAA history.

The entry fee for the new championship was 2/6. It was arranged that clubs in a county would play out their ties first; the winner of the final would be entitled to represent the county. It was scheduled that the county championships would be run off between 1 February and 17 March, and that the All-Ireland final would take place in the last week in April or the first week in May.

Twelve counties entered the first All-Ireland football championships. The draws resulted in a new time-scale, which was also too ambitious. County teams were confined to the champion club of each county, with the inter-county draw as follows:

Wicklow v Clare, Athlone, Tuesday, 19 July
Kilkenny v Cork, Dungarvan, Sunday, 24 July
Louth v Waterford, Dublin, Sunday, 24 July
Galway v Wexford, Dublin, Sunday, 24 July
Meath v Limerick, Dublin, Sunday, 24 July
Tipperary v Dublin, Mountrath, Saturday, 30 July

Within weeks there were objections. Wicklow pulled out because 'While Galway, Waterford, Louth, Meath, Wexford and Limerick are accorded the privilege of playing at Elm Park Merrion … we must decline to ask any team to go to Athlone at this season for a match.' Dublin champions, teacher training team Erin's Hope, asked for a postponement because many of their players were on holiday. It also emerged that Galway were interested in fielding a team in the hurling championships only. Galway's football champions Kilbecanty protested, but the Galway County Board scarcely acknowledged them.

That left nine counties in the competition. But the championship was slow to get going. It was April 1888 before the 1887 championship was completed. Even then it was a bit of a miracle that the final took place at all.

At the start of 1887 the GAA had two official journals and an impending crisis between clergy-led and IRB-inspired officials. They also had a highly politicised central committee, all of whom were entitled to attend any county committee meeting. That meant that the GAA's executive, IRB men all, could overrule any local decisions with which they disagreed for the price of a few train tickets.

In June and September 1887 athletics meetings held by Grocers' Assistants and Freeman's Journal clubs were proscribed by the executive in a row over the handicapper for their sports (but which really related to the IRB question). November's convention in Thurles featured a one-hour pitched battle between the Fenians and Parnellites, with fists flying, catcalls and tables being overturned, before the clerical delegation eventually walked out. Croke intervened and in January 1888 a reconstruction convention put the priests and Parnellites back into office.

25 APRIL 1888. LIMERICK COMMERCIALS 1-4 AND NO FORFEITS, DUNDALK YOUNG IRELANDS 0-3 AND NO FORFEITS, CLONSKEAGH

> 'The Commercials began to press and the famous Malachi, getting possession of the ball, added the second goal to the Commercials' credit.'
>
> *Freeman's Journal*, 25 July 1887

When attention eventually turned to the playing fields, it was urban teams that dominated the first championships. The townspeople that Jim Forrest had talked about had started workplace clubs, often with the blessing of the employers. They were able to work out an approach to the new rules, and parkland such as the Mardyke, Market's Field or the Phoenix Park was easily accessible around large towns. And whereas rural clubs were strongest in athletics and hurling, urban clubs gained an early foothold in the football power struggle. Compared with Tipperary, who had 130 clubs in 1887, Dublin had just 40, less than Louth.

Commercials pre-dated the GAA, having played Limerick Butchers in a challenge in 1883, and in 1884 played Meelick and St Patrick's in well-supported matches on Limerick's canal fields. The driving force behind the club was Shannon Rowing Club oarsman Dan H. Ryan, a farmer's son from Park, Rossmore, Thurles, and an old boy of Jarlath's in Tuam. Commercials had an advantage over their urban rivals. At Limerick Market's Field, unlike the Phoenix Park, admission could be charged to the event. In 1886 a monster athletics sports organised by Commercials went on for three successive Sundays and raised £310.

When Dan H. Ryan was transferred to Dublin and set to work organising the Dublin drapery houses in the Kickham's club in 1887, Pat Treacy, although not a player, took over the captaincy.

Limerick had two county championships, split by the politics of the time and the attitude to football's big competitor in the city, rugby. In 1886 Dan H. Ryan had sided with the GAA against the Munster Association rules on the grounds that they were 'too like rugby'. A year later he stood by the old IRB board during the split of 1887, chaired by Paddy 'Twenty' O'Brien in opposition to the county board, chaired by a priest who was a brother of Nationalist MP David Sheehy.

Commercials' big city rivals, St Michael's, won the play-off arranged for Croom in front of a crowd of 5,000. The inter-county championship fixtures in Saturday's papers listed St Michael's as Limerick representatives, but it was Commercials who travelled to Dublin for the first round. In the meantime, St

Michael's found that five of their rugby-playing members were barred under the new 'foreign games' ban.

This was only the first round of the new championship, but the Commercials teenager was already a star. 'The famous Malachy, not yet seventeen', scored the second goal from midfield in Limerick's 3-2 to 0-2 victory over Dowdstown of Meath. A crowd of 10,000 gathered at Lord Ffrench's estate in Elm Park, and the star of the day was invited to tea with the host landowner afterwards.

According to Limerick GAA historian Séamus Ó Ceallaigh, he was chaired from the field by an opposing team after a match against Kilmacow in the next round, whom they beat 1-3 to 0-5 in a replay, Templemore of Tipperary by 1-8 to 0-4 in another replay, and Dundalk Young Irelands of Louth by 1-4 to 0-3 in the final. The referee at the first All-Ireland final, John Cullinane, later an MP, was just out of jail for his activities in the Land War.

Young Irelands' techniques of that first championship included 'dandling' the ball with one hand, hopping it and striking the ball with the forearm. According to the GAA's first historian, Thomas F. O'Sullivan, 'It was not unusual to see players sending the ball a distance of almost fifty yards by this fashion.'

'Hand-play punting of Dundalk was a credit to the side,' the *Freeman's Journal* reported, while 'fast, determined charging won the match for the Garryowen team.' It was William J. Spain, later to win a hurling medal with Dublin, who scored Limerick's winning goal eleven minutes into the second half of that first All-Ireland final. It came after a long, dribbling run almost from his own 21 yard line by McNamara, and a three-man hand passing movement. His goal changed the course of the game. Dundalk, having won the toss, played with the wind in the first half, led 0-3 to 0-1 at half-time, and had what looked like an inevitable goal saved. They objected, unsuccessfully, to William Spain afterwards, thus initiating another GAA tradition.

After the match the Commercials dispersed. When their medals were eventually presented 25 years later, many were dead or had emigrated. Some stayed in the drapery trade when they moved to places such as Dublin. Michael Slattery left for Australia; James Purcell went on to the Philippines; William J. Spain, Timothy Fitzgibbon, Richard O'Brien, Ned Casey and Denis Corbett all went to the United States.

Malachi O'Brien's career was short as it was spectacular. In 1890 he moved to work in Clery's in Dublin before leaving for New York. He returned to his native Ballinvinna in 1929, where he died in August 1953, and is buried in

Emly. His 1887 medal, sent to him in Bridgeport, Connecticut, and 'one of the surprises of my life after so many years', passed to his niece May Dundon of Knocklong and was purchased by the *Limerick Leader* newspaper in 1990.

He would have become the first footballer of the year, had there been such a thing at the time.

23 SEPTEMBER 1888. KILKENNY 1-4, WEXFORD 0-2, THE FIRST LEINSTER FINAL, NEW ROSS

> 'Both teams wore green and black, which was most disagreeable for the spectators, who found it very difficult to distinguish the players.'
>
> P. P. SUTTON, *Sport*, 9 June 1888

Given the success of 1887, the decision to abandon the championship of 1888 was unfortunate. Attendances at Leinster championship matches and the reported 12,000 at the final showed just how popular the new inter-county formula could become, with its intricate combination of parochial and territorial rivalries.

The championship started auspiciously in June. Special trains brought several thousand people up from Kildare for the first Leinster championship match played between Fiach McHughs, a team chosen from the 'French' College, Blackrock, representing Dublin, and Clane of Kildare. Both sides wore green and black which was described as 'very disagreeable for the spectators, who found it very difficult to distinguish the players'. Three of the best Clane players had emigrated since the Kildare championships, and Dublin won 1-6 to 0-1.

Wicklow champions Annacurra tested the notion of selected county teams five years before it was legal to do so, when they picked two players from Avoca and one each from Brittas and Aughrim to help them against Wexford. 'The Wexford lads were tidy, hardy, active kind of fellows, the kind of lads to be found around a town', Wexford native P. P. Sutton recorded in *Sport*, adding that the match became 'rough—vicious', and had to be abandoned after supporters stormed the field to join in a fracas. An Annacurra player, Kirwan, had to leave his clothes behind as he escaped the mob by climbing over a wall. The replay became the first match played at the site of the present Croke Park on Jones's Road, and the first to go into extra time before Wexford won by a point.

A crowd of 5,000 attended the Leinster semi-finals at Clonskeagh, where the brawny phalanx of men from Kilmacow, Co. Kilkenny, beat the hand pass experts Dundalk Young Irelands, and Wexford's hardy townies, the Blues and Whites, beat Blackrock College. The crowd was even bigger for the Leinster final at New Ross, the last match of the 1888 championship to be played. Kilkenny and Wexford were tied at 0-1 each at half-time and at 0-2 each with five minutes to go before Kilmacow scored a lucky breakthrough goal and followed up with two insurance points to win 1-4 to 0-2. Wexford objected that some of the Kilkenny players had been chosen from outside Kilmacow parish, but were unable to prove their case. According to Sutton, the Kilmacow men were 'brawny countrymen, magnificent kickers who possess a good turn of speed'.

Alas, that brought the championship to an end, depriving Kilkenny of the chance of what might have been their only All-Ireland football championship. The GAA embarked on an ill-fated athletics tour of America which landed it in debt for several years, leaving behind no administrators to organise the play-offs between Kilmacow, Ulster champions Inniskeen, and Bohercrowe of Tipperary.

Defending All-Ireland champions Limerick Commercials were beaten by Newmarket-on-Fergus in the first round of the new Munster championship, but Newmarket were then disqualified for the increasingly familiar complaint that they had fielded players from outside clubs.

Bohercrowe, one of five separate football teams based in Tipperary town, were scarcely a year in existence when they became surprise champions of Tipperary. They won the county semi-final against Grangemockler on an objection after losing on the field of play. They then surprised undefeated Fethard, for whom Dick Cummins had earned a reputation as possibly the finest footballer in the country, by four points to one in the Tipperary final.

Bohercrowe defeated GAA founder John McKay's highly rated Cork champions Lees in the Munster semi-final and were declared champions when Limerick Commercials failed to turn up for the final, cunningly fixed for a weekday in November when drapers might be expected to be going about their duties.

20 OCTOBER 1889. TIPPERARY 3-6, QUEEN'S COUNTY 0-0, INCHICORE

> 'No doubt the present championship was anything but a representative one.'
>
> *Freeman's Journal*, 22 October 1889

Another Munster footballer, Willie Ryan, was to emerge as the outstanding player of several championships in the 1890s after winning his first All-Ireland with the Bohercrowe team of 1889.

Since their surprise Munster championship in 1888, Bohercrowe had enhanced their reputation with what was effectively a national tour, playing

36 matches against teams such as Erin's Hope in Dublin and Drogheda Gaelics, the best known a fundraising match for the Oblate fathers' new church in Inchicore.

In the Munster championship they beat the Waterford champions Aglish-Ballinameela, got a walkover from Kildysart of Clare before they beat Midleton (champions of Cork 'under the old county board') 1-2 to 0-3 in a hectic 1889 Munster final. Midleton defeated J. P. O'Sullivan's Laune Rangers from Kerry on the same day as the final.

Just three of the ten Leinster counties bothered entering the championship, and a semi-final between non-existent Ulster and Connacht champions was advertised without the slightest chance of the matches taking place. Winning a Leinster title for Maryboro should not have been difficult, considering that only Louth, Dublin and Queen's County were affiliated at the time. Bray Emmetts, later to win an All-Ireland title representing Dublin, turned out as the Wicklow champions because they were the only Wicklow club which recognised the Central Council at the time, despite the fact that Annacurra and Valleyknockan were advertised to play in the Wicklow final a few weeks later.

When Bray beat Newtown Blues of Drogheda 1-7 to 1-4 on 15 September, they claimed they had won the 'final of Leinster' because Queen's County and Kilkenny had not shown up for semi-finals and a final that were to be played on the same day. Kilkenny club Kells said they failed to show for their semi-final against Louth because they were fixed to play in the local county final on the following weekend and wanted to train for that match. Nobody seemed to be in control of affairs at the venue to decide whether Louth and Wicklow were entitled to walkovers. Messengers were dispatched to seek out Central Council members while the teams played their 'Leinster final' anyway.

It took just four days for the result to be quashed and Bray to stop their celebrations, and Maryboro found themselves facing a new semi-final and final on 13 October. Despite having to beat Wicklow 0-9 to 0-4, while Drogheda had beaten Dublin six weeks earlier, if anything, Maryboro were fresher in the second match. Kildare opted out because a Maynooth man, Thomas Cullen, had died as a result of injuries sustained playing against eventual county champions, Mountrice club Wilfred Scawen Blunts.

The St Patrick's Field near the Oblate church on Inchicore Road was the venue for the All-Ireland final. The Oblate church had been largely funded by the proceeds of GAA matches on the ground. The present Tyrconnell Park housing estate was built on the site of the field.

In the final, Maryboro (for whom five Cushions were playing) beat Bohercrowe (with five Ryans on the team) in a 'wildly exciting game' by three points to two. It was played on an appalling day. The pitch was speckled with pools of water. *Sport* mourned: 'It must be designated the roughest match yet played at Inchicore' with 'too much tripping, catching and general fouling.' That complaint was to continue to punctuate GAA coverage for over a decade. Among the 3,000 spectators at the game were several police spies who gleefully reported on every incident of violence.

Bohercrowe had an easy task in what was advertised as the All-Ireland semi-final against Maryboro, but what was eventually recorded as the final. Bohercrowe kicked an early goal, led 1-5 to nil at half-time, and eventually won a tempestuous game 3-6 to nil. P. P. Sutton wrote that a fourth Tipperary goal was 'rightly disallowed', as the ball had crossed the line, and there were 'one or two scenes' as the 'match was characterised by entirely too much roughness'. Each altercation was accompanied by a crowd invasion.

The police were not the only ones to notice that IRB members were taking back the positions they had lost at the 1888 reconstruction convention. The clergy were actively campaigning against the GAA in many areas and the Association was practically wiped out in parts of Ulster, especially in Fermanagh and Monaghan. Priests in Newry, Enniskillen and Clones, and bishops in Clogher and Dromore, condemned the GAA from the pulpit. In Laois one priest demanded that a shopkeeper remove a notice advertising a GAA game, and then stood at a crossroads turning people away on their way to the match.

Bohercrowe were the most spectacular casualty of the political turbulence that followed. Joe Ryan, the club president, was of the IRB wing of the Association. The team trained on his land and Jack Frewen also gave fields for GAA purposes. The Land War saw many club members involved in the New Tipperary fight in 1891 and Willie Ryan was imprisoned. The Parnell split, in which Joe Ryan was fervently involved on the pro-Parnell side, eventually caused the club to break up in disarray in 1892. Willie Ryan was among the club members who returned to play with Arravale Rovers in 1893.

15 JUNE 1892. CORK 2-4, WEXFORD 0-1, CLONTURK PARK

'Confusion worse compounded.'

P. P. SUTTON's description of the arrangements for the 1890 All-Ireland final in *Sport*, 22 November 1890. The final was aborted and eventually played eighteen months later.

The 1890 championship started optimistically. Then shortly before the match was due to begin, the referee Dan Fraher discovered he had no ball. Nor had anyone else in the grounds. Someone was sent downtown to get one and it was seven o'clock before the game started, which meant that most of the

Wexford supporters missed the steamer back to New Ross.

The pitch was reduced in size to no more than 50 yards wide by advancing spectators, and crowds of them stood in front of the goalposts during the game. Due to a transport difficulty, Ballyhale from Kilkenny started with nineteen men instead of 21-a-side, when the original fixture was replayed in Dublin two months later, and withdrew complaining about roughness early in the game.

Blues and Whites from Wexford went on to beat Drogheda Davitts 0-3 to 0-2. The Leinster final was originally fixed for Avondale, scene of the successful exhibition matches that had been held in front of Charles Stewart Parnell's house in 1886. But the game was refixed at a late stage to a more accessible venue, the famous Clonturk Park.

Clonturk was first used as the venue for the 1890 athletics championships and went on to replace Inchicore and become the major GAA venue of the early 1890s. The venue for four football and four hurling All-Ireland finals, it was comfortable and accessible, situated in a natural hollow on the banks of the Tolka opposite where St Patrick's College is today, but soon it proved impossible to control access to the ground and gate receipts suffered. The housing estate now built on the site is called Clonturk Park.

Blues and Whites took a 1-3 to nil half-time lead against Ringsend-based Dublin champions Isles of the Sea and held out by the skin of their teeth to win 1-3 to 1-2. Isles of the Sea complained that the final whistle was blown four minutes early. The attendance was disappointing, mainly consisting of about 400 supporters who came by special train from Wexford.

Midleton won the Munster championship when team captain Jim Power, a noted sprinter from Ballywalter in north Cork, who later joined Lees in Cork city when he set up a drapery shop in Cork, scored a spectacular drop-kick point 'with his hands still on his hips'. John Langford had kicked the ball out from the ten yard line. A slight wind made the ball veer to where Power was standing 'in a white uniform with a white handkerchief around his neck'. Power prepared to catch but changed his mind when a Killorglin man got ahead of him, stepped back a pace or two, put each hand on a hip and met the ball with a drop-kick as it hit the ground to send it back to drop under the crossbar. As well as Power, Midleton had a flying winger with fine ball control, Ted 'Tit' Downey.

Their first attempt to play the Munster final against J. P. O'Sullivan's Killorglin ended prematurely when the ball burst three minutes from the end and a replacement could not be found, the Killorglin men 'having neglected to bring a ball'. Killorglin's Jer Hayes sat out the replay, hobbling along the sideline on crutches 'with his racing cards', after having his 'knee cap kicked off' in the drawn game.

The All-Ireland final was fixed rather hastily for Clonturk Park on 16 November 1890 at a special meeting of the Central Council the previous Monday at Limerick Junction. A vague notice arrived in Dublin about the events, two football semi-finals set for Sunday and both hurling and football finals, with an addendum that the four provinces would be sending teams. But rumours persisted that neither Connacht nor Ulster would show.

Ulster's first semi-finalists showed up all right. Armagh Harps emerged as one of the foremost clubs in Ulster during tournament matches in 1889, and there was not much surprise when they defeated Antrim 3-7 to 0-1 and Cookstown Owen Roe O'Neills 2-8 to 1-2 on the same day to win the provincial championship. Armagh Harps arrived at Amiens Street at 11.30 on Sunday morning with the William O'Brien's fife and drum band and 250 supporters. They did not manage to get past the half-way line, trailed 0-7 to nil at half-time and lost by 1-14 to nil, as two Cork men helped force the game's only goal entering the last quarter.

There followed a stand-off. Midleton captain Jim Power said he had been told the final would be played on Monday, so he kept his team overnight in Dublin. They togged out and claimed the match, secure in the knowledge that Wexford Blues and Whites had already gone home on Sunday night. They claimed the title, and as the GAA tore itself apart over the Parnell affair, the issue went unresolved. A replay was arranged for 13 March 1892 but was cancelled because of a fair in Midleton that day. Then in June 1892, eighteen months after the original fixture and after the conclusion of the 1891 championship, the final was played, and Midleton eventually beat Blues and Whites 2-4 to 0-1.

Wexford were short four of their team and missed a great goal chance as they fell 1-3 to 0-1 behind at half-time. Then came a stop-start second half: thirteen minutes of play, eight minutes seeking a substitute for an injured player, three minutes more play, seven minutes of delay as a Cork man was injured near the sideline. Three minutes later the first Wexford goal, then a second goal immediately afterwards.

Connacht didn't turn up, probably due to the incredibly inefficient organisation, roundly blamed on Mr Clery by P. P. Sutton, who declared that 'Sunday was more or less a failure.'

17 NOVEMBER 1890. CAPTAIN WILLIAM O'SHEA, WALKOVER, CHARLES STEWART PARNELL, SCRATCHED

> 'That this Convention is resolved to support the policy of independent opposition and freedom of opinion under the leadership of Mr Parnell.'
>
> GAA resolution, 27 November 1890

Just seven counties were represented at the 1890 GAA convention. There they learned that the Association was in debt to the tune of £1,000, largely as a result of Davin's athletics tour of the US in 1888.

Things were to get worse. Ten days before the convention, Captain O'Shea was granted a decree for divorce. Charles Stewart Parnell, named as co-respondent, was offering no defence. On 7 December, 44 of Parnell's Parliamentary Party seceded, leaving 28 Parnell supporters behind. The split throughout Irish society that ensued was to last for eighteen years. Most surprisingly, some of the people who were supporting Parnell against an increasingly more hostile clergy included many of the old IRB nationalists who had opposed him most vehemently three years before.

The GAA backed Parnell, the losing side in the electoral battle that ensued, and met the hostility of the clergy. Club numbers plummeted from 1,000 in 1888 to 220 in 1892. Only six counties were represented at the 1892 convention. Unfortunately, among those who turned against Parnell was its patron, T. W. Croke. Croke removed a bust of Parnell from his home and described the uncrowned king of a few months earlier as 'a moral leper, a measly pig in a litter who infects all the rest'.

In Sligo, priests were directed to infiltrate and undermine the Association. In Carlow, Louth and Tipperary it was opposed. In Laois, Kildare and Waterford it was boycotted. In Galway and Mayo it was pulpitted by the bishops of Ossory, Elphin, Achonry and Sligo.

Dublin fared better than rural areas as the GAA tore itself apart in the wake of the Parnell split. A quarter of the delegates at the 1890 convention were from Dublin, proclaiming undying support for Parnell. Clubs disbanded and broke up throughout the country. Even in Dublin attendances fell and teams played short.

28 FEBRUARY 1892. DUBLIN 2-1, CORK 1-9, CLONTURK PARK (2,000)

> 'Clondrohid sent the ball under the crossbar twice and the ball between the point posts seven times. However, one of the goals was disallowed by the referee.'
>
> *Freeman's Journal*, 29 February 1892

Dublin Young Irelands were developing a strategic 'catch and kick' style at practice sessions in the Phoenix Park, near the brewery where the team members all worked. They began their spectacularly successful run with their (and Dublin's) first All-Ireland in 1891.

Arrangements in Leinster were characteristically poor for the time. Kildare champions Mountrice would not play Moyanna of Queen's County because of 'the near approach of their sports', and Clane, nominated in their place, did not hear about the match in time. Moyanna would not take the walkover, so Mountrice were eventually enticed to play with the promise of a special train from Monasterevin. After beating Moyanna, Mountrice refused to play Young Irelands later the same afternoon and conceded a walkover.

The Ulster final at Bailieborough broke up in disarray because Armagh scored a goal after the referee had blown for a foul on one of their players. The referee decided not to give a decision on the incident until the next council meeting. In the replay Cavan Slashers had to erect the posts when they arrived for this final against Armagh Harps, using a rope as a crossbar, then scored 1-11 without reply to win the county's first championship. They were heavily beaten by Dublin Young Irelands in the semi-final 3-7 to 0-3. Young Irelands went on to play Cork club Clondrohid, who had beaten Kerry champions Ballymacelligott 2-5 to 0-2 and Waterford's Dungarvan 3-2 to 1-1 for the Munster title.

The All-Ireland final, fixed for 21 February 1892, was postponed for a week because of snow. When it was played, Clondrohid were declared the winners by 2-9 to 2-1. But their second goal was disallowed because a Cork man had picked the ball off the ground. This was not at all clear at the end of the match. Three hours after the game, the referee confirmed that he had disallowed Clondrohid's second goal.

Dublin won little sympathy with their tactic of lining the goal in the second half to prevent Cork denting their 2-1 to 0-2 half-time lead. At the time a goal outweighed any number of points, so Dublin were now the winners on the scoreline. The inevitable replay was ordered by the Central Council. Young Irelands were eventually awarded the title when Clondrohid refused to travel for a replay fixed for Thurles on 9 April 1893. The matter was further contested and another replay was ordered for 17 September 1894.

By that time Clondrohid had disbanded and, although they were probably never officially awarded the title, Dublin are recorded as the 1892 All-Ireland champions.

26 MARCH 1893. DUBLIN 1-4, KERRY 0-3, 1892 ALL-IRELAND FINAL, CLONTURK PARK

> 'The crowd encroached on the pitch when Kerry looked like scoring.'
>
> Complaint from Kerry representative after Killorglin Laune Rangers were beaten by Young Irelands in the All-Ireland final.

Five years into football history, the modified Davin rules were showing the strain. Few matches were being played on full-size pitches. Most 21-a-side games ended up as mud-wrestling bouts. Some counties (such as Kildare in 1892) had already taken the initiative and organised their championships with teams of sixteen-a-side. This enabled smaller clubs to field teams, but above all it helped clear some space on the playing field where a footballer could move without fear of disembowelment.

Clubs were persistently selecting players from outside their own area for inter-county matches. There was a growing lobby who proposed that the practice should be legalised. The argument for selected county teams was virtually sealed when one Kerry hurling club, Kilmoyley, disbanded specifically so that their best hurlers could join another club, Ballyduff, and win the All-Ireland championship in 1891.

The GAA had another reason to change the rules. They wanted to avoid a repeat of the fiasco of lining the goal that ruined the 1891 All-Ireland football final as a spectacle. As early as 1890 Kerry had suggested that a goal should be made equal to five points. So in January 1892 three important rule changes were made. Teams were reduced from 21-a-side to seventeen-a-side; the goal was made equal to three points; and champion clubs were allowed to select players from any club in their own county for inter-county games.

Matters off the field were not helping the football follower either. Matches were falling through in the aftermath of the Parnell split. The fiasco of the 1892 Leinster championship semi-finals and final, fixed for the same day on 12 March 1892, was a case in point.

The first semi-final went ahead when Young Irelands used their new catch-and-kick tactics to beat Kildare who, according to *Sport*, 'played genuine Gaelic football and unlike Dublin teams abhor catching'. But because the special train from Queen's County left six minutes early, their representatives, Maryboro, could only find six players for the second semi-final against Drogheda Emmetts of Louth. Referee J. P. Cox awarded the semi-final to Louth and asked them to play off against Dublin in the provincial final.

A short while later, a band of men arrived claiming to represent Queen's County and demanding a semi-final match against Louth. The referee stuck to his decision (the Queen's County secretary had also conceded the match) and said that a challenge match might be played. Louth protested that the Queen's County team was not genuine, and independent observers suggested that there were quite a few Dubliners in the newly recruited team.

The Queen's County 'recruits' took possession of the field and refused to leave until they were given a game, while spectators stood around in confused groups. Dublin too felt that Louth should play a match to even things out. 'Feeling ran pretty high,' it was reported and 'a couple of Queen's County players met with hostile demonstrations from sections of the Dublin supporters.'

Late in the day Dublin lined up. Whether Louth had gone home, or whether they had still not cleared the Queen's County recruits from the field is not clear. Dublin got the walkover and their place in the record books that they would almost certainly have won on the field of play.

Two weeks later Young Irelands were All-Ireland champions amid more acrimony. A bout of pugilism brought the All-Ireland semi-final to a premature end. Athlone T. P. O'Connors, who had represented Westmeath against Dublin in the 1890 Leinster championship and lost by 6-11 to 0-2, had reinvented themselves as Roscommon club and won the Connacht championship. This time they were beaten 1-8 to 1-0.

The match started late because 'some of the Athlone players had to attend Divine Service'. Athlone arrived with several bands and a large contingent of supporters, but soon after they had scored their first goal, a Dublin player hit one of their players off the ball and Athlone withdrew.

Cork's chances of a Munster title were scuttled by an extraordinary series of events in the local championship. Clondrohid's second team won the Cork county football championship, their first team having been beaten in the first round. Confusion over who was entitled to play for the club in the Munster final meant that some of the Clondrohid players did not travel to the game.

Kerry's Killorglin Laune Rangers won their first Munster title when they defeated Dan Fraher's kick-and-rush style Erin's Own club from Dungarvan and overcame an understrength Cork in the Munster final by 3-6 to 0-5.

Laune Rangers were children of the railway construction project between Killorglin and Caherciveen, where most of the footballers were employed. J. P. O'Sullivan was the paymaster. The Killorglin captain was retrospectively hailed as the father-figure of coaching in Kerry. He was a fluent Irish speaker and a dancer. His father accompanied the County Court judge on his circuit as his interpreter.

He won the all-round athletic event at the 1891 GAA championships (for which he was given a championship belt, boxing-style) and was a 120 yard champion hurdler and second in the long-kick championship. He spent most of 1892 training to defend his title, but pulled out of the event due to the death of his sister.

His free-taking was commemorated by later writers such as Paddy Foley. According to Foley, he never tried for a point, but always for a goal. When within range he placed the ball in front of the crossbar and let a forward charge by his men do the rest.

O'Sullivan brought his Laune Rangers north with a powerful reputation, but they ran up against an in form George Roche in the Young Irelands defence. According to the Cork newspapers, the Killorglin visitors found the field 'badly fenced off', and they were surrounded by a hostile mob, with no protection. But the Dublin newspapers said they had 'never seen a match pass off so quietly and orderly', although the usual 'knot of wall-climbers and street-urchins' took to boohing the referee when he awarded three frees in succession to Killorglin in the first half.

According to the *Kerry Sentinel*, the Dubliners 'hooted and groaned the Kerry men in the midst of play in a manner that was not alone discreditable to those guilty of it, but calculated to take the spirit and heart out of the Killorglin men which they did effectually'. In the end a defensive mistake let Dublin in for the winning goal with ten minutes to go, after Kerry had dominated the second half.

Laune Rangers lasted only as long as the construction project. J. P. played for Firies later on, keeping goal until he was 43 years old. He dropped dead leaving a coursing meeting in Cork. J. P.'s son Eamonn later became the Kerry coach for half of the twentieth century and the leading proponent of orthodox fixed-position football well into the 1960s.

24 JUNE 1894. WEXFORD 1-1, CORK 0-2, PHOENIX PARK

> 'North Cork Mili-tia, North Cork Mili-tia'
>
> Wexford supporters' chant at the 1893 All-Ireland final

Politics put a stop to Young Irelands' gallop. The great disquiet among the GAA grassroots at the pro-Parnell stand of the Central Council meant that Dublin did not defend their title, and just five counties entered the 1893 championship, three of these in Leinster. But just to be sure, another Young Irelands from Wexford town stayed on the field until full time before claiming victory against the reigning champions.

Young Irelands, trained by Watty Hanrahan and captained by Tom 'Skull' Hayes, trained three nights a week and, headed by Watty, they would do a road run of three to five miles. They ended up as the Leinster champions after an astonishing walk-off. The usual pattern in 1890s football was for the losing team to walk off, claiming some indignity or other. In the Leinster championship of 1893 it was the winning team that walked off, Kilkenny captain Dick Kealy taking his men off the field and refusing to continue, in protest at Wexford's 'rough tactics'—despite the fact that Kilkenny were leading by five points to one at the time. Kilkenny moaned that five of their players were injured at the time they withdrew, and the rock-hard pitch was not suitable to their style. In the tradition of the time, Kilkenny expected a walkover, but the match was awarded to Wexford instead.

Late in the first half the referee intervened two or three times as 'play got exceedingly warm', according to P. P. Sutton. This is the only time in GAA history that a winning team walked off the field. Wexford's other game was an easy 2-6 to 0-1 victory over Westmeath, who started the game two men short and scored first.

In Munster, north Cork club Dromtarriffe reached the All-Ireland final without having played a match. Cork and Kerry were fixed to play in the final three times, twice at Millstreet and eventually at Mallow, but Laune Rangers did not show up.

The 1893 All-Ireland final was shambolic, even by the standards of the time. Originally fixed alongside the hurling final for the Ashtown trotting grounds, it was transferred to the nearby Phoenix Park because the secretary had forgotten to get the grass cut. The match was eventually played after the hurling final at the Phoenix Park. Cork scored the first point after fifteen minutes of Wexford pressure. Wexford returned with a rushed goal forced from a high ball to go 1-1 to 0-1 ahead at half-time.

According to the reports at the time, a Cork player fouled a Wexford man and kicked him on the ground. The crowd, never ones in those days to restrain themselves from joining in, invaded the field to exact retribution from the Cork man. Cork, who were playing with what used to be called 'the incline', felt they had a good chance before the fracas. They were also becoming incensed at the chants of the Wexford supporters: 'North Cork Mili-tia, North Cork Mili-tia', a reference to the yeomen stationed in Wexford in the aftermath of the 1798 Rebellion. Wexford's Tommy O'Connor told John D. Hickey 60 years later that the spectators were at fault, not an altercation between the players. 'One of the onlookers rushed in to hit Paddy Curran, but a man who was obviously a Wexford supporter repaid the wallop. Up to the time the spectator hit Paddy it was a grand match altogether.'

The referee decided to send a player off from each side and tried to get the teams to resume with substitutes replacing some of the injured casualties of the riot. Wexford got into position, but when Cork did not reappear, the match was awarded against them.

Nick Lacey emerged as the leading forward of his time. Wexford goalkeeper Thomas Maloney-Redmond was one of the first players to turn the position into a specialist area of its own. Another Redmond, Thomas 'Hoy' Redmond, was the epitome of great ground play, a man who campaigned that the 'catching' tactics used by Young Irelands should be banned. Wexford Young Irelands, according to a 1953 account, played 108 matches and lost just three—to Kilmore and Volunteers in Wexford and their Dublin namesakes, Young Irelands.

21 APRIL 1895. CORK 1-2, DUBLIN 0-5 UNFINISHED, THURLES (10,000)

> 'No one can blame a schoolboy or a street urchin for climbing a wall to see a game, but it was truly galling and humiliating to see the number of respectable looking men who adopted this means.'
>
> P. P. SUTTON, *Sport*, 20 October 1894

The 1893 championship saw the first appearance in an All-Ireland final of Tom Irwin of the new pro-Parnellite club Redmonds, the outstanding Cork sportsman of his generation. Irwin won an 1892 All-Ireland hurling medal, played in three football finals, was one of the best cricketers in the country, was in line for an Irish rugby cap at one stage, and later served as the Cork county secretary for 21 years.

The following year Irwin switched his allegiance to Nils Desperandum, a team that spent most of the decade interpolating between rugby and Gaelic. In the 1894 county championship, their first and second teams met in the county semi-final. They went on to beat Tipperary twice.

Arravale Rovers of Tipperary (with many Bohercrowe players among them) successfully objected to an illegal Kerry team in the semi-final. Arravale then found three of the Kerry players they had met in the semi-final playing against them again in the 1894 Munster final. They objected again. A replay was ordered, and they lost by an even bigger score.

The two Young Irelands clubs from Dublin and Wexford met in the Leinster semi-final, an initial meeting on 12 August having fallen through because Wexford could not get a special train to Dublin. Dublin dished out one of the heaviest defeats ever to the reigning All-Ireland champions when they won 1-11 to nil in an unusually clean game, where the referee only had to intervene twice, 'the second time to issue a mild reprimand'.

The other semi-final was more rancorous. Kilkenny captain John Fitzgerald was bitter about his side's defeat, and wrote to the papers saying that he did not expect Meath to show and the team 'had to select substitutes from the sideline'.

When the Leinster final was played, the crowd at Clonturk Park was the biggest since Dublin v Tipperary in 1890, and proved once again that the days of Clonturk Park as a major GAA venue were coming to an end as officials ran out of patience with the gatecrashers, despite the orderly fashion in which the crowd was controlled, with 'nobody allowed to stand at the Richmond Road end of the ground'.

The All-Ireland final in Clonturk Park resulted in a draw, the finest game in the history of the championship till then. Cork's equalising goal was scored when the Dublin goalkeeper missed the ball completely, mainly due to having to play 'with a Corkman hanging around his neck'. In the exciting closing stages Cork had another goal disallowed and Dublin's Luke Kelly hit the post. Cork refused to play extra time, claiming that the referee 'had played 40 minutes instead of 30 in the second half'. Cork also argued that a Cork man had been struck by a Dublin man, thus starting the problem. The Central Council agreed with Dublin and ordered a second replay.

When the teams arrived in Thurles for the replay, they found two club teams ready to take the field, unaware that the All-Ireland was fixed for that day. A record crowd of 10,000 offered the GAA a preview of the days of mass support which were just a decade away. They were attracted by the prospect of another thriller like the last one.

The 13 stone Dick Curtis, six times Irish wrestling champion, scored an equalising goal for Dublin after he moved to the 'extreme forward position'. P. D. Mehigan quoted how Curtis was recalled with affection in later years: 'The longest hour was a holiday to him, when men were men.'

Dublin then withdrew because the crowd were not 'under control'. The *Freeman's Journal* would support this view: 'Order was very fair until the last ten or fifteen minutes when the throng in their enthusiasm broke in and as twelve of the Young Irelands [Dublin] players were assaulted by some Cork supporters and the feeling of the crowd getting somewhat heated, disorder then reigning supreme, the Young Irelands refused to continue.'

Dublin were awarded the All-Ireland title. Cork withdrew from the GAA in a sulk, a move that almost bankrupted the Association. The county board struck a special set of 'All-Ireland champions' medals for Nils, who spent the year playing in the unofficial Munster Sunday rugby competitions.

The number of clubs in Cork increased from 40 to 54. They took affiliations from Limerick and Waterford clubs, and it appeared at one stage that Cork might set up a rival association. Limerick man Pat Ryan, the Mallow town park committee, and eventually the Association's patron, Archbishop Croke, worked to bring Cork back into the fold.

15 MARCH 1896. TIPPERARY 0-4, MEATH 0-3, JONES'S ROAD

> 'The referee J. J. Kenny refereed the match to the entire satisfaction of all concerned.'
>
> *Freeman's Journal*, 16 March 1896

The Guinness brewery team, Young Irelands, were beaten by the Ringsend club, Isles of the Sea, in the 1895 Dublin championship, and John Kennedy lost his captaincy of Dublin.

Isles began the customary clear-out that characterised the days when the champion club had sole control of selection. This augured well for the prospects of Meath Navan O'Mahonys.

Navan were spearheaded by Dick Blake, the polemicist and GAA official who was the cause of much rancour in the GAA at the time, particularly his clashes with the Cork delegate Michael Dineen. Blake had played a leading role in the suspension of Nils, bringing about Cork's withdrawal from GAA affairs. He was also responsible for steering through a temporary reprieve on the ban on foreign sports, which was removed from GAA rule books from 1896 to 1906. He also felt that the game needed to be changed.

The seventeen-a-side formation of one full back, two quarter backs, five half backs, two wing men and nine forwards caused a continuous scrimmage that moved backwards and forwards along the field. Blake felt that the formation should be broken into clear lines with more space for players to move. Too much importance was still attached to a goal. Blake masterminded the rule changes of February 1896:

- Goal to be made equal to three points.
- Scores direct from a sideline throw to be banned.
- Opposing players to be required to be outside the 21 yard line for kick-outs.
- Players to remain in their own half of the field while the ball is being kicked out from their own goal.
- The 40 yard kick (later the 50) to be awarded when a player sends the ball over his own end line, taken from opposite where the ball crossed the line.
- A goal stopped by a bystander to be allowed if the referee adjudges that the ball would have crossed the line otherwise.
- A player who gets bottled up to concede a hopped ball.
- The goalposts to be 21 feet wide, the crossbar 8 feet high, and the point posts 21 yards on either side of the (still soccer-style) goals.
- Dress to be defined as knee-breeches, stockings and boots.
- Nails and iron tips on boots to be banned.

The 1895 championships were already under way when the rules were decided upon. Cavan made their first and only Leinster championship appearance that year in a handsome rig-out of pink knicks and white jerseys. Cavan, who could find no opposition in Ulster at the time, led 0-1 to nil at half-time against Louth, having pressed for much of the first half. But three quick points from Louth early in the second half upset their hopes of a historic breakthrough, and Louth won 0-5 to 0-1.

Making its last appearance as a venue was Clonturk Park, where the second round match between Kildare and Louth on 10 November 1895 was staged.

P. P. Sutton's report gives an idea of why it was abandoned: 'Encroachment of the crowd during play was simply deplorable. Non-paying classes of the community scaled the walls. The club that has the greatest following usually gets there in this arena.'

Not that Maurice Butterly's Pleasure Grounds on Jones's Road, tried out for the first time a week earlier, were much better. The grounds, later to become Croke Park, had only one gate, and the crush at the semi-final between Dublin and Kildare reminded one journalist of 'boxing night at the Old Royal'. Making a first appearance in the Leinster final were the coloured flags for umpires to signal scores, red for a goal and white for a point.

Meath eventually ended Dublin's reign in that final at Jones's Road by 1-3 to 0-2, having won themselves no friends when they refused to allow a Dublin substitute on to the field after Tom Knott was hurt. This was evidently a matter that had to be agreed between the teams at the time. Meath's refusal was couched in defiant terms: 'No Isle will come in here.' P. P. Sutton pondered: 'This may be just. But is it manly or sportsmanlike?'

Arravale Rovers of Tipperary were heirs to the Munster title in the absence of Cork. The Tipperary County Board had ordered Arravale to replay the final twenty minutes of their county semi-final against Grangemockler (captained by world record hammer thrower Tom Kiely) in the local championship. Arravale came through to beat Waterford 2-7 to 0-1, and Limerick Commercials who, with not a single survivor of the 1887 triumph on board, had trounced Kerry's Ballymacelligott 5-6 to 1-1 in the semi-final. Arravale brought the last one-club selection to play in an All-Ireland final and defeated Navan O'Mahonys' Meath selection with what folklore has decided was a controversial point, but which the newspaper reports of the time ignore.

The referee, champion sprinter J. J. Kenny, is said to have written to the newspapers admitting a mistake: one of Tipperary's points should not have been allowed because it was scored from inside the 21 yard line. Meath did not demand a replay. Instead Navan got to play for a set of medals from the Central Council because of the 'point that wasn't'. The teams drew 0-5 each (although Meath felt they had scored six) before Tipperary settled the issue by winning 2-13 to 1-4 at the new Jones's Road, where 'the rough surface contributed to the high scores'.

Arravale's Willie Ryan, who scored all of Tipperary's four points, the winning one from a free with seven minutes to go, may have been the player of the decade. Ryan's exploits included, according to the Tipperary papers, kicking the ball into the air, racing after it, catching it and launching the equalising score. Alongside Tom Irwin of Cork, Peter Clarke of Meath, George Roche and Luke Kelly of Dublin, he was a member of an Irish football team that played London on Whit Monday.

6 FEBRUARY 1898. LIMERICK 1-5, DUBLIN 0-7, JONES'S ROAD

> 'The Dublin goalkeeper was playing in the centre of the field where his presence was often not needed.'
>
> P. P. SUTTON, *Sport*, 12 February 1898

The evolution of the playing rules continued in 1895 when the crossbar was reduced from ten and a half to eight feet and a goal was made equal to three points. But the game was still rough, tough and physical.

Dublin Young Irelands' first-round meeting with Wicklow in the 1896 championship was left unfinished because a Wicklow player refused to leave the field when sent off. 'The Wicklow men played a game utterly unknown in Dublin,' *Sport* commented. 'They charged their opponents roughly and with an obvious intention to hurt.' When the teams met again in the Croke Cup, a special subcommittee was appointed to report on rough play by the teams.

Dublin weathered a great second half fight back by Kildare, which brought them from 2-10 to nil down back to a respectable four-point defeat. Then against Meath in the final they took control in the first half, went 1-4 to 0-1 ahead at half-time, and recaptured the title by 2-4 to 1-5.

Their opponents were Limerick Commercials, who surprised the representatives of reinstated Cork by 1-2 to 1-1, and defending champions Tipperary 2-4 to 0-6, before defeating Waterford 0-4 to 0-1 in an unfinished provincial final in Mallow. Limerick's fourth point came when the ball rebounded off a spectator, and Waterford walked off the field in protest, despite the fact that Limerick offered to ignore the score.

Training had a lot to do with Limerick's success. Tall, wiry trainer Con Fitzgerald walked his charges six miles to Cratloe every Sunday for a practice match with the local team and then six miles home. They played in two football All-Ireland finals and won both.

Dublin's star forward Jack Ledwidge knocked himself unconscious against massive 6' 3" Limerick man Larry Roche, 'like spray dashing against the Cliffs of Moher'. Roche was a hefty weight-throwing champion who was later instrumental in changing the rules of the game.

Young Irelands spurned scoring chances to go for goals. One 40 yard free by distinguished captain George Roche grazed the crossbar. They regretted that miss as they lost by a point in the end. They were unfortunate to lose their best scorer, Bill Conlan, who got the first of two points after just ten seconds before the players had dashed back into position from the throw-in.

Limerick was already 'a rugby stronghold' in the late 1880s, according to a 1953 retrospective by Séamus Ó Ceallaigh. In 1898 Limerick staged its first rugby international. Through a combination of the suspension of the GAA's ban on competing football codes between 1892 and 1902, the twelve successes of Garryowen in the first sixteen years of the Munster rugby cup, the rapid decline of Commercials after 1907, and the foundation of Young Munster from the docks community in 1902, Limerick became the only Irish city where rugby was the most popular football game.

Another massive crowd turned out to see Dublin Young Irelands beat previous All-Ireland champions Arravale Rovers by four points to three in the first Croke Cup final. It was a game the old-timers recalled fondly for 40 years, some maintaining it was better than the 1903 All-Ireland and the 1913 Croke Cup finals.

5 FEBRUARY 1899. DUBLIN 2-6, CORK 0-2, JONES'S ROAD

> 'It is doubtful if there were ever more interest in a football match played under the rules of the GAA than that which came off yesterday.'
>
> *Freeman's Journal*, 6 February 1899

Having lost to one set of drapers for the All-Ireland championship, Young Irelands promptly lost to another in Dublin. C. J. Kickhams promptly cleared out all except Luke Kelly of the 1896 All-Ireland final team. Seven of the new Dublin team worked in Clery's, four in Arnott's and one each in Todd's and the Henry Street warehouse. Among their acquisitions was Limerick Commercials star of 1896, William Guiry, who transferred to Dublin and was the scorer of two goals in the All-Ireland final.

The Leinster championship started with a hiccup when Longford and Westmeath were included in the draw, but were subsequently found not to be affiliated. Then Kickhams' new Dublin team ran into problems in the semi-final because one of their players, Canavan, played for both Meath and Dublin in the championship. But they survived to earn a replay because Wexford withdrew ten minutes from the end of the semi-final in protest at a free awarded against them.

The final was the scene of more controversy. Wicklow, champions for four days in 1889, went three days better in 1897 when they became the Leinster champions for a week. The final was fixed for 30 October alongside the All-Ireland hurling semi-final between Kilkenny and Galway, but torrential rain reduced the track around the Jones's Road grounds to a muddy mess, and the field was not much better. Dublin presumed the match would not be played and went home.

The referee awarded a walkover to Wicklow, but the following meeting of the Central Council ordered the match to be replayed on 13 November. This time Wicklow would not play and sent word to that effect on Saturday evening at 7 o'clock. Dublin easily won the replay by 1-9 to 0-3 after the original match was postponed.

Cork native P. J. Walsh, who had played against Dublin in the controversial 1894 final, now captained Dublin. It was a one-sided final, Dublin winning 2-6 to 0-2. Dunmanway's play was described as 'slovenly' by the *Freeman's Journal.* 'Somehow their play lacked finish. Nils, Lees and Clondrohid played a different kind of football, a game pleasanter to witness.'

The disappointed attendance included some special guests—the Irish and English rugby teams. Cork kept their players behind the ball and often had a single forward against Dublin's massed defence.

There was an explanation for Dunmanway's slovenliness. After travelling from west Cork from early Saturday morning, they arrived at 2 am in the city. By accident or design, they discovered that nobody had booked them into a hotel, and various jarveys brought them from house to house in the city looking for accommodation. They wandered the streets until 4 am when they eventually gained admittance to a hotel in Amiens Street.

8 APRIL 1900. DUBLIN 2-8, WATERFORD 0-4, TIPPERARY

> 'The workhouse wall used to be availed of in the past by visiting non-paying spectators who did not dread the brand of that institution so long as it saved them gate money.'
>
> Central Council comment on the problems staging matches in Tipperary town

Dublin went through more sweeping changes in 1898. Geraldines took over the team selection, Matt Rea the captaincy, and Tom 'Darby' Errity was back. Dublin faced a protest over an illegal player, but beat Wexford so convincingly by 2-6 to nil in the unfinished Leinster final that it did not matter. The game ended in a brawl, as the referee reported: 'In the second half, after 20 minutes play, a Dublin and a Wexford player had a small row at the sideline which I think could easily have been quelled but for the intervention of an outsider who rushed in and struck the Wexford player.' In the 'interests of the Association' the referee called the match off.

Dungarvan club Erin's Hope, one of the dominant clubs in Waterford County since the GAA was founded, won their only Munster title in the most convincing manner possible in 1898. Despite the fact that they still had a rival club claiming to be Waterford champions at the time because the county board was split, they beat Tipperary by nine points to nil and Fermoy's Cork selection 1-11 to 1-3 in a historic final at Lismore. Limerick and Clare were both disqualified for failing to field in a first round match: they had arranged between themselves to play in Limerick rather than Tipperary to cut costs.

There were to be no more upsets. Dublin beat Waterford 2-8 to 0-4 in the final. Jack Ledwidge struck just before half-time and again in the second half with goals that foiled the rags-to-riches story. Ledwidge went on to play for Shelbourne and won two Irish caps in 1906. Left wing Bill Sherry, who came from Bellewstown, Co. Meath, was followed by a massive group of young fans wherever he played with Geraldines or Dublin.

The Central Council was by now half-considering winding up the GAA and leaving its organisation to the county boards because of financial problems and organisational ineptitude. But the 1899 All-Ireland final may have changed its mind, as special trains brought valuable shillings from Dublin, Limerick, Lismore and Waterford.

10 FEBRUARY 1901. DUBLIN 1-10, CORK 0-6, JONES'S ROAD

> 'The men of that period, the 1890s, were of tougher fibre than the men of today.'
>
> JOHN D. HICKEY, *Irish Independent*, 27 November 1952

Cork won back the Munster championship in 1899, thanks to a breakdown in a custom of the time—that each team provide a ball for one half of the match. Cork played with their ball in the first half of the first final with Tipperary. They trailed 2-1 to 0-1 at half-time, and cutely demanded Tipperary's ball for the second half. When Tipperary were unable to produce one, Cork said theirs had burst. The referee P. J. Hayes dispatched a messenger to the town twenty minutes later. He failed to return and the matter ended there, although it does appear that Cork agreed that a second half-hour could be played in Cork.

The replay lasted 30 minutes as well: at half-time Tipperary (trailing 1-2 to 0-1 and without their star footballer Willie Ryan) insisted that the aggregate scores over the two matches be counted, which would leave them 2-2 to 1-3 winners, and refused to continue. Tipperary did not agree with the decision to stage a second replay, and when twelve Tipperary men defected, nobody really believed the newspapers when they attributed it to the weather. Cork beat a makeshift Tipperary team 3-11 to 0-1 in a downpour before a large crowd.

In Leinster, Dublin beat Wexford 1-7 to 0-3 in the provincial final, thanks to a goal from Pat Fitzsimons after just five minutes that put them 1-4 to nil ahead at half-time, despite 'not playing up to standard'.

The 1899 All-Ireland final between Geraldines' Dublin selection and Fermoy's Cork selection was the poorest in the history of the championship so far. T. J. Mahony in the *Nation* referred to Geraldines as 'a big powerful combination, but lacking knowledge of the game'. Jack Ledwidge scored an early goal. At half-time Dublin led 1-7 to 0-2, and although Tom Irwin inspired a Cork comeback in the second half, Dublin won by 1-10 to 0-6. It was poor value for the Cork fans who paid a return fare of 1/3.

The championship had fallen into chaos. The Dublin county secretary Frank Burke first learned that his county had been fixed to play Queen's County in the newspapers. And what's more, Geraldines club had already represented Dublin there and won.

Wexford were disqualified for not turning up to play Meath (the first they heard about the fixture was their notice of disqualification). To add to the confusion, they were later rescheduled to play against Kings County instead.

The malaise reflected the state of GAA organisation generally. The Association had alienated the Catholic clergy in 1887 and 1891. Although Croke was attending games again from 1895 on, all but two of the Catholic hierarchy were still suspicious of the Association, and there were allegations of clerical opposition right up to 1906. Now the Association appeared to have alienated its nationalist support base as well. Dublin had only twenty affiliated clubs in 1899. It was chronically short of money (for which Blake was blamed). It got a boost from the revival of nationalism that came with the 1798 centenary celebrations, but was in no position to consolidate or build upon it.

In early August 1900 both the Wexford and Kilkenny county boards threatened to leave the GAA unless the organisation was improved. Watt Hanrahan, a Wexford man, suggested that the provincial councils take over the running of the provincial championships. It was a proposal that saved the Association. The September 1900 congress approved the suggestion, and the Leinster council was formed in October 1900.

And so the GAA survived into a new century. For a young body it had survived a frightening series of crises. With power transferred to the provinces, it was to thrive.

21 SEPTEMBER 1902. TIPPERARY 2-17, GALWAY 0-1, TERENURE

> 'Bob Quane reappeared in the home colours and, when recognised, was given an ovation worthy of his honoured past.'
>
> PHILIP FOGARTY, *Tipperary's GAA Story*, describing Tipp v Limerick Munster semi-final

Clonmel Shamrocks were entrusted with the task of restoring Tipperary's reputation in the championship of 1900. They did so spectacularly, winning the All-Ireland and then imploding in a row with the Central Council afterwards. Tipperary beat Cork by the hardly extravagant scoreline of three points to one, and then beat Limerick 2-4 to 2-1. Kerry's Laune Rangers selection, whose team list included such strange names as P. E. Valkenburg, showed a 'lack of training' in the Munster final, and Tipperary won 1-13 to 1-3.

Meanwhile, Kilkenny's Slate Quarries team, and most notably Pat Wall, were winning the county's second Leinster championship comfortably. They beat Carlow by 2-11 to nil, Wexford by five points to four, and in the Leinster final trounced Louth by twelve points to nil.

Defending champions Dublin ran into an internal dispute. Geraldines refused to travel and Kickhams had to field for the first round tie against Wexford at short notice, their one-club selection losing 1-7 to 0-8. After that most attention focused on the Kilkenny-Wexford semi-final, played at the strange-sounding location of Christendom, to where the Slate Quarries team travelled from Carrick-on-Suir by train. Two invasions by the rather unchristian spectators interrupted the game—Kilkenny claimed that one of their points had really been a goal and another point should not have been disallowed.

There were other protests: Wicklow objected to Louth in the other semi-final, and Meath felt aggrieved because not one of the Drogheda Independents side that beat Stamullen's selection came from north of the Boyne. They were all technically resident in County Meath.

But the biggest protest of all came from Tipperary after Kilkenny defeated them 1-6 to 0-7 in the All-Ireland semi-final. Tipperary objected that five of the Kilkenny players lived on their side of the border. Tipperary won the All-Ireland final with the help of these five moving quarrymen: Jim Cooney, Pat Wall, Dan Harney, Bill O'Toole and Jack Shea. When a replay was ordered, Tipperary selected five 'Grangemockler' players: the same five, including Jack Shea, who had been sent off while playing against them. Kilkenny refused to turn out.

Theoretically, the beaten home finalists Tuam Krugers could have objected to Tipperary and won the title. Instead, they offered little opposition. A bitter row over a county final between Tuam and Dunmore led to Dunmore refusing to release their players for the final, and Tuam then refused to hand over team selection to the county board. Having qualified for the All-Ireland final without playing a match, Tuam managed just one point with their own club selection, strengthened with a few players from Caherlistrane, Ballinasloe, Galway city and Athenry, and lost by 2-20 to 0-1.

Britain had been declared a province of Ireland at the previous congress with an irony befitting the nationalist GAA, and that meant that London Irish got a bye into the All-Ireland final for the first time. The team, which included Sam Maguire and his brother John, arrived at 2 am on the Sunday morning and had a few hours' sleep in the North Star Hotel before the match.

Tipperary's Davey Smith scored the goal that started a 3-6 to 0-2 landslide, having led 2-2 to nil at half-time. Guest politicians at the match included J. C. Harrington, Lord Mayor of Dublin, and Westminster MP James McCann. The politicians were beginning to support the GAA again. In July 1902 Tom O'Donnell MP attended a Kerry convention. Willie Duffy in Galway, Willie Redmond in Clare and William McKillop in Armagh all donated cups. Being associated with the GAA was becoming expedient for politicians.

5 JULY 1903. DUBLIN 1-2, CORK 0-4, TIPPERARY

> 'When I went to Dublin in 1900 I found the attractive catch-and-kick style dominant. Players rarely handled a ball in the west Cork fields of my youth. Half the team, in those distant days, crowded around midfield and swept the ball with them goalward. Rivals met in waves.'
>
> P. D. MEHIGAN, *History of Gaelic Football* (1941)

Back at full strength under the leadership of captain Dan Holland, Ringsend's Isles of the Sea (Dublin) deposed Leinster champions Kilkenny by 3-13 to 1-2 in the first round of the following year's championship and never looked back. They beat Louth twice in the semi-final and Wexford by 1-9 to 0-1 in the Leinster final, Michael Whelan having taken the pass from his brother to score a first half goal.

Before the All-Ireland home final against Cork, Dan Holland resigned not just the captaincy but his place on the Dublin team to David 'Gush' Brady of Dolphins, as the club now had control of selection. Isles disintegrated and were replaced in 1904 as the dominant sporting force in Ringsend by a new soccer club based around Shamrock Terrace, Shamrock Rovers.

At first, this surprise move seems to have derailed the Dubs. They trailed 0-1 to 0-3 at half-time against Cork, but a goal at the start of the second half earned them a narrow victory. The match was delayed because Dublin's train arrived late. Dublin were invited to a reception in the Mansion House afterwards, a sign that nationalists were at last enjoying some political power in Ireland.

Thanks to the Dolphins' influence, this Dublin team was more ecumenical than ever before, enjoying the temporary reprieve of the ban on foreign games. Val Harris of Terenure Sarsfields went on to play soccer for Shelbourne and Everton and was capped twenty times for Ireland. P. McCann played for Belfast Celtic and Glenavon and won seven caps.

But defeated finalists Cork had versatile sportsmen too. Con Walsh, who drove the heavy leather ball of the time 69 yards and two feet to win a long kick championship in 1902, went on to win a bronze medal for Canada in the hammer at the 1908 Olympics.

Mayo took part in their first All-Ireland semi-final, having beaten Galway 2-3 to 0-3 in the first Connacht final at Claremorris, despite a great display by Galway captain J. J. Nestor. The Connacht council was established at a meeting in Ryan's Hotel afterwards.

R. Marsh was Mayo's star. Willie Parsons captained the side. Tom Patten opened the scoring for Galway, who had earlier beaten Roscommon by five points to three. In the semi-final against Cork, a Mayo player 'got a fit on the field', and Cork got a fit in the second half, running up a scoreline of 4-16 to 0-1 after leading by just 0-5 to 0-1 at half-time. Two players were sent off.

Ulster had their first representatives in action since Cavan played in the 1895 Leinster championship. Dublin led 0-8 to nil at half-time against Antrim and had a Madigan goal at the start of the second half to help them to a 2-12 to 0-2 win. The Ulster championship had been confined to Antrim clubs. In the final Tír na nÓg beat Red Hand 3-5 to 2-5 at Belfast a week before the semi-final.

24 JULY 1904. DUBLIN 0-6, TIPPERARY 0-5, KILKENNY

> 'Handsome, debonair, he was the darling of the time and the team. He stood head and shoulders above great players. A tireless, brainy footballer with craft and pace, he beat whole teams by his own individuality. He would tear through big men on his way to the goal. He could kick at fine length with either foot—on ground, overhead, and across his shoulder.'
>
> P. D. MEHIGAN on Willie Ryan of Tipperary, *History of Gaelic Football* (1941)

Tipperary recaptured the 1902 Munster title against a county that was emerging as one to watch. The Munster final on 4 October 1903 against Kerry was a draw, 0-4 each. Tipperary narrowly won the replay 1-6 to 1-5. Three Tipperary veterans from 1889, Willie Ryan, Bob Quane and Dan Quane, starred in this last championship fling. Willie proved the star of the replay.

But the days of Willie Ryan and him 'tearing through big men' was coming to an end. Dublin football was considerably more advanced than its country cousins as a result of the efforts of Young Irelands, Isles of the Sea and Kickhams.

Into this fray came a group of Wicklow men. A tournament in Greystones, where they beat the powerful Terenure Sarsfields, convinced Bray Emmetts that they should concentrate their efforts on winning the Dublin championship. Bill Sherry was among those attracted to the town. Jack Dempsey, born in Monamilla, Co. Wexford, captained Bray to their first county title in April 1903. Bray selected nine outsiders on the Dublin team, and despite the fact that Wicklow have never won a provincial title, went on to win the All-Ireland.

A crowd invasion stopped the Leinster final at Carlow with thirteen minutes to go, but Dublin, 2-5 to 0-2 leaders at the time, won the replay 1-5 to 0-5 in Kilkenny. All twelve counties had competed. Offaly surprised Wexford with a first round draw (the teams met a third time as a result of an objection). Wexford also needed a replay to beat Kilkenny in the semi-final.

Tipperary's Willie Ryan got the crucial first goal after fifteen minutes against Galway in the semi-final, and Bill Barrett added a second to go 2-1 to 0-1 ahead at half-time. Defending champions Mayo actually retained the Connacht title later in the year. The Mayo team was selected by Charlestown in 1902, and beat Galway 2-1 to 0-2, despite Galway claims that one of their points was actually a goal.

The long grass hindered play in the other semi-final in Drogheda, where against Dublin 'Armagh's dribbling tactics were spoiled by the luxuriant sward'. Dublin led 1-10 to 1-3 at half-time.

Pat 'Cocker' Daly was the star of Dublin's victory over Tipperary in the home final. An exceptional performance, followed by the two points that helped Dublin come from behind to win, saved Dublin after Tipperary overhauled them as a result of veteran Bob Quane's inspirational scores midway through the second half. The ball burst in the Dublin square after just five minutes of play. It was Willie Ryan's last fling for Tipperary, and he opened the scoring before Grace, Jack Dempsey and Stephen Mulvey sent Dublin 0-3 to 0-1 ahead at half-time. The sides were level twice in an exciting second half. A delay to enable Tipperary find a sub for an injured player 'did not help the state of the ground, already considerably diminished in width by the spectators'. Tipperary later beat Dublin 0-7 to 0-3 in a testimonial game for Tom Kiely. Cork's Lower Park was the venue for the final proper, when Dublin beat London by 1-8 to 0-4. Thus another era ended with neither a bang nor a whimper. Tipperary and London represented the power-base of 1890s Gaelic football.

At the end of 1903 it was Kerry's combination, selected from the Tralee and Killarney clubs, which was generating a lot of interest. Could they provide successors to Tipperary's Willie Ryan, Tom Irwin and Denis Murphy of Cork, to Dubs George Roche, Dick Curtis and Tom 'Darby' Errity? Their disciplined, passing style had won them a lot of admirers in the Munster final, the orders of their Killarney Crokes captain Eugene O'Sullivan being 'quickly and heartily responded to'. Ponderous comparisons were made with J. P. O'Sullivan's Laune Rangers, but one sportswriter concluded: 'Changes in the rules are so many and the field work so different that such a task could not be attempted.'

P. P. Sutton wrote of the Kerry 1902 team: 'A fine athletic lot they were, whose very appearance inspired confidence.'

It was to Kerry that the twentieth century belonged.

Chapter 2 ~

1903–27: A POPULAR GAME

Kerry, Kildare and the arrival of the All-Ireland final as a national event

'Many brilliant football forwards we have seen but never a one in quite the same class as Dick Fitzgerald of Killarney. Others footballers had talent. Dick Fitz was a football genius born. Tall and slim, he played a share of straight football before going to school in Cork. At 16 he played in the Cork senior championship with the Nils. Returning to Killarney he was soon the leader of the Crokes club. By 1904 he was on a plane apart.'

P. D. MEHIGAN, *History of Gaelic Football* (1941)

There is something biblical about Dick Fitzgerald. In the beginning was Dick, and Dick wrote the words, and Dick *was* the word.

'Dick sits at the beginning, the Statue of Liberty looking out over its people, the gateway to the new world', Joe Ó Muircheartaigh wrote in his definitive 2008 guide to Kerry footballer-heroes, *Princes of Pigskin*. He was the key personality in the game as football entered the spectator age in the years between 1903 and 1913. Not until then had Gaelic football established itself as the sport of choice outside rural parts of Munster and Leinster. Between 1903 and 1930 football won the battle of the balls, and thereafter was the best supported and most played large ball game on the island. Dick died on the eve of the 1930 All-Ireland final, his mission accomplished.

Fitzgerald wrote in 1914:

> Gaelic football of the present day is a scientific game. It is necessary to lay this down at the beginning because some people have got an idea into their heads that the game is unscientific, and they have no scruple about saying so.

There was a time indeed when the game was anything but a scientific exposition. This was the case twenty years ago [in the 1890s] when the rough and tumble and go for the man system obtained. Then it was rather a trial of strength and endurance than an exhibition of skill. But all that is long gone since.

In a certain sense Gaelic football of the present day is more scientific than any existing football game. In other forms of football, such is the constitution of rules governing them, there is very often too much of the element of luck.

In the native game, however, there is no such preponderance of luck, and this is to be accounted for by the fact that the rules provide the two kinds of score, the point as well as the goal.

Everybody knows the tendency of outdoor games of the present day to reduce the individual player to the level of a mere automaton. In a manner, the individual in modern games is a disadvantage to his side, if his individuality asserts itself strongly, so strongly that he tends to be too much of an individualist and too little of the mere machine.

How dry is the description one often gets of those great matches in which perfect combination alone is the only thing commended. In them there is no hero, no great individual standing out from the whole field. If he did stand out, he would cease to be a machine, and his usefulness to the side would cease likewise.

Such is the genius of the game itself, that while combination will always be prominent, the brilliant individual gets his opportunities times out of mind, with the result that, after the match is over, you will generally have a hero or two carried enthusiastically off the field on the shoulders of their admirers.

Gaelic football is what may be called a natural football game. There is no incentive in it towards rough play. One player can hamper or impede another in one way, and only one way, and that by means of the shoulder. Hence it is that severe tackling, rough handling and all forms of tripping are banned.

4 JUNE 1905. KILDARE 0-9, KILKENNY 0-1, JONES'S ROAD

> 'Kildare were splendid footballers, every one. I would say they were more polished than Kerry, but any drawbacks there may have been in our finish was more than compensated for in fire and dash. In my long career I never remember seeing more determined games. Both counties gave football a fillip that marked the starting point of the game as we know it today.'
>
> DICK FITZGERALD, article in *Sunburst*, 1913

The folkloric success of the 1903 All-Ireland championship was wholly unexpected. There is an impression that the progress of the game was unstoppable after Kerry's first success in a twice replayed final against Kildare in 1903.

The series of matches itself was partly responsible for the gathering momentum behind football. It coincided with a period when the GAA had the good sense to restructure on provincial lines, and the better sense to realise that Dublin city was not yet ready for its game. The catharsis of 1903 took place far away from the capital, in Tipperary and Cork.

In preparation for the 1903 All-Ireland 'home' final, players tried out new experiments, new tactics. Kildare footballer Michael Kennedy tried dropping the ball on to the toe, to be gathered again at stride's end with the hands.

His colleagues worked on an open palmed pass along the ground that enabled a wet, sodden and misshapen leather ball to be propelled much more accurately.

Kildare and Kerry teams started regular three-times-a-week practice sessions for the first time in the history of the game. Joe Rafferty in Kildare and Eugene Sheehan and Tim Gorman in Killarney and Tralee introduced sprints, leap frogs and route marches into training to increase stamina and flexibility on the playing field. Kildare training on Tuesday evenings at the Knocks, Naas, consisted of half an hour with the ball, then runs of 40, 60, 100 and 180 yards, and a composite race (run 440 yards, walk 440 yards). On the Roseberry grounds on Thursdays, half an hour with the ball was followed by a run to the college cinder track, and half an hour of sprints.

Both county teams were built around an intense two-club rivalry. In Kerry it was between Tralee John Mitchels and Killarney Doctor Crokes. In Kildare it was between two clubs and two workplaces, Roseberry, almost all of whom worked for the Dominicans on the farm and school at Newbridge College, and Clane men, most of whom were working for the Jesuits at Clongowes College. The Clane jerseys, hand-me-downs from a house rugby team at Clongowes, were used for the county. By an act of fate, they were white, so the team added white shorts and some of them dyed their boots white to add to the effect.

Kerry's bifurcated squad played each other in challenge matches at both towns and at Listowel. Two Kerry players came from outside the Tralee-Killarney axis, Denny Breen of Castleisland and a Kilmacthomas, Co. Waterford-born athlete, later to become a judge at the 1932 Olympics, Rody Kirwan. An official at the National Bank, Kirwan was shifted from New Ross (where he had already been selected for the county team) to Castleisland just in time for the 1903 championship. Denny Breen told the *Irish Press* in 1963 that his employer would allow him to leave early on Tuesday and Friday evenings to get to Killarney 'where the probables played the possibles'.

In Munster, Kerry beat Waterford 4-8 to 1-3 in the first round, Clare by 2-7 to 0-3 at Limerick, and Cork in the Munster final by 1-7 to 0-3.

Kildare, where a Cork-born county secretary Dick Radley, now based in Prosperous, re-organised structures in the county, heavily defeated All-Ireland champions Dublin 3-11 to 1-3 at Geashill, then had an easy 4-5 to 0-1 victory over newly renamed Laois (after a 1903 proposal that Kings County and Queen's County be called Offaly and Laois for GAA purposes). They then had to play Kilkenny three times in the final. The first match finished 1-2 to 0-5. They came back from 1-4 to 0-1 down for an apparent victory in the replay, pending an objection over a disputed Kilkenny point. For the first time in eighteen years a referee's decision was overturned in Leinster by the new provincial council. Excursion trains carried 5,000 people to the second replay which Kildare won convincingly 0-9 to 0-1. Kilkenny's only point resulted from a Kildare player Tom Hyland kicking the ball in the wrong direction.

There were three draws in the Ulster final too. But this time the explosion in support was curtailed by the hostility of the Great Northern Railway Company. The Great Northern refused to run an excursion train for the final between Cavan and Armagh on 10 April, so the match was fixed for Easter Monday. The attendance was a large 3,000, the teams drew five points each on two occasions, and although miserable weather kept the numbers down the second day, the estimated 7,000 turnout for the second replay was a new record.

Cavan won by eight points to five at Newbliss, but then lost the All-Ireland semi-final against Kildare by eight points to nil. The hurling semi-final was played the same day and it took half an hour to clear the field so the football match could be started.

Considering the fame that the Kerry team has been accorded in retrospect, the Mayo men of 1903 deserve some credit. In the other semi-final Kerry narrowly led Mayo 1-1 to 0-3 at half-time, but pulled away in the second half for a four-point victory.

Even though Mayo contested the 1903 All-Ireland semi-final, they were not Connacht champions. Galway were awarded the Connacht title without kicking a ball when Mayo and Roscommon were found to have fielded illegal players.

23 JULY 1905. KERRY 1-4, KILDARE 1-3, TIPPERARY
27 AUGUST 1905. KERRY 0-7, KILDARE 1-4, CORK SHOWGROUNDS

'I shouted PRESS, but the crowd just pressed harder.'

The rugby correspondent of *Sport* describes his attempt to get in to see the All-Ireland final of 1903, 3 September 1905

For an epic, it started inconspicuously. The *Freeman's Journal* accorded just 21 lines to the All-Ireland 'home' final, most of that describing the unruly crowd scenes at the match.

It was the Kerry supporters who had most difficulty getting to the venue, Pat McGrath's badly fenced field just outside Tipperary town. Their train broke down between Ballybrack and Killarney. A relief train was sent from Tralee, but it missed the connection at Limerick Junction. The team was taken by Bob Quane's brake to the field; thousands of others decided to walk. And when they arrived, the match was well under way. Without proper embankments they began to spill on to the field.

Frank 'Joyce' Conlan scored a goal for Kildare. This led to a fifteen minute dispute, with Kerry claiming that the ball had been played along the wing behind the spectators who were well beyond the sideline. A Dick Fitzgerald goal for Kerry with two minutes to go led to another crowd invasion. Although the umpire, Mr Lundon, raised the white flag, his colleague claimed that the Kildare goalkeeper, Jack Fitzgerald, had not been forced over the line when he stopped the ball. With the final score at 1-4 to 1-3 for Kerry, referee Pat McGrath decided that discretion was the better part of valour and delayed his decision until the Central Council meeting that was scheduled to follow.

In contrast to the match itself, extensive newspaper coverage was given to the aftermath of that game, and a lengthy dispute over where the replay should be held. There were more council chamber debates, some rousing speeches from both sides, and a couple of delightful newspaper parodies, including one based on the *Merchant of Venice*. Cork was agreed as a venue for the replay only after two Central Council decisions in favour of Jones's Road, despite GAA president Jim Nowlan's comment that 'it was little better than an open plain' and Thomas Sullivan's complaint that 'Jones's Road is not a neutral or enclosed ground.' Suggestions that the replay take place in London's Crystal Palace or Belvoir Park in Belfast did not gain any support.

The replay was the best of the three games. Kerry took an 0-5 to 0-3 half-time lead, but Kildare saved the game with a great Jack Connolly goal four minutes from the end. It was said that just four Kildare players touched the ball from the kick-out at the other end. This was followed by an inspirational save by goalkeeper Jack Fitzgerald from Kerry's Jim 'Thady' O'Gorman. Kildare man Jack Murray put his foot through the ball with one almighty kick during the game. Rody Kirwan dribbled the ball out of defence, then jumped over the crouching Frank Conlan. 'After the match, numbers were heard discussing the game in voices husky from enthusiasm', the *Irish Independent* reported. Again there was confusion. At first the referee announced that Kerry had won, but realised his mistake and announced a draw, Kerry 0-7 Kildare 1-4, before the cheering had died down.

Many on the special trains travelling to Cork for the second meeting saw only the second half. It was reported: 'Players had no reason to fear any encroachment of the ground as the paling was firmly put down and during the course of the game there was nobody but officials and press on the inside grounds.'

13 OCTOBER 1905. KERRY 0-8, KILDARE 0-2, CORK SHOWGROUNDS

> 'Kerry seemed slightly the lighter of the two but what they lacked in weight they brought up in speed. Kildare, however, outclassed the Southerners in tactics.'
>
> *Kerry Sentinel*, 20 October 1905

Kerry dominated the third meeting, leading 0-3 to 0-2 at half-time and scoring five points without reply in the second half to win 0-8 to 0-2. The talking point of the day was Kerry's sixth point, scored from an extraordinarily acute angle by Dick Fitzgerald. Kildare's first point that day was an 'own point' scored by Kerry's Rody Kirwan.

Joe Rafferty was marked by two Kerry men on the third day, and was blamed for sending a free wide off the upright the second day, a miss that cost Kildare victory.

The crowd were chanting for Joyce Conlan to take the free. Jim Scott was also an accomplished free-taker on the Kildare side. The scenario led to a whole set of legends about 'Rafferty's secret', or why the 1903 All-Ireland went to a third replay.

If Rafferty had a secret, it accompanied him to the grave. In the one extended interview he gave, John D. Hickey described his regret at the incident in 1956, but added 'from other sources I learned that Joe should not blame himself. The ball was caked in mud and he had to kick it out of a pool of water. Indeed it has been handed down from father to son in Kildare that that kick was about the best Joe ever took.'

The interview recorded Rafferty's recollection of how the first match ended. No one knows better how it finished up. 'After the ball went over the side I went over to throw it in and Mickey Crowe, the greatest referee that ever lived, took out his watch and said, Joe you have played six minutes and thirty seconds over time. With that I turned around and kicked the ball over the poorhouse wall and that was the end. There was no other ball to be had. After I kicked the ball away a number of lads squared up to me, demanding what did I mean. I will answer any of ye that stands out, I said.' And, as Hickey told it, 'the party dissolved'.

The grateful GAA allocated an extra £25 expenses to each team and presented defeated Kildare with gold medals to mark their achievement. After years of penury, the games brought gate receipts at Tipperary of £123, £187 at Cork, and £270 at the second replay at Cork.

Kerryman writer Pat Foley claimed that the phrase 'Up Kerry' was invented for the series. It was borrowed from John Baily's local election cry in Ballymacelligott: 'Up Baily.' Rosettes and flags were another innovation.

It wasn't even the real final, but after all that excitement, few people paid any attention to Kerry's victory over London. They won by ten points to three at Jones's Road.

1 JULY 1906. KERRY 0-5, DUBLIN 0-2, CORK SHOWGROUNDS

> 'It was a dour game. Kerry's masterly high fielding and perfect positioning close to goal outshone a polished Dublin side.'
>
> *Kerry Sentinel*, 7 July 1906

Kerry had no time to rest. Four weeks after beating London-Irish to win the county's first All-Ireland title, they ran up against Tommy O'Halloran and his Clashmore selection from Waterford that included Percy Kirwan, a younger brother of Rody. Waterford took an 0-3 to 0-1 lead over Kerry early in the second half of the Munster final and eventually held Kerry to a draw, 0-3 each, despite having a man sent off. Waterford could have won, had not Tom Ducey missed a vital free kick at the end of the game.

At half-time in the replay, Waterford trailed by only 0-2 to 0-1, largely because Kerry had hit the post with their best effort. Then came a goal, five minutes into the second half, scored by one of Kerry's additions to the 1903 All-Ireland team, Billy Lynch, from which Waterford never recovered, and Kerry went on to win 2-3 to 0-2.

Kerry's All-Ireland semi-final was easier. Cavan beat Monaghan 0-7 to 0-3 in the Ulster final, lost the title on a Monaghan objection, then won it again on appeal to the Central Council. Kerry defeated them by 4-10 to 0-1 at Jones's Road.

But it was in Connacht that standards were rising fastest. In 1904 Ballina Stephenites took over selection of the Mayo team from Castlebar Mitchels and then played two challenge matches against All-Ireland champions Kerry. To universal surprise, they drew the first 0-1 each, then won 1-2 to 0-4 three weeks before the Connacht final.

It became evident that this had been a wise move when they beat Galway 0-7 to 0-4 and Roscommon 3-6 to 0-1 to win their third Connacht title in four years. When it really counted, in the All-Ireland semi-final, they lost by just two points, 0-8 to 1-3, to Dublin before 10,000 spectators in Athlone.

With selection back in the hands of Kickhams, Dublin got their revenge for the 1903 drubbing (when they had ten newcomers on the team) by beating defending Leinster champions Kildare 0-9 to 0-5 in the first round. Kildare goalkeeper Jack Fitzgerald walked off the field because he objected to a free awarded against him, then later apologised publicly in a letter to the papers.

Dublin went on to beat Louth 0-11 to 0-6 in Dundalk and Kilkenny by a single point, 0-5 to 1-1, with the help of a few exiled Kilkenny players such as Jack and Pierce Grace. Spectators were so far advanced on one side of the field at the Leinster final in Wexford that wing play was impossible. Lamogue's Kilkenny selection had been formed in 1900, won the 1901 championship and went on to further greatness, coming back from three-nil down to beat Wexford in the Leinster semi-final.

Despite having no organised training in the manner of 1903, Kerry led the very first Kerry-Dublin All-Ireland final by four points to two at half-time, and Dick Fitzgerald got the only point of the second half to retain the title 0-5 to 0-2.

The match was disappointing and commenced in a downpour that made the ball difficult to hold and the ground slippery. Within minutes an accident forced John Thomas Sullivan to retire, and he was left unattended in the dressing room for the duration of the game. Kerry also had a point disallowed for over-holding near the end.

16 JUNE 1907. KILDARE 1-7, KERRY 0-5, THURLES

> 'I am sure I am voicing the opinion of the whole team when I say the referee's decisions at Thurles were, as they have always been, absolutely impartial.'
>
> AUSTIN STACK defends the All-Ireland final referee in his own county

Kildare beat Leinster champions Dublin in August 1905, then beat Offaly in Geashill and started against Louth in the final, playing with a blinding sun to help themselves to a 0-10 to 0-1 half-time lead before having to defend it against a Louth onslaught that reduced the margin to 0-12 to 1-7 at the end. Kilkenny beat Louth in the Leinster semi-final 0-6 to 1-1, but they had played an illegal player. This only heightened Kilkenny's grievances because the substitute referee settled all the disputes in this game by hopping the ball between players.

Dublin defeated London 1-9 to 1-4 as nominees of Leinster in the All-Ireland quarter-final, but were out of the championship by the time the semi-final came round.

Although there were no games played in Ulster, the *Anglo-Celt* was able to claim in 1907: 'Cavan have now won the Ulster championship for three years in a row.' Some of the selected Cavan team did not show up as the county went out by 4-16 to 0-2 to Kildare in the All-Ireland semi-final. A *Leinster Leader* columnist concluded: 'Cavan would not even win the junior championship of Kildare.'

The momentum created by a challenge match success over Kerry the previous year had run out for Mayo, who were beaten by Roscommon 0-7 to 0-5. Mayo objected to their first-ever Connacht championship defeat because Roscommon played an illegal player and also because there were no umpires or linesmen, but that does not seem to have been unusual at the time.

A Roscommon goal from a free got the All-Ireland semi-final off to a great start, but two goals just before half-time sent Kerry into a 2-4 to 1-3 lead and an eventual 2-10 to 1-3 victory.

Kerry's challengers in Munster showed none of the promise or heart of Waterford the previous year. Cork initially gave Kerry a walkover in the Munster semi-final because the date clashed with a local St Finbarrs v Dungourney fixture. Kerry kept Limerick inside their own 25 for much of the Munster final.

With all the pretenders out of the way, it was back to real business, Kildare v Kerry. The customary wrangle over the venue for the final took three Central Council meetings to resolve. Kildare refused to travel to Munster to play, and at one stage the title was awarded to Kerry on a walkover. Eventually, on a beautiful June afternoon in Thurles, Kerry and Kildare resumed their by now famous relationship. Kerry won the toss and chose to play against the breeze. That was a mistake. Kildare went 0-6 to 0-1 up at half-time and held on to win 1-7 to 0-5. Joe Rafferty's 'deft punching' caused havoc at centrefield, and Kildare got the game's only goal when Jack Connolly hit the crossbar, only to power his own rebound over the line 'after a few minutes of life-and-death struggle'. Wing play was credited with the victory.

The telephone was used for the first time to send the result back to ecstatic Kildare supporters.

19 NOVEMBER 1905. LEINSTER 1-8, CONNACHT 0-5, LIMERICK

> 'The dying year has been a remarkable one in the whole history of Gaelic pastimes in Kildare. Our Gaelic pastimes are becoming more popular with all classes of public. It is no longer vulgar to witness Gaelic games on Sundays.'
>
> Edward Ramsbottom ('Thigeen Roe'), *Leinster Leader*, December 1906

The new enthusiasm for the game was responsible for the creation of two more competitions.

Famous 1903 final referee, Mick Crowe, was an employee of the Great Southern and Western Railway Company. He prompted his employers to donate shields for an inter-provincial competition in 1905. The shields would remain in competition until they were won twice in succession, or three times in all. The football shield lasted just three years, and the hurling four.

The footballers got the shields off to a great start. Leinster hurlers beat Munster in the first semi-final, 3-10 to 1-7, but the football semi-final between the same teams was drawn, 0-7 to 1-4. Three weeks after the 1905 trilogy between Kerry and Kildare in the All-Ireland football championship Munster (with eleven Kerry men) met Leinster (with ten Kildare men) in the replay. Kildare's Mick Fitzgerald kicked a point from 85 yards during that game, which Leinster won by eight points to five. Wexford's Mike Cummins became the first dual inter-provincial medallist when he played on two winning Leinster teams that year. The Munster footballers won both the 1906 and 1907 shields, so got to keep the trophy.

The Croke Cup was much older, having been donated by the Association's first patron, Dr Croke, in 1896. The Croke Cup quickly became the GAA's second most prestigious competition. They were first organised on a knock-out basis parallel to the All-Ireland championship, but caused so much fixture congestion that after victories by the Dublin footballers in 1896 and the Wexford footballers in 1897, the trophies were awarded to the All-Ireland champions. In 1904 the competitions were revived, and London-Irish were invited to play in the Croke Cups rather than the All-Ireland finals of 1904. In 1905 they were confined to the four beaten provincial finalists.

They were eventually discontinued in 1916 and were succeeded by the Wolfe Tone tournaments. Now the trophies are awarded to the National League champions.

20 OCTOBER 1907. DUBLIN 0-5, CORK 0-4, ATHY

Dublin took the Leinster title back when they beat Kildare 1-9 to 0-8 before 5,000 supporters at Kilkenny with a late goal from Mick Madigan set up by Jack Grace. They had trailed 0-8 to 0-2 at half-time and the crowd spilled on to the field to join in as the match grew to an exciting climax.

By then Kildare had already been in action in the All-Ireland championship against a Monaghan team that ended Cavan's run. The 'difference in refereeing was a drawback', it was reported, when Kildare beat Monaghan 2-10 to 1-6 in Belfast.

Dublin got the nomination from Leinster to beat London 2-7 to 0-3 in the semi-final at Wexford, after London held Dublin to 0-2 each at half-time in their semi-final. In the other semi-final Cork beat Mayo 0-10 to 0-6 at Limerick's Market's Field. Ballina made up for the previous year's lapse, thrashing both lethargic Galway 2-16 to 0-1 and champions Roscommon 2-13 to 0-5. Their star in the Connacht final was Davey Ryder, who ended a great rush 'by neatly screwing a goal'. Then Mayo gave the crowd eight minutes of excitement towards the end of their semi-final against Cork. Earlier in the game Cork had a player sent off, but a Mayo player followed him to the line after Cork got a score. Kerry were flagging from early in the year. A last-minute point brought Kerry a narrow victory over Tipperary, 0-7 to 1-3, in the semi-final. Then Cork stopped Kerry's four-in-a-row bid by 1-10 to 0-3 at Tipperary. Cork had introduced a league system twelve months before, and this was expected to contribute a lot to their performance.

In October 1907, Athy Showgrounds was the new venue for the All-Ireland final as Dublin came from behind to beat Cork 0-5 to 0-4 with points from Kelly and Walsh, having trailed three points to two at half-time. Giant Kerry man Paddy Casey, at 6' 6", one of the tallest men to play in an All-Ireland final, strengthened the Dublin line-out.

25 JANUARY 1908. FERMANAGH WALKOVER, MONAGHAN SCRATCHED, CLONES

> 'The public came in large numbers to witness the game, by train, brake, car, bicycles and on foot, and after waiting two hours had to return home, many of them long distances, disgusted. Some 200 or 300 people went into the field, paying their sixpence at the gate, and waited in patient expectation until 3.45, at which time the referee lined up Fermanagh team and awarded them the match.'
>
> *Anglo-Celt*

Fermanagh almost contested an All-Ireland semi-final in 1907, 97 years before they qualified for one by right and, famously, almost shocked Mayo. The saga began when Fermanagh were awarded a walkover over Monaghan at Clones in January 1908 and were nominated by the Ulster council to represent the province in the All-Ireland semi-final.

Monaghan's Castleblayney-based players failed to show, and although the Carrickmacross contingent were there, the referee, Mr Donnelly from Belfast, awarded the match to the Fermanagh team, which was mainly composed of players from Derrylin. The anti-Sunday sport timetable of the Great Northern Railway made it impossible for them to travel to Dundalk for the match and Monaghan took Fermanagh's place in the All-Ireland semi-final instead.

Newbliss man Paddy Whelan, Monaghan county councillor and Ulster GAA chairman, partly solved the trains crux by travelling to the Railway Commission hearings in London on 13 March 1908, to complain successfully about the lack of facilities for GAA teams. He told the commission, chaired by Belfast shipbuilder William James Pirrie:

> I am the President of the Gaelic Association of Ulster, a body numbering 20,000 members. The Great Northern Railway have absolutely refused to give facilities to this organisation for Sunday travelling.
>
> A competition was in operation between the counties of Cavan and Antrim some years ago. The railway company agreed to run an extension of the Sunday morning train from Belfast to Clones on along to Cavan, a distance of from twelve to thirteen Irish miles. All arrangements were completed and a guarantee agreement, signed by the secretary was handed in to the company's officials, at the company's request. However, the company withdrew the arrangement and from that time to this they have never granted any facilities to the organisation in regard to travelling.
>
> Our members are generally employed in the rural districts, young farmers and the sons of agricultural labourers. They have no day off except Sundays, and after attending their respective places of worship on Sundays they wish to have a little amusement, and they have no facilities for those amusements or for travelling under the Great Northern Railway system.

Pirrie asked, somewhat rhetorically, whether Whelan thought it fair and unreasonable that people with rigid views with regard to Sunday observance who happen to be directors of a railway, should obtrude their views into the management of the railway to such an extent as to deprive poor people, who have very little leisure, of the one opportunity they have for amusement.

Fermanagh's revival was short lived. They lost heavily to Cavan 3-7 to 1-3 in Ulster's new Gold Medal tournament, and three weeks later went down to Cavan by five points in the championship.

Monaghan went on to beat Antrim 2-10 to 1-2 in the 1906 Ulster final. But despite being out of the 1907 championship, Monaghan were back in the semi-final the following year, losing to Dublin 1-5 to 0-2.

Antrim won the 1907 Ulster championship in September 1908, a success due to some extent to the decision to set up a league for the city clubs that summer, which created a pattern of regular competition in the county for the first time.

After an uncertain start against Down, when they were held to a draw in the quarter-final at Newry, Antrim heavily defeated Cavan 1-8 to 0-4 in the Ulster final. Drumlane players had refused to turn out for Cavan in the semi-final, but when Drumlane won the Cavan championship, twelve of the club side were selected to play against Antrim.

5 JULY 1908. DUBLIN 0-6, CORK 0-2, TIPPERARY

> 'Science was not lacking, but something like combination was, and that was not exactly on the part of the enthusiastic representatives.'
>
> *Irish Independent*, 6 July 1908

A blinding hail storm spoiled the crucial tie in Leinster between Kildare and Dublin. Dublin won 0-11 to 0-7, and Kildare's claims that the Dublin goalkeeper had stepped over his own line were not upheld. Offaly reached their first final, a late goal foiling Meath by 1-6 to 0-4. Hugh Mallin, Jack, Peter and Joe Dunne all starred in Offaly's breakthrough. Dublin retained the championship by 1-10 to 0-4 with their scores coming from Paddy Cox and Michael Kelly.

Meath's quarter-final match with Kilkenny was abandoned in darkness the first day after a long delay caused by a Meath player breaking his leg. An ambulance ferried him to the Mater Hospital. Wallis scored the replay goal for Meath.

In Munster, Cork beat Kerry by a convincing six points, 1-9 to 0-6, in the semi-final, scoring a goal just before half-time. Another powerful first half performance helped them beat a Tipperary team that selected thirteen Grangemockler men. A rushed goal midway through the first half gave them a 1-7 to 0-1 lead. Mayo then walked off against Cork with seven and a half minutes to go when a free was not awarded to them.

Dublin's train was delayed on the way to Tipperary for the All-Ireland final, causing the match to start late for the second time in seven years. Their winning point was scored by Kilkenny man Pierce Grace, Dublin having led 0-6 to 0-2 at half-time.

In the 1908 Leinster final, Kildare captain Jack Murray won the toss and played with the breeze in the first half, but failed to get enough scores. Dublin had a charged goal from Jack Shouldice and Pat 'Cocker' Daly midway through the second half for a 1-7 to 0-3 victory. Kildare struggled against Louth; a last-minute point from Kit Brien forced a 0-5 each draw and a replay where Murray got the vital goal in a 1-6 to 1-5 win. Louth struggled in the quarter-final against Kilkenny, three late points from Lynch earning a replay. The second meeting was impossible for spectators to follow 'owing to the crushing and swaying of the crowd'.

Antrim's Fagan scored a point late in the first half to help them hold Dublin to 0-1 each at half-time, but lost 1-8 to 0-2. Antrim's selection, from

Belfast city clubs, played with a strong breeze in the first half. MacAuley's second half goal ended their hopes.

Kerry beat Waterford, newly reunited after a damaging three-year county board split, by 0-7 to 0-2. Waterford beat Cork 1-7 to 1-2 with a late goal in the semi-final.

Mayo hoped to build on their achievements earlier in the decade. Players like Andy Corcoran worked to get Ballina's selection to inter-county standard. By 1909 they were probably at their peak but were still unable to reach the All-Ireland final. The month after beating Roscommon in the Connacht final, they held Kerry to one point to nil at half-time in Limerick, but were beaten heavily. The following August they beat Kildare 0-7 to 0-4 in an unfinished Croke Cup final, to bring Connacht its first national trophy.

In the All-Ireland 'home' final, Dublin pulled away in the second half to beat Kerry. A 30 yard point from Daly sent them narrowly ahead 0-3 to 0-2 at half-time. Hugh Hilliard, Martin Power, Tom MacAuley, Hilliard again and Tom Walsh set off a five-point spree in the second half, to which Kerry's only reply was a point from Con Murphy, alas too late to bring them back into the game.

Dublin went on to beat London easily in the final proper, despite having a man sent off after 25 minutes. They were also billed to play New York Irish during August, but the match never took place.

Pat 'Cocker' Daly, undoubtedly the star of the championship, continued to play football until 1926 when he was 53 years old.

5 DECEMBER 1909. KERRY 1-9, LOUTH 0-6, JONES'S ROAD

> 'From every point of view it was undoubtedly the finest exposition of the Gaelic code ever witnessed.'
>
> *Freeman's Journal*, 6 December 1909

Johnny Skinner was the hero as Kerry won their third title in 1909. They first won an acrimonious Munster final against Cork. Although Kerry protested that the referee was allowing too much rough play and walked off the field, they were persuaded to return but lost the game 2-8 to 1-7. But immediately afterwards they objected that one of the Cork players, Jerry Beckett, was a native of Kilgarvan, who had returned and played for Kilgarvan in a tournament game in Kerry. Beckett argued that the tournament was an unofficial one, but that did not excuse him, and so Kerry earned a replay. In a superb replay at Cork, Cork-born Johnny Skinner scored the winning goal for Kerry. Receipts from the replay of £116 were donated to the family of former Tipperary footballer, Bob Quane, who had died suddenly in October.

In the Connacht final, Eamonn Boshell's shot broke the crossbar in Mayo's 1-4 to 0-5 victory over Galway, and play was held up for several minutes while it was being repaired. Earlier in the championship Sligo refused to travel to Mohill to play Leitrim 'because of the rough treatment they had received on their previous visit to the venue'. Kerry beat Mayo 2-12 to 0-6 in the All-Ireland semi-final at Ennis in November.

The Ulster championship got off to a bad start when an Armagh player refused to leave the field after he was sent off, and the first round match between Armagh and Monaghan was abandoned. When Monaghan played Antrim in the Ulster semi-final, the referee complained that he feared there would be a riot if he sent off any of the Monaghan players. Monaghan were suspended for twelve months after the match, a suspension lifted afterwards.

Gates were still paltry: despite a 6*d* admission charge, they totalled £49-4-10 for the championship. Belturbet's £9-10 for the final, in which Antrim beat Cavan 1-9 to 0-5, was the best: about 380 spectators.

Kerry had new opponents in the All-Ireland final. Goals from Tom Matthews and Jack Carvin helped Louth beat Kilkenny 2-9 to 0-4 for their first Leinster title. Kilkenny led briefly by two points to one. Louth had beaten Dublin 1-11 to 0-7 in the Leinster semi-final and went on to beat Antrim 2-13 to 0-15 in the All-Ireland semi-final as Antrim put up a good display at Belfast and trailed by only 0-5 to 0-3 at half-time.

Kildare did not even compete in Leinster: a bitter dispute arose out of the Croke Cup final which was prematurely halted by a crowd invasion and whether Kildare were prepared to continue playing against Mayo or whether they were just waiting for the pitch to be cleared. Some of Kildare's Leinster rivals proposed that they should be suspended, so Kildare withdrew from the championship.

Kerry completed a comprehensive victory against Louth in the final. The ball passed through four players without touching the ground before the last point was scored by Johnny Skinner.

When Dublin met London in heavy rain in the quarter-final on one of the wettest days of the year, there was another attendance record—the wrong sort. At the time of the throw-in, there was not a single spectator in the ground, but as the rain eased eventually about 200 people turned up to watch.

1910. KERRY V LOUTH, JONES'S ROAD

> 'Let it be said the attendance exceeded by thousands any that has yet assembled under either of the three rules played in the Metropolis.'
>
> *Freeman's Journal*, 6 December 1909

Collecting sixpences at the entrances to the playing fields was turning into a profitable pursuit for the GAA. The great gate rushes of the 1900s had shown up the potential of Gaelic football as a spectator sport. In 1909 the Association had collected £317-3-6 from 12,000 spectators at the Kerry v Louth final.

Despite the enthusiasm of the newspaper reports, they were still smaller than rival spectator attractions. Dublin was staging an international rugby match each year. Pavilion facilities were better and admission charges were higher, but rugby receipts reached £1,200 on occasions. Soccer matches were being staged with more regularity in Dublin. Gaelic was still regarded as a country man's game, but was making inroads in the capital. The GAA realised that the survival of the game depended on the organisation of spectator facilities in the city.

Louth itched for revenge over their Kerry rivals. They retained their Leinster title in 1910 with an overwhelming 3-12 to 0-10 victory over Kildare (after spectator-winning efforts were all undone by classic Gaelic unpunctuality and the match started an hour and twenty minutes late), and a torrid three points to nil success against Dublin before 6,000 spectators in Navan. Dublin hit the post twice in that Leinster final, and John Brennan scored the points for victory after Louth led 0-1 to nil at half-time. Jack Grace captained Dublin for the last time in this final: the outstanding player of the previous decade had won five football All-Ireland medals, contested eleven All-Ireland finals, six in football and five in hurling, and played with both Kilkenny and Dublin. Robust rather than speedy, his motto was 'Give me one yard clear and I fear no man.' P. D. Mehigan recalled: 'A thoroughly fair player, he hurt every man that crashed into him. He could run all day, and break up half a team when roused.' Louth's achievement in holding Dublin scoreless, Tom Burke stated afterwards, underlined their claim to be the greatest team of the era: 'Kerry took their cue from that and refused to meet Louth in the All-Ireland football final later that year. Let who will put forward any other reason.'

2 OCTOBER 1910. DUBLIN 3-5, ANTRIM 0-2, JONES'S ROAD

> 'The play showed a distinct improvement in the form of the Ulster team when compared to what we were accustomed to witness only a couple of years ago from Ulster provincial teams.'
>
> *Freeman's Journal*, 3 October 1910

Kerry were also careering back towards a repeat of the 1909 final. They beat Cork, for whom Charlie Paye was emerging as one of the leading marksmen of the era, by 0-4 to 0-2 in the Munster final, but had nothing as spectacular a victory in their semi-final against Mayo's Stephenites selection. Just before half-time Mayo led 0-4 to 0-1, and even Kerry's single point was disputed by Mayo. Kerry hit with a goal and controlled the second half for a comfortable 1-7 to 0-4 victory.

The Ulster championship, meanwhile, was staggering through its difficulties with unruly railway authorities, unruly administrators and even more unruly spectators. The first round match between Cavan and Fermanagh was abandoned when the ball burst and there was no replacement. Then arrangements for admitting spectators to the Monaghan v Antrim semi-final left a lot to be desired: 'One man with a bag giving out tickets . . . one spectator waited half an hour to get the change from a shilling.' But the scenes were worse when the match ended and spectators leaving the ground found they had to pass out the same gate in single file, one at a time. Antrim beat Monaghan twice, having to replay because of an objection, while Cavan beat Tyrone in the unlikely venue of Bundoran.

Antrim eventually settled the issue between themselves and Cavan with an overwhelming 3-4 to 0-1 victory. They used a unique, fast, hand passing style developed in training by players who were based close together in Belfast city. The *Anglo-Celt* mourned: 'Cavan were dead slow. You can't cut finished footballers out of a hedge. Muscle in the county is running wild for want of cultivation. Our players have no style, a clumsy catch and awkward delivery.'

London, wearing bright green jerseys and captained by Sam Maguire, scored 1-1 in the opening minutes of the second half of the quarter-final against Louth, but Louth hung on to win 2-5 to 1-2. Louth did not play in the All-Ireland semi-final. Instead the Leinster council nominated Dublin, who beat Antrim 3-5 to 0-2, so Leinster were represented by Louth in the quarter-final against London, Dublin in the semi-final against Antrim, and Louth again in the All-Ireland final. Dublin easily beat Antrim's stylish footballers.

There was at least some good news in Ulster in April 1910 for the Ulster council when a meeting between the GAA and the Great Northern Railway board appeared to secure, at the third attempt, train facilities for teams on Sundays.

13 NOVEMBER 1910. LOUTH WALKOVER, KERRY SCRATCHED

> 'The final tie of the All-Ireland football championship, which was fixed to be played at Jones's road ground tomorrow, has been declared off, as the Kerry team has refused to travel. It was thought early yesterday that the crux had been bridged over, but later in the day a telegram from Tralee stated that as the demands of the Kerry team were not conceded in full by the railway company, they would not travel to play Louth.'
>
> *Freeman's Journal*, 12 November 1910

No sooner was one railway dispute in the north ended, than another erupted in the south. Just as it appeared that Louth would earn their revenge against Kerry, they never got their chance after an extraordinary row over the price of train tickets to Dublin for Kerry's supporters that prevented the 1910 All-Ireland final taking place.

Kerry were furious that the Great Southern and Western Railway Company would not give a cheap excursion fare for their followers. They received vouchers for seventeen players, but no promise of a reserved carriage on Thursday, 10 November. The following day, the superintendent for Inchicore, S. Cooper Chadwick, extended the offer to a reserved carriage for twenty players. Kerry then said they would travel if vouchers were provided for the players and twelve close supporters and mentors.

On Saturday a notice in the papers declared that the match was off, all trains were cancelled, and Kerry stood accused of lowering the GAA's reputation in pursuance of a local dispute with the railway company. Despite the fact that railway companies and the GAA were going through a rough relationship at the time, the GAA Central Council sided with the railway company.

Kerry supporters published a list of complaints against the Great Southern Railway Company, or the 'Great Sourface Railway' as D. P. Moran described it in his journal, the *Leader*. They listed among their grievances excessive fares (compared with round trip fares of 4/- for a rugby match in Cork and 13/- return from Tralee to Cardiff). On two occasions Kerry supporters returning from Thurles were forced to board from the 'cattle bank'.

The GSWR, they alleged, never let Kerry players travel by the early train on Saturday from Tralee, the 1.50, forcing them to share the overcrowded 3.20 with market day passengers who boarded in Killarney. A promise that there would be room on the 3.20 was dismissed by Kerry. Ennis Gaelic Leagues passed a motion of support, citing their own treatment by the GSWR. The Nationalist Party, who complained they had difficulty getting train facilities for Home Rule meetings, supported Kerry's move. While 800 followers waited for the verdict outside, a delegate proposed that Kerry be suspended for five years for bringing the Association into disrepute. Eventually the title was given to Louth, who still said they would prefer to win it on the field of play. Kerry were not suspended, avoiding an 1894-style confrontation, as Cork were threatening to 'go into the wilderness with Kerry'.

The Central Council lost heavily. Their receipts from the year were paltry: Louth v London in Dundalk earned £46, Kerry v Mayo in Tuam £50, and Dublin v Antrim in Jones's Road £20.

'If the Kerry players in our time can journey in comfort to Dublin in corridor carriages,' veteran *Kerryman* correspondent Paddy Foley wrote in 1945, 'if teams through the country are accorded first-class travelling facilities, let them remember these concessions were only secured by the sacrificing of an All-Ireland through the arches of the years. Let all Gaels applaud Kerry's gallant 1910 stand-down.'

When Louth and Kerry eventually met in a 1913 Croke Memorial tournament final, it broke all existing attendance and receipt records.

The rules had to be changed to get rid of some of the pulling and dragging out of the game.

The scoring area had been reduced twice in the early 1900s. The old point posts were seventeen feet on either side of the goals, which were 21 feet wide. In 1901 they were brought back to fifteen feet on either side of the goal. In 1903 they were fixed at twelve feet on either side of the goalposts. In 1909 a motion that point posts be abolished led to the establishment of a subcommittee which reported back in 1910 that point posts should go, goal nets should be introduced, and the goals should be 21 feet wide. The old ten yard line in front of the goal, inside which no scores could be obtained, was replaced by a parallelogram. This brought an end to the era of the 'whipe', usually a forward of the overweight variety who lurked around the goalmouth specifically to intimidate opposing backs. He effectively marked the goalkeeper. As one writer commented: 'Previous to the change, it was not unusual to see the goalkeeper and the full forward having a friendly chat together while the ball was thrown down the field.'

Another innovation was getting the backs into position when the ball was thrown in. Until then it was possible to get a quick score before the defenders had reached their positions. Collison of Dublin got the last of these 'snatch' goals in the opening seconds of the 1910 Leinster semi-final against Wexford. Although M. Conlon of Dublin managed a point before the defenders were in position in the 1894 All-Ireland final, there was no snatched score in a football final as prominent as the goal scored after just five seconds of the 1906 All-Ireland hurling final by Tipperary's Hugh Leonard. Only forwards were required to line up for the throw-in.

Goal nets helped sort out disputes about scores, although as late as 1929, a Connacht championship match between Sligo and Leitrim was played without goal nets.

14 JANUARY 1912. CORK 6-6, ANTRIM 1-2, JONES'S ROAD

> 'The game was advertised for 1.15, and about that hour the Meath team took the field, few, if any of the Kilkenny team being on the ground at the time.'
>
> *Irish Independent*, 23 October 1911

Both Louth and Kerry made early exits from the 1911 championship.

Waterford, eighteen-point losers the previous year, won a famous 1-2 to 1-0 Munster semi-final victory at Mallow over the Kerry men, who had been unbeaten since 1908. Waterford conceded the first goal, sent to the net off the post, but scored an equaliser soon afterwards and picked their way back into the game as a slight drizzle turned into a downpour. While neither side added to their score in the second half, it was Waterford who did most of the attacking, captained by P. Lynch, one of eleven Rathgormack players on the side. Kerry had seven of their 1910 selected All-Ireland team, but no Killarney players: the entire Killarney team had been suspended for walking off the field in the county semi-final against Tralee.

The success proved more than Waterford could follow, and Cork beat them 2-5 to 0-1 in the Munster final. As beaten provincial finalists, Waterford qualified for the Croke Cup but were beaten in the final by Meath, who were achieving their first national title. Cork went on to beat Galway 3-4 to 0-2 in the All-Ireland semi-final at Maryboro.

Louth went out to more powerful pretenders, Dublin, 3-2 to 1-4 in the Leinster quarter-final at Navan. The elated Dublin men in turn lost to Meath, surprise 1-3 to 0-2 winners in the semi-final. There was a further surprise when Meath in turn went on to lose to Kilkenny 2-4 to 1-1 in a confusing Leinster final.

Meath were awarded the match at 2.05, because Kilkenny were twenty minutes late. They refused to accept the title but were beginning to change their minds when Kilkenny arrived at 2.25. By now Meath wanted a challenge match instead. The game went ahead; Meath were beaten in a downpour, and their protest afterwards was rejected, so Kilkenny won their third and their last Leinster football title.

For the winners it was largely a family affair. Patrick and Richard Dalton of Knocktopher got Kilkenny's goals. Richard also got two points and William another point. Gate receipts of £100 went to the Wexford foundry workers who were locked out in a trade dispute. The GAA were identifying themselves with the Trade Union movement at the time, stipulating that their rule books be printed with trade union labour.

Just as the GAA in Connacht and Ulster seemed to have turned a corner, both provinces hit organisational stagnation in 1911. The rise in the standard of football was not being matched by an end to official ineptitude. Galway and Mayo's proposed clash on 24 September in Claremorris in the Connacht final was postponed as a result of a rail strike and was never replayed. Even more extraordinary was a case in Ulster where the new provincial secretary W. P. Gilmour was ill for most of the year and never got around to organising a championship. Getting the 1910 Ulster final played a year late was the height of provincial council activity for the year. A new acting secretary was appointed at the end of the year, and all correspondence and minute books were collected from Mr Gilmour.

Running the Ulster championship was a loss-making operation. Gate receipts were never large enough to cover teams' travelling expenses. The Ulster council had no funds to provide their provincial champions with medals until 1919. Even the medals for the 1920s were presented retrospectively in 1930. And yet Antrim achieved a breakthrough for Ulster by reaching the All-Ireland final. Their surprise 3-1 to 1-1 semi-final victory over Kilkenny resulted in a Central Council investigation into the overt roughness of the game. Kilkenny's James Doyle was suspended for five years as a result. Antrim introduced 'toeing off' the ball from goal which non-plussed the Kilkenny men.

Ulster's joy was short lived. Cork's record 6-6 to 1-2 score in the final against Antrim caused a lot of comment, but might not have been all that it seemed. Newspaper commentators agreed that one of the Cork goals should have been a point.

Nevertheless, it was a fine achievement by the Belfast men, drawn from the Seaghan O'Neill (from which captain Harry Sheehan led their bid), Ollamh Fodhla, Mitchels, Sarsfields, Cuchulainns and Dalcassian clubs. The first goal of the game fell to Antrim when William Lennon boxed P. D. Kelly's centre to the net. O'Neill had another Antrim goal disallowed in the second half. By then Charlie Paye, from a Billy Mackessy pass, had helped Cork go 1-4 to 1-0 ahead at half-time. Mackessy followed with a goal at the start of the second half (the first of three by the dual star), and Cork piled in four goals in the last quarter.

Goalscorer Charlie Paye from Fermoy had once won a soccer medal with Cork Celtic and was one of the first transatlantic players. In 1908 he spent his summer in New York playing for the Cork club. Willie Mackessy, who was born in Buttevant and later played with Kinsale, was a sprinter. Team captain Mick Mehigan, 35 years old at the time of the final, later went on a 24 day hunger strike at Wormwood Scrubs.

3 NOVEMBER 1912. LOUTH 1-7, ANTRIM 1-2, JONES'S ROAD

> 'Antrim has produced in recent years some fine scoring men who can dribble trickily and drive beautifully.'
>
> DICK FITZGERALD, *How to Play Gaelic Football* (1914)

According to the met men, 1912 was a wet summer, at 308.6 cm of rainfall, the fifth wettest summer on record. Rain 'destroyed the Leinster semi-final between Louth and Offaly as a spectacle' and caused the postponement of a Dublin-Kilkenny quarter-final replay on 4 August. When the replay took place in Enniscorthy, Dublin dumped the provincial champions by 3-4 to 0-1. Dan Kavanagh, a Wicklow native remembered for playing in his distinctive slouch hat, led Dublin's charge against Wicklow in the Leinster semi-final and reporters complained that the Wicklow men 'could have had more regard for the rules in the second half'.

At that stage Dublin looked likely finalists. Dublin were Leinster's All-Ireland semi-final nominees against Harry Hession's Roscommon team at Jones's Road in September. Roscommon missed a first half penalty, Hession got a goal soon after half-time, but F. Brady and D. Manifold goals made sure Dublin secured a final spot for Leinster, winning 2-4 to 1-1. Roscommon were surprise Connacht champions after Jim Brennan got the only two points of the provincial final in the first half, and they went on to beat Galway 0-2 to 0-0 at Castlerea.

But in October 1912 in Navan, Louth defeated Dublin 1-2 to 1-1 to take the title back. They failed to score against the wind in the first half and went in 1-1 to nil behind at half-time. Then Dublin too failed to score against the wind in the second half, and Louth squeezed through by a point.

With fifteen minutes to go it was 1-1 to 0-1. Louth forced a 50 near the corner flag. Joe Mulligan's kick sailed unaided to the net. Louth came back with a long solo run from 'Gentleman' Jim Smith, who was exhausted by the time he reached 21 yards from the Dublin goal. Team mate 'Whack' O'Reilly pushed him off the ball and scooped it over the bar.

Again the match was destroyed by what used to be called 'inclement conditions'. The rain was so heavy that hundreds who travelled to the match remained in the railway carriages. Many suspected the match would be postponed and four of the players, all from Dublin, cried off because of the weather.

That gave Louth a chance to meet Kerry and gain revenge for both 1909 and the railway ticket fiasco. But Kerry disobligingly lost their semi-final against Antrim on another rainy day by a massive 3-5 to 0-2. Antrim were led by Louth-born Johnny Coburn. Born in Mount Pleasant, he captained Sarsfields from 1908 to 1918.

It was a shock that has gone into legend. Antrim led 0-3 to 0-2 at half-time, having played against the breeze. Early in the second half, play became rough and Antrim had their full back sent off five minutes after half-time. This should have inspired Kerry. Instead, Antrim came forward for a Joe Mullen goal, followed by two more breakaways as Kerry showed signs of strain. Later Kerry blamed a wedding the day before, but Antrim's great display in the final suggests this was only part of the story. As *Sport* wrote, 'Antrim have improved in style. They practised for all they were worth.'

Antrim ran out of luck before the final, losing a player under the 'foreign games' rule, a rule which hindered the development of the game in Belfast for half a century. It took fourteen minutes for Louth's Tom Matthews to open the score. They still managed to lead by two points with fifteen minutes to go. Mullen equalised, Louth led 0-2 to 0-1 at half-time, and then Antrim had a goal for the last quarter lead. Jack Bannon, Johnny Brennan, Paddy Reilly and Stephen Fitzsimons got Louth's four points for a 1-7 to 1-2 victory. The attendance included 611 spectators who paid 1/-, 300 at 2/- and 1,000 at 1/6.

They still had an Ulster championship to defend for a spot of consolation. A week after the All-Ireland final, Antrim lined out in the Ulster final against Armagh in Castleblayney with five changes to the team and won 2-2 to 0-1.

Armagh had qualified for the Ulster final in the most bizarre of circumstances. Seven Cavan players failed to turn up to play in the semi-final against Armagh. Cavan were forced to play in their work clothes in the driving rain that distinguished that summer of 1912, and they included Fermanagh player George Wilson in their line-out. They still won 1-2 to 1-1, but that illegal player cost them the match afterwards on an objection.

Armagh had problems of their own that day: the county's entire GAA following was stranded in most unblissful circumstances in Newbliss. The excursion train went home without most of the players and spectators because of delays getting the match under way.

4 MAY 1913. KERRY 0-4, LOUTH 1-1, CROKE PARK
29 JUNE 1913. KERRY 2-4, LOUTH 0-5, CROKE PARK

> 'The county was smitten by a football fever unequalled in the old Kerry-Kildare days, or since.'
>
> PADDY FOLEY, writing in 1945

Louth had won the championship. But they still had to wait for the Croke Tournament final the following spring to meet Kerry and get a real chance of revenge for the no-show in 1910. When they did so, a replayed final set a new GAA attendance record of 30,000. The GAA was ecstatic that the attendance record set by a rugby match at Lansdowne Road had been beaten.

The game itself was recalled for two generations afterwards. The long periods of action in which the ball 'did not touch the ground or go out of play' went into the folk memory.

It was Kerry who decided the issue between the teams by winning the replay 2-4 to 0-5 after a 0-4 to 1-1 draw. Between the draw and the replay Louth introduced full-time training, causing a storm when it was announced that former Scottish soccer international George Blessington and Belfast Celtic trainer Jim Booth were to train them for the final. Since 1905, Kerry players trained separately in Tralee and Killarney and came together on Sundays for practice matches. Kerry now followed suit by bringing their team together to Tralee and Killarney on alternate weeks to train under local athletes Jerry Collins and Bill O'Connor. A 40-year tradition of teams going into full-time training for big matches was begun.

Receipts of £750 and £1,198 at the football finals, and £2,734 in all from just six matches in the tournament, gave the GAA a higher than expected fund for a memorial to Archbishop Croke in Thurles. Much to the chagrin of the Thurles people, who resented the hijacking of their memorial funds, the GAA used the surplus to purchase Jones's Road from their secretary Frank Dineen for £3,641-8-5, and rename it Croke Memorial Park. The Association paid over £1,641-8-5 in cash. Thurles was given a further £300 towards its confraternity hall to quell its protests.

The new rules were on trial at that replay for the first time, and their success was guaranteed for ever after. The decision to reduce teams from seventeen-a-side to fifteen-a-side gave the game a long overdue boost. Other new rules were the decision to allow players who had been knocked to the ground to fist the ball away, and to take kick-outs from the 21 yard line after a score.

'Some forty thousand people witnessed each of these strenuous tussles for supremacy,' Dick Fitzgerald wrote, 'and it has been said on all sides that never in the history of outdoor games in Ireland have people gone home so well pleased with what they saw.'

14 DECEMBER 1913. KERRY 2-2, WEXFORD 0-3, CROKE PARK

> 'It is so long since I attended a football match I don't know how it is going to start.'
>
> JOHN DILLON, guest of honour at the 1913 All-Ireland final

Former Dublin All-Ireland medallist Paddy Breen had taken over as chairman in Wexford. Under his leadership Wexford won the Leinster junior championship in 1911 with an impressive 3-1 to 0-2 victory over Dublin. Among the successful juniors were Paddy Mackey, Aidan Doyle, Gus O'Kennedy and Tom Murphy.

In 1912 Wexford had suffered one of their most humiliating championship defeats to date, beaten 4-4 to 1-3 by Wicklow in the first round. In 1913 a new Wexford team, based around New Ross and the county town, gathered together in the spring. Egged on by nationalist journalist Seán Etchingham and fired by the growth of the local volunteer group (the Volunteers, said to be entirely a Sinn Fein grouping, and even had a Gaelic football club), they selected the county's best-known sportsman as a trainer. Jem Roche had fought Canada's George Burns for the world heavyweight title in 1910. What matter if, at one minute and 28 seconds, it was one of the shortest professional fights on record. Jem's training evidently worked. Wexford were missing a key player, Eamonn Phelan, but they still beat Dublin 2-3 to 1-0 in the Leinster semi-final in Wexford. Teenager Aidan Doyle, soon to become a household name, scored the winning goal for Wexford.

In the other Leinster semi-final, Meath managed to hold Louth to a 0-2 each draw at half-time, but eventually went down by 2-3 to 0-2. Provincial champions of three years earlier, Kilkenny, had fallen on hard times. Mascot Peter Dunne was forced to line out for his county against Louth to make up the team and lost 2-5 to 0-1.

Louth were odds-on favourites to challenge Munster for All-Ireland honours. They represented Leinster at the start of the All-Ireland series, travelling to Kensal Rise in early August to beat London. But Wexford surprised even themselves when they stopped Louth's run by 2-3 to 2-2 in the Leinster final in September.

Jim Rossiter, the only player from the Wexford Volunteer club, snatched victory five minutes from the end of the final. He had already contributed a goal at the start of the second half. Winning the Croke Cup in June was poor consolation for Louth. Wexford were therefore Leinster's representatives in the All-Ireland semi-final win over Antrim.

Antrim were in decline. Unrated Fermanagh, with George Wilson back, surprised them with a Cassidy goal to give them a 1-3 to 0-1 half-time lead in the Ulster semi-final. Then Antrim lost two of their leading players. Both moved away from Belfast the same month. In the circumstances Antrim barely held their Ulster title by 2-1 to 1-2 against Monaghan with the help of two soft goals from Ward and Gorman. Frank Duffy got a goal to help Monaghan come back from seven points behind, 2-1 to nil, at half-time, leaving Monaghan with only their goalkeeper to blame for his nervous start. Goals by Wexford's Johnny Rossiter, Dick Reynolds and Gus Kennedy ensured there would be no giant-killing this time as Antrim crashed 4-4 to 0-1.

Kerry too were having troubles, this time with Tipperary. In the Munster championship, Kerry's Dick Fitzgerald scored the late equaliser that Kerry needed to draw 0-2 each with Tipperary. Davey Stapleton's goal made life difficult for Kerry in the replay; it put Tipperary 1-0 to 0-1 ahead at the beginning of the second half, but Kerry won 0-5 to 1-0, and then beat champions Cork in the Munster final by the surprisingly large margin of 1-6 to 0-1 before a record £308 crowd.

It was clear that Dick Fitzgerald, who scored 1-4 in that match, was having his best-ever season. Now 26, he was in the process of writing his *How to Play Gaelic Football*, which was published at the beginning of 1914 and was giving ample lessons to opponent and spectator alike on the playing field. Galway too ran into the Fitzgerald factor as Dick scored 1-4 against them in a 1-8 to 0-1 victory in Maryboro—'as dreary an exhibition of Gaelic football as was ever seen', the *Kerryman* mourned.

For the first time, what a later generation of headline-writers would call 'final fever' broke out in advance of the game in Kerry. Thanks to the stand Kerry had taken in 1910, supporters now had ample train facilities to bring them to Croke Park. Sister Dominick was enlisted to treat an injured Tom Rice, and her nursing skill enabled him to play in the final. Even £1,000 a year county surveyor Singleton Goodwin was inspired to give a shilling to the Kerry training fund—the *Kerryman* newspaper highlighted it in bold type in their subscription list. A new training camp was established at the residence of Kerry supporter Jack McCarthy in Dunboyne before the All-Ireland final.

Fitzgerald was the outstanding character as Wexford faltered after a promising start in the final. As Kerry beat Wexford 2-2 to 0-3 before a crowd of 17,000, he scored a goal and a point in the first half, had another goal disallowed (as Kerry led 1-1 to 0-1), and then notched the opening points of the second half. After fifteen minutes of the second half, Johnny Skinner had a wrap-up goal for Kerry.

Pat O'Shea from Castlegregory gave a wonderful display. His high fielding earned the comment ''Tis an aeroplane he is' from opponent Johnny Doyle. It earned him the nickname 'Aeroplane' after the device invented ten years earlier by the Wright brothers. The *Kerryman* reported that he 'did some fine aeroplane turns in midfield, catching the ball at almost incredible heights'. His previous nickname with the Erin's Hope club had been 'Springheel'. O'Shea was only 5' 8", but was a great judge of the ball. He claimed later: 'I'd see the trajectory of every kick and knew when to go for it. Two handed for the reasonable ones, pulling down the high ones one handed; go up like a diver feet together; come down like a hurdler on one foot and kick it with the other. The momentum gave me length and I'd have a map in my mind where the forwards were.'

The attendance reached 17,000 and the talk on the banks was of replacing the camáns that the Volunteers used for drilling with real guns sometime soon. There was a flavour of triumphant nationalism everywhere. James Upton, one of the nationalists who seemed to dominate the sporting press at the time, wrote in the *Kilkenny Journal*: 'Gaeldom is marching today and has attained a position that seemed very remote fifteen years ago, or ten years ago, or even five years ago. And best of all, my brothers, we have reached that position without striking our colours or erasing a single syllable from the principles of an uncompromising faith in Ireland's right to full and independent nationhood.'

The Volunteer spirit had seized the GAA. When a challenge match in Drogheda on Easter Sunday 1915 ended with the Louth players calling for three cheers for Kerry, Dick Fitzgerald called for three cheers for Eoin McNeill instead.

In January 1914 the GAA president James Nowlan called upon members to 'join the Volunteers and learn to shoot straight'. Delegates finished the April 1914 Congress with a hearty rendition of 'A Nation Once Again'. By then the UVF guns had landed in Larne and the Irish Volunteers were negotiating to get some of their own.

1 NOVEMBER 1914. KERRY 1-3, WEXFORD 0-6, CROKE PARK (13,000)
29 NOVEMBER 1914. KERRY 2-3, WEXFORD 0-6, CROKE PARK (20,000)

> 'It has been quite noticeable how the reduction of the number from seventeen aside to fifteen aside has given the players more scope to indulge in dribbling, passing with the foot, and dispensing a good deal with the handling of the leather, and it requires no prophet to foretell that, if the number be further reduced, let us suppose to thirteen aside—the Ground Game will be much more in evidence.'
>
> DICK FITZGERALD, *How to Play Gaelic Football* (1914)

Kerry and Wexford looked forward to a repeat final, and a friendship was growing between the counties that the Kerry-Louth rivalry never achieved. Wexford entertained Kerry at the county feis in New Ross and brought them on a boat trip along the Barrow and Suir. When Wexford repaid the visit, they were treated to a 'motor drive through Ardfert to Ballyheigue' on Sunday morning, a drive around the Killarney lakes on Monday, and a return by boat. Among the oarsmen was 1903 Kerry goalkeeper Pat Dillon. Kerry were relaxing too by all accounts. Wexford won 3-5 to 0-2 and, according to the *Kerryman*, 'A team of old-age pensioners would have given a better display of football.'

But when the serious business began, Kerry retained their Munster title by beating Tipperary 2-2 to 0-2 in Dungarvan and Cork by 0-5 to 0-1 at Tralee, doing most of their scoring in the first nine minutes of the second half after they had gone 0-1 to nil up at half-time.

Wexford felt they were now ready to take the Kerry men on. Wexford beat Meath, Kilkenny and Dublin in the space of five weeks to reach the provincial final. But the most ironic event of an undistinguished championship occurred when, in the first round, Kildare 1905 star 'Joyce' Conlan eliminated his former colleagues from the championship with a last-minute goal for Laois (he was working on the railway at Maryboro, later Portlaoise, at the time). Laois failed to Louth, 5-3 to 0-3, in the semi-final.

Wexford eventually annihilated Louth by 3-6 to 0-1 after a slow start in the Leinster final. Fittingly, Seán O'Kennedy, their natural leader who cycled a round trip of 80 miles to train the team, got their first goal after fifteen minutes. McDonald made it 2-3 to 0-1 at half-time, and Johnny Rossiter got a third in the second half. Meanwhile, Louth had the misfortune of having a goal disallowed and then hit the crossbar with another shot.

A record crowd paid £58-13-8 to see Cavan trail six-in-a-row seekers Antrim 1-1 to nil at half-time in the Ulster championship quarter-final, but they took control in the second half and their 2-3 to 1-2 victory ended a winning sequence that extended back to the chaos of 1907. Three weeks later Cavan went down to Fermanagh 2-1 to 0-4—a surprise considering Cavan had earlier won the Ulster Medal tournament by beating Derry 1-3 to 0-2 on 31 May in Newbliss. The Ulster semi-final between Monaghan and Armagh on 7 August at Carrickmacross was a scoreless draw—the only full-length GAA championship match to finish scoreless in 100 years. Monaghan ended a great Fermanagh run when they beat the Teemore selection 2-4 to 0-2 in the Ulster final.

In the All-Ireland semi-final against Wexford, Monaghan had a second half goal disallowed as they went down 2-6 to 0-1 to goals from Gus O'Kennedy and Johnny Rossiter before a paltry 3,000 attendance in Croke Park. Kerry had easily beaten Roscommon 2-4 to 0-1 in the other semi-final at Maryboro a week earlier. Roscommon had the advantage of having persuaded Connacht's leading player, Harry Hession from Roscommon town, to captain his native county that year, while the Fuerty and Kilbride areas contributed most of Hession's team.

Wexford were back for another crack at the title, and goals from Seán O'Kennedy and Aidan Doyle early on in the All-Ireland final suggested they might succeed this time. But the 2-0 to 0-1 Wexford half-time lead crumbled seconds after the restart when Paddy Breen took Dick Fitzgerald's pass for a Kerry goal. A last-minute point from Fitzgerald earned a replay, 1-3 to 2-0.

Kerry, the replay specialists, took their time about winning the second time round. Again they trailed at half-time, this time by six points to nil. Paddy Breen repeated his drawn match 'psychological' goal to start the second half, Johnny Mahoney piled in another from the kick-out, the irrepressible Dick Fitzgerald kicked two points and Johnny Skinner landed a third. Kerry became outright winners of the Railway Cup by 2-3 to 0-6, having won the All-Ireland twice in succession.

The provincial finalists played off in the Croke Cup semi-finals. Minnows Fermanagh met Louth at Newbliss on 8 November, and the 1912 All-Ireland champions barely survived because Fermanagh missed two penalties and Louth won 1-1 to 0-1. When Louth lost the Croke Cup final to Cork by 2-1 to 0-3 in February 1915, it was to all intents and purposes the end of the road for Owen Markey and the others.

It was also the end of the road for the Croke Cups themselves, after eighteen years. With running expenses of £180 and receipts of only £115, it had clearly failed to arouse any interest among the new generation of sports spectators.

7 NOVEMBER. WEXFORD 2-4, KERRY 2-1, CROKE PARK

> 'We had great football but no rough play; and frees were not nearly as frequent as they are today. The meeting of friends was looked forward to from year to year. We talked of things other than football, of events of the future that were in the making. One gained in strength of spirit and hope renewed through contact with these Kerrymen and it did not surprise me when the time came that Kerry ranked high in Ireland's role of honour.'
>
> JIM BOLGER in *Gaelic Athletic Memories*, ed. Séamus Ó Ceallaigh, 1944

Sometime in the spring of 1915, Wexford got the organisation right. Organised selection, organised club football and organised training could win an All-Ireland. Schoolteacher, sprinter, jumper, hurler and footballer Paddy Breen had proved one of the best wingers on Erin's Hope teams early in the century, at a stage when Dublin had the best footballers and half the All-Irelands ever played in the bag. At home in Wexford Breen set up the organisation that would win four All-Irelands in a row. It was only a matter of time before they broke through. When they did, it rapidly became a question of who would crack a new formula, the one to stop them.

In the 1915 Leinster championship, Wexford brushed aside Kilkenny and Offaly easily enough. Only for a few minutes at the end of the Leinster final did Wexford's provincial three in a row begin to look doubtful—when two Seán Lawlor goals for Dublin forced them to a replay, 2-2 each. Seán O'Kennedy, who scored Wexford's first goal in the drawn match, scored 2-2 in the replay as Wexford eventually triumphed by 2-5 to 1-3. Support was swelling beyond 1913 or 1914 levels. Record crowds of 8,000 (paying £229) and 13,000 turned out to watch the Leinster finals.

Two goals midway through the first half from newcomer John Wall and team captain Seán O'Kennedy, and another goal from Wall in the second half, helped Wexford to master improving Cavan by 3-7 to 2-2. Cavan at least managed a respectable scoreline, their comeback into the game inspired by Quinn and Rogers goals.

Cavan had had a stormy Ulster championship. They had to play Antrim twice on the grounds that they were late on the field the first day, winning 1-3 to 0-2 and 0-3 to 0-1. They drew the final against a Monaghan team for whom Eoin O'Duffy was having an increased organisational and playing input, and when they appeared to have won, Monaghan objected to their 0-4 to 0-3 victory on the grounds that 'the crowd had been on the pitch for the final ten minutes of the game', that 'the goalposts were broken, rendering it impossible for them to score', that 'the umpire saved a certain Monaghan goal three minutes from the end', and that Cavan's star, Felix McGovern, had played in Leitrim. The McGovern objection was upheld, Monaghan were nominated to play in the All-Ireland semi-final of the following year, and a replay was ordered for 10 October in Belfast. Cavan refused to play and were declared, uniquely, 'champions without medals'.

Kerry were beginning to falter even before they faced Wexford in the All-Ireland final. M. Donovan and young Jack Rice got the Kerry goals that brought them from behind in the second half to beat a Roscommon team captained by future GAA president Dan O'Rourke, 2-3 to 1-1. A week later Roscommon lost the Connacht final to Mayo 3-1 to 1-3.

Kerry trainer Jerry Collins had been transferred to Limerick, star player Johnny Skinner was working in Clonmel, while Johnny Mahoney emigrated to New York. Then full back Jack Lawlor broke his thumb in a trial match in Tralee. He was sent on to the field to play with his thumb encased in plaster of Paris and a bandage. This was crucial to the result of the game.

For a third year in succession the outstanding fielding of Pat 'Aeroplane' O'Shea of Castlegregory was the highlight of the All-Ireland midfield battle, rapidly becoming the most important sector of the field under the new fifteen-a-side rule. His skills impressed a crowd of 27,000, who paid £1,040, but not Wexford, who got their revenge in the final, winning 2-4 to 2-1.

Wexford owed their victory, not as might be expected, from the O'Kennedy brothers of New Ross, but this time from the place-kicking of Jim Byrne of Wexford town. Byrne kicked two points from 50s and landed the winning goal from another in controversial circumstances. The goal was to be talked about for years to come. Byrne was not clear about the scoreline as he stepped up to take the third 50. He misread the signal from a colleague, indicating that he should opt for a point, and dropped the ball in for a goal instead. Full back Jack Lawlor went to catch the ball with his bandaged hand and then changed his mind. Dinny Mullins tried to save too late and barely touched the ball, which was allowed to strike the underside of the crossbar and drop into the net.

Aidan Byrne had got the first goal that sent Wexford 1-2 to 1-0 ahead in reply to a goal by Kerry's Denis Doyle. Dick Fitzgerald hit the post in the first half and the crossbar in the second half before charging the goalie into the net for Kerry's second goal.

So, Wexford had become champions at the third attempt and collected the new Railway Cup as a reward.

17 DECEMBER 1916. WEXFORD 2-4, MAYO 1-2, CROKE PARK

> 'The ground was barely playable and I was very anxious about my players.'
> Wexford captain SEÁN KENNEDY, *Irish Independent*, 18 December 1916

It appeared that there was another battle between the finalists in store, this time for the Wolfe Tone tournament, arranged to replace the Croke Cup. But Louth defeated Wexford by a single point, 2-3 to 2-2, in the quarter-final.

Kerry had already beaten Cork in another quarter-final 4-0 to 0-2. By the time the final came to be played, political fortunes had changed. So many of the players found themselves in Frongoch prison camp in Wales after the 1916 Rising that the final was played there, and Dick Fitzgerald's Kerry team defeated Tom Burke's Louth by a point.

A separate tournament was taking place outside the prison camps between four weakened teams, producing victory for Mayo over Kerry, and Louth over Monaghan, before Louth beat Mayo in the final. The final was the last appearance, at the age of 43, of Jack 'Sandman' Carvin. In a career with Kickhams of Dublin, Drogheda Independents and Tredagh, 'Carvin of the 100 battles' was slow to run but had a pair of arms which were reputed to reach down to his knees.

The round-up of insurgents after the Easter Rebellion had put several notable GAA players behind bars. Shocked and confused by the unexpected rebellion, the authorities had targeted GAA members because, according to their now hopelessly inadequate files, the GAA was rife with Sinn Féiners. GAA president James Nowlan and prominent Waterford referee Willie Walsh were among the first to be arrested. But they knew nothing about the rising.

The strongest GAA connection with the rising was in Wexford, where Seán Etchingham and Seamus Doyle were among the rebels that held Enniscorthy for several days, having used an Easter Sunday GAA fixture to foregather. Kerry GAA man Austin Stack was arrested after the landing of arms for the rising was bungled. Individual clubs were devastated. The Croke club had 40 members: 32 fought in the rising; two were killed. The Maynooth Volunteers marched to join the rising in Dublin, as a result of which the local club could not field in the Kildare championship.

Four Dublin players from the 1915 Leinster final team were among those who fought. Jack Shouldice was sentenced to death after the rebellion. Frank Bourke, the most decorated dual star in Gaelic history, was also in the GPO, as were Frank Shouldice, P. J. Walsh and Michael Collins elsewhere in action. Con O'Donovan and Harry Boland were rank-and-file GAA members. Among those executed, Pearse was a GAA colleges council member and Seán McDermott, Con Colbert, Michael O'Hanrahan and Eamonn Ceannt had GAA connections. But the GAA responded to the rebellion by denying that it had any connection, that these individual members were acting independently, and distanced itself from the rebels.

There was no stopping Wexford now, especially when Kerry withdrew from the 1916 championship because they wanted 'to play matches on their own'. As was the case in Galway, arrests had devastated the local GAA scene, and the suppression of the *Kerryman* newspaper had cut off communications bringing club activities to a halt.

Kerry had already eliminated Tipperary by 2-2 to 0-1, so Cork and Clare were left to fight out the final. Somewhat surprisingly, Cork were forced to hold on grimly and won 2-2 to 1-4 as Clare came storming back to within a point of them, having led 2-2 to 0-1 at half-time.

Wexford's other main rivals, Dublin, decided to opt out when Frank Bourke and other football colleagues were dispatched to Frongoch in the aftermath of the Easter Rising. Appropriately enough, Dublin won a Leinster championship 'final' played inside the camp when they beat Wexford, captained by 1901 veteran John Vize, by 1-8 to 2-3. Under martial law, travel and practice was becoming increasingly difficult. The police even banned training sessions in Cavan, Down and Fermanagh.

Despite losing their Maynooth men to the rigours of martial law, Kildare still made it to the Leinster final with a new teenage star, 19-year-old Larry Stanley. 'Stanley, who was taking part in senior football for the first time, covered himself in glory', *Sport* enthused. Wexford won 1-7 to 0-4 as Aidan Doyle struck with a goal just before half-time to make the score 1-4 to nil and kill off any hopes of a Kildare revival.

Although the Leinster final in October attracted an attendance of 10,000, the military was increasingly using its power to cancel special trains within a fortnight, a power often used arbitrarily and late. The result was that the All-Ireland final and semi-finals drew some of the lowest attendances in years. For the semi-final in Athlone on 22 October, local businesses prepared to cater for 10,000 visitors to the town, but all trains were cancelled at the last minute and the piles of ham sandwiches went unsold.

Mayo were the rising team in Connacht. Some 4,000 attended the Connacht final against Roscommon. Mayo trailed by 0-1 to 0-3 at half-time and their recovery was started by a point from Harry Hession who had been, in a previous guise, Roscommon captain and star of 1914.

Mayo won that semi-final 1-2 to 0-2 and achieved a breakthrough for Connacht, but because one of the Mayo team, Durkin, had lined out in the Cork championship, Mayo were forced to replay the All-Ireland semi-final against Cork, and a Lyons goal and Reilly and Courell points helped them beat Cork 1-2 to 1-1 the second day in atrocious conditions. The gates were not opened because heavy rain in the morning left a doubt over the game. It eventually went ahead in front of 'a few hundred brave enthusiasts' who gained admission at the last minute. The Railway goal was 'in the middle of a lake' and there were pools of water inches deep elsewhere on the pitch. Four points from Gus O'Kennedy and three from Jim Byrne helped Wexford overcome Monaghan by 0-9 to 1-1, inspired by Joe Keeley's goal, in the other semi-final in Carrickmacross, where an impressive total of 5,000 turned out.

Despite the political crisis having brought Gaelic games to a standstill in Belfast and several other parts of Ulster, the championship got under way in June. Down caused a good deal of surprise when they held Antrim to level terms at half-time in the Ulster semi-final, but they failed to score in the second half and lost 1-3 to 1-0. Monaghan got revenge for the Felix McGovern affair by beating Cavan 4-3 to 1-5 in the other semi-final, then beat ailing Antrim 2-3 to 0-2 in an anticlimactic Ulster final at Clones.

No special trains were allowed for the All-Ireland final, so the crowd of 3,000 was described by the *Freeman's Journal* as 'surprisingly large'. The streets of Dublin were sheeted in ice, and overnight frost meant the pitch was extremely hard, despite the fact that straw had been spread on it. 'We doubt if any match has been played under such wintry conditions as prevailed', the *Irish Independent* commented. In later years spectators were better able to recall their journey to and from the game than the match itself.

At 2 o'clock the ground was pronounced playable and the O'Kennedy brothers quickly established Wexford's superiority and they won 2-4 to 1-1. John snatched two first half goals and gave to Gus in the second half for a third. Mayo's reply was a late goal by Tom Boshell and first half points from Harry Hession and Frank Courell. During the match Mayo's goalkeeper placed his hat against the net behind the goal.

There was an attempt to run a rival All-Ireland championship in 1916 by the National Association of Gaelic and Athletic Clubs (the NAGAC, or five-letter folly, as the GAA ridiculed it). It had its origins in a dispute over the setting up of a separate junior board in Dublin, and one of Dublin's most traditional clubs, Kickhams, seceded from the GAA in 1913. In February 1916 delegates from Galway, Sligo, Tipperary and Wexford met to join Kickhams delegates and form the NAGAC in Dublin. Among the issues that brought a diverse group of dissident clubs together was opposition to the Volunteer takeover, and also opposition to Dublin control at the expense of Thurles. In 1919 Kickhams rejoined the GAA.

9 DECEMBER 1917. WEXFORD 0-9, CLARE 0-5, CROKE PARK

> 'From an hour before the appointed time large crowds were heading for the venue, the Munstermen resident in the city being largely represented. The Model County also had a large following, while large numbers came by car and bicycle. Wexford were first to take the field followed a little later by the Clare players, who, headed by a Republican flag, were loudly cheered.'
>
> *Irish Independent*, 19 December 1917

As they had difficulty completing local club matches, it was no surprise that Kerry were out again in 1917, but Dublin were back for an impressive 0-12 to 1-4 victory over Louth and a 0-5 to 0-3 victory over Laois to face Wexford in the Leinster final.

Their year's absence caused some hiccups. Dublin struggled for 45 minutes in the semi-final against Laois, and trailed 0-1 to 0-2 at half-time. But they were getting their act together with the help of a new 6' 3" midfielder, Paddy McDonnell of O'Toole's. Wexford needed a dramatic late winner to beat Dublin 1-3 to 1-1 before 7,000 spectators. Jim Byrne's sideline ball was fisted on by Seán O'Kennedy for the winning goal, again scored by Aidan Byrne. Seán Lawlor got Dublin's only goal in the final, from a drop-kick, after Wexford had held on to a 0-1 to nil half-time lead, despite having played into a stiff breeze.

Wexford missed Tom Mernagh and Val Connolly for their 6-6 to 1-3 semi-final victory against Monaghan, but managed to recall former star Fr Edmund Wheeler, unavailable since his ordination. Wheeler played under the three pseudonyms, J. Quinn, James Furlong and Ed Phelan to avoid ecclesiastical censure and helped in their victory.

The province from which Monaghan had qualified, as usual, had its fair share of disputes. Most of them revolved around the Ulster semi-final between old rivals Monaghan and Cavan. In the Ulster semi-final, Monaghan won 3-1 to 0-2, but were late on the field. Cavan were awarded the match by the Ulster council when Monaghan rejected an offer of a replay. The Central Council ordered a replay, but this time Cavan refused, claiming Monaghan had too much influence on the Ulster and Central councils (a tribute to the persuasive skills of Monaghan's Eoin O'Duffy). The acrimony between the two wasn't doing the coffers any harm: £60 was taken at Cootehill, compared with £10 at the final, where Monaghan beat Armagh 4-2 to 0-4 with the help of three goals from Joe Keeley, as they came back from 0-2 to 0-3 behind at half-time.

There was no such income from the Antrim-Down shambles in the first round, advertised for 3 o'clock 'Irish time'. Hundreds turned up at 3 o'clock 'present time' and when they heard they would have to wait an hour and a half for the match, most of them went home in disgust. The clock had been tampered with to save fuel during the First World War and this led to total confusion about exact starting times.

Kerry's absence enabled a powerful Clare team to emerge in Munster for their first and only championship, 2-6 to 0-3 victors over Waterford, 0-5 to 0-4 victors over Tipperary, and massive 5-4 to 0-1 victors over Cork in the Munster final at Tipperary town. The flag they followed on to the field read 'Up De Valera'. Kilkee man and Kildare native Jim Foran, all 6' 3" of him, organised the training for the side with 1914 hurler Sham Spellissey.

In the All-Ireland semi-final, Clare beat Galway 2-1 to 0-4 at Athlone. Martin McNamara and Ned Carroll got the second half goals that put Clare into the final, Turlough 'Tull' Considine the point in the first half.

Travel restrictions in the wake of insurrection meant the whole draw in Connacht had to be rearranged. Sligo v Roscommon in Boyle could not be played because of martial law restrictions, and the draw was rescheduled so Sligo would play Mayo instead. Galway stopped Mayo in their tracks with a 1-4 to 1-1 victory in the Connacht final at Castlerea, Pat Roche getting the vital goal.

Because of these restrictions, just 6,500 turned out to watch the final. A group of Wexford players and supporters were fined five shillings with costs at Arklow petty sessions for defying restrictions and using a motor car to travel to the game. Driver Jim Fortune commented: 'Had the members of the RIC, who halted us on our way home from the game, made a search of the car, instead of taking us as mere football enthusiasts, the story would have been different.'

Wexford were expected to complete the three in a row rather easily. As it happened, they needed a lot of luck to prevent a shock Clare victory, although the 0-9 to 0-5 scoreline was a comfortable one in the end. Wexford led 0-6 to 0-4 at half-time, and after a dispute over a disallowed goal by Aidan Doyle, they came under pressure in the second half. Tull Considine from Ennis, one of the outstanding GAA personalities of his generation and a player in the All-Ireland hurling final as late as 1932, broke through but was tripped from behind. Then Clare had a goal disallowed and Wexford held on for a four-point victory, mainly thanks to Jim Byrne's sharpshooting, while Martin McNamara of Clare was doing some of his own.

The Clare players turned to a different kind of shooting in the years that followed. Two of them lost their lives during the War of Independence.

16 FEBRUARY 1919. WEXFORD 0-5, TIPPERARY 0-4, CROKE PARK

> 'It was decided due to the large numbers of players down with flu, not to make any fixtures.'
>
> *Anglo-Celt*, 2 November 1918

There were signs that all the political problems the GAA had narrowly avoided so far would eventually catch up with them in 1918.

Kerry signalled their return to championship football in 1918 by beating defending Munster champions Clare 5-3 to 1-3. But in the Munster final they failed to Tipperary by 1-1 to 0-1. Tipperary started with a goal from Bill Grant minutes after the throw-in. Con Clifford scored a Kerry point before half-time, but Davey Tobin scored a winning second half point for Tipperary. A tiny attendance watched in Cork.

Leinster provided the shaggy ball story of the championship. The ball burst before the Laois-Kildare match could get under way on 30 June. The game lasted only ten minutes as numerous attempts to repair it proved fruitless.

But everywhere politics was intervening. Public meetings were banned in thirteen counties on 4 July, with the rules framed to include the GAA, but not cricket or lawn tennis games. With the RIC demanding permits for the holding of football matches under the Defence of the Realm Act and the GAA refusing to apply for them, a confrontation was inevitable. During the long, hot month of July, soldiers baton charged matches in Offaly and Down, took down goalposts in Kildare and occupied playing fields in Cork.

The biggest show-down took place before an Ulster championship match between Cavan and Armagh at Cootehill in July, where a large body of troops occupied the playing field where 3,000 had gathered. Local parish priest, Fr O'Connell, addressed the crowd, asked them to disperse quietly and no incidents occurred. A match was fixed for the same field on the following day. This time the police attended, but bayonets were not drawn and the game took place.

On 4 August the GAA replied by mobilising 54,000 players at games throughout the country. All the matches started at the same time. Parishes and townlands which had not fielded a team for a generation lined out, and there was no RIC interference. The permit issue was allowed to die.

The championships quickly swung back into action. Antrim and Derry played at a new Belfast venue, Celtic Park, home of the Belfast Celtic soccer club. Cavan were sulking and had to be persuaded to enter the championship at all. Following the objections saga of 1917, they had considered playing in Connacht instead. Then they proposed a new fifth province of Tara, to include themselves, Longford, Westmeath, Louth and Meath. The proposal was not taken seriously.

As it happened, Cavan totally dominated the final against Antrim and won 3-2 to nil. They had first half goals from John Malone and Pat Fay as, meanwhile, Antrim managed to get across the halfway line only once. In the second half Antrim managed just one dangerous attack, while Cavan had a third goal from J. P. Murphy. Gate receipts were only £5-17-4.

Wexford faced a renewed challenge from Louth in Leinster. Louth beat Meath, Dublin and Kildare. Louth's attempt to stop Wexford was not helped by the fact that four of their players never made it to Croke Park because the car in which they were travelling broke down. In October, Louth were Leinster's last nominated semi-finalists and needed two second half goals from Frank Byrne to beat Cavan 2-4 to 0-4 before a small attendance of 3,000.

But Wexford were not finished yet. In January, Jim Redmond and Gus Kennedy's first half goals sent Wexford into a commanding interval lead of 2-3 to 0-2, and they held on to beat Louth 2-5 to 1-4 before a 10,000 attendance. Noel Butterley got the goal that brought Louth back within two points midway through the second half. Politics, not football, was the topic of conversation among the spectators. The first Dáil met the following day.

Having survived the political crisis of 1918, the GAA faced an even more serious one, a killer influenza epidemic carried back from the trenches of France by the returning soldiers from October onwards.

All-Ireland finalists Tipperary were badly hit by the 1918 black flu. Davey Tobin scored two goals that gave Tipperary the cushion to pip Mayo 2-2 to 1-4, despite Eamonn Courell's shooting. He was one of the flu victims who missed the final.

Then, nine days later, came the Solohead shootings which kicked off the War of Independence on 21 January 1919. Tipperary training had to be halted as a military clampdown followed.

Sport enthused that Wexford's team was 'the best ever' after the Leinster final. Nevertheless, Wexford had the closest victory of their four in the All-Ireland final, 0-5 to 0-4, in front of a replenished attendance of 12,000. Tipperary could have won. Gus McCarthy, scorer of two Tipperary points, had another disallowed for 'whistle gone'. Former Kerry footballer Jack Skinner and Tommy Ryan got the other Tipperary scores as Byrne, Pierce and Redmond put Wexford 0-3 to 0-2 up at half-time, and Pierce and O'Kennedy went on to complete a historic victory.

At the tail end of the game, Gus McCarthy was inches wide with a 30 yard free, and Tipperary also claimed the ball bobbed across the line before a Wexford back scooped it away. Wexford had created a record by winning four in a row, but only by the skin of a whitewash line.

28 SEPTEMBER 1919. KILDARE 2-5, GALWAY 0-1, CROKE PARK

Three nonpareils Kildare can claim
Honourable, clean and manly
Their names can grace the hall of fame
Dempsey, Conneff and Stanley.

ANONYMOUS KILDARE BALLAD (1919)

When Wexford ran out of steam, it was not Louth or Kerry who succeeded them. Dublin's star, in an 0-11 to 1-2 semi-final victory over the seven-in-a-row seekers Wexford, was midfielder Paddy McDonnell. Dublin were under threat from a proposed ban on all civil servants who had taken the oath of allegiance. It had already been used against one of McDonnell's club mates and could have caused large headaches for the GAA if Dublin had gone on to All-Ireland level. But Dublin were beaten 1-3 to 1-1 by Kildare in the Leinster final.

Kildare were inspired by 22-year-old midfielder Larry Stanley who demonstrated his legendary 'one-handed catch' against McDonnell. Rugby star Jim O'Connor was Kildare's goalscorer in the final. He had scored 4-1 in the semi-final against Westmeath.

Louth's bid was short lived. In the first round, Meath came back from six points down to earn a draw with Louth, forced another draw, and beat them 2-5 to 2-4 in a second replay.

In Ulster, Cavan won the championship while the Ulster council celebrated the province's first £100 gate. Armagh beat Monaghan and then lost to Antrim in turn. The council had thought of a unique way of getting rid of their financial problems, having started the year £230 in debt. It organised three meetings between the finalists, at first arranging that the 'best of three matches' would decide the championship. As this would be of doubtful legality, the first two meetings were redesignated 'build-up friendly matches' to boost interest in the game and, more importantly, the funds of the Ulster council.

Cavan won the first match 5-3 to 1-4 in Belturbet; the second meeting resulted in a draw, Cavan 2-4, Antrim 1-7; and when Antrim rejected Belturbet as a venue for the final proper, it was staged at neutral Clones. Cavan won 5-5 to 0-2. Council receipts soared from £144 in 1918 to £359, and the Ulster champions were presented with medals for the first time.

Kildare beat Cavan 3-2 to 1-2 in the semi-final at Navan. Frank 'Joyce' Conlan, a survivor from 1905, scored 2-1 for Kildare in the first few minutes of the game, and had a breakaway shot from the throw-in barely saved.

Kerry took back the Munster title after five years and also had a new star, marksman John Joe Sheehy. Kerry ousted champions Tipperary in the first round by 2-4 to 2-3, and Sheehy got the first half goal that sent Kerry 1-7 to nil ahead of Clare at half-time in the Munster final at Ennis. Then he started the second half goalrush that led to a massive 6-11 to 2-0 victory.

But Kerry lost to the Connacht champions in the All-Ireland semi-final. Michael 'Knacker' Walsh was to become Connacht's best-known forward of the 1920s. In 1917 he scored one point for Galway; in 1919 he turned the match around just when Roscommon had gained an 0-5 to 0-1 lead, scoring a dramatic goal and a point immediately afterwards to give Galway a 1-6 to 0-5 victory over Roscommon in the Connacht final before 3,000 spectators at Tuam. Walsh's exploits continued in the All-Ireland semi-final, as Galway drew 2-6 to 3-3 with Kerry, when J. Egan got two goals in answer to two from Baily and a lucky Kerry goal from O'Connor, and then won the replay 4-2 to 2-2 three weeks later. In the replay Walsh's sixth and sixteenth-minute goals helped Galway to a 3-0 to nil lead with another goal from John Hannify, while Michael Flannelly scored a fourth twelve minutes from the end. Kerry's two goals came late in the game.

Kildare devised a plan to keep Knacker Walsh from upsetting their All-Ireland prospects. The goalkeeper and full back would change places, and the goalkeeper would body charge Walsh while the full back stood on the line. As the goalkeeper was the massively built veteran from 1903, Larry 'Hussey' Cribben, whose giant physique would tear up the Croke Park turf like a bullock as he paced the goalmouth, the body charge was expected to work. After one near miss there was a crunch of body-to-body impact, and after that Galway's only point in the game came late in the second half from John Egan.

Meanwhile Larry Stanley, playing at midfield with Mick Sammon, helped Kildare dominate the game, while Galway's placing was described as wretched. For the final, Kildare's goals came from another 1903 survivor, Frank 'Joyce' Conlan, after seventeen minutes, and Jim O'Connor who tipped a Mick Sammon 50 to the net nine minutes after half-time. Kildare had taken a 1-2 to nil half-time lead. Kildare newcomer, 19-year-old Paul Doyle, who played his first championship game because Peter Grady had flu, proved one of the finest lifters of the ball so far.

Stanley, one of the contenders for the tag of 'greatest ever', was to play just seventeen times for Kildare, and failed to line out in 1920 because he was disgusted at being suspended for 'not trying' in a match. The suspicion was that he was helping someone win a bet. Bookmakers were common at GAA matches until the 1920s. One of the best stories of a betting footballer was told about Johnny Brennan, who asked a friend to put 7/6 on Dublin at 6/4 in the 1913 Croke Cup competition. Brennan then kicked seven frees to help Louth beat Dublin, the team he had backed, 0-7 to 0-5. After the game he found out his friend had forgotten to lay the bet in the excitement.

But the bookmakers were a minor threat to the GAA compared to what was coming. A new round of bans had just been introduced, against Sinn Fein, the Irish Volunteers, Cumann na mBan and the Gaelic League. The GAA had escaped, but on the eve of the All-Ireland final, the *Freeman's Journal* complained that the authorities 'place every obstacle in the movement of devotees to Irish native games'. But, for Gaelic football, the political obstacle course was only beginning.

11 JUNE 1922. TIPPERARY 1-6, DUBLIN 1-2, CROKE PARK

> 'The 1920 football final, played yesterday at Croke Park, will rank with the best and most exciting championships in the history of the GAA. On a baked ground and under a broiling sun the pace was set a cracker and never flagged, but rather intensified to the last whistle.'
>
> *Freeman's Journal*, 11 June 1922

While the GAA braced itself for a new round of political problems in 1920, Leinster's problems were born of old-fashioned football rivalry.

Kildare's threats to withdraw from the 1920 Leinster championship, after Larry Stanley had been suspended for allegedly 'not trying' in a challenge against Kerry after the 1919 All-Ireland, brought out the old county rivalries within the Leinster and Central councils.

While old rivals proposed that Kildare be suspended for anything up to five years, Stanley played for Belfast Celtic and, although he lined out for the 1924 All-Ireland final with Dublin, he was not to play for Kildare again until 1926.

When Kildare were eventually persuaded to enter, tragedy resulted. Kildare's first round match with Wexford resulted in an injury to William Hodgins from which the Wexford player later died due to a complication.

Kildare met Dublin in the Leinster final on 29 August, losing 1-3 to 0-3. St Enda's headmaster and successor to Pearse, Frank Bourke, scored the final point against his native county, having set up a first half goal for Paddy Carey.

The All-Ireland semi-final took place on 9 September, in which Dublin beat the Ulster nominees Cavan 2-6 to 1-3. Cavan had just beaten Dublin 2-6 to 0-6 in a challenge match in Virginia on 5 September. Then, to Cavan's chagrin, the Central Council postponed the match from 12 September for two weeks. When it went ahead, John Synnott killed off Cavan with two early goals, while Frank Bourke scored a third at the beginning of the second half. J. P. Murphy got Cavan's goal just before half-time.

As it happened, despite the argufying, Leinster was one of only two provinces to complete their championship in 1920. While less sporting troubles brought competition to a halt in Munster and Ulster, seven days before the Leinster final Connacht had completed their championship when Mayo beat Sligo in the final at Castlerea before 2,000 spectators.

Tom 'Click' Brennan, Paddy Colleran and Mick Kilcoyne were the stars of the Sligo team which beat Mayo in the final of the 'other' Connacht competition, the Railway Cup of 1920. Sligo were soon to make a big impact on the championship itself, but not for two more years. Mayo were eventually saved by first half goals from P. Robinson from a free, and D. F. Courell with a fine overhead effort, to defeat Sligo. A group of Sligo supporters from Templeboy commissioned a motor lorry to bring them to the game.

Ulster's championship had reached the final stages by then, but the final between Cavan and Armagh was not played until August 1923. In a noteworthy championship, Down shocked Antrim, now just a shadow of their former strength, and a run-of-the-mill motor breakdown depleted Tyrone's team for the match against Armagh.

But it was Munster which felt the winds of war the strongest. Kerry had beaten Cork in the first Munster semi-final on 20 June before play came to a stop there. Tipperary were due to play Waterford, but did not get a chance to do so until 19 February 1922. By then all had changed utterly. Several closed days had disrupted the GAA calendar, and Tipperary had long been out of action when a letter from the secretary and captain of the Tipperary football team appeared in the *Freeman's Journal* on 1 November 1920: 'We understand that Tipperary's superiority over Dublin in football, despite two decisive victories by Tipperary, is being questioned by Dublin. We therefore challenge Dublin to a match on the first available date, on any venue, and for any objective.'

Dublin replied. The Central Council fixed a match for 21 November in aid of an injured Gael. The Gael was not named, but in Dublin Castle they had no doubt that the game was to raise funds for the IRA. The day was to become known as Bloody Sunday.

Early in the morning groups from Michael Collins's squad entered eight separate houses and shot dead twelve British spies and wounded several other agents sent to assassinate republican leaders.

In the afternoon soldiers and police went to Croke Park and fired upon the crowd. Twelve people died on the day, and a thirteenth later in hospital. Nine people, including three children, were shot dead. A woman was crushed to death in the panic. Another man died from shock. A statement issued from Dublin Castle that the troops had been fired upon was contradicted by press reports and by the subsequent investigation by Dublin Castle's own police force on the ground, the Dublin Metropolitan Police.

Among the dead was Tipperary footballer Michael Hogan. The Hogan Stand at Croke Park was named in his honour in 1925; a second stand was built in 1959 and the third in 2002.

The outrage brought Gaelic games to a halt for six months. On 11 July 1921, a truce was signed between the Irish Republican and British Forces, but it was another ten months, eighteen months after Bloody Sunday, before the Munster championship resumed.

Tipperary beat Kerry 2-2 to 0-2 in the provincial final. Meanwhile, the country braced itself for a civil war which would tear both counties apart.

So the All-Ireland semi-final eventually took place on 7 May 1922 and Tipperary beat Mayo 1-5 to 1-0 before a surprisingly large crowd of 15,000. Tom Powell got the goal at the end of the first half. William Lydon got Mayo's goal. Pat Robinson was Mayo's best player as Seán Lavin did not reproduce his Connacht championship form.

When Tipperary started out in the 1920 championship, Dan Breen was on the run. By the time the All-Ireland final was played between Tipperary and Dublin eighteen months later, Breen was a hero of the revolution and invited to start the match by throwing in the ball before a crowd of 17,000. Tipperary won 1-6 to 1-2. Frank Bourke, another hero of the revolution, scored a magnificent 30 yard goal for Dublin to send them 1-2 to 0-3 ahead at half-time, but Tipperary came back to equalise eighteen minutes into the second half and went ahead with a Mick Arrigan point before Tom Powell got a clinching goal. Ned O'Shea was the best of their backs, Tom Powell, Gus McCarthy, Mick Tobin and Vincent Vaughan their best forwards.

An *Irish Independent* colour writer opined:

> I should like to have set a thermometer in the covered stand of Croke Park yesterday. I could fancy it chasing itself roundabout and upside down in its effort to make the mercury record the degrees of temperature. When I arrived I found men in the throes of politeness saluting the sun with hats off. Scores of them cooled with coats off. A vista of Sunday-shirted men and bare-necked women looking for the breeze. I tried to get in the line of the breeze that blew down from the railway, but a flag post and a Limerick Junction farmer blocked the way.
>
> In yesterday's spectatorate I venture to say there were as many girls and women as there were others. Clergymen darkened the background,

bandsmen and pipers splashed the place with colour, and there were Irish military officers in sufficient strength to run a life sized revolution.

One thing becomes clearer and clearer with every visit to this arena of athleticism. It is that people come here to see the game. To Lansdowne Road throng thousands drawn by the desire to see and be seen. Curiosity, and perhaps divarshun will entice onlookers to slide up to an election meeting; bookmakers and sideshows and fashions attract to race meetings. But at Croke Park the game's the thing that counts.

17 JUNE 1923. DUBLIN 1-9, MAYO 0-2, CROKE PARK

> 'Those who didn't come were more noticeable than those who did. Politicians were there by the score, of course. But there is an election at hand, and you know all Irish politicians suddenly discover in such a crisis that they have been lifelong patrons of Irish games.'
>
> *Irish Independent*, 18 June 1923

A week after the 1920 All-Ireland final, champions Dublin beat Monaghan 2-8 to 2-2 in the 1921 All-Ireland semi-final.

Leinster had completed their championship by September 1921 despite a drawn final, but some teams were badly prepared for championship action. Kildare's 9-8 to 1-1 annihilation of Carlow stood as a record for 58 years. Both counties expected the game to be prohibited by the British authorities, but it went ahead and the better-prepared Kildare were sent on course with a goal from local man Ed 'Sapper' O'Neill, later to star on New York and US Tailteann teams.

Leinster found the going tough throughout 1921. The attendance at many early rounds did not cover the costs of the games, as motor cars had to be used because the railway system had broken down. The salvation came from a £2,974 windfall from the replayed football final. The drawn final drew an estimated 20,000—the biggest attendance since Bloody Sunday.

The inactivity of the months since had been used to carry out £12,000 of improvements to the grounds, with a view to staging the Tailteann Games, now a real possibility since the Dáil had given it the go-ahead. A new stand had been erected in Croke Park (or Crow Park, as it was called in the British House of Commons after Bloody Sunday) and the length of the pitch was increased by fifteen yards.

Albert O'Neill got Kildare's goal for a 1-3 to 0-6 draw, and Joyce Conlan, the 1903 All-Ireland final goalscorer who was still going strong, missed the chance of a winning point. Dublin won the replay 3-3 to 1-3 and went on to beat Monaghan with an early goal from Bill Fitzsimmons. Dixon scored a second goal after ten minutes, and Dublin led 2-3 to 1-0 at half-time before going on to win by six points. Michael Deery scored both Monaghan goals.

Monaghan's preparations for the semi-final included six weeks spent in jail after they were kidnapped by B Specials in Dromore, Co. Tyrone, on 14 January 1922, while on their way to play in the Ulster final against Derry. Half the team were in the old IRA, including Dan Hogan, Officer in Command of the 5th Northern Division, and brother of Bloody Sunday footballer-victim Mike Hogan of Grangemockler. But the War of Independence had ended with a truce the previous July, and the IRA was now the army of the new Free State. They were travelling in six cars in convoy to Derry for the game. Documents were found on them relating to plans to release three prisoners due to be executed in Derry Jail. Pro and anti-treaty factions united in efforts to get the players released.

Then things turned nasty. In February, 42 loyalists were kidnapped by the IRA and held as hostages for the footballers. Eventually the three prisoners were reprieved and the footballers released on 16 February, after the intervention of Michael Collins and after instructions had been passed to Sir James Craig from Winston Churchill.

The match was postponed while the players spent those six weeks in jail, but in the confusion afterwards, arranging a replay proved difficult, and Monaghan represented Ulster in the All-Ireland semi-final against Dublin in June. The final was eventually played (after the 1922 and 1923 finals had been completed) on 28 October 1923 when Monaghan beat Derry 2-2 to 0-1 to confirm their nomination to represent Ulster as provincial champions that year. 'The Ulster Council are nothing if not persistent', Dublin newspaper *Sport* commented. Their persistence had to extend to locating their entire funds. The account had been transferred so often from bank to bank that the treasurer claimed he had mislaid it.

And according to the *Anglo-Celt* of 13 May 1922, the prize for a game between two local teams at Ballyjamesduff the following day would be a machine gun.

In Connacht, Mayo played one match each year, beating Roscommon in November 1921, Galway in June 1922, and Roscommon in March 1923 to win the Connacht championship. A Roscommon v Sligo match fixed for Tubbercurry fell through—both districts were controlled by anti-treaty forces during the early stages of the Civil War. Mayo got a walkover from Tipperary in the semi-final.

The Munster council got through their fixture pile-up and wriggled out of an impasse with some ingenuity, deciding that the 1920 finalists should play the 1921 provincial finals. This was designed to get over a difficult objection by the Limerick hurlers to a Cork player. It suited the hurlers, but Tipperary and

Kerry had still not played before the Civil War took full effect from July 1922. With fighting especially severe in the Kerry mountains and around Carrick-on-Suir, a November Munster council meeting decided to postpone all championships until 1923.

The Civil War issue would not go away in Munster. In April 1923 Tipperary finally conceded a long-fought, on-again off-again All-Ireland semi-final against Mayo on the issue of the republican prisoners, officially because they found it 'impossible to field a team'.

Eventually in June 1923, Dublin beat Mayo 1-9 to 0-2 in the All-Ireland final of 1921. They had the game sewn up when Bill Fitzsimmons scored a late goal to augment their scoreline. Dublin took fifteen minutes to open the scoring and led 0-4 to 0-1 at half-time.

The spectators watched a new tactic in operation that day. Mayo point-scorer Seán Lavin was one of the first to perfect the hand-to-toe technique and was later to represent Ireland in the sprints at the 1924 Olympics, at which Dublin and Kildare midfielder Larry Stanley competed in the high jump. Ireland had a flag of its own by then. The birth of the nation had been painful.

7 OCTOBER 1923. DUBLIN 0-6, GALWAY 0-4, CROKE PARK

> 'The most mixed up championship that I remember has ended gloriously.'
> *Irish Independent*, 8 October 1923

The rest of 1923 would be spent cleaning up the backlog of fixtures. Leinster, alone of all the provinces, completed their 1922 provincial championship on time as tensions mounted.

Anti-treaty forces had seized the Four Courts in April 1922. British troops began withdrawing from the barracks on 17 May, and the Four Courts bombardment started the Civil War on 28 June. As a result the Dublin-Kildare semi-final was postponed from 9 July to 1 October. When the game got under way, 'local incidents and prevailing circumstances' caused five of the Kildare team not to turn up and they lost 2-5 to 0-1.

For the Leinster final, Kilkenny recalled their 1911 goalscorer Paddy Dalton out of retirement to play in goal, but were missing two of their current players because of a motor breakdown. It was Kilkenny's last appearance in the Leinster final as they lost 1-7 to 0-2 to rampant Dublin. Paddy McDonnell ran up 1-4 without interruption at the start of the second half, breaking the dogged Kilkenny defence open after Dublin were held 0-2 to 0-1 at half-time.

Inside Newbridge internment camp, where 1,200 anti-treaty campaigners were imprisoned, Kildare had defeated Dublin 3-6 to 1-5 in the internees' Leinster final in October 1922. The campaign to get those prisoners released was increasingly intruding on Gaelic games throughout that summer of 1923.

Munster was the scene of the worst excesses of the Civil War. South Tipperary was reorganised in August 1923, but Kerry was still undergoing postwar confusion. Tipperary had a walkover from war-torn Kerry, but different types of walking were involved before they beat Cork in the Munster semi-final. They had to walk part of the way, travel partly by car and partly by rail past blocked roads and blown-up bridges on the way to Cork. After all the exertion, Jim Ryan got the vital goal as Tipperary beat Limerick 1-7 to 0-1 in the Munster final. That the final was played at all was regarded as a triumph for the GAA as a unifying force over the bitterness of the Civil War.

Monaghan won the Ulster championship with a last-minute goal from Mickey McAleer to put them 2-7 to 2-6 ahead of Cavan. Armagh managed to field a team for the semi-final against Monaghan at Ballybay, despite the fact that they had no county board at the time and half their team were on the run on both sides of the border. The newly established border was causing more than a little discomfort for GAA followers, and most of the matches in the championship were held south of the border.

Monaghan failed to get a single score against Dublin in the semi-final at Dundalk in July 1923, and lost by 2-5 to nil. John Synnott got both Dublin goals in the second half after they led 0-3 to nil at half-time.

But the talking point of the 1922 championship was the saga of how Sligo won an All-Ireland semi-final and never played in the final. In the Connacht final Sligo beat Galway by a point, 3-2 to 1-7, thanks to goals from Tom 'Click' Brennan, Mick Kilcoyne and Vincent Cunningham. Objections dogged Sligo throughout the campaign: they had to beat Roscommon twice in the first round. The inevitable objection from Galway eventually cost them their hard-won Connacht title.

Sligo had beaten Tipperary in the All-Ireland semi-final by the time Galway's objection was upheld. Three points down at half-time against Tipperary, they took the game by storm and won 1-8 to 0-7. Michael Kilcoyne got three points, James Colleran added another, a Sligo goal was disallowed, and with ten minutes to go, Nick Devine scored the winning goal.

The Connacht final replay acted as a curtain-raiser to the All-Ireland hurling final. This time Galway won 2-4 to 1-5 as Pat Roche and Denis Egan struck for goals in the first half in front of a not very impressed crowd of 20,000. Bernie Colleran replied for Sligo, who were short James Colleran, Peter Harte and Ned Colleran.

So Galway went straight into the All-Ireland final and Sligo remained the only team to have won an All-Ireland semi-final but never played in a final.

The *Irish Independent* hailed the broadening of the competition, and the support base.

> It not only gave us an hour of multiplying thrills but it proved beyond yea or nay that not only has Gaelic football greater vigour of life today but that henceforth the Connachtmen are to be placed in the front rank of footballers, beside the best that can come from Kerry, Dublin, Tipperary or Kildare.
>
> Twenty three special trains, not to speak of hundreds of Fords, Overlands and Crossleys, and hybrid lorries of mysterious origin and weird appearance landed their cargoes from early morning till the match was almost over.
>
> This time, too, there was little danger the visitors would go home hungry. Hotels and restaurants that never before helped to break the fast on the Sabbath not only threw open their doors but made sure we should learn all about it from posters, advertisements and decrepit sandwich boards.

Dublin came from behind to beat Galway 0-6 to 0-4 in the final. Captain Paddy Carey scored the last point from a 50. Joe Synnott, Paddy McDonnell and Frank Bourke also scored before Martin Walsh and Leonard McGrath pushed Galway ahead. For the first time there was a real possibility of getting the 1923 series out of the way and bringing the championship back up to date.

The little comedy left the Connacht council in an embarrassing situation. What war had done to disrupt the GAA was nothing compared to what the Connacht council would achieve over the next three years.

28 SEPTEMBER 1924. DUBLIN 1-5, KERRY 1-3, CROKE PARK

> 'Why not the provision of adequate gates for the speedy clearance of the enclosure, and so eliminate the utter savagery or ferocious pushing and shoving at the exits. The erection of suitable lavatory accommodation is another crying need, for the present sanitary arrangements, on the unreserved side of the ground at least, are an absolute disgrace. And when is a scoring board going to be erected on the railway wall?'
>
> *Irish Independent*, 29 September 1924

Ulster was a model of efficiency in 1923 in probably the most adverse circumstances of all. Three Ulster finals in all were played in 1923, four if you include the drawn 1922 final, including the 1921 final played in October before a gate of £7 15s. Derry, contestants in that delayed 1921 final, had been kicked out of the 1923 championship for playing an illegal team, and Donegal was given their place in the semi-final. Donegal failed to show, and eventually Cavan beat Monaghan 5-10 to 1-1 in the 1923 Ulster final at Cavan before a gate of £104. This gate bonanza meant the Ulster council could grant a set of medals to internees on the *Argenta* in Larne and at Ballykinlar camp in County Down, as the troubles began to die away.

Dublin were managing to continue a normal GAA life in the midst of all the trouble and were favourites to retain their All-Ireland title in 1923 as the effects of Civil War inactivity were felt in the rural counties. Kilkenny ousted an out-of-practice Kildare rather spectacularly from the 1923 championship by 2-3 to 2-1, after the sides were level 1-0 each at half-time. Dublin beat Meath 3-5 to nil in the Leinster final.

Dublin then beat Mayo 1-6 to 1-2 in the All-Ireland semi-final with a goal from Frank Bourke at the start of the second half, in reply to one by White on another cold, miserable day.

In Munster, the memories of Tipperary's semi-final no-show and the return of Kerry would be sure to test the frayed nerves of GAA followers. Kerry's pro-treaty team won the Munster championship without any help from their interned colleagues, beating Limerick 4-5 to 1-3, Cork 3-4 to 0-3 and Tipperary 0-6 to 0-3. But all was not well. Only two players had turned up for Kerry's first training session of the year, and three players had to be recruited from the sideline to make up the fifteen to play Cork in the semi-final.

In April 1924 Kerry defeated Cavan 1-3 to 1-2 in the All-Ireland semi-final. Kerry had to endure an enthralling finish against Cavan in terrible weather conditions. Tom Egan got Cavan's first half goal that put them two points ahead. With six minutes to go, they still led by two points when, in the quagmire that passed for a Cavan goalmouth, the ball was forced over the line demolishing the net and almost demolishing the Cavan goalkeeper Jack Heslin. Amid protests, the goal was awarded. J. P. Murphy's equalising point for Cavan came seconds too late. Cavan had the help of Kildare stars Paul Doyle and Jack Higgins stationed in the army in Cavan.

But playing off the 1923 All-Ireland finals was now proving to be more difficult than at first thought. The Free State government continued to hold a large number of prisoners in jail. In August, de Valera joined them. An October hunger strike created public hysteria, and in Waterford GAA games were halted to draw attention to their plight. Grounds in Cork were vandalised by sympathisers. Although the hunger strike was called off on 23 November, two days later several delegates walked out of a Kilkenny County Board meeting when it refused to stop all matches until anti-treaty prisoners were released.

For six months of 1924 there was no sign of a mass release of the political prisoners. Dublin would not accept a walkover awarded in June 1924, when Kerry refused to travel for the All-Ireland final in protest at the imprisonment of county board chairman Austin Stack, among the last Civil War prisoners released alongside Eamon de Valera in July 1924.

Most of Munster GAA backed the anti-treaty side. After hasty suspensions were dished out to football finalists Kerry, hurling finalists Limerick and junior hurling finalists Cork for refusing to fulfil All-Ireland fixtures, the Munster council joined the protest by refusing to participate in the Tailteann festival, and Connacht followed suit. Only a special congress in August 1924 prevented a split in the GAA.

Kerry benefited in the end. When the internees were released, they beat the county team by twelve points in a replayed challenge match. There were eleven changes in the team for the All-Ireland championship.

The 1923 All-Ireland final eventually got under way on 28 September. A 20,000 attendance paid receipts of £1,622. Although Dublin won 1-5 to 1-3, Kerry started with a storm. Con Brosnan crashed home a 50 yard shot to give them a 1-2 to 0-1 half-time lead, but Kirwan had a goal for Dublin from John Synnott's cross on the restart, and Paddy McDonnell, Jack Murphy and Joe Stynes (2) got the points to secure a four-point win. Whereas Brosnan, later to stand for Cumann na nGaedheal in the 1932 General Election, and many of the Kerry team were pro-treaty, John Joe Sheehy, Kerry's second half scorer, was definitely anti. When Sheehy was hiding out on the run, he had heard the land-mine blast in Ballyseedy when nine prisoners were killed in one of the most horrific episodes of the Civil War, and rescued a survivor, Stephen Fuller, from the scene. He was constantly on the run from August 1922 to May 1924. When he emerged from his Cnocán dugout to play in a match in aid of republican prisoners in Tralee (700 from the town were in internment camps), no attempt was made to arrest him. In Kerry, football was helping to dress the wounds of Civil war.

Paul Russell, who was 17, had never played before for Kerry at any grade when he was selected to play in the final.

26 APRIL 1925. KERRY 0-4, DUBLIN 0-3, CROKE PARK

A free to Kerry, Con Brosnan took it
With steady foot and unerring aim
He scored the point and again we led them
'Twas the final point of the hard-fought game
Hats off to Brosnan, our midfield wonder
He's par excellence in feet and hands
Oh, where's the Gael can pull down the number
Of Kerry's idol from Newtownsandes.

KERRY BALLAD (1924)

The Kerry men halted Dublin's bid for four in a row at the last hurdle in the 1924 All-Ireland final, not played until April 1925.

Three weeks before the 1923 All-Ireland final, two first half goals from Bill Landers helped Kerry's reunited team beat Cork 4-3 to 2-1 in the Munster semi-final. Then, a fortnight after the All-Ireland defeat, they beat Clare 3-10 to 2-2 in the Munster final. Con Brosnan dominated midfield and three Kerry goals insulated the champions against two late goals in reply by Clare for an eleven-point victory.

Kerry had a Dublin man on board. Jimmy Bermingham later went on to play for Bohemians in their record-breaking 1927–28 sweep of FAI Cup, League of Ireland, Shield and the Leinster Cup.

Reaching the final was an achievement for still-divided Clare, whose county board had split after the execution of county secretary Pat Hennessy and fellow GAA activist Con MacMahon by the Free State forces in January 1923. By the time the 1924 Munster final was played, the two county boards were suspending players who played in the other board's competitions. It was the summer of 1925 before the situation was resolved. Ironically, Con Brosnan hatched a plan to allow his republican team mate, John Joe Sheehy, to play in that Munster final. Sheehy was guaranteed safe passage to and from that game though he was still on the run in north Kerry. He made his own way to Limerick, appeared out of the crowd, was handed a jersey, played the game and disappeared back into the crowd at the final whistle.

Kerry continued their comeback march as winter closed in. In December 1924, John Ryan scored a goal at the end of the first half of Kerry's semi-final against Mayo for a 1-4 to 0-1 victory before a £460 crowd. Mayo had won the Connacht championship after a unique 0-1 each draw with Galway when the final was first played. Meanwhile, Wexford reappeared in the forefront in Leinster. Martin O'Neill scored their 1-1 total in the semi-final to help them beat another re-emerging county, Kildare, for whom 1903 hero 'Joyce' Conlan was making his last appearance. In the other semi-final, Dublin had a man sent off in a 2-6 to 2-4 victory over Louth. They also missed their adopted midfielder, Larry Stanley, who was competing with the first Irish Olympic team in Paris.

It took Dublin two efforts to beat Wexford in the final. On the first day, a late goal from another internee, Joe Stynes, saved Dublin from defeat, 1-4 each. In the replay Dublin took an early 2-1 to 1-2 lead with goals from Joe Stynes and M. O'Brien. In fact Dublin led by nine points approaching the end of the replayed final, before Martin O'Neill's goal for Wexford cut back the margin to 3-5 to 2-3.

The only controversy was, thankfully, an old-fashioned 'biased referee' football dispute. Dublin objected to ex-Kerry footballer Dick Fitzgerald being appointed to referee their semi-final against Cavan because of his decision as an umpire to allow a Mayo goal against them in 1923. Despite J. P. Murphy scoring a second half goal from a free he followed up himself, Dublin won easily 0-6 to 1-1. Cavan's goalkeeper, R. Black, was outstanding.

Dublin's run came to a halt as a rejuvenated Kerry defeated them 0-4 to 0-3 in a fabulous game watched by 28,844 spectators. The gate receipts of £2,564 became the cause of a libel case against the *Freeman's Journal*, who claimed 'there was surely 40,000 at the match'. Kerry's man of the match was Con Brosnan, who scored the winning point after a tremendous tussle. It took twenty minutes to open the scoring. Dublin's Joe Synnott pointed the first free of the game from 40 yards, then Landers punched an equaliser for Kerry. Peter Synnott restored Dublin's lead two minutes later, but John Baily and then Con Brosnan gave Kerry a 0-3 to 0-2 half-time lead, and Joe Synnott pointed an acute-angle free to equalise. In a final enthralling sequence, Baily had a goal disallowed for 'whistle gone' before Brosnan's winning point.

Spectators paid five shillings to sit in the newly erected wooden Hogan Stand, named after the Tipperary footballer who died on Bloody Sunday. A new scoreboard on the Railway wall was in use for the first time. It was a tremendous game which was probably the best in Gaelic football history to date. 'The Kerry favours were everywhere in evidence and to judge from the volume of cheering Kerry had by far the bigger following among the spectators', the *Irish Independent* reported.

Kerry had their wing forward, clerical student Redmond 'Mundy' Prendiville, spirited out of All Hallows College in defiance of the rules then in force for seminarians, reportedly replying to Donal Ó Ciobhain, 'Would a duck swim?' when asked if he would play for Kerry. Mundy won an All-Ireland and it did no harm to his career. He later became Archbishop of Perth. His grave was the subject of a pilgrimage by some Kerry players during the International Rules series.

So good was the match that it reminded the *Sport* correspondent of Arravales v Young Irelands. This was quite an achievement, because Arravales never played Young Irelands in the All-Ireland championship, but in a forgotten 1894 Croke Cup final. Even in 1924, nostalgia was not what it used to be.

18 OCTOBER 1925. GALWAY 1-5, MAYO 1-3, TUAM

> 'A curious Decision—The All-Ireland football championship has, we learn unofficially, been awarded to Galway. As a result of objections and counter-objections the title, we understood, had gone automatically to Mayo. The decision to declare Galway champions was, it appears, made

after midnight at a meeting of the Central Council, when several of the Connacht delegates had left. In the absence of Mr O'Toole, Secretary GAA, from town yesterday, we are unable to obtain an official statement on the matter.'

Irish Independent, 7 November 1925

Just when the GAA had apparently extricated itself from a political minefield, it carefully constructed a home-made one which sabotaged the 1925 championship.

A sad and confused championship resulted from a motion to the 1925 Congress that players could opt to play for their native county. It was designed so that rural counties could plunder the wealth of talented footballers who had migrated to Dublin and were debarred from championship football. At the 1925 Congress, Barney Fay of Cavan won the case with a plea: 'We only ask for a chance that players who are not wanted by Dublin teams to assist counties where they have trained.' The motion was accepted with a small amendment.

Rural teams scrambled to reclaim their exiles. Dublin, whose three in a row had helped bring the motion about, went out of the championship at the first hurdle, 2-4 to 1-6 victims of Wexford. Two goals inside the first minute of the second half from Martin O'Neill and Jack Lucey turned a five-point deficit into a lead that Wexford never surrendered. Ironically, Martin O'Neill was one of the declaration players, but he was not living in Dublin. He resided in Bray at the time. He went on to score four goals for Wexford against Meath and Wexford went on to take the title. Kilroy and Synnott got the goals in a 2-7 to 0-3 victory over a shaky though promising Kildare team in the final.

After Kerry beat Cavan 1-7 to 2-3 and Mayo beat Wexford 2-4 to 1-4 in the All-Ireland semi-finals, things started to go wrong. Cavan man James P. Murphy, ironically from the county which first proposed the rule change, was the new rule's first casualty because of his somewhat complicated lifestyle.

He had played with Dublin club Keatings in 1924, but also with Cornafean in 1925 while he was living in Mullingar. It emerged that he went home at weekends and had taken a month's sick leave before the All-Ireland semi-final. On a 9-5 vote he was found to be illegal because the declaration rule was not clear enough in defining a player's home. One Galway delegate pleaded: 'A man's home is where he earns his bread and butter.'

Murphy's contribution to the All-Ireland semi-final had been outstanding, particularly his innovative hand-to-toe solo runs, the first time the tactic had been seen by many Kerry men (although it had first been used by 1903 Kildare footballer Michael Kennedy, and John D. Hickey later claimed it was invented in the 1920s by Seán Lavin of Mayo).

Kerry man Phil Sullivan was next on the doubtful list. He played for his college, UCD, against the Civic Guards in a Dublin hurling league match and for Faughs in the Dublin hurling championship, so Kerry too were eliminated on spurious grounds.

Kerry demanded a special congress to sort out the crux, but the GAA stuck to their rule book, and meanwhile Connacht muddled their way through an eleven-match championship that fell hopelessly behind schedule. When a Connacht application to postpone the All-Ireland championship was refused by the Central Council early in the year, the Provincial council nominated Mayo to take part.

So when Kerry and Cavan were thrown out of the championship, everyone assumed Mayo became champions by default. Defeated semi-finalists Wexford had a go on the objection merry-go-round as well, but their claim, that Mayo player Michael Mulderrig had played for Tipperary against Kerry in the Munster junior championship, failed on another 9-5 vote. It was a pity because the semi-finals had both been exciting: Jack Henry and Williams got Mayo's first half goals to beat Wexford by a goal, and John Joe Sheehy's tenth-minute goal spurred Kerry to a one-point victory over Cavan.

Connacht's championship was still plodding along. Roscommon and Sligo played six times. Despite the fact that Sligo qualified in the end, two of the matches were won by Roscommon. After the first meeting in Boyle, Sligo objected that a disallowed goal of theirs should have been allowed. Sligo's Mick Noone forced a draw with a late goal the second day. Sligo's 'Click' Brennan forced a second draw with a late point, and they forced a third draw with two second half goals after they trailed 1-3 to nil at half-time. Roscommon won the fifth match with a disputed goal on which the referee 'reserved judgment' until the next council meeting, and eventually Sligo won at the sixth attempt by the decisive margin of 2-3 to 0-2.

Leitrim forced Galway to two draws, refused to play extra time, and were eventually beaten 2-3 to 1-4 at the third attempt. Mayo had already been declared All-Ireland champions when the Connacht final was played. Galway beat them 1-5 to 1-3. A free from old 1919 warrior Michael 'Knacker' Walsh at the start of the second half hit the net in response to a similar goal from Mayo's Jack Henry. Galway (who reportedly had not trained) were now Connacht champions. But even they were surprised by the news that the All-Ireland title had been awarded to them at a Central Council meeting on 23 October. A Galway delegate proposed that Galway become champions after Seán T. Ruane of Mayo left the meeting, and the motion sneaked through.

Galway were champions for two weeks before anyone knew anything about it. An *Irish Independent* report on 7 November leaked the information that sometime after midnight at the 23 October 1925 meeting of the Central

Council, the All-Ireland championship had been awarded to Galway. In the 1925 championship, a council chamber lobbyist had proved more important than fifteen men on the field.

The embarrassed Central Council organised an 'in lieu' competition that had no real credibility because Kerry refused to compete. Galway did save some blushes by winning it with two three-goal sprees from Bannerton, Egan and James when they beat Wexford 3-4 to 1-1 in the semi-final, and from Roche (2) and Egan when they beat Cavan 3-2 to 1-2 in the final. Kerry instead replayed their 1924 All-Ireland final against defeated Leinster finalists Dublin in a much-heralded challenge match, but lost 2-6 to 1-6.

Galway got their only dual medallist out of the chaos, Leonard McGrath, who had forsaken rugby to play in the 1925 championship (and may have been illegal if anybody had bothered to object against Galway). Once claimed as a native of Australia, McGrath was claimed as a native of Leitrim, a parish between Athenry and Ballinasloe, in the 1967 *Our Games Annual* by Séamus Ó Cualláin. The GAA suffered from more than a tarnished image: funds were down from £2,553 to £1,553 because the in lieu tournament was poorly supported.

It was not all bad news, however. The 1924 Tailteann Games had seen the revival of inter-provincial competition when Munster, captained by Phil Sullivan of Kerry (he had eight colleagues, with four Clare men and one each from Limerick and Cork on his team), beat Leinster, captained by Dublin's Paddy Carey. And the unhappy mess might have helped boost interest in a new Central Council competition, the first 'secondary' competition since the Wolfe Tone tournament of 1916–17.

While the declaration rule was being introduced, another motion to the 1925 Congress established the leagues. A four-county league set up by Louth, Monaghan, Cavan and Meath had proved highly successful in 1924. National leagues were proposed by Seán McCarthy of Cork and seconded by Liam Clifford of Limerick (both were to become future presidents of the GAA).

The Central Council set up a subcommittee to formulate the league and they presented their findings on Sunday, 8 August 1925. The competitions were seen as a threat to the traditional power base of the GAA, the club competition, and the club structure has had a stormy relationship with the league at times in the years since.

The competitions began in 1926. Unlikely group winners emerged: Antrim, Laois, Longford and Sligo, as well as Dublin and Kerry. Laois footballers won their first national competition by beating Kerry 1-6 to 1-5 in the semi-final and eventually beat Dublin before 1,000 spectators in New Ross in the first final.

Until 1935–36, the football league was run on a regional basis with three divisions and a series of play-offs between the divisional winners.

5 SEPTEMBER 1926. KERRY 1-3, KILDARE 0-6, CROKE PARK
17 OCTOBER 1926. KERRY 1-4, KILDARE 0-4, CROKE PARK

> These are the men you spoke of in the game your fathers loved;
> These are the men who blazed the trail and made it fair.
> In my dreaming now I see them as I saw them long ago,
> Green and gold and white limbs leaping
> when our Kerry played Kildare.
>
> SIGERSON CLIFFORD

Kerry and Kildare restored pride and funds to the GAA with another classic replayed final in 1926.

The year had not started well for Kerry, still seething over the declaration fiasco of 1925. Cork shocked Kerry in the Munster semi-final with two early goals from Jim Fortune and Duggan. But a Paddy Farren goal left the teams level at half-time, and Jackie Ryan, Joe Barrett and Tom O'Mahoney points gave Kerry a 1-9 to 2-1 victory and a final against Tipperary—which was just as well because the final had been advertised on Railway company posters before the semi-final was even played.

Kerry beat Tipperary 0-11 to 1-4 with the help of six points from John Joe Sheehy and would have won by more only for Barrett's late goal for Tipperary. Kerry's Jeremiah Moriarty and McCarthy of Tipperary were sent off for fighting in the first half, at the end of which Kerry led 0-5 to 0-3.

In the semi-finals, Jackie Ryan's first half goal and four points were enough to exact revenge for Kerry over Cavan, the last nominated team in an All-Ireland semi-final who 'abandoned their old aggressive game', only to be mesmerised by Kerry's deft, quick passing and lost 1-6 to 0-1.

The news that Kerry's opponents were going to be old 1903 and 1905 adversaries Kildare was greeted with delight by old-timers. Kildare began their comeback by hammering Louth 5-8 to 1-5 in Leinster. A good first half display (with Joe Curtis and George Higgins goals) deposed Dublin 2-5 to 1-2 in the Leinster semi-final. They had Bill 'Squires' Gannon in goalscoring form (he scored both goals as they beat Wexford 2-8 to 1-5 in the final) and Larry Stanley back under the declaration rule.

A 12,000 crowd watched the Leinster final as Kildare built up a seven-point lead, and Patsy O'Connor's goal came too late to save Wexford. Kildare looked even more impressive as they tore apart the All-Ireland champions Galway 2-5 to 0-2 with goals from Curtis and Ryan, although some Knacker Walsh scores had given Galway an early two-point lead.

The final survived the threat of another 1910-style boycott: north Kerry players were asked not to travel to the match in a protest over the quality of train services.

This match was worth waiting for. Bill Gorman got one of the most dramatic equalising goals in GAA history after 29 minutes of the second half, five minutes short of the final whistle, and forced a 1-3 to 0-6 draw.

Jack Murphy from Caherciveen played an excellent game at centre half back, but apparently put on his clothes without bothering to take off his playing gear afterwards. The following Wednesday a selector, Euge Ring, noticed he was in pain. A doctor was summoned, and he was sent to hospital in Tralee where he died of pneumonia, leaving his colleagues to win an emotional All-Ireland 1-4 to 0-4 in his honour.

Larry Stanley became embittered by the grilling he got on the field from Phil Sullivan in the replay. Curtailing Stanley in the final paid off for Kerry: he was regarded by now as the greatest player to have pulled on a Gaelic football jersey. Each of his three scores in the drawn match came from frees. Eight minutes into the second half he pointed a free kick from an angle so acute he had to remove the corner flag to kick it. He also scored a point in the replay, despite some rough treatment.

Tom O'Mahoney scored Kerry's valuable second half goal in the replay. Kildare hit the woodwork three times as the squashed followers cheered the match to the echo. P. D. Mehigan relayed the match to a couple of thousand radio listeners. 'Pirate' programmes were on sale for the first time.

Attendance figures brought a bonanza for the impoverished Central Council. The drawn match drew 37,500 spectators, paying a total of £3,540; 35,500 turned up for the replay, paying £3,374. The GAA could pay its bills again.

25 SEPTEMBER 1927. KILDARE 0-5, KERRY 0-3, CROKE PARK

> 'Dublin City was so fully represented that the famous Hill 60* has rarely been so crowded, and the cheers which greeted Kildare successes surely came mostly from city throats. In the manner of cheering it could not help being remarked that there seemed a singular absence of enthusiasm which one associated with similar events some years ago.'
>
> *Irish Independent*, 26 September 1927

* The bank on the eastern corner behind the Railway goal used to be known as Hill 60 after a landmark in the Dardanelles. It later became known as Hill 16.

Kildare and Kerry's rivalry had been passed on to an enthusiastic new generation. Revitalised and filled up with 'if only' stories from one of the greatest finals ever, Kildare stuttered back into action in the 1927 championship. Meath led 0-2 to 0-1 at half-time in the semi-final before succumbing to Kildare who came back to win 1-5 to 1-2.

Kildare retained the Leinster title by 0-5 to 0-3 as sharpshooter Paul Doyle scored four of his side's points. He was resuming an old free-taking rivalry with Kerry man Paul Russell, the captain of Dublin for the year. Russell changed allegiance because his club, Garda, had won the Dublin championship. It was rumoured that Garda sought a declaration from all its team that they would play with Dublin to help win the 1927 All-Ireland championship. The outcome of all this was that Larry Stanley, the most famous Garda of them all, opted to play for neither Dublin nor Kildare.

Paul Russell helped Dublin defeat Wexford 0-8 to 1-1 in a replayed semi-final, one of the last matches at Kilkenny's old St James's Park. The venue certainly left its mark on those who occupied the specially rented grandstand. It collapsed beneath their weight and sent six inch nails protruding through an occasional backside, with not a whisper about public liability insurance in those innocent times. The man who was responsible for all aspects of the organisation of the game, the Leinster secretary, was unaware of all this. Instead, Martin O'Neill was busy in the Wexford attack. He and Seamus Hayes had scored Wexford's goals as they drew 2-5 to 0-11, and Dublin's Mohan was forced to save the match with a late equalising point.

Hayes, surprisingly, did not score any of the record thirteen goals in Wexford's previous game when they beat Longford 7-10 to 6-2 in the first round. Longford had just been suspended for twelve months as a result of a row over a challenge match with Dublin in 1926, and at one stage the Connacht council asked that Longford be allowed to join them.

Kildare reached the final once again, but had to recover from their customary slow start to beat Monaghan 1-7 to 0-2 with a second half goal from newcomer Tom Keogh, later to star with Laois.

In Ulster, Monaghan were tired of losing replays to Cavan, so they spiked Cavan's five-in-a-row bid in style, 2-6 to 1-6, thanks to two early goals from Shevlin and T. J. Weymes and a penalty save by goalkeeper Tommy Bradley. Bradley stopped Jim Smith's kick splendidly when there were three points between the teams minutes from the end. After that, the final should have been easy against the previous year's All-Ireland junior champions, Armagh. Not so. Monaghan were forced to come from behind to win 3-6 to 2-5.

Connacht resumed their traditional histrionics. Mayo and Sligo's first round match lasted just three minutes before the crowd invaded. One angry newsman wanted to know why the crowd did not wait until three minutes from the end before they invaded and allow everybody to get their money's worth. The referee had changed his mind and disallowed a Sligo goal after Mayo defenders protested, and two Sligo men, George Higgins and Mickey Noone, left the field in protest. Sligo were disqualified from competition for twelve months, a punishment that was to have extraordinary consequences for the Sligo men.

But 1927 was the year of Leitrim's breakthrough. Leitrim's good displays of 1925, when they drew twice against Galway, stood them in good stead as they captured their only Connacht title in 1927 with the help of James O'Hehir's training (James was the father of the veteran radio commentator, Micheál, and trained the Clare hurlers to success in 1914) and with a little good luck.

Their Connacht semi-final opponents Roscommon had to line out without five players whose car had broken down, and Leitrim won a replay encounter by 0-7 to 1-0. Roscommon deserved a replay as some of their team had been recruited from the sideline when Leitrim beat them 1-3 to 0-2 the first day. 'Nipper' Shanley led the Leitrim attack to a 2-4 to 0-3 victory over Galway in the Connacht final and earned a place on the Irish team to play America in the Tailteann tournament.

Contacts with American GAA structures had reached an advanced stage in 1926, and Kerry played Cork earlier than usual in the Munster championship to allow time for a prestigious first-ever US tour. The time spent together in America benefited Kerry when they came home, and they had an easy run in the championship, beating Cork 1-7 to 0-1, Tipperary 2-6 to 1-1, and Clare 4-4 to 1-3, and then faced Leitrim in the All-Ireland semi-final.

Leitrim's only appearance in a semi-final was a stormy affair in Tuam: as Kerry won 0-4 to 0-2, the referee did not send anyone off. He stayed out of controversy, ironing over awkward situations by getting the two players involved to shake hands. Two John Joe Sheehy frees gave Kerry the cushion they needed to go 0-3 to 0-2 up at half-time and gradually wear down the outsiders.

The All-Ireland final between the old rivals was exactly what the spectators ordered. A record 36,529 of them turned up to see Kildare beat Kerry 0-5 to 0-3 in a game that failed to live up to 1926 levels, but had enough to talk about all the same. Kildare trailed by three points to nil early in the game, but Tom Keogh, Paul Doyle, Squires Gannon, Joe Curtis and Doyle again scored points to restore Lily White pride. It was not a classic, but the inevitable comparison with the previous year was not entirely inappropriate. Kerry again broke through with five minutes to go, but this time John Joe Sheehy hit the post.

26 FEBRUARY 1928. ULSTER 2-8, MUNSTER 2-6, CROKE PARK

Immediately, Kerry began strengthening their hand for the 1928 championship. One of their first moves was to attract back their exiled Garda, Paul Russell, now a veteran at 20 years of age.

Russell hit the headlines early in 1928 when he found he was picked by both the Munster and Leinster inter-provincial teams. Because he had declared for Dublin in 1927, though having already played for Munster in the 1927 Railway Cup, Leinster thought he would be eligible for them. Munster picked him because he had declared for Kerry for the 1928 season. The Central Council ruled that he should play for Leinster in the end. It enabled him to win his second Railway Cup medal in two years with different teams.

Meanwhile, his Munster colleagues stormed off the field because of a dispute over a goal by Ulster in the semi-final. Ulster took a quick throw-in and scored a goal that gave them a lead of 2-8 to 2-6, but the Munster players refused to kick out the ball, claiming that the throw-in should have been Munster's. Their walk-off led to a six-month suspension, but the controversy gave the new Railway Cup competition a welcome boost.

The successful Railway Shields experiment was just a memory when Pádraig Ó Caoimh proposed that inter-provincial competition be resumed in 1926. In 1927 the Railway Cups were inaugurated, again donated by the Great Southern and Western Railway Company, to be contested annually between the four provinces, with the finals to be played on St Patrick's Day. A crowd of 10,000 turned up to see Munster beat Connacht in the first final, despite the fact that Connacht underwent a special course of training in Ballinasloe. For nearly 40 years this formula was to prove highly successful.

Chapter 3 ❧

1927–47: HAND ACROSS THE ATLANTIC

Gaelic football and its significance for the Irish at home and Irish migrants abroad

'The Sam Maguire memorial committee have intimated to the Central Council GAA *that they have decided to present to the Council a silver cup to be known as the Sam Maguire Memorial Cup, annually to the winners of the All-Ireland championship. The cup will be a replica of the Ardagh Cup, with a gold panel and gold medallion of the late Sam Maguire, who was a lifelong worker in the* GAA*, particularly in England.'*

Irish Independent, 30 April 1928

The medal on the chest, that militaristic derivative that has become the cornerstone of the recognition of athletic achievement, was no longer enough for football champions. Twentieth-century team sportsmen sought silverware. A trophy for the tableware, with its own plinth, an identifiable piece of glittering precious metal that could be held aloft at the end of the match, was now required as well.

An eclectic assortment of cups had been awarded to Gaelic football champion teams since the earliest days. The idea was, like many of the GAA's best ideas, borrowed.

The craze for sports silverware had been floating around for 200 years. Silver plate was a fashionable reward for winning horses in the race-matches that were run on the Curragh and other Irish grasslands from the 1740s on. The Scottish two-handled loving cup was introduced for soccer competitions from the 1870s in England. Irish sporting events, including football competitions, had a few of these themselves. Cups had been presented by Archbishop William Croke in 1896 for a separate football competition, but this was merged for a time with the All-Ireland championship. The original

Croke Cup, the oldest competed for by county teams, was for a time awarded to the National League champions before ending up in the GAA museum in Croke Park.

The first Railway Cup presented in 1913 ended up in Kerry because it was won for two years in a row. The one for 1915 ended up in Wexford for the same reason. But for twelve years it was not replaced.

Presenting the cup to a winning captain was a ceremony that attracted as much attention as the match, the focus shifting to the trophy rather than the abstract concept of the victory. The 1927 English FA Cup soccer final win by a non-English team, Cardiff City, with a Dublin-born goalkeeper on their side, brought a new focus to the trophy awarded there. Newsreel footage of the Cardiff captain receiving the cup was shown throughout Irish cinemas during the summer of 1927.

Gaelic football's All-Ireland championship needed a cup of its own. Then, in February 1927, Sam Maguire died at a young age.

> 'The funeral took place at his native place Dunmanway of Mr Sam Maguire, who up to a year ago, was a well-known official of the GPO Customs dept. He had 25 years service in the GPO London, where he was a close friend of the late General Collins, with whom he was very intimately identified in the movement which led up to the rebellion. He held the rank of Lieutenant General in the Volunteers, and was director of Intelligence in Great Britain during the Black and Tan period. He came into the Saorstát PO Service after the Treaty. He played a leading part in the transport of arms and ammunition to this country in pre-truce days.'
>
> *Irish Independent*, 9 February 1927

Even decades after his death nobody has been able to evaluate Sam Maguire's contribution to the independence movement. He is the subject of three biographies, by Barra Ó Donabháin, Raymond Lyons and Margaret Mary Walsh. His name was instantly recognisable to readers solely because the trophy that a Sam Maguire memorial committee donated to the GAA had become the most sought after in Gaelic football.

That the initiative came from England was interesting in itself. London GAA fans had already donated a trophy for the hurling championship, for Liam MacCarthy in 1921. It was in the shape of the mether, seen at the time as a peculiarly Irish version of the Scottish loving cup, used as a model by the English and Scottish soccer associations. Methers were a popular symbolic piece of silverware in the 1910s.

By the 1920s the focus had switched to the Ardagh chalice. It was the star of the show in the National Museum of Ireland's collection, even more so than the Tara Brooch, or the later attention given to the Book of Kells and the neolithic chamber at Newgrange.

Handball's doubles trophy awarded early in 1928 was also based on the Ardagh chalice. And the Ardagh chalice was chosen, unsurprisingly, as the model for the new Sam Maguire Cup. On 30 April the Maguire memorial committee intimated that they were presenting a silver cup worth about £200 (about €6,000 in 2008 using the retail price index) to the Central Council of the GAA for presentation to the All-Ireland football champions. On 5 May it was recorded by the Central Council as 'nearing completion'.

Nobody was sure who Sam was. He was from Dunmanway, and the cup was introduced at a time when energetic Cork man Seán McCarthy was the GAA president. 'A lifelong worker in the GAA, particularly in England' was P. J. Devlin's introduction to his readers.

His brief obituary recorded that he was 'a close friend of the late General Collins with whom he was very intimately identified in the movement which led up to the rebellion'. The obituary described how he 'held the rank of Lieutenant General in the Volunteers and was Director of Intelligence in Britain during the Black and Tan period' and 'played a leading part in the transport of arms and ammunition to his country during the pre-truce days'.

The fact that he was a member of the Church of Ireland was not a matter of any surprise at the time. It became much commented upon later, particularly in 1970s and 1980s Northern Ireland, when the GAA was the subject of a sectarian campaign of murder and bomb attacks on its properties, and was often accused by the perpetrators, as is the nature of these things, of itself having sectarian characteristics. The desire of Protestants to bring 'wee Sammy back to Londonderry' was the subject of a somewhat laboured joke during Derry's championship campaign of 1993.

Margaret Mary Walsh's work has uncovered much more about his life. But as many questions remained as answers. The nature of Maguire's contribution to the independence movement may have been too enormous to acknowledge in the 1920s, when his allegiance to the treaty was under a cloud and his dismissal from the Irish Post Office service that he briefly joined after the foundation of the Irish Free State was still the subject of controversy. Like all leaders of secret movements, we can try to assess his involvement only from small hints and unreliable and often hostile sources.

His GAA involvement as an organiser and captain of the London Hibernians is easier to track, but given London's non-performance at the time, not conducive to superlatives. Hurling fans have no difficulty reconciling the Christy Ring and Nicky Rackard cups with the pursuit of excellence. But Sam Maguire was a mysterious choice of name for the All-Ireland football championship cup. Maybe he was just the right patriot at the right time. Or maybe there was more to it than subsequent generations can ever understand.

There was no mention of the cup in the reports of the 1928 All-Ireland final. If there was a winning speech by the captain, as is unlikely, it was not mentioned. It was 1933 before we hear of a presentation speech. Jim Smith, the Cavan captain of the day, gave a brief acceptance speech on how his life's ambition had been recognised. It was the first in a long tradition of speeches, which by the 1950s had adopted a rote form: 'Is mór an onóir dom, an chorn seo a brhonnadh so son an fhoireann.' (It gives me great pleasure to accept this cup on behalf of the team.) Speeches have become longer and more unconventional, often accompanied by a song. Ray Silke's speech in 1998 bears the record for longevity.

Back in 1933 the GAA president was Maguire's fellow Cork man Seán McCarthy, prime mover on the Central Council of the campaign to commemorate Sam Maguire with a trophy. He mentioned in his presentation speech that the love of nation and love of Gaelic games had come together in the spirit of the Sam Maguire Cup.

And that is probably as close as we shall ever come to learning how the most coveted trophy in Irish sport became known to most football supporters simply as 'the Sam'.

29 MAY 1927. NEW YORK 3-11, KERRY 1-7, POLO GROUNDS, NEW YORK

> 'Kerry never tried to play and say they never mean to play what is Celtic Park football again.'
>
> Telegram back to Ireland in the name of DICK FITZGERALD, 29 May 1927

Who was going to win it first? Would it be one of the great rivals of the decade, Kerry or Kildare? The same congress that accepted the new cup had made a decision that threw up an intriguing possibility.

They decided to rotate the draw. Kerry and Kildare would meet in the All-Ireland semi-final. The final should be easy for them, but maybe not. Ulster and Connacht teams had the possibility of snatching the trophy away with one big performance.

Football history has, before and since, been filled with surprise successes by teams that came through the weak side of the draw and won a championship, Clare in Munster in 1992 the best recent example. There was a distraction as well. The big football event of the summer of 1928 was not the All-Ireland final at all. It was the Tailteann football international between Ireland and the US.

The Tailteann Games had been a surprise success in 1924. That success was repeated in 1928 with crowds of 12,000 attending most of the days at Croke Park. It meant that the All-Ireland semi-finals were shipped out of Croke Park so there would be no distraction from the main event.

And so it was. The great international contest of 1928 was a key attraction of the Tailteann Games precisely because of the possibility that America's Gaelic footballers might beat the Irish. Transatlantic rivalry had been fired up by the first tour abroad by Kerry in 1927. The tour was inspired by the Tipperary hurlers' one-sided world tour in 1926. When the Kerry footballers followed them in 1927, it brought Gaelic football on to the sort of distant fields that Cusack and Davin had dreamed of at that meeting in Thurles back in 1884.

Timothy 'Ted' Sullivan (1851–1929), Clare-born serial baseball manager of teams in the various leagues that appeared and disappeared with alarming regularity in nineteenth-century America, often credited as the originator of the word 'fan' for sports follower, was the man chosen to promote the tour. Sullivan had been captivated by the growing baseball movement he had found when his family emigrated to St Louis, and was first listed as a baseball umpire for a match in Chicago in 1876. He had organised a barnstorming trip around the world in 1913–14 by the Chicago White Sox and New York Giants baseball teams. He set the GAA tour up on a similar basis, that he got 40 per cent of the profit after all expenses had been paid.

He set up matches at New York Giants Stadium, the Polo Grounds and baseball parks in Springfield, Mass., Boston, Hartford, Chicago and a training stint at New Haven before the second match with New York for what he billed the 'World Championship', with a baseball-inspired zeal for hyperbole.

The assistant manager was Muiris 'Kruger' Kavanagh, the Dunquin publican famously embroiled in a libel action with Patrick Kavanagh. Fr E. Fitzgerald, brother of Dick, travelled out to make preliminary arrangements for the tour. Fr Fitzgerald's telegram home after the first match of the tour was to cause a controversy that threatened to bring the entire project to a halt.

The arrangement came unstuck before the last match of the tour, Kavanagh claiming that Sullivan made off with an alleged profit of $11,000 from the tour, either through avarice or, more likely, an inability to meet the expenses of the poorly supported matches in smaller locations.

A letter from Sullivan to the *Irish Independent* praised the Kerry players who 'brought credit to them not only as exponents of Ireland's national game but as the highest type of citizen of Ireland'. But he didn't mention the county board, whose bickering over the first match defeat turned the entire tour into a loss-making venture.

While in excess of 30,000 attended the first New York game, it was down to 15,000 when Kerry returned to New York amid recriminations two months later. Other attendances were 6,000 in Boston, 8,000 in Chicago, 4,000 in Springfield and negligible in Hartford. No subsequent American GAA tour ventured beyond New York.

In the end, the Kerryman's Association in New York had to raise $500 to cover the team's expenses. Never again would the GAA allow a private promoter to become involved in any of their activities.

Kerry not only lost the money they hoped to use to buy a field in Tralee; they were hammered in the battle for Sullivan's 'World Championship' and a trophy provided by Denis Florence McCarthy for the matches.

According to Paddy Foley, Gaelic football was booming in America as a stream of post-Civil War emigrants arrived in the ports. 'In Transatlantic cities where the electric light is in vogue, the big ball is easier on the eyes than the fast flying sliotar.'

The Kerry team began their journey on 15 May and lined out against New York four days after landing on 29 May, losing 3-11 to 1-7. New York, who had a panel of 35 players training for the contests, were captained by Martin Shanahan of Tipperary and fielded three players from Mayo and Wexford, two from Kildare and Leitrim, and one from Cavan, Cork, Louth and Waterford.

Sullivan secured the use of the Polo Grounds, home of the New York Giants, for the matches against New York. It was the first of several baseball experiences for the GAA. 'The grounds were somewhat short and much too narrow,' Foley observed. 'A big patch of the sward had been worn brown by the feet of baseball players. Grass on the remainder was scorched by a blistering sun. The sod was almost as hard as concrete. Three cornet players stood in the middle of the arena and played the "Star Spangled Banner", followed by the "Soldier's Song". The stars and stripes, with the Irish tricolour, fluttered from the masthead. New York's Pipers bands played the teams on to the middle and the cheering was hair-raising.'

Joe Stynes of Kildare, whose grandnephew was later to become Ireland's first famous export to the Australian Rules code, played havoc on one wing, Shanahan on the other. Seán Carr of Mayo had a goal for New York straightaway, and they never looked back. The description of New York's third goal by *Irish Advocate* reporter, Limerick-born James Reidy, gives a hint of the style of play. 'Bailey had taken a free and the forwards rushed the Kerry defence, sweeping the goalkeeper off his feet while the ball was placed in the net by Tommy Flynn.' Joe Stynes regarded the play was fair and Kerry were simply 'outclassed by a better combination'. That wasn't how newspaper readers at home received it. 'The game was a very poor sample of Gaelic football on a field too small for any real evolution', a telegram home in the name of Dick Fitzgerald, but later found to have been written by his brother, said.

Foley recounted afterwards that 'certain reports appeared in the Irish papers of the day alleging roughness on the part of the New Yorkers. They created a bad impression on their speedy transmission to New York. But the honest fact remains, as this writer pointed out at the time, there could be no excuse for Kerry's defeat. They were soundly beaten on all aspects of the game by a superior New York side.' He quoted 1903 hero Dan McCarthy, now resident in Brooklyn, as saying, 'Not one of them could catch a ball with the players of his day.'

The row about the allegations of rough play in Fr Fitzgerald's telegram dogged the entire tour. Another Chicago fan, J. Murphy, wrote that Kerry's version of Gaelic football was 'a hundred years behind the times' after their appearance there. When on their return the Kerry County Board passed a motion 'disclaiming all responsibility' for the telegram, Dick Fitzgerald dissented from the motion.

The second match went ahead only after a 'secret meeting' of Kerry County Board attended by the players, of which John Joe Sheehy argued strongly that the game should go ahead. Sheehy subsequently recalled that the team could not feel in form after their arrival and could not expect to be in their home standard unless they were in the States for twelve months, the climate being so heavy for them. 'When we came back to play the second match this cablegram was before us and lowered our prestige. We were practically hooted as men who could not take a beating.'

He denied rumours circulating in Ireland that the team had differences over politics, claiming 'the members of the team were perfectly united throughout the tour', despite the fact that it coincided with the first of two bitterly fought elections in 1927.

In the event it was football that became the chief talking point of the tour. Kerry lost the final game of the tour to goals by Joe Stynes and Tommy Flynn, 2-6 to 0-3. It was a match marked, according to Reidy, 'by bitterness, its rough and tumble character bringing many casualties'. Gene Carr of New York was put out of the game with a badly strained leg, and Paddy Clifford of Kerry suffered a gash over his left eye.

The folkloric status of the game was later to focus on one of the great goalkeeping displays of all time on that hard, short pitch by Waterford-born Eddie Roberts, 'the sorest thorn in the sides of the Kerry men', according to Reidy's report of the opening match.

Foley recounted how a Mrs McCrohan came to him after the game.

'Is that the great Kerry team?' she asked.

'That's the great Kerry team,' I answered.

'Sure they are only ordinary boys after all.'

'That's all ma'am,' said I.

19 AUGUST 1928. IRELAND 2-9, US 1-4, CROKE PARK

> 'McGoldrick the American centre back was voted the brightest star, although some of the Irish players were not far outshone.'
>
> *Irish Independent*, 20 August 1928

The complaints about rough play fired up interest in the New York footballers even further. The appetite for international competition had been whetted, and the Tailteann international was the first chance the crowds in Dublin had of satisfying it.

In the absence of Martin Shanahan, who could not get time off work to travel, Tom Armitage of Tipperary captained an American football team. Ten of New York's victors over Kerry played, including 1923 All-Ireland medallist Joe Stynes, 1921 All-Ireland medallist Bill Landers and 1924 and 1926 All-Ireland medallist Johnny Moriarty. Cork-born Paddy Lenihan had won a National League medal with Laois in 1926. The Ormsby brothers had both played with Mayo. Furlong of Wexford and Tuite of Louth had junior championship medals. M. Moloney from Clare had played on the Munster team at the 1924 Tailteann Games. While Tommy Flynn had been a goalscoring star of the 1927 matches against Kerry, another Leitrim man, Johnny McGoldrick, was to be a star of the 1928 international.

Ireland selected five Kerry men, Joe Barrett, Con Brosnan, Paul Russell, John Joe Sheehy and Jack Ryan, four army players from Kildare, Matt Goff, Jack Higgins, Frank Malone and Paul Doyle, the McDonnell brothers from Dublin, Tom Shevlin from Roscommon, Paddy Colleran from Sligo, Jim Higgins from Cavan and J. Shanley from Leitrim.

A crowd of 30,000 showed up to see Ireland win 2-9 to 1-4 on a rain-spattered day, and there was a hint of former controversies. P. J. Devlin wrote: 'A good game would have been still better had the American players given more attention to the ball and discarded tactics that would certainly not be permitted in the home championships. In America there is no play during rain but there was a steady downfall yesterday and had an adverse effect all round, but particularly on the exiles who were appearing under the heavier handicap. The American style is over-vigorous, if not bordering on actual roughness.'

The controversies on the field of play were nothing compared with what was going on in the background. Because the Aonach Tailteann was essentially seen as a Cumann na nGaedheal government project, John Joe Sheehy and Jack Ryan refused to play for Ireland. Mick O'Brien of Dublin, who scored both goals, and Martin O'Neill of Wexford played instead. It meant that eleven of the Irish team were either Free State soldiers or Gardai, while almost all the American team were opponents of the treaty, some of whom, like Stynes, had been forced to emigrate because their politics made work difficult to find. Martin O'Neill later recalled the atmosphere between the teams as near-poisonous.

A week late, the American team played Kerry at Tralee before a crowd of 7,000, a record for the venue. The rematch for Ted Sullivan's world championship was a draw, ten points each. The Kerry team were to win back the world championship and McCarthy's cup by 0-9 to 1-2 in 1931 before a record crowd of 60,000, at that time the biggest for a football match on either side of the Atlantic.

Even as the cheers were receding from the 1928 match, it was clear that the Tailteann project was running into trouble. The games had been successful only in spots. What success they enjoyed was due to the fact that they were staged immediately after the Olympic Games and persuaded some competitors from Paris in 1924 and Amsterdam in 1928 to drop into Dublin on the way home, leading to the large attendances at the athletics and swimming competitions of 1924 and the boxing competition of 1928. But the 1932 Olympics were already scheduled for Los Angeles. It was proposed by director J. J. Walsh, and indeed decided, that the Tailteann Games be moved to 1931. The decision was subsequently overturned. The 1932 Tailteann Games went ahead in a drizzle without the best Irish athletes, who were busy competing in our best-ever Olympics on the track and in boxing. They were overshadowed by the Eucharistic Congress and the subject of something resembling determined ambivalence from the new Fianna Fáil government.

The international football and hurling contests against America could not sustain the Tailteann Games on their own, and the project was wound up.

30 SEPTEMBER 1928. KILDARE 2-6, CAVAN 2-5, CROKE PARK

> 'No one will expect onlookers unduly to withhold their enthusiasm and ardour on the occasion of big matches, and Irish human nature seems to revel in a good shout, whether of triumph or reproach.'
>
> DICK FITZGERALD, *How to Play Gaelic Football* (1914)

Away from the glamour, Tipperary had unexpectedly dumped Kerry out of the Munster championship.

The Railway Cup, in just its second year, ushered in an incident-packed year for Kerry. An all-Kerry team representing the province of Munster led Ulster by two points with two minutes of the semi-final left. Ulster then scored a would-be winning goal as the Kerry players were protesting a line ball awarded by Mr Ward of Laois. Kerry withdrew from the field and were dealt a six-month suspension by the Central Council, which was lifted by congress just in time to beat Kildare in a National League final listed by Paddy Foley as 'the best ever played in the league series' and by the *Leinster Leader* as 'the fastest and most exciting played at Croke Park'.

Foley said, 'Generally speaking Kerry do not take this competition seriously and except on this occasion never fielded at full strength.' It set Kerry up as favourites to win back Kildare's All-Ireland title.

Disaster struck for Kerry on what should have been a triumphant return to Tipperary town for their first championship match there since the 1903 All-Ireland final. Foley recalled that at half-time, with Tipperary leading 1-5 to 0-2, a bookie behind the press table was shouting 'Four to one against Tipperary', but had no takers, such was the belief that Kerry would prevail in the end. Goals from Kerry's Jack Sheehy and Paul Russell came too late in the game to make any difference. 'Scenes of the wildest enthusiasm followed,' Foley wrote. 'Tipp followers charged in over the pitch and chaired the victors.'

After exit Kerry, it was exit Tipp, rolled over in the Munster final 4-3 to 0-4 by a Cork team that included goalscorers in a one-sided final which included two physicians, Doctors Kearney (who got two) and J. O'Callaghan. Cork's semi-final defeat by Kildare before a crowd of about 15,000 at their own Leeside Athletic Grounds was even more emphatic. Paddy Martin got two of the Kildare goals and Joe Curtis the third as they raced 1-5 to nil ahead at half-time and eventually won by fourteen points, 3-7 to 0-2.

On the other side of the draw both champions perished early. In Connacht defending champions Leitrim drew with Galway on a unique scoreline of one goal and no points each, then won the replay. They were then surprised by Sligo, who were enjoying their first outing after undergoing a twelve-month suspension, dished out for walking off the field in protest at a disallowed goal in the first round of the previous year's championship and provoking a crowd invasion after just three minutes. Sligo beat Mayo in the Connacht final, Nickey Devine delivering the pass to Milo Flynn for Sligo's crucial goal.

Monaghan went out in the Ulster semi-final to Armagh, 0-4 to 0-1, in a semi-final that was played at 5.30 in the evening to allow Commissioner Eoin O'Duffy's car to travel north with four Monaghan players who had played in the Army v Garda challenge game earlier in the day. Regular bulletins were issued from the Garda barracks in Castleblayney as to how the journey was progressing.

Armagh later won an objection, lodged by Monaghan on four separate points. In the Ulster final, brothers Charlie (Armagh) and John (Cavan) Morgan played in opposing goals. Cavan trailed 1-2 to 0-2 at half-time, thanks to Gerry Arthurs' goal for Armagh. A breather in the second half, when Armagh led 1-4 to 0-5, helped Cavan. The ball was kicked into an adjoining field of oats and it took several minutes to find it. Cavan's J. P. Murphy and Andy Conlan had the ball in the Armagh net twice in the space of two minutes when play resumed.

Cavan then qualified for the final after trailing Sligo by a point at half-time. Two quick-fire goals from Conlan and Devlin at the start of the second half put them into the final.

30 SEPTEMBER 1928. KILDARE 2-6, CAVAN 2-5, CROKE PARK

> 'Let it be written quickly: P. Loughlin threw the ball to the Cavan net.'
>
> P. D. MEHIGAN, *The Irish Times*, 1 October 1918

Kildare stuttered somewhat on their way to the final. They beat Laois in the first round 0-4 to 1-0, having been 'shattered' by a goal from Brown in the first half. Goals from Pat 'Darkie' Ryan (2) and Peter Pringle ensured a smoother passage against Longford, who were beaten 3-6 to 0-2. Neither played in the final.

The Leinster final against Dublin was one of those downright dirty matches in GAA history, with the referee attacked after the match and, as his report put it: 'Were it not for the intervention of the Dublin players and the Leinster officials I would have got a rough handling.' McDonnell's move to escort the referee, who had sent him off during the match, after the final whistle was a major factor in preventing any assaults. It along with his co-operation with the referee when ordered off, led to a minimum suspension and eligibility for the Tailteann Games for the Dublin captain.

Kildare won by a point, 0-10 to 1-6. The trouble started as Kildare led 0-9 to nil soon after the start of the second half, when two people confronted the referee with stories about what would happen to him unless he gave Dublin a fair show. Subsequently, Joe Synnott's men cut the Kildare lead away, and only a Joe Curtis point with ten minutes to go saved Kildare. Kildare's efforts were hampered by the fact that a 'juvenile element' gathered round the Dublin goal in the second half and refused to go back to their places.

The semi-final brought Cork and Kildare together for the first time in a competitive match, although they had met in a challenge as early as 1908. Crowds of people gathered in Barrack Square, Naas, and in Athy Showgrounds to listen to Paddy Mehigan's broadcast of the match. Kildare won with surprising ease, 3-7 to 0-2. A Bill Mangan goal in the opening minutes shattered Cork's confidence. Mangan and Paddy Martin added goals in the second half.

Kildare were so confident of beating Cavan in the final that hundreds didn't travel. The attendance, 24,700, was 12,000 down on the previous year and 6,000 less than the Tailteann football match.

The *Leinster Leader* put Joe Curtis's absence from the final down to a cycling accident before the Cork match. In a later interview Curtis claimed he had three broken ribs as a result of a collision with a goalpost during the semi-final.

When it was discovered that Pringle might be ineligible if Cavan objected, Curtis was strapped up, given a shot of whiskey and sent out to play. Kildare's record of two All-Irelands with the same fifteen players was established.

Peter Pringle was a small and fighty wing forward from Rathangan. His combination with Paul Doyle on the opposite wing led inevitably to their fame as 'Peter and Paul'. Even 55 years later he could not disguise his heart-broken disappointment at missing that final against Cavan. He was getting a rub down from Joe McDonald in the dressing room before the match when a delegate from Cavan came into the room with a photograph of Peter playing in Laois. 'It was not right. I don't know where they got it from. I got my medal and my gold watch afterwards. But it broke my heart.' In Kildare they say it was a hockey dance that deprived Peter of his final place. Joe Curtis, broken ribs and all, was fed a baby Powers, strapped up and sent on to the field in Pringle's place.

Curtis appeared on the team, Pringle didn't play, and Kildare made history by fielding their 1927 fifteen. They started badly and Cavan had three points before Mangan's first goal put Kildare 1-2 to 0-3 up at half-time. Kildare went into a three-point lead, but Young equalised for Cavan. Kildare responded with a goal from Paddy Loughlin, starting a controversy that raged ever afterwards. Sportswriter Paddy Mehigan produced one of the most damning lines in GAA history when he wrote: 'Let it be written quickly: P. Loughlin threw the ball into the Cavan net.' The open-handed pass was the source of much controversy in its day, but never more so than the hand pass for Sam in 1928.

Infamous as it was to become, Loughlin's goal was not decisive. Devlin scored another equalising goal for Cavan, and with minutes left it was 2-5 each. Kildare had Bill Mangan to thank for a vital winning point in the dying seconds.

The Sam Maguire Cup was presented by Dr MacCartan, a close friend of Sam Maguire. It was taken home for display in Conlan's shop in Newbridge, where disappointed Kerry fans could view it on their way home.

22 SEPTEMBER 1929. KERRY 1-8, KILDARE 1-5, CROKE PARK

> 'It was a test for men that surpassed that of any other competition in Ireland. Football is our popular game.'
>
> *An Phoblacht*

As the 1920s drew to a close, weaker counties were getting a look-in. Inspired by Sligo and Leitrim, Longford led Dublin twice in the Leinster quarter-final of 1929, but were stunned by a Paddy McDonnell goal with ten minutes to go, and eventually lost 3-7 to 2-6. Kilkenny's physically strong team won their last-ever senior championship match 0-10 to 0-4 with a great first half display against Louth. They then held Kildare level at half-time in the semi-final before succumbing to two last-quarter goals from Albert O'Neill, 2-11 to 0-3. Meath too gave notice of changing times: attacking theologian Fr MacManus scored a late point to earn a replay, 1-5 each. Bad luck was promised to Kildare when they committed the cardinal indiscretion of objecting to the priest before winning the replay 3-5 to 0-9. 'Ye will never win another All-Ireland', they were told—and they never did!

In the Leinster final Kildare got another fright from a maturing Laois team before winning 2-3 to 0-6. They trailed 0-1 to 0-2 at half-time, but two Peter Pringle goals and a series of great saves by goalkeeper James O'Reilly came to their rescue.

Laois showed their capabilities when they beat Wexford 3-3 to 0-7 in the quarter-final, using an unprecedented five substitutes, and then qualified for the final by beating Dublin 5-5 to 3-10. O'Shea secured their historic final spot with a doubtful-looking final point. Dublin had already been shaken by goals from Jack Delaney, Harry Browne, McDarby, a Dublin defender's own goal, and Callanan at that stage.

Derry re-established their county board in 1929, and once more there were 32 counties in the competition. But the 1929 Ulster championship is remembered for a tragic incident in the Ulster semi-final between Cavan and Armagh as Cavan's Jim Smith clashed with Jamesy Kiernan of Crossmaglen. Kiernan died two days after the incident, and a storm erupted around the affair. Kiernan's death was due to peritonitis following an operation, the doctor in Belturbet having made light of Kiernan's injury after the match. During the inquest Smith was implicated by the questions of an RUC head constable and charges were initiated against him in Cavan. Smith was cleared when preliminary evidence was heard, but the incident cast a shadow over Ulster football for several years.

When Monaghan and Cavan met again in Ulster, the match was a draw, 1-4 each. In the replay Jim Smith was barracked throughout the match as a consequence of the Jamesy Kiernan incident. To add to Cavan's problems, Monaghan won 1-10 to 0-7, thanks to a goal from T. J. Weymes with ten minutes to go, following up his own shot that came back from an upright. Monaghan faded early against Kildare in the All-Ireland semi-final, were 0-6 to 0-1 down at half-time, and lost 0-9 to 0-1.

But Kildare's old rivals were stirring. Cork led Kerry by 1-2 to 1-1 at half-time, but Kerry avoided another semi-final exit by 1-7 to 1-3 with a John Joe Landers first half goal. When Kerry met Clare in the final for the fourth time in seven years, Clare showed their strong defensive qualities but precious little else. Kerry went 0-10 to nil up at half-time, despite having a goal disallowed, and they raced away to a 1-14 to 1-2 victory as Miko Doyle made his debut for Kerry.

In the Connacht championship, Sligo and Leitrim played the last senior championship match to take place without nets on the goalposts. After they lost 1-4 to 0-6, Leitrim's objection was ruled out of order because it was not on Irish watermarked paper. Meanwhile, Mayo laid the foundation of a great 1930s team by winning the provincial title. Six D. F. Courell points combined with a goal from Kenny helped them beat Galway 1-6 to 0-4 after mauling unfortunate Roscommon by twenty points in the semi-final. Mayo went into three weeks' full-time training under Garda boxing instructor Tommy Moloney at Enniscrone, but they were crushed by Kerry in the All-Ireland semi-final 3-8 to 1-1. The closest they got to the final was shortly after half-time when they came within two points of the Kerry men.

In the All-Ireland final, Kerry survived a rattling second half comeback by Kildare that kept the record attendance of 43,839, paying receipts of £4,010, on their feet to the end.

Ned Sweeney's first half goal, shot in off the upright after a Jackie Ryan free, proved enough. John Joe Sheehy and Paul Doyle scored five points each in a duel of free-taking. Paddy Martin landed a 30 yard drop-kick into the net at the start of the second half to inspire Kildare. John Joe Landers and John Joe Sheehy points killed off the challenge when Kildare came back to within a point of Kerry, against the sun and the wind. But instead of Kildare's three in a row, Gaelic football braced itself for Kerry's four.

In the National League, Kerry beat Kildare, again by a single point, 1-7 to 2-3. The rivals had much more to offer. But first an interlude.

28 SEPTEMBER 1930. KERRY 3-11, MONAGHAN 0-2, CROKE PARK

> 'Monaghan's good backs, who had mastered Kildare's attack, were helpless against the brains and brawn of these Kerrymen.'
>
> P. D. MEHIGAN, *The Irish Times*, 29 September 1930

The Kerry v Kildare rivalry had not passed its peak. The sides should have met again in 1930, but things started going wrong. Just as Kerry's concentration had slipped in the run-up to the big match in 1928, Kildare's slipped in 1930. The result was a breakthrough for Monaghan who had such humiliating results that the Monaghan supporters wondered was it worth the effort.

Monaghan had no real opposition in Ulster. They qualified for a final meeting with Cavan when they beat Armagh 2-2 to 0-5 with a goal each from Mason and, in the last minute, from Charlie McCarthy. The fearful referee had to be escorted from the field by RUC men after he sent off Armagh star Jack Corrigan. At least they only had to play one team in the Ulster semi-final.

Cavan, on the other hand, had to play the Ulster semi-final twice against two separate opponents! Antrim did not include Patrick Gunning in the list of players handed to the referee when they beat Fermanagh 3-3 to 2-5, with the help of two own goals by defenders. Cavan had already beaten Antrim in the semi-final when Fermanagh's objection was upheld. So Cavan had to beat Fermanagh as well.

The final was endangered when Cavan objected to travelling to Carrickmacross's showpiece grounds, opened two years earlier, because of the abuse Jim Smith suffered there in 1929. The Ulster council secretary, Cavan man Benny Fay, and colleague Standish O'Grady recruited a rebel Cavan team on the morning of the match, mainly from Cornafean and Crosserlough.

It was heavily beaten, having trailed 3-3 to nil at half-time and eventually lost 4-3 to 1-5 to goals from Fischer (2), McCarthy and P. J. Duffy. Cavan County Board reacted by suspending all the rebels and 'selectors' Fay and O'Grady. Cavan were in turn suspended for failing to turn up at the Ulster junior final two weeks after the senior final. They also missed a National Football League match against Down on 3 August. As confrontation loomed, a special convention on 27 September tried to defuse the situation and reinstated Cavan.

Monaghan were the underdogs for their All-Ireland semi-final. But it was a good year for underdogs. In the Leinster semi-final Dublin were already struggling against underdogs Meath in the semi-final before Tom McGennis's goal plunged them seven points down, and P. Colclough added another goal in the dying minutes for a 3-6 to 1-4 surprise win for Meath.

Larry Stanley had been called out of retirement to help Kildare beat underdogs Meath in the Leinster final. Tom McGennis had forced them all back to Croke Park with a goal near the end of the final. They needed two meetings before Meath eventually succumbed by 2-6 to 1-2, to goals from Jack Higgins and Larry Stanley at the tail end of the first half.

Monaghan's win over Kildare in the All-Ireland semi-final ranks as one of the shocks of the century. A breakaway goal midway through the second half left the score 1-6 to 0-3, but Kildare were not unduly worried—until the Kildare comeback efforts went wrong. A Harry Burke goal was disallowed for 'whistle gone'. Another Burke piledriver was stopped by a dazed goalkeeper. And rain bucketed down as Monaghan held on to win by two points, 1-6 to 1-4.

Ulster did not have the monopoly on objections. Galway beat Mayo 0-7 to 0-1 in the Connacht semi-final, but Mayo got to the final anyway on an objection. There they beat Sligo too, after some anxious moments. Sligo had a great start. At half-time it was 0-4 to 1-1 and M. Moran got Mayo's goal soon afterwards to bring about a 1-7 to 1-2 victory. In the All-Ireland semi-final, Mayo tried to do a Monaghan and took a four points to three lead against Kerry at Roscommon, but John Joe Sheehy's goal and his second half sharpshooting sorted out all suspicion of a shock with a resounding 1-9 to 0-4 win.

The upsets ended when Kerry hammered an unfortunate Monaghan team by 3-11 to 0-2 without their goalkeeper touching the ball! Sportswriter P. D. Mehigan described them as 'the best Kerry team since 1925'.

They certainly managed to play with a swagger in this match. Jack Riordan was the goalkeeper, Dee O'Connor, Joe Barrett and Jack Walsh kept the full back line; Paul Russell, Joe O'Sullivan and Tim O'Donnell played in the half backs; Con Brosnan and American-born Bob Stack were at midfield; Jackie Ryan scored three points from right wing; Miko Doyle was at centre half and scored 0-2; athletic champion Eamonn Fitzgerald played left wing; Ned Sweeney scored a goal from the right corner; John Joe Landers scored 1-2 from full forward; and John Joe Sheehy scored 1-3 from the left corner.

And they beat Kildare 0-9 to 0-2 in the specially arranged Count McCormack challenge match after the All-Ireland, just to prove the point.

A Monaghan County Board official described the final as a 'bullfight'. Monaghan scored first and a second point made it 0-4 to 0-2, then John Joe Landers punched over the goalkeeper's head, making it 1-6 to 0-2 at half-time. Sweeney punched another goal eight minutes into the second half, Sheehy got a third almost from the kick-out, and the crowd invaded the pitch near the end after an altercation between two players. It was a rough one. Four Monaghan players retired injured, and Seán O'Carroll had his leg broken. Matadors' luck.

27 SEPTEMBER 1931. KERRY 1-11, KILDARE 0-8, CROKE PARK

> 'The mountaineer is a better fighter than the man of the plains. From his infancy he has something to look up to, something to surmount. He is impelled to climb the highest peak, to see what lies beyond. The child of the plains has no such incentive.'
>
> *An Phoblacht* ponders the significance of the result of the All-Ireland final, 3 October 1931

Kerry set off on another triumphant United States tour. Their appearances in Yankee Stadium, New York (with a capacity of 82,000, much larger than the Polo Grounds), brought out crowds of 60,000 and 55,000. There were 45,000 in Comiskey Park, Chicago, to watch them play. Kerry won all their matches this time. The tour promoter was rumoured to have made £20,000 without taking the trouble to abscond, and Kerry came home with enough profit to purchase Austin Stack Park in Tralee.

This time Kerry, never ones to exaggerate, came home with a 'Champions of the World' tag by virtue of their wins over Irish American teams and hammered Tipperary 5-8 to 0-2 in the Munster final, having been given a bye because of the tour.

Kerry's next opponents were to prove more difficult. New scoring star Gerard Courell scored 2-4 to help Mayo fight off Roscommon's best challenge in fifteen years before 6,000 spectators in the Connacht final at Sligo, Mayo winning 2-10 to 3-2. In the All-Ireland semi-final Jackie Ryan got a goal for Kerry against Mayo in the very first minute. Kerry led 1-5 to 0-1 at half-time, but Culkin boxed a Mayo goal at the restart to cause Kerry a lot of worry. Mayo had a goal disallowed and the pitch was invaded before Kerry eventually won 1-6 to 1-4.

Cavan beat Armagh 0-8 to 2-1 in the Ulster final, the first meeting between the teams since the Jamesy Kiernan fatality in 1929. Dundalk was chosen as a safe venue. A nasty situation was averted when an attempted invasion of the field after an Armagh player was injured did not come off, and all ended peacefully. Unhappiest team in Ulster of 1931 were Donegal, thrown out of the championship for being late on the field after a breakthrough victory over Antrim, their first major win in senior football championship history.

Back in the All-Ireland semi-final with a full team, Cavan threatened to avenge 1928. Their attempt to 'do a Monaghan' on Kildare started with a Colleran goal at the end of the first half, which left the score 0-2 to 1-4, but Kildare's 'Peter and Paul' combination (Pringle and Doyle) linked up with Pat Byrne and Paddy Martin to storm back to victory by two points, 0-10 to 1-5.

So Kerry had familiar opponents in the All-Ireland final. After drawing with Meath for a record third year in a row, Kildare reached the final thanks to Paul Doyle's contribution of 1-3. Rain spoiled the Dublin-Louth match and caused the initial Meath-Louth game to be abandoned on one of the wettest days in Irish meteorological history: the Boyne burst its banks and large areas of the east coast river valleys spent days under water. Kildare had new opponents in the Leinster final. Westmeath, the 1929 junior champions, thwarted Dublin in the Leinster semi-final with goals from P. Bracken and J. Smith, and had a shock 2-4 to 1-4 win. Kildare started with a sensational goal from Paul Doyle, shot to the net from 40 yards, and won by 2-9 to 1-6, but another Doyle, from Westmeath, kept Westmeath in the reckoning throughout their first Leinster final with a vital goal at the start of the second half.

Kerry were missing John Joe Sheehy and Ned 'Pedlar' Sweeney. Somewhat dramatically, Johnny O'Riordan was dropped in the dressing room minutes before the final was due to begin, and his place in goal given to Dan O'Keeffe.

Kerry settled the argument by 1-11 to 0-8 in the final, thanks to a somewhat lucky goal from Paul Russell and a series of ingenious switches at half-time.

A good second quarter performance helped Kildare to a lead of 0-6 to 0-4 at half-time. Paddy Whitty was switched to left wing, Jackie Ryan to full forward, Eamonn FitzGerald to right corner forward, and Stack and Brosnan switched sides.

Kerry had already taken a 0-10 to 0-7 lead as a result of those switches when Russell's long shot was allowed to drop into the net because the goalkeeper and the full back misread each other's calls.

25 SEPTEMBER 1932. KERRY 2-7, MAYO 2-4, CROKE PARK

> 'The superiority of Kerry as a football power is now a serious problem for Gaelic administrators.'
>
> *Daily Express*, 26 September 1932

> 'There are three things which tend to make the playing of football, and in a sense, the playing of every outdoor game, specially difficult, and these are the sun, the wind, and the rain.'
>
> DICK FITZGERALD, *How to Play Gaelic Football* (1914)

Of the twenties twosome, Kildare ran out of steam first. Leinster had new champions in 1932.

The question was, who would succeed them? At first Wexford looked likely pretenders. Wexford's Nick Walsh and Martin O'Neill got the goals to thwart Kildare's seven-in-a-row bid at the semi-final stage by 2-8 to 2-5, despite conceding an own goal in the first minute when a defender fly-kicked into his own net. Davey Morris set a new individual scoring record with 5-1 for Wexford against Laois.

There were two other hopefuls. The previous year's finalists, Westmeath, eventually ran out of steam after leading Dublin by two points in the semi-final. Willie Bracken and P. Doyle got the Westmeath goals. Meath also led Dublin by two points in the quarter-final, before collapsing in the second half.

In the end it was Dublin who took on Wexford in the Leinster final, and old-timers Paddy Synnott (2) and Paddy McDonnell scored the goals to give them a thirteen-point half-time lead (3-5 to 0-2) and sure victory over Wexford by 3-7 to 2-5 in a bad-tempered replay. Wexford's Nick Walsh had earned that replay with a spectacular late point from near the halfway line for a 2-5 each draw. Only one Dublin man had made the Leinster team for the Railway Cup that spring!

As Kerry found no clear-cut rivals in Munster, Clare beat Cork 3-5 to 1-6 with the help of a new hero. Georgie Comerford's best football, however, was to be with Dublin with whom he won a Leinster medal two years later. But Kerry beat Tipperary in the final and faced another much-heralded Munster -Leinster semi-final, against new champions Dublin.

It merited the full-blooded build-up, as the new *Irish Press* and older *Irish Independent* competed for the GAA readership with far more extensive coverage. Both teams played a remarkable scoreless first half. Dowd got a Dublin goal, another Dublin goal was disallowed, and Kerry were in serious trouble before Paul Russell got their winning goal with four minutes to go. It was a lucky goal: Russell's long speculative shot caught the goalkeeper unawares and put Kerry into the All-Ireland final. The *Irish Independent* eulogised: 'This was one of the greatest displays of football ever witnessed in Croke Park or elsewhere. It was a wonderful struggle, packed with thrills from start to finish, and as an exhibition of speed and dash, grit and vigour, and all the best qualities that contribute to the best that there is in the Gaelic game, new heights were reached. Dublin, beyond a shadow of a doubt, are unlucky losers.'

That left Connacht and Ulster to fight out the other semi-final. In Ulster, Cavan were set for their 2-9 to 0-2 victory in the provincial final from the moment an unfortunate Armagh defender dropped the ball over his own line. Jack Smallhorn added a second half goal, and the match ended prematurely when the crowd invaded three minutes from the end, with Cavan leading by 2-9 to 0-2. According to the Ulster council, a detective Garda had produced a gun, triggering off the invasion. Ironically, earlier in the year a storm was created when Antrim proposed a motion debarring Garda members and Free State soldiers from GAA membership! Against Cavan in the first round, two

Donegal players had failed to turn up and four others involved in a motor accident in Clones were unable to play.

Mayo had begun to show the innovative style that captured six National League titles in the 1930s. Paddy Moclair of Mayo was reputedly the first 'roving' full forward. They won their fourth Connacht title in a row, beating Galway 3-5 to 1-3 at Castlerea before a record 11,000 attendance, and Sligo by 2-6 to 0-7. When the provinces met, Mayo won 2-4 to 0-8. Moclair's two goals against a disallowed goal by Smith of Cavan were enough to protect their semi-final lead.

Mayo had a boxer on board. Substitute Dick Hearins was seven times Irish light heavyweight champion and won 173 of his 198 amateur bouts. In a startling football career he played inter-county with Roscommon, Longford, Donegal, Cork, Dublin and Mayo.

Kerry almost let the four in a row slip. They were three points down at half-time, 1-1 to 1-4, Paul Russell getting the Kerry goal, Courell the Mayo goal, and Moclair most of the points. The Kerry selectors switched Jackie Ryan and Tim Landers at half-time. On the restart Bill Landers struck for a lightning goal, Con Brosnan had another disallowed, and Forde's goal with only four minutes to go was shell-shocked Mayo's only score in the second half. Courell missed two late frees, the second from just 30 yards range, that might have saved the day for Mayo.

Kerry were missing Eamonn Fitzgerald, chosen to represent Ireland in the triple jump at the Los Angeles Olympics. He finished fourth, missing the bronze medal by just over four inches. Three Landers brothers played together in the final. Bill, who had returned to Ireland from America in May as part of the touring 1932 American GAA team, came on as a substitute for the injured Con Geaney to join his brothers Tim and John Joe on the team. The youngest of the three brothers, Tim, was undoubtedly the man of the match, according to P. D. Mehigan: 'Elusive as an eel, hopping like a rubber ball, quick to strike as a serpent in attack, he made bohereens through the Mayo defence.' He was probably the first Kerry player to turn down an offer of a professional soccer contract. Among the Kerry men who played on all four winning teams was Miko Doyle—he was not yet 21!

Heavy rain delayed the start of the match and kept the attendance down for the final: 25,816 spectators who paid receipts of £2,247. They watched the end of Kerry's greatest era to date. Being Kerry, the target of four in a row sought to inspire rather than intimidate future generations of footballers.

24 SEPTEMBER 1933. CAVAN 2-5, GALWAY 1-4, CROKE PARK

'An event of international importance.'

Anglo-Celt, 30 September 1933

Who would beat Kerry? Evidently nobody in Munster. Kerry got another bye to the provincial final because of a US tour. They travelled to another new venue, Clonmel, the seventh in eight years for what was among the worst attended of the provincial finals at the time. This time it was not so easy. The teams were level three times in the first half, and Tipperary took the lead early in the second half before two goals put Kerry back in the driving seat, and they won 2-8 to 1-4. Paddy Foley concluded in the *Kerryman* that victory was 'not due to superlative merits on their part, but rather to the home team's inefficiency'.

Not a good sign. Leinster would appear to provide the main contenders. Meath were destined to succeed Kerry as the 1932–33 National League champions, beating Cavan in the final by a single point, 0-10 to 1-6. But when it came to the championship, Meath came back to equalise against Dublin before a late P. Perry goal saw them off, 1-8 to 1-4.

Laois forced a replay against Kildare with late goals from Chris Delaney and Johnny Brennan, but Tom Keogh (later to play with Laois) scored a last-minute goal for Kildare to win the replay 2-11 to 1-5.

Louth were disappointed and scoreless during the second half of their match against Dublin as they watched their one-point lead dwindle to a nine-point defeat.

Wexford led 2-7 to 0-3 at the three-quarter stage, then saw their lead reduced to three points before beating Kildare 2-8 to 1-8. Wexford led through a Martin O'Neill goal, 0-4 to 1-4 at half-time.

In the end Dublin came back to equalise with eleven minutes to go and won by 0-9 to 1-4. Dublin became Leinster champions with an eye on the title they last held ten years earlier.

Connacht had two contenders. Mayo were National League semi-finalists (and were not to be defeated in the competition again until 1946), but Galway had been threatening to depose rampant Mayo for two years. It happened as Mick Donnellan sprang a surprise early goal to give Galway a 1-5 to 0-2 lead. Mayo got a goal at the start of the second half, Gerald Courell reduced Galway's lead to a point shortly before the end, but Galway went on to win by two, 1-7 to 1-5.

Cavan had the advantage of having the first sniff at an increasingly vulnerable Kerry team after they ran away with the Ulster championship. To get there, Cavan beat Armagh 1-8 to 0-2 and Tyrone 6-13 to 1-2 in the provincial final.

That was not too difficult. Tyrone's Dungannon players had all defected an hour before the match and stormed out of the Railway Hotel in Cavan, leaving the county board to scout for replacements to make up their fifteen players.

The Cavan men who faced Kerry had just five survivors from the 1928 near miss. The 1928 goalscorer, Willie Young, was in goal; Willie Connolly, Patsy Lynch and Mick Denneny were the full backs; Tommy Coyle, team captain Jim Smith (an international in the 1928 and 1932 Tailteann Games) and Packie Phair were the half backs; at centrefield were 'Big' Tom O'Reilly from Cornafean and Hughie O'Reilly; converted goalkeeper Donal Morgan, Patsy Devlin and Jack Smallhorn were the half forwards; while Vincent McGovern, Louis Blessing and 'Son' Magee were the full forwards.

On 27 August 1933, a crowd of 17,111 looked on in Breffni Park as Cavan stopped Kerry's run. Kerry were within two minutes from the five-in-a-row chance. Vincent McGovern booted to the net after Devlin had laid on a ball previously received from Smith, making the score 1-5 to 0-5. Tim Landers was just wide on an equalising mission for Kerry, and the crowd went wild. The excitement had boiled over earlier when the crowd raided the field when a Cavan player was fouled.

That put the All-Ireland up for grabs between the weaker provinces who sought to break the Munster-Ulster stranglehold on the championship. A week earlier Galway too had had a tight squeeze as they watched their 0-8 to 1-2 half-time lead get whittled back to a single point, 0-8 to 1-4, and Synnott had a Dublin goal disallowed before a 7,596 attendance at Mullingar.

The public loved the change. Despite blinding rain, a record 45,180 crowd showed up and 5,000 were locked out when the gates were closed twenty minutes before the start. They listened to the match on loudspeakers outside the grounds.

Radio listeners had an unexpected interruption. At half-time, a group of men bustled commentator Eamonn de Barra away from the microphone and called for the release of republican prisoners. Engineers at the various broadcasting stations realised what was happening and turned the microphones off. Athlone acted more quickly than Dublin or Cork.

'The standard of play was dull for half an hour', but that did not disturb the fans who watched Cavan win Ulster's first title 2-5 to 1-4 with two first half goals. Louis Blessing put Jim Smith's 50 into the net after 22 minutes, and sent a pass to 'Son' Magee for the second in lost time at the end of the first half. That gave Cavan a 2-3 to 0-2 half-time lead.

Galway played better in the second half, but struggled to come back to terms with that deficit. A goal, two minutes into the second half, was variously credited to Mick Donnellan and Brendan Nestor. Fly-kicking and rushes from midfield made Cavan worry, and Dermot Mitchell hit the post. But Cavan held on in a finish broken by several stoppages for injuries.

Cavan returned on Monday to a parade through the town to the Farnham Arms Hotel, led by the Cavan Labour band. Jim Smith, twice Cavan's only representative on Ireland's Tailteann sides, said: 'My life's ambition is now realised. After fourteen years of struggle I have what I want at last.' The *Anglo-Celt* did not understate the importance of this win, describing it as 'an event of international importance'.

That description was accurate when applied in New York, at least. When Cavan went on tour to America in May 1934, Mayor La Guardia welcomed them to City Hall, wishing them 'everything in the world except victory. After all I am from New York.' The welcome did not extend to the exile Gaelic footballers. When there was a heavy tackle on Jack Smallhorn towards the end of the match against New York before 40,000 people in Yankee Stadium, it took police, firemen and stewards to clear the ground, and mounted police stood by in anticipation of a wholesale riot.

23 SEPTEMBER 1934. GALWAY 3-5, DUBLIN 1-9, CROKE PARK

> 'The closest and greatest fight for All-Ireland football honours in the history of the GAA has come to an end, and Galway are proud holders of the title.'
>
> *Connacht Sentinel*, 25 September 1934

As All-Ireland champions, Cavan had found the going much tougher in the 1934 Ulster championship. They appeared to lose to Tyrone in the first round, but qualified on the official scoreline of 2-5 to 2-4. When the match ended, Tyrone celebrated, thinking they had won by two points. As the Tyrone players were chaired off the field by jubilant supporters, it was pointed out that one of their second half goals, by Seamus Campbell, had not been allowed, so it was Cavan who had won.

Allegations that Tyrone had deliberately shortened the pitch were withdrawn. Other allegations were made that Tyrone had 'deliberately roughed up' the Cavan men. In reply to that, the referee said, 'It was the cleanest match I ever refereed.' Those shenanigans over, Cavan set off on their triumphant American tour and returned for an impressive win over Fermanagh, 3-4 to 1-3.

When Cavan eventually beat Armagh 3-8 to 0-2 in the Ulster final, a record crowd for the province (£511 worth) made their way along the two miles from Castleblayney to the field in the Hope Estate, where the Ulster final got under way somewhat late. The second half did not start until 5.20!

Galway had that rarity, a dual goalkeeper, Michael Brennan, in action. They too were convinced they could go a step further in 1934, particularly after Michael Donnellan captained Connacht to victory in the Railway Cup for the first time. Donnellan retired immediately and missed another honour, although that hardly seemed likely as Galway got a shock from Roscommon in the first round of the Connacht championship when they trailed 0-1 to 0-3 at half-time, before they came back to win 2-7 to 0-4. They easily beat Mayo in the Connacht final at Castlerea before a 16,000 attendance. John Dunne and Martin Kelly from Ahascragh got the goals for a 2-4 to 0-5 victory.

The show-down between Cavan and Galway, a repeat of the 1933 All-Ireland final, was fixed for Tuam on 12 August. There was no banking whatsoever to facilitate the 28,000 spectators who turned up. The impending crisis was evident from an early stage. The sideline seats were filled from halfway through the curtain-raiser, a hurling match. The racecourse stand was unusable, as it was 200 yards away from the pitch. Entrepreneurial locals were charging five bob for a box to stand on.

When the match got under way the ground was hopelessly crowded with spectators fifteen yards over the east sideline. The despairing linesmen started giving throw-ins whenever the ball hit a spectator. Rain at half-time made the situation worse as thousands were pushed on to the field by latecomers with a poor view. At times it was possible to shake hands across the field, so close were the spectators on the other side of the pitch.

The pitch had to be cleared five times in a match peppered with stops and starts, that one Cavan official, T. McCormack, commented: 'I saw five minutes of the game and three glimpses of the ball in the second half.' Six Central Council members convened at half-time to decide whether the match should continue. Galway, 1-5 to 0-5 ahead at that stage and about to face the wind, agreed. Cavan's captain apparently said no, although this was disputed vociferously by Cavan at a council meeting afterwards, claiming that they wanted the match to go ahead as a friendly. 'The question arose at half-time whether the game should be continued and we understand that the Galway officials and their team were unanimous though holding the lead at half-time to have the game declared off and replayed at Croke Park if Cavan so wished. They consulted among themselves and captains of teams and the Cavan side expressed a desire to have the match finished in Tuam.'

The match went ahead. Son Magee missed a late penalty and at ten past six, two hours and four minutes after the throw-in, Galway emerged winners by virtue of Dermot Mitchell's early goal, 1-8 to 0-8. Not everybody thought the game was out of control. John Joe Sheehy claimed: 'I never saw the sideline at all, but the encroachment was not a serious handicap.'

Dublin had a hard, tough mixture of natives and blow-ins in action. Their goalkeeper was John McDonnell, the only survivor from the last victory in 1923; full backs were Des Brennan, Michael Casey from Clare, and Frank Cavanagh; half backs were Paddy Hickey, Ned McCann and Paddy Cavanagh, brother of Frank of Dolphins; the midfielders were Bobby Beggs (Finglas born but later to win All-Ireland medals with Galway and Railway Cup medals with Connacht) and Kerry-born Murt Kelly; and the forwards were Gearóid Fitzgerald from Kerry, Georgie Comerford from Clare, Mick O'Brien, Michael Wellington, Willie Dowling, and Michael Keating from Wicklow, who were expected to prove more than a match for their Leinster opponents.

The Leinster final between Dublin and Louth went to three meetings. Louth appeared to have won at the first attempt when Murt Kelly struck back with 1-1 towards the end, and they relied on a Seán Cullen equaliser for a 0-5 to 1-2 draw. Eventually, in the second replay, Dublin came from behind to win 2-9 to 1-10 at Drogheda after trailing 1-9 to 2-2 early in the second half. Sligo-born Paddy Colleran's first half goals laid the foundation for their victory.

In contrast to Tuam, Tralee set a great example in the second All-Ireland semi-final, with brand new banking adequate to cope with a record 21,438 attendance. Everything went according to plan except the home team's performance. They went four points up before they succumbed, by a hefty 3-8 to 0-6, to goals from Georgie Comerford in the first half and Michael Wellington and Paddy Colleran in the second. The Dublin players changed out of their jerseys in Limerick on the way home. 'The Kerry crowd wasn't happy,' Murt Kelly recalled afterwards, 'and the Dublin lads didn't hang around after the game.'

Having beaten Kerry, Dublin were now favourites. But they never recovered from their bad start in the All-Ireland final, and before 36,143 spectators Galway brought Connacht its second title and answered the critics of the 1925 title by a decisive 3-5 to 1-9. Most of the triumphant Galway team were in their early twenties. They won with two first half goals from 23-year-old Kerry-born UCG student Michael Ferriter. The 28-year-old Martin Kelly got the third at the start of the second half before Dublin began to edge their way back into the game. The 10.8 second sprinter from Miltown Malbay, Co. Clare, George Comerford, slotted over four of Dublin's final five points as they pushed the margin back from eight to two points. This was as near to an All-Ireland medal as Comerford came. It was once wrongly claimed that he had won a Railway Cup medal alongside fourteen Kerry men. Comerford's contribution to football history was as an outstanding player in the wrong counties at the wrong time—he played for six inter-county teams in all.

22 SEPTEMBER 1935. CAVAN 3-6, KILDARE 2-5, CROKE PARK

> 'Chanders, the pick and shovel man, but a good goalkeeper was turned down to make room for Maguire, a cuff and collar man and a bad goalman, because in the eyes of the selection committee the game was already won—a trip to America was contemplated, and the newcomer to the goal would be a more suitable traveller and more deserving of All-Ireland honours.'
>
> Letter to the *Leinster Leader*, 28 September 1935

Fermanagh have always been regarded as the weakest GAA county of them all. They have, as one county secretary called it, 'the population of Leitrim divided by two because of religion' to chose from. Underage games were organised at eleven-a-side and thirteen-a-side for many years because of the shortage of players. Poor pitches, the difficulty in obtaining land because of the hostility of the unionist community, and a dispersed population, all combined to leave it the sole Ulster county which has never won an Ulster championship.

In 1935 Fermanagh had their best championship run for a generation with the help of northern wandering star, Jim McCullough. The former Armagh player also played with Tyrone as his job with the Northern Ireland Electricity Board brought him through several different counties in a twelve-month period, confusing officials and incurring suspensions (which he always seemed to avoid by moving to another county) with his meanderings.

Fermanagh had won the McKenna Cup in 1933, then McCullough had helped them reach the 1935 League final in the most momentous year in their history. He was an inspiration in their great championship run. Fermanagh beat Tyrone 1-11 to 2-6 at the second attempt, and Armagh by 3-4 to 2-2 also at the second attempt, to face rampant Cavan in the Ulster final.

It was David and Goliath stuff, especially when Son Magee scored a seventh-minute goal. Louis Blessing hit another, and Cavan led 2-3 to nil approaching half-time. Bill Maguire got a goal before half-time, Eddie Collins got another in the second half, and after Fermanagh's defeat, they reminisced on Maguire missing another chance with the goal at his mercy.

Munster were weaker than usual. A Kerry county convention decided the county should withdraw from all championships in protest at the treatment of republican prisoners at the Curragh. As an uneasy alliance between the IRA and de Valera fell apart from the time the Cumann na nGaedheal military tribunal was re-established in August 1933, Kerry GAA was once again drawn into the political controversy. They had withdrawn from a December 1933 National League match because twelve Tralee youths were arrested on the night that Blueshirt leader General Eoin O'Duffy visited Tralee.

So Tipperary beat Cork 2-8 to 1-2 to win their last Munster championship and Cavan's 'last-minute goal' survival technique had another trial against Tipperary in the All-Ireland semi-final. Tipperary had made their way back from five points down to lead 0-8 to 0-7 when they faced a Jim Smith 50. There was silence as Smith sent the ball in to Louis Blessing, who punched through to Hughie O'Reilly (from Mullahoran), who tipped it to the centre of the net for a sensational goal and a 1-7 to 0-8 victory.

Smith's place on the Cavan team had not been secure right up to the throw-in. The Dublin County Board were meeting in Croke Park almost until the throw-in to consider whether he should be suspended over a club incident. O'Keeffe had a Tipperary point disallowed in the second half. Tipperary objected, but to no avail.

The Leinster championship had a changed look about it as Westmeath and Meath defied tradition by playing their Leinster quarter-final tie on a Thursday night, and the 1933 junior champions Carlow had a historic 5-7 to 1-6 victory over Wexford. Kildare eventually took the Leinster title back. Christy Higgins and newcomer Paul Mathews combined to take control of midfield for Kildare against Mathews' native Louth, and they won the provincial final 0-8 to 0-6.

Mayo protested about the Connacht council's choice of Roscommon as the venue for the provincial final, then won out the much-heralded clash between National League (Mayo) and All-Ireland champions (Galway) by a comfortable 0-12 to 0-5 before 26,000 spectators. Mayo then went down to Kildare 2-6 to 0-7, thanks to goals from Geraghty and Keogh in the first ten minutes of their semi-final.

Four points was the margin in the final. Cavan got revenge for 1928 by 3-6 to 2-5 before a record 50,380 attendance, and Kildare simmered for months afterwards over the dropping of regular goalkeeper Pa 'Cuddy' Chanders. Although he had not conceded a goal in the championship, he was replaced by a converted corner back, Jim Maguire, who had never played in goal because of the belief that his nerves would not be up to it after he let in six goals in a challenge match against Meath. But, according to a *Leinster Leader* correspondent, there was more to it than that: 'Chanders, a pick and shovel man but a good goal-keeper, was turned down to make room for Maguire, a cuff and collar man and a bad goalman, because in the eyes of the selection committee the game was already won—a trip to America was contemplated, and the newcomer to the goal would be a more suitable traveller and more deserving of All-Ireland honours.'

Legends still survive in Kildare that an attempt was made to reinstate Chanders on Saturday night, that the Kildare full back Matt Gough announced 'we'll test this goalkeeper' at the start of the game to his own backs, that a section of the team left the bus and refused to travel to Croke Park, and that instead of Tom Keogh's usual rousing song on the team bus, he sang an old mourner that summed up the melancholy mood of the Kildare men. It was all very petty in view of the fact that none of the three goals could be blamed on the goalkeeper, and that Cavan put three goals past Chanders when they won a November League match in Newbridge.

None of this deterred the fans. An official 50,300 turned up, and when the gates were locked at 2.50, some 5,000 more waited outside to listen to the match on the loudspeaker relay.

Cavan won the match in the first half, when the O'Reilly pair, Hugh from Cootehill and 'small' Tom from Mullahoran, took control at midfield. 'Kildare were put off their game by faster and fitter footballers, who were a transformed team since their last appearance against Tipperary.'

Son Magee scored a point after just twenty seconds, the fastest opening score since 1896. Packie Boylan landed 24th and 31st-minute goals in the first half and Tom Reilly a third in the second half to make amends for the tragedy in Tuam in 1934. Kildare improved in the second half and fought to regain the lost ground with 1-3 in the last quarter, Mick Geraghty's goal complementing one by Tom Mulhall just before Boylan's second in the first half.

'It is possible,' P. D. Mehigan wrote, 'that Kildare's change of goalkeepers was ill-advised, for Chanders never had a goal scored against him in the championship. Through the second half Maguire cleared good balls, and he was opposing a much-improved group of forwards.' What is left unsaid is that Cavan's first two goals should not have been scored.

27 SEPTEMBER 1936. MAYO 4-11, LAOIS 0-5, CROKE PARK

> 'There was a time when one could name with fair accuracy on New Year's Day the counties that would reach the ensuing finals. That day has long since passed.'
>
> *Irish Independent*, 28 September 1936

Newly crowned champions Cavan were given a bye to the Ulster semi-final because they decided to follow the 1930s tradition of taking an American tour. On their return they beat Armagh and Monaghan to recapture the Ulster title by 1-7 to 0-4 with the help of an early goal from Louis Blessing. Monaghan's Christy Fisher missed his side's best chance when he put a penalty over the bar at a stage when Monaghan trailed by 1-7 to 0-4 midway through the second half. Both goalkeepers gave a display of great saves late in the game.

Cavan's run was ended by Laois, who had taken back the Leinster title after

47 years, when it seemed Kildare had won the real final against Louth. The semi-final was attended by 15,576, who saw Kildare win 1-8 to 1-4, the final. Just 13,567 showed up for the Leinster final, and they watched in surprise as John O'Reilly engineered the 3-3 to 0-8 victory with three goals. In the All-Ireland semi-final Laois came from three points down at half-time for a Chris Delaney penalty to launch a second half comeback, fired on by former Kildare player Tom Keogh to victory.

Back in the Munster championship, Kerry lived dangerously. They fell 0-1 to 0-5 behind at half-time against Tipperary but won 1-5 to 0-5. Kerry then fell 0-1 to 0-2 behind against Clare. Clare blew their chances with a bewildering series of misses, and Kerry got through by a comfortable 1-11 to 2-2.

Mayo became Connacht champions in a replay after Galway's Brendan Nestor engineered a thrilling 2-4 to 1-7 draw. Nestor almost caused a riot in the process. Galway trailed by three points when Nestor forced the ball over the line. A Mayo defender punched it back, the umpire hesitated, and Nestor raised the flag himself. The crowd invaded the field, and it took several minutes to clear it so the last few seconds could be played.

After that excitement it was back to Roscommon, where first half goals from Josie Munnelly and Patsy Flannelly settled the issue 2-7 to 1-4 in Mayo's favour. Roscommon was the venue for the All-Ireland semi-final too, where Patsy Flannelly scored the vital goal in the first half as Mayo beat Kerry 1-5 to 0-6.

The 50,160 who attended the final did not expect to see Mayo hammer a stage-struck Laois team by eighteen points, 4-11 to 0-5. The cause of the disaster was an unfit player. Laois midfielder Bill Delaney limped through the game with two broken bones in his foot, while Mayo's Patsy Flannelly cleaned up at midfield: 'He raced through and shot to the square, to the net, and high between the posts—he seemed to inspire his side who played runaway football . . . Flannelly fielded and raced to either wing, paving the way for Munnelly's and Moclair's overwhelming scores. A temperamental team always, the Western champions opened so brilliantly they were always on top of the wave. Speed to the ball was their trump card.' Paddy Munnelly had goals in the tenth and twelfth minutes of the first half, Paddy Moclair followed ten minutes into the second half, and Paddy Munnelly scored again after four minutes of injury time.

Laois had four Delaney brothers from Stradbally in action, Jack, Chris, Mick and Bill. Their uncle Tom played at full back. Goalkeeper Tom Delaney was no relation to the others. The four brothers were to win seventeen Railway Cup medals. A legacy of the defeat was a superstitious horror of getting a trainer from outside the county to help future Laois teams, a reluctance that lasted until 1981. 'Laois were beaten for pace and seemed stale and over-trained' was the verdict. 'Never handling a ball confidently, they muffed many openings.'

Mayo's team had matured. Their team was worth more than one All-Ireland: throughout the 1930s they solidly dominated the National League, winning six titles in a row between 1934 and 1939, opting out (for Galway to win it) in 1940, and coming back to regain the title in 1941. They had Tom Burke in goal; John McGowan, Paddy Quinn and Purty Kelly in the full back line; Tommy Regan, J. Seamus O'Malley (captain) and George Ormsby in the half backs; Patsy Flannelly and Henry Kenny at centrefield; Jackie Carney, Peter Laffy and Tom Grier in the half forwards. Paddy Moclair scored 1-5 in the final from right corner; Josie Munnelly who scored 0-3 from full forward was back 21 years later to win an All-Ireland junior football medal in 1957; and Paddy Munnelly scored three goals from left corner.

26 SEPTEMBER 1937. KERRY 2-5, CAVAN 1-8, CROKE PARK
17 OCTOBER 1937. KERRY 4-4, CAVAN 1-7, CROKE PARK

> 'That hour which had been so crowded with excitement was a bit of glorious life which one might not see a second time. Could there ever be a game just like it between these teams again? For three weeks the drawn final had been replayed through the length and breadth of the land, each one who had seen it carrying with him an excitement which was being shaped into expectation of seeing it for the second time as a still more intense series of thrills.'
>
> BRINSLEY MACNAMARA, *The Irish Times*, 18 October 1937

Nine years had passed since a 'goal that wasn't' was scored against Cavan to deprive them of the All-Ireland. In 1937, in a cruel role reversal, Cavan saw a point of their own disallowed, depriving them of another.

Two Cavan newcomers caught the eye as they romped through the Ulster championship, corner back Paddy Smith and a wing back from Cornafean, John Joe O'Reilly.

They had to look to Connacht for a semi-final opponent. There, All-Ireland champions Mayo won another classic final 3-5 to 0-8 as Galway refused to give up against overwhelming odds. Mayo's first goal came from a mêlée in the opening minutes, their second from Josie Munnelly at the start of the second half, and their third from Peter Laffey near the end which clinched the issue.

The Connacht semi-final between Galway and Sligo degenerated into what was described as a 'miniature riot' near the end. The referee had failed to show and Jim Farrell of Roscommon was recruited as a stand-in from the sideline.

He probably regretted his readiness to do so afterwards, as he was forced to make a speedy exit as soon as he had blown the final whistle, chased out of the ground in his togs by a horde of screaming spectators.

At Mullingar, in front of 26,000 spectators, Cavan eliminated All-Ireland and League champions Mayo in a much-interrupted All-Ireland semi-final by 2-5 to 1-7 with late goals from Son Magee and Louis Blessing. It ended a remarkable run of 57 games without defeat by Mayo.

The other semi-final was turning into a dogfight between Kerry and Laois. In Leinster, Laois had surprised their critics with a good championship run. Tom Keogh put his old colleagues from Kildare out of the championship by 2-10 to 2-7 with a last-minute goal, just as Joyce Conlan had done in 1914.

But Laois had some troubles of their own. Twice against 1935 junior champions Offaly, they found themselves in a crisis situation. First they trailed at half-time, retook the lead, and Byrne's dramatic last-minute free earned a draw for Offaly, 1-9 to 2-6. Then came two late goals to beat Offaly in the replay, 2-7 to 1-7. The first by Keogh led to a crowd invasion and several minutes of confusion. When order was restored, Keogh passed to Harkins for the last-minute winning goal. Laois eventually beat Louth 0-12 to 0-4 before a 15,317 crowd in the Leinster final.

Laois could have gone further than their eventual semi-final defeat against Kerry. They had regrets after travelling to Cork to draw 1-6 to 2-3, thanks to a late goal for Kerry from Con Geaney. They had more to regret after losing the replay 2-2 to 1-4 in Waterford to a similar late Kerry rally. Laois made a great second half comeback in that replay, inspired by a fabulous left-footed drive into the corner of the net from 'Boy Wonder' Tommy Murphy, a 16-year-old Knockbeg College student. But Kerry's 'tall, young rearguard of six-foot striplings' thwarted their efforts to go further.

Kerry struck back to win the semi-final with a Tim Landers goal at the end. The full back failed to come out to meet O'Sullivan's long ball. Landers snatched it, and for the second time in a fortnight Laois saw their three-point lead against Kerry snatched away in the dying minutes. Then Martin Lyne added the winning point to send Kerry into the final.

The final brought old warriors Kerry up against the new Cavan team. As one commentator put it, 'Kerry's tall backs against Cavan's brainy forwards.' Some of the tall backs were mere striplings of lads. Tadhg Healy and Joe Keohane were still eligible for minor. Cavan did the celebrating, but only because they had been announced as winners on the radio and the Croke Park loudspeakers. The referee had other ideas, however. He said he had disallowed Cavan's winning point.

Cavan goalscorer Packie Boylan was the scorer of what should have been the winning point, disallowed for throwing three minutes from the end. Few of the spectators noticed that a free out was taken instead of a kick-out, and it was announced over the loudspeakers that Cavan had won. Radio commentator Fr Michael Hamilton told the nation that Cavan were the champions, and many supporters were at home in Cavan before they realised a replay was needed. Hamilton had been selected as the 'GAA man' after a running battle between Radio Éireann and the GAA over who should chose the All-Ireland commentator had blacked out the season's fixtures, including the All-Ireland hurling final.

Cavan had shown great sparkle in coming back after an appalling start to draw 1-8 to 2-5, after John Joe Landers had the ball in the net twice for Kerry from beautiful swerving raids in the first thirteen minutes. In the 21st minute of the second half, a great solo run by Jim Smith sent Cavan's Packie Boylan through for a dramatic goal—'the thrill of the hour'—that put Cavan ahead by one point. Kerry launched two scintillating counter-attacks from returned exile Gearóid Fitzgerald to level and Tim O'Donnell to regain the lead. Son Magee put the sides level again with six minutes to go, and then Boylan and Magee changed places, and with 'Kerry's young backs showing signs of wear', Boylan flung the ball over the bar from close range for the 'winner that wasn't'.

A massive 52,325 crowd nearly got squashed to death in their attempts to see the game. The Cusack Stand had not yet been built, and when the gates were forced open by the crush at 2.45, anything up to 10,000 more could have got in.

Kerry won the replay rather easily, 4-4 to 1-7. Hamilton commentated again, his folksy style earning the plaudits of some newspapers, but he mistakenly announced that Jim 'Gawksie' O'Gorman was the substitute who came on for Tim O'Donnell, rather than Tom 'Gega' O'Connor, who made his Kerry debut.

Mehigan complained: 'The play was broken too frequently by minor accidents to compare with the drawn match as a continuous and gripping sporting spectacle. It was too earnest, too fierce to be a classic. It was more severe as a test of men than the drawn match, and it introduced us to a young team of footballers who would do credit to any nation.'

The tackling was indeed 'robust'. Cavan's Tom O'Reilly and Jim Smith were both injured. Timmy O'Leary flicked Kerry's first goal to the net after twelve minutes. It was 1-0 to 0-3 at half-time. Miko Doyle got a second goal six minutes after half-time, O'Leary the third twelve minutes into the second half, and John Joe Landers the fourth after 28 minutes.

Tim 'Roundy' Landers, as he was known because of his small stature at 5' 6", was said to have been approached by soccer scouts after he caught the ball at midfield, dropped it to his feet and dribbled soccer-style to the fourteen yard line before launching his shot for a goal.

25 SEPTEMBER 1938. GALWAY 3-3, KERRY 2-6, CROKE PARK
23 OCTOBER 1938. GALWAY 2-4, KERRY 0-7, CROKE PARK

> 'The Kerry centre field had the best of the exchanges for most of the hour, but the western backs negatived this by as grand a display of defensive football as we have seen for some years in an All-Ireland final.'
>
> SEÁN BONNER ('Green Flag') in the *Irish Press*, 24 October 1938

Kerry lost their title after another replay in 1938. They had only three players over 25 on the team that beat Cork by twenty points in the Munster final. Then they met Laois in the semi-final for the second year in a row. After this, it was decided to rotate the semi-finals among the provinces.

The semi-final saw the new Cusack Stand opened with a blast of community singing by Seán Ó Síocháin. Kerry's Charlie O'Sullivan and Murt Kelly eliminated Laois from the championship by 2-6 to 2-4 with two goals in 90 seconds early in the second half.

Offaly had been surprise semi-finalists in Leinster: Hughes got the goal that started their comeback from six points down against Wexford to win their first round tie 1-9 to 1-5. His declaration to play for Offaly was found in order by an appeals board just 24 hours before the match! But it was Laois who gave a classic display in beating Kildare 2-8 to 1-3 in the Leinster final.

Galway took the Connacht title back from Mayo by 0-8 to 0-5. They also felt sore at having a goal disallowed, but they kept their heads. Their 'Kerry recruit', Jack Flavin, started popping over the points, and Galway collected their reward in the All-Ireland final at Croke Park.

There was a surprise in Ulster as Monaghan interrupted what would have been a fifteen-in-a-row run for Cavan, and for the only time in an incredible 30-year period from 1927 to 1957. Before 8,000 people, Armagh beat Cavan in the semi-final 2-7 to 1-4. After Monaghan beat Armagh 2-5 to 2-2 in the Ulster final, the referee, Cavan star Hughie O'Reilly, had to be escorted off the field. An objection by Armagh, that Monaghan's team list was not complete and the referee was not impartial, failed.

When they met in the All-Ireland semi-final at Mullingar, a new 18-year-old radio commentator was describing the match on the airwaves. Dubliner Micheál O'Hehir was to earn the nickname 'the voice of the GAA' during a 40-year career relaying games on radio and television. O'Hehir was not a full-time commentator until 1959. At first he worked in the civil service and was paid a guinea for his services. He replaced a number of commentators such as Paddy Mehigan, Eamonn de Barra, and Fr Michael Hamilton who had given out the wrong scoreline at the end of the 1937 All-Ireland final. The best story about O'Hehir, that he was in hospital listening to a commentary on radio and felt he could do better, was not true.

Galway beat Monaghan 2-10 to 2-5, thanks to two quick-fire goals from Martin Kelly and a John Burke 50, to qualify to meet Kerry in the final. When Kerry drew with Galway, 2-6 to 3-3, the final whistle went early and a would-be winning point by substitute John Joe Landers was disallowed. Kerry complained that no time had been added for stoppages. A goal five minutes from the end by Timmy O'Leary had left them counting down to the championship, but Ralph Griffin propelled Brendan Nestor's free over the line for Galway's breath-saving goal three minutes from the end. Ned Mulholland and the outstanding Nestor got the other two for Galway.

The replay was even more bizarre. When the crowd invaded prematurely, the whole match had to be restarted. Galway, 'the more uniform, the more secure, the more united team', broke Kerry's knack of winning replays (they had previously won three), despite having a penalty claim turned down in the first half. Goals from Galway's Ned Mulholland and Martin Kelly set up their 2-4 to 0-7 victory, confirmed after ten minutes of total confusion.

The crowd mistook the final whistle when the referee blew twice for a free two minutes from the end. The free had been awarded to Kerry. A Galway man stood too close to the ball, and when the referee whistled again, the crowd swept on to the field. Even the Kerry players were fooled: nine of them went away to tog off at the Central Hotel. Four more had gathered around John Walsh, who was having hip and shoulder injuries dressed in the new Cusack Stand dressing room. Seán Brosnan and Tim O'Leary were still on the field and probably the first to hear loudspeaker pleas for the players to resume. Myers, Casey, Dillon and Paddy 'Bawn' Brosnan had gone.

Brosnan had been called in to replace Joe Keohane, but his career was in abeyance for ten years after dropping the ball over the line for one goal and being bustled over the line for another. Mort Kelly, the injured Joe Keohane (who had watched the rest of the final from the stand dressed in his Sunday suit), Murphy, Ned Walsh and Jack Sheehy filled some of the places, but Kerry finished the match without their complement of fifteen. Despite this they scored a point in the remaining minute! Moyvane-born Johnny Flavin won his second All-Ireland medal in successive years, first with Kerry, then for Galway against Kerry!

Styles had changed completely from the fast hand passes of the 1920s. Hands were gone. Shoulders were in for the forties.

24 SEPTEMBER 1939. KERRY 2-5, MEATH 2-3, CROKE PARK

> 'We feel sure we are merely giving expression to the feelings of the loyal supporters of the green and gold in saying that we never felt so proud of Meath in victory as we do in defeat.'
>
> *Meath Chronicle*, 30 September 1939

Galway fell at the first hurdle in 1939. Connacht football had outgrown its facilities—when Mayo met Galway in the Connacht final, the old Roscommon grounds could not hold the 20,000 crowd. It took 30 minutes to start the match and the spectators overflowed on to the pitch in the second half. Mayo were clear 2-6 to 0-3 leaders at that stage, thanks to Paddy Moclair's seventh and 23rd-minute goals and 1-3 in a vital seven-minute spell which gave them a 2-5 to nil half-time lead. The match ended prematurely in an invasion with two minutes to go.

In Munster, Kerry went off on another American tour, so they were given a bye into the provincial final, where Tipperary qualified to meet them by beating Cork 1-9 to 2-2 and Clare 4-5 to 1-6. Goals at the start of each half from Tom McAuliffe and Murt Kelly secured the title for Kerry, 2-11 to 0-4, on their return.

Ulster provided another unfinished final. Cavan were leading Armagh 2-6 to 2-4 in the unfinished first match, fought out on a steadily shrinking pitch in Castleblayney, as the crowd (receipts £693) advanced further and further beyond the touchlines. They invaded, eventually, when Conaty got an Armagh goal in the first half. And when Armagh captain Jim McCullough (the Fermanagh wanderer) was punched by one of the crowd as he was taking a throw-in, a mêlée followed. The referee abandoned the match when the pitch was not cleared. It had been rough going; the match had started at 4.15 and was called off at 6.45, the crowd having swept across the field four times in all.

Cavan won a sedate replay in the unfamiliar surroundings of Croke Park with goals from T. Clarke and Tom O'Reilly in a two-minute spell in the second half.

Spectators joined in a previous fight in Castleblayney during the Monaghan-Armagh semi-final as well, as Loughman scored a late equaliser for Monaghan, and had to repeat the performance when Armagh went ahead again. Armagh finished the 1930s, despite their reputation, stranded in the middle of their most barren spell, having lost three Ulster finals in a row and a total of eight finals in twelve years. The 1938 and 1939 McKenna Cups were a poor consolation for their woes. Gate news was good for the Ulster council: £693 for the abandoned match and £400 from the All-Ireland semi-final gate of £2,615, where the replay acted as a curtain-raiser.

Samuel MacKenzie's heavily stylised representation of an 1820s street football match is in contrast to the condemnatory tone of many newspaper reports of the time. Local customs in organising and playing games, including differences between urban and rural games, become apparent as more 18th-century newspaper references come to light.

The founder president of the GAA and the man who drew up the rules for football, Maurice Davin, at his home in Deerpark near Carrick-on-Suir in Co. Tipperary, with his sister Bridget, Pat and Eileen Davin and their daughter Mary Bridget.

UNITED IRELAND

[SATURDAY, FEBRUARY 7, 1885

FOOTBALL.

1. There shall be not less than fifteen or more than twenty-one players aside.

2. There shall be two umpires and a referee. Where the umpires disagree the referee's decision shall be final.

3. The ground shall be at least 120 yards long by 80 in breadth, and properly marked by boundary lines. Boundary lines must be at least 5 yards from fences.

4. The goal posts shall stand at each end in centre of goal line. They shall be 15 feet apart, with a cross-bar 8 feet from the ground.

5. The captains of each team shall toss for choice of sides before commencing play, and the players shall stand in two ranks opposite each other until the ball is thrown up, each man holding the hand of one of the other side.

6. Pushing or tripping from behind, holding from behind, or butting with the head, shall be deemed foul, and the player so offending shall be ordered to stand aside, and may not afterwards take part in the match, nor can his side substitute another man.

7. The time of actual play shall be one hour. Sides to be changed only at half time.

8. The match shall be decided by the greater number of goals. If no goal be kicked the match shall be deemed a draw. A goal is when the ball is kicked through the goal posts under the cross-bar.

9. When the ball is kicked over the side line it shall be thrown back by a player of the opposite side to him who kicked it over. If kicked over the goal-line by a player whose goal-line it is, it shall be thrown back in any direction by a player of the other side. If kicked over the goal-line by a player of the other side, the goalkeeper whose line it crosses shall have a free kick. No player of the other side to approach nearer than 25 yards of him till the ball is kicked.

10. The umpires and referee shall have during the match full power to disqualify any player, or order him to stand aside and discontinue play, for any act which they may consider unfair, as set out in Rule 6.

The first rules of football as published in February 1885. It is not clear whether the game is a propulsion or a carrying game. The early rules made it too difficult to score, leading to a succession of scoreless draws. Football, apparently under agreed local rules, was already being played under the auspices of the GAA before the rules were published.

FOOTBALL

THE INTER-COUNTY FOOTBALL CONTEST.
WICKLOW *VERSUS* WEXFORD.

On yesterday the great inter-county contest in football between Wicklow and Wexford took place at Avondale, the seat of C. S. Parnell, Esq, M P. This is the first contest which has been held under the auspices of the Gaelic Athletic Association, and from the manner in which everything went off was a most unqualified success. The position selected for the contest was a most picturesque one, overlooking the Avonmore and but a short distance from the Vale of Ovoca. On all sides as far as the eye could reach, the scenery could scarcely be excelled, and this, combined with the excellent weather which favoured the gathering, the sun shining through a cloudless sky all day, contributed not a little to the success and enjoyment of the day. The ground, though rather rough, was in excellent condition, and was surrounded on three sides by those huge beech trees which are to be found so plentifully on the demesne of the Irish leader. Throughout the day the order of the people was most creditable to themselves, but the arrangements made by those responsible for the laying out of the ground were wretched. The side lines were so badly roped that the spectators had burst in through them before play commenced, while the end lines were not protected at all, the result being that the people crushed in and filled the goal and side spaces, which rendered it difficult to decide in cases of scoring. Dur-

Report of a gala football tournament in front of the Parnell homestead in Avondale in 1886. As well as allying the GAA to the Home Rule movement, it proved a turning point in the history of football, initiating the lucrative and attention-grabbing concept of inter-county competition.

Limerick Commercials did not win their local championship in 1887, yet went on to win the All-Ireland championship when five members of the St Michael's club were found to have played rugby. They provided the first football playing star, the teenage hero Malachi O'Brien. Limerick won two football All-Irelands with a team of out-of-town shop assistants before the city turned its attention to rugby in the early 1900s.

Tipperary defeated Meath by a point in the 1895 All-Ireland football final with seventeen Arravale Rovers players, the first to be played in what is now Croke Park. This was the match that established Willie Ryan's reputation as the outstanding footballer of his generation, scoring the winning free. The referee wrote to the *Freeman's Journal* after the match, saying that he should not have allowed one of their scores because it was scored from inside the 21 yard line. As late as 1952 one of the surviving spectators still nominated it as the greatest match of all time. Mick Ryan went on to play rugby seventeen times for Ireland, participating with his brother Jack in the tumultuous 1899 triple crown-winning match against Wales.

Many of the Young Irelands team that dominated Gaelic football in the late 1890s were employed in the Guinness brewery. Luke O'Kelly, John Kennedy, George Roche and Tom Errity, all to the right on the front row, were the stars of the team.

Some of the earliest Gaelic football action photographs featured in the *Irish Weekly Examiner* and are from the second replay of the 1903 All-Ireland football final between Kildare and Kerry, showing the old-style point posts and soccer goals without nets. Kerry's goalkeeper is Patrick Dillon, later to lose his arm in an accident. Waterford-born Rody Kirwan, Con Healy and Bill Myers are also in action, as is Frank 'Joyce' Conlan of Kildare. The crowd stayed well behind the railings at Cork Athletic Grounds, unlike the chaotic scenes at the first match in Tipperary which ended without a clear winner. Gate receipts were a record £270.

Louth's emergence as a power in 1912 was due to some tactical innovation, a coach who had studied soccer methods and, controversially, full-time training. A pavilion was added at the newly acquired Jones's Road grounds in north Dublin before the final in which Louth beat fancied Antrim. Louth's place in history was secured in a replayed Croke Tournament final in 1913. The first high-profile fifteen-a-side match, it was nominated by Dick Fitzgerald and others as the greatest game of its era.

Looming out of the ink-blackened pages of the *Freeman's Journal*, the 1913 final was one of the first to have photographic coverage. The exertions of Pat 'Springheel' O'Shea at midfield helped swing the game for Kerry. Louth won the All-Ireland semi-final, but Wexford had superseded Louth as Leinster champions before the final. Wexford captained by 'Tearing' Tom Doyle lost the final, attended by Irish nationalist John Dillon.

Dick Fitzgerald was the most influential footballer of the first quarter-century of the GAA and wrote the first instructional manual on the game. His death in 1930 came as a shock to football. The stadium in Killarney is named in his honour. 'Gaelic football is what may be called a natural football game,' he wrote. 'There is no incentive in it towards rough play. One player can hamper or impede another in one way, and only one way, and that by means of the shoulder. Hence it is that severe tackling, rough handling and all forms of tripping are banned.'

Inspired by team captain Seán O'Kennedy, his brother Gus and goal-scoring forward Aidan Doyle, Wexford were the first of three teams to win four All-Ireland championships in a row, between 1915 and 1918.

THE FREEMAN'S JOURNAL. MONDAY. NOVEMBER 22. 1920.

FOURTEEN KILLED

Amazing Deadly Round-Up of Military and Auxiliary Officers in Dublin

STARTLING STREET BATTLE

Civilians Make Sortie From House and Fight With Crown Forces

Dublin was a city of amazing tragedy yesterday.

In a series of morning visits by armed men to hotels and boarding-houses, at least ten officers, two civilians, and two auxiliary policemen were killed, and several officers were wounded.

In Lower Mount street, where a civilian was shot in bed in mysterious circumstances, a regular battle took place between armed civilians emerging from the house where the shooting took place and auxiliary police, and two of the latter, it is said, were mortally wounded.

The attacks by the armed raiders were practically simultaneous, and most of those whom they shot were, according to the Dublin Castle report, military officers associated with the Government's policy in Ireland.

The record we give of the day's events may not be complete, for until a late hour reports were coming in of other shootings in the city—two dead bodies were found in Merrion street—but owing to the operation of the Curfew regulations it was extremely difficult to secure full details or confirmation.

14 KILLED: 5 WOUNDED

The official list of casualties resultant on the shootings of officers yesterday morning is as follows:—

KILLED.

Major DOWLING.
Captain D. L. MACLEAN.
Captain T. H. SMITH.
Captain BENNETT.
Lieut. AIMES.
Lieut. NEWBURY.
Lieut. BAGGALLY.
Lieut. FITZGERALD.
Captain McCORMACK.
Captain PRICE.
Mr. MacMAHON.
Mr. L. A. WILD.
Cadets CARLIN and MORRIS.

WOUNDED.

Mr J. CALDOW.
Captain KINLEYSIDE.
Colonel WOODCOCK.
Colonel MONTGOMERY.
Lieut. MURRAY.

Most of these officers, says an official statement, were connected with courtsmartial, and the attackers were in search of documents found in the typhoid plot. Captain Fitzgerald was some months ago shot at and left for dead in Co. Clare, but by shamming death he got away with a broken arm.

AMRITZAR REPEATED IN DUBLIN

Armed Forces of the Crown Kill Player and Spectators in Croke Park

AGONISING SCENES ON FOOTBALL FIELD

Eleven or Twelve Persons, including a Woman, Killed, and from Eighty to One Hundred Wounded

Scenes of bloodshed on a football field, unparalleled in the history of the country, were enacted at Croke Park yesterday by armed forces of the Crown.

Almost 15,000 spectators had gathered to witness a football match between Tipperary and Dublin, when suddenly, the game being in progress, shots rang out, fired by the armed forces, and Michael Hogan, a prominent member of the Tipperary team, fell dead, shot through the mouth. Many of the onlookers were also seen to fall, dead or wounded.

A woman is among the killed.

The casualty list, the extent of which has not been definitely ascertained, is a long one. It is estimated that eleven or twelve persons are dead, and from 80 to 100 wounded, in varying degrees of seriousness.

The armed forces, according to many of the onlookers, gave no warning to the spectators to disperse, beyond a preliminary volley of shots in the air. Then the bullets came as thick as hail, dealing out death in their swift passage; a wild scene of panic ensued, and women and children were knocked down and walked on.

A priest, who was a spectator of the tragic occurrence, says: "I found poor Hogan lying on his back in a pool of blood. His feet were on the playing pitch, and his body on the gravel walk."

The Dublin Castle official report, which gives the number of dead at about 10 and the number of wounded and injured about 54, states "It was believed that a number of gunmen came up to-day under the guise of wishing to attend the Gaelic football match between Dublin and Tipperary, but that their real motive was to take part in the series of murderous outrages which took place in Dublin this morning."

PRIEST DESCRIBES THE SCENES OF BLOODSHED

Terrible scenes took place during the Tipperary and Dublin match at Jones' road yesterday. [...] being searched individually and allowed to pass through the gate. Owing to the delay caused by the [...] a considerable amount of blood oozing from his left side, seemingly. Another priest came over, and he afterwards went for the [...]

Although coverage of the Bloody Sunday massacre, as in this *Freeman's Journal* report, was heavily censored and the documents suppressed for decades after the event, attempts to manage the coverage of the event in England were unsuccessful amongst a media and a public becoming disenchanted with British policy in Ireland. English liberal opinion was appalled, despite the best efforts of Dublin Castle's propagandist, former *Daily Mail* war correspondent, Basil Clarke. Documents released in recent years show that even the Dublin Metropolitan Police contradicted the claims of the Black and Tans that they were fired upon as they approached Croke Park.

A section of the crowd at the 1926 All-Ireland final. The stadium had grown from a single pavilion in 1911. A running track and grandstand were added for the 1924 Tailteann Games and a long stand also placed on the Jones's Road side of the ground.

MONDAY,

37,500 AT FOOTBALL FINAL

KERRY AND KILDARE DRAW

GREAT CHAMPIONSHIP STRUGGLE AT CROKE PARK

KERRY - 1-3. KILDARE - 6 PTS.

The great struggle between Kerry and Kildare in 1903, when the counties met three times in the championship final, was recalled by yesterday's test in the 1926 All-Ireland football final, which resulted in a draw of six points each.

The attendance of 37,000 set up a record for Croke Park, which was taxed to the utmost of its accommodation, the spectators crowding on to the edge of the pitch, but not encroaching on the actual field of play.

The story of the match, which is fully told, both below and in our news columns, may be summarised by stating that it was a fine exhibition; that Kildare, although the more scientific side, lacked the strength and lasting powers of the Kerry players, who were gallantly led by John Joe Sheehy; and that a draw was a fitting result, taking all happenings into account.

Larry Stanley once more gave a magnificent display for Kildare, being the master hand in nearly all the scores; while Gorman, as a marksman, made an auspicious *debut* in an All-Ireland final for Kerry.

HONOURS EVEN AT END

KERRY'S FINAL BURST REWARDED

A great game, stubbornly contested, and fiercely fought all the way, it was played amidst scenes of enthusiasm and excitement that will live in the history of Gaelic football. With over 30 special trains arriving in the city the gathering was representative of every corner of Ireland. Kerry, which had sent a contingent of over 1,500 with the players on Saturday evening, predominated, and the familiar green and gold colours were in evidence everywhere.

Large numbers travelled by road, and every conceivable shape of motor conveyance appeared to have been brought into requisition. The grounds were packed to their utmost capacity, and some of the more daring of the spectators climbed to points of vantage in the most extraordinary and unlikely places. On the whole it was an orderly, easily-disciplined host, that followed the fortunes of the game with the keenest interest.

PERSONNEL OF TEAMS.

Both sides fielded out with confidence. The Kildare team was, to a man, the same that beat Dublin and Wexford in the Leinster Championship. P. Martin, who, owing to illness, had been off against Galway in the semi-final, resumed his

EXCITING STRUGGLE

KILDARE LEAD AT THE INTERVAL

Kildare, 0-6; Kerry, 1-3.

Winning the toss, Kildare played towards the railway goal with a breeze in their favour. Doyle put Kildare attacking from the throw in, and Stanley forced a "50." Jack Higgins's kick was received by Doyle, whose shot was stopped by Riordan (Kerry goal), but went over for a point for Kildare. **Time, 1 minute.** From the kick out Sheehy opened up for Kerry, but the Kildare backs saved, and in a flash the Kerry end was visited. Kildare went in with vigour, but were repulsed by a sound defence.

Kildare worked back from a free by Jack Higgins, but Doyle in possession fouled by hopping twice. P. Sullivan's free was returned by Jack Higgins (Kildare), but the Kerry backs were all there. Sheehy again left Kerry on the offensive, but the Munster forwards made little headway. Kildare going in marred a likely chance by fouling, and Kerry pressed without avail. In a hot onrush by Kildare Stanley was fouled and injured, but resumed amidst cheers. Kildare went in from J. Higgins's free, and from a second free on the right wing **Stanley** kicked a point for Kildare. **Time, 12 mins.**

FREES AND INJURIES.

Kildare returned from the kick out, and a perplexing hand-to-hand move, which brought the play well into the Kerry ground.

T. Clifford (Kerry), who had come on as a substitute in the first half, went off injured, and was replaced by J. Slattery. On a hop in Kerry ground Paul Doyle (Kildare) was temporarily knocked out of action, and from the resulting free **Stanley** added a point for Kildare. Loughlin (Kildare) beat off a fine effort by Sheehy, and on a return Buckley cleared for Kildare. There was an easing off in the pace, but both sides were still going strong, and the tackling was as keen and vigorous as ever.

After the Kildare end was crossed, Doyle and Stanley got away on the kick-out, Curtis centred for Kildare, but Riordan (Kerry goal) saved from O'Neill. A renewed onslaught by Kildare ended in an over. Kerry bounded off from the kick-out, and **Gorman**, receiving from Sheehy, put over a high point for Kerry.

Kildare were now leading by 5 points to 1 for Kerry.

Kildare got the better of a midfield exchange, and then went in from a free after Stanley had been fouled. **Loughlin** added a point for Kildare, who had now a lead of 3 points. Kerry forced the play in dogged style, but failed against the Kildare defence.

A SOUND DEFENCE.

Kerry came in from **a free by Brosnan**, but halted before the Kildare defence. From a second free by Barrett Kerry again went over. The Kildare backs, now bearing the brunt of the struggle, were putting up a brilliant defence against a succession of spirited onsets by Kerry. Loughlin and Jack Higgins cleared in turn, and the Kerry attack was broken after a period of tense and exciting play.

Kerry worked back in determined style, and an exchange between Brosnan and Walsh was passed on to **Gorman, who beat Cummins for a great goal for Kerry.**

With the scores level (Kildare, 0-6; Kerry, 1-3), Kerry followers cheered frantically, and Kerry again took up the offensive. Kildare backs did not waver, and the scene was one of remarkable excitement. There was a delay in keeping the crowd off the line, and on resumption Kerry attacked and went over. In a return Kerry spoiled by fouling, and two frees eased for Kildare.

Kerry again attacked, and Sheehy sent over from 40 yards out. Kerry finished the stronger, but the backs held the game for Kildare.

Mr. T. Shevlin (Roscommon) was an impartial referee.

THE TEAMS.

Kildare—J. Loughlin (capt.); J. Cummins (goal); M. Buckley, W. Goff, H. Graham, F. Malone, J. Higgins, J. Hayes, P. Martin, G. Higgins, L. Stanley, P. Doyle, A. O'Neill, W. Gannon, J. Curtis.

Kerry—J. J. Sheehy (capt.); J. Riordan (goal); P. Sullivan, J. Barrett, J. Murphy, P. Russell, J. Walsh, J. Moriarty, C. Brosnan, R. Stack, J. Sullivan, D. O'Connell, J. Ryan, James Baily, W. Gorman. Subs.—P. Clifford, J. Slattery.

Crowds spilled on to the field as far as the sideline for the 1926 All-Ireland final between Kildare and Kerry which drew an attendance of 37,500. By 1929 Gaelic football had superseded soccer as the best attended field sport in the country.

Paul Doyle scores Kildare's first point in the 1926 All-Ireland football final, deflected over the crossbar by Johnny Riordan. Kerry earned a replay with a dramatic last-minute goal. Jack Murphy died in hospital before the replay, which Kerry won by three points. Replays have defined much of the growth of the GAA. That of 1926 pushed football on to the front pages of the newspapers as well as the sports pages. In 1929 an attendance of 43,839 superseded the attendance records for soccer and rugby for the first time.

Sam Maguire's role in the GAA and independence movement was necessarily obscure, to the extent that we will probably never know the full scale of his activities. The tendency to identify major sporting occasions with iconic trophies in the mid-1920s led a group of London Irish to raise £200 for a trophy in his honour. The minor trophy is also named for a fellow IRB man, Tom Markham.

By 1932 Kerry had established hegemony in the game they never subsequently lost, becoming the second county to win four All-Irelands in a row.

The wining goal from Cavan's Vincent McGovern two minutes from the end of the All-Ireland semi-final of 1933 prevented Kerry winning five in a row.

The old Cusack Stand at Croke Park is under construction in the background, as Dan O'Keeffe of Kerry and 'Son' Magee of Cavan contest a ball during the drawn 1937 All-Ireland final.

Kerry v Galway 1938. Dinny O'Sullivan (NO. 4) and John Burke (NO. 9) under pressure in the drawn All-Ireland final, regarded as one of the greatest games ever. To the right of the action are Bobby Beggs and Charlie O'Sullivan.

WELL TAKEN!

The spirit of Gaelic football—dashing, vigorous, clean—is conveyed in this picture taken by an "Irish Independent" photographer.

There's life in all the photographs, news, and commentaries by

IRISH INDEPENDENT
EVENING HERALD
SUNDAY INDEPENDENT

Independent Newspapers, Ltd Dublin.

An advertisement for the *Irish Independent* featuring an action photograph from the infamous 1946 All-Ireland semi-final between Kerry and Antrim. Kerry devised a tactic to intimidate the fast-passing Antrim men, tackling the man about to receive the ball in a manoeuvre that had dubious legality. Two players were sent off, with the radio commentator diplomatically ignoring the warfare despite a chorus of boohs which almost drowned him out.

Bringing the 1947 All-Ireland final to New York was a bigger project than anyone realised at the time it was decided—in somewhat controversial circumstances—at the 1947 Congress in City Hall. The attendance was disappointing and the venture not without its critics, by the time Bohola-born Mayor William O'Dwyer threw in the ball ten minutes after the scheduled time; but the game was not under way yet. The police band, which had played 'Faith of Our Fathers' and the two anthems, had not yet left the field and referee Martin O'Neill threw in the ball again to start the real match. Cavan won, in the words of Mitchel Cogley, 'fighting back like tigers after a start that was too bad to be true'.

John Joe O'Reilly is chaired off the field after Cavan's spectacular comeback to win the Polo Grounds final. The pageantry of the home-coming added to the impact of the final being staged in New York to commemorate the centenary of the worst year of the famine. O'Reilly returned to play for the national Army in a club match, allowing his vice captain to bring the cup home to Cavan town. Double tragedy struck the Cavan team after their dual All-Ireland triumph of 1947 and 1948: first P. J. Duke and then O'Reilly himself both died prematurely. There are those who say Cavan football never quite recovered from the psychological blow.

A group of supporters from Portadown at the 1953 All-Ireland final. Interest in the final brought an unprecedented 86,155 spectators to the game, the first indication the GAA had of the enormous level of support for hitherto unsuccessful northern teams. Bill McCorry missed a penalty and Armagh, in defeat, took 49 years before they found redemption. Ironically, their 2002 victory was accompanied by another missed penalty.

Meath v Kerry in the 1954 All-Ireland final. Exchanges were ragged and broken and there were few passages of good play, causing the first real debate over the amateur ethos of the GAA. For the first time full-time training for teams was banned before the match, leading to speculation that this had precipitated a decline in the standard of football. Kerry were odds-on favourites but succumbed to a second-half comeback by Meath after Peter McDermott opted to play against the breeze in the first half.

As a player, administrator and as football's first high-profile team manager, Kevin Heffernan was one of the most influential personalities in Gaelic football history. He first made his mark in hurling with an explosive first-minute goal for St Joseph's against St Flannan's in the 1945 All-Ireland colleges hurling final. Dublin's 1955 defeat against Kerry, when he was regarded as the outstanding forward in the game, was to unleash a near-obsession with the southern county that was to colour the 1970s and swell interest in the game. As manager Heffernan was credited with reigniting interest in football in the capital and saving the game's urban credentials. His other achievements include reviving the Trinity College GAA club when attending college there in 1955. His goal from 40 yards against Royal College of Surgeons in the Duke Cup semi-final of 1955 was one of the best in the history of third-level colleges competition.

In a moment resplendent with symbolism, Down's victorious 1960 team carries the cup across the border. The tactics of the 1958–68 Down team were not as revolutionary as many of their supporters have claimed, but their innovations were to change the way teams everywhere prepared for games.

Mick O'Connell emerged on to the Kerry team during the 1956–7 League campaign, winning national recognition with his performance at midfield in the 1957 League semi-final against Cavan. Over the next fifteen years his distinctive high-catching style and commitment to the game brought him near mythic status. Many regard him as the greatest fielder the game has ever seen. It was no surprise that, of four potential Kerry players to be selected on the team of the millennium at midfield, he was the one chosen. He travelled a 100-mile round trip from Valentia Island to training sessions, rowing a boat to the island in the days before it was joined to the mainland.

Leinster had new champions. Meath had been one of the easier opponents in Leinster since Dick Blake's days. Ten years after first showing signs of changing that with priestly help, they got the Leinster title they deserved, beating Laois 1-9 to 1-7, Kildare 2-10 to 2-8, and Wexford 2-7 to 2-3. Last-minute goals featured in the 1939 Leinster quarter-finals: Louth went out to one by Somers of Wexford; and Laois to one by Willie Brien of Meath.

Meath's semi-final victims, Kildare, protested that Cummins's goal for Meath should not have been allowed, calling their defenders to give near-identical statements before the Leinster council, insisting in turn that they had 'stopped playing when they heard the whistle' for a free in. The referee changed his mind, awarding the goal instead. Clarke scored another goal against the disoriented Kildare men, and Meath ate away a nine-point half-time lead. When the council refused to reverse the referee's decision, Kildare withdrew from the National League in protest.

When they fell behind in the Leinster final against Wexford, it was 24-year-old Tony Donnelly who started the revival. He had starred since a debut against Cavan in the 1932–33 League at the age of 17. Matty Gilsenan and Peter Clarke (with a second half goal) brought Meath back from behind in the final against Wexford, who had struck with two timely goals from Smyth and Roche immediately before half-time.

The troublesome tradition of 1939 was continued at the All-Ireland semi-final between Kerry and Mayo, as Kerry came back from two points down at half-time to draw amid displays of pugilism and considerable trouble for Fermanagh referee Dunne, who was dispossessed of the ball after the match.

After the teams drew 0-4 each, the replay was at least an improvement, and Spring and Sullivan goals in the dying minutes of the first half and another from Walsh within a minute of the restart saw Kerry through by 3-8 to 1-4. The first goal confused many people (Spring was a late call-up to the team in place of Miko Doyle) including radio commentator Micheál O'Hehir, who was passed an illegible slip of paper telling him about the team change and described the full forward as Dan Shine throughout the game.

A great first half display and a Cummins goal to start the second half brought Meath through the first of many famous local derbies with Cavan, 1-9 to 1-1, and into their first All-Ireland final.

Meath won the toss to wear their familiar green jerseys, so Kerry won their thirteenth All-Ireland in the red jerseys of county champions Dingle. Kerry had to fight to beat off the new challenge of Meath. Dan Spring got two goals for Kerry in a 2-5 to 2-3 victory. The first was awarded only after some hesitation on the part of the referee, who consulted his umpires. Then one of the best goals in GAA history, from Mattie Gilsenan just before half-time, and another from Jim Clarke midway through the second half, brought Meath back into the reckoning.

After kicking eleven wides, Meath lost by two points in the end. The first goal, a lucky effort awarded only after the referee had consulted the umpires, saw Kerry through in a match described euphemistically as one where 'hard knocks were given and taken'. According to the *Kerryman*, 'It was a triumph of backs over forwards.'

This was the spirit of the 1930s—no elaboration, but hard knocks and hard shoulders.

22 SEPTEMBER 1940. KERRY 0-7, GALWAY 1-3, CROKE PARK

The silver Feale and sweet Tralee,
Killarney's heavenly plan;
And though our foes be sterling men
And strive as heroes can,
There's none can beat the Kingdom sweet
At horse or hound or man.

BRYAN MACMAHON

Despite Kerry's successes, support for football in Munster was not very high: a crowd of about 2,000 (gate £90) turned out for the 1940 provincial final in Waterford city, which meant football in Munster was now running at 10 per cent of hurling final support. With Cork losing to Tipperary in the first round, and Kerry beating Limerick at a temporary pitch in Glin (4-9 to 0-2), Tipperary (4-8 to 1-5) and Waterford (1-10 to 0-6) by big scores, the disinterest was perhaps justified. Despite this, Waterford led 0-5 to 0-2 at half-time after playing with a strong breeze. After that, a scoring spree from Seán Brosnan, who finished with 1-4, ended their dreams.

Perennial Ulster champions Cavan trounced Antrim in a replay 6-13 to 0-4 after Antrim had drawn with a skeleton Cavan team in Corrigan Park 3-3 to 0-12, then met two aspirants, Donegal (0-12 to 3-2) and Down (4-10 to 1-5) in the semi-final and final before a crowd of 6,000. Down were on the way up: they had astonished the Gaelic football world by reaching the National League semi-finals in 1940 and again in 1941.

Down's first appearance in a final began with a flourish when J. Carr scored a goal and Michael Lynch a point before Cavan settled down. But a Vincent White penalty before half-time sent Cavan in with a five-point lead, and when Pat Boylan, Donal Morgan and Joe Stafford added goals in the second half, Down's dreams were demolished. Down felt the wartime travel restrictions and abnormal times unfairly penalised them, and protested over the fact that the match was fixed for Breffni Park in Cavan, but to no avail.

Earlier in the year Down had settled their long-standing dispute with Armagh over the border areas around Newry.

Munster and Ulster met in the semi-final thanks to the rotation system. Kerry had an exciting 3-4 to 0-8 win, having fallen 0-2 to 0-5 behind ten minutes into the second half. Jim 'Gawksie' O'Gorman's two easy goals and another immediately afterwards from John Walsh destroyed Cavan's bid to avenge 1937. On the same day, in a double bill semi-final that brought 33,251 spectators to Croke Park, Galway defended their six-point half-time lead against a Meath onslaught in the second half to win 3-8 to 2-5.

Mayo may have made a mistake when they opted out of the National League after winning six in a row in 1940. Galway won the League in their absence, and their inactivity led to troubled signs when Mayo played Sligo in the Connacht semi-final and were held to a draw, 1-7 to 2-4, as only a last-minute goal struck by Mick O'Malley from twenty yards out saved Mayo embarrassment against Sligo, for whom McLoughlin scored two goals. Paddy Moclair with two goals and a third from Jim Laffey settled the issue in the replay, 3-2 to 0-7.

When the Connacht final came around, Galway showed that their League victory was well merited. Bobby Beggs gave one of his best-ever displays as they beat Roscommon 1-7 to 0-5 in Roscommon. Few turned out to see it, probably because they had been half-crushed to death the previous year. Galway trailed by two points at half-time, levelled midway through the second half and then took control with a Brendan Nestor goal.

To retain their Leinster title before 29,351 spectators against Laois, Meath had to come back from three points down at half-time. Dan Douglas got a goal for Laois midway through the first half, but J. Mayo struck twice in the second half for a Meath victory, 2-7 to 1-7, as Tony Donnelly tacked on the winning points.

Laois were on to something. Their semi-final defeat of Offaly by 2-7 to 0-7 started with a 2-4 scoring spree in six minutes at the start of the game—observers noted that 'their hand passing resembled Kildare at their best'.

Dublin's first-ever all-native selection were seven points down at half-time in the quarter-final against Louth, but came back to win by one and bowed out to Meath in a bad-tempered semi-final. With Galway's victory over Meath, that left Kerry with a chance of revenge for 1938. They got it by a solitary point, 0-7 to 1-3, as 60,821 spectators roared them on.

After touring the United States together in 1938, these teams knew each other well—perhaps too well. 'The game was not productive of great football. The play was scrappy all through and hard knocks abounded.' There were more fisticuffs. Jimmy Duggan's goal for Galway set the game alight, booted to the net from a tangle of players after a John Dunne free just before half-time. Then when Galway added just one point as they lost their 1-2 to 0-3 lead in the second half, tempers began to boil over. John Burke's attempt at a winning point for Galway came back off the post and was cleared. Soon afterwards Charlie O'Sullivan shot the winning point for Kerry with a left-footed shot from 40 yards after 37 minutes of second half play.

The introduction of 'Bawn' Brosnan set Kerry away on the trail of the four points they needed to win. Galway were awarded 38 frees to Kerry's 24, a total of just over a free a minute. One report claimed that the number of times Galway players slipped when going for the ball indicated that their boot studs were faulty!

Despite the tough edges to the game and the pouring rain, there was a marvellous moment when a duck, clad in green and gold, was let loose to waddle across the field.

That left Kerry within sight of the three in a row for the second time in fourteen years.

7 SEPTEMBER 1941. KERRY 1-8, GALWAY 0-7, CROKE PARK

> 'You may be neutral in the war but you can't be neutral in this contest, said the small boy who tried to sell me team colours. One of the wartime changes noticeable during the match was the absence of sweets and fruit in the baskets of the refreshment vendors. They replaced these commodities by bottles of minerals. They are even less elegant in manipulation, with the froth streaming out of them, than the traditional and now defunct orange.'
>
> GERTRUDE GAFFNEY, *Irish Independent*, 8 September 1941

Like Cavan in Ulster, the lack of opposition in Munster did not seem to deter Kerry. They were given a bye into the provincial final while the other Munster counties played off for the McGrath Cup, which was recently presented by the Munster convention. Tipperary were certainly no longer a threat. They barely survived a first round championship match with Waterford when Ahearne had a last-minute goal disallowed. Tipperary then decided to concede a walkover to Clare because foot-and-mouth worries sent the county into quarantine. Clare won the mini competition, and despite the efforts of returned football nomad, 1934 Dublin star Georgie Comerford, Clare trailed 1-3 to 0-3 at half-time and went down by 2-9 to 0-6, thanks to a Murt Kelly goal at the start of the second half.

But any of the provinces could have mounted a challenge to Kerry at the semi-final stage, and Dublin's 'native players' policy was paying dividends in Leinster.

They started with a draw. Matt Fletcher scored Dublin's last-minute equaliser against Louth, which left the score level at 2-7 to 3-4. Even the referee was confused that day: he initially announced Louth the 3-5 to 2-6 winners, then consulted his umpires and admitted his mistake. Fletcher popped up again in the replay for the winning goal near the end. Then Dublin ousted champions Meath 1-8 to 1-6 at Drogheda. Fletcher got both goals for Dublin as they survived a late Kildare comeback in the semi-final to win 2-11 to 2-10.

It was a year of replays in Leinster. Surprise packets Carlow survived a four-match marathon against Wexford, eventually winning 2-8 to 0-3 with goals from Rea and Byrne. They looked home and dried the second day, but Wexford came back from eight points down.

Dublin could have gone the whole way. In the semi-final, which resulted in an 0-4 each draw, only a late Murt Kelly free saved Kerry from defeat. Dublin ran into transport problems when they replayed the semi-final in Tralee. Those who travelled from Dublin on Sunday morning arrived to discover that the other half of the team had not yet arrived. The ones who thought it a bright idea to overnight in Limerick were still snailing along en route to Tralee by turf-train. Dublin failed to reproduce their Croke Park form and went down 2-9 to 0-3.

Dublin were therefore out of the championship by the time the Leinster final was played, thanks to the foot-and-mouth cattle disease scare. Fletcher, Fitzgerald, O'Connor and Banks scored the goals to beat Carlow 4-6 to 1-4.

In Ulster, Tyrone made their bravest bid yet. They beat Armagh 3-13 to 0-1, 1940 surprise team Down (who had fairly hammered Antrim 5-4 to 0-4) by 1-10 to 1-9, and went into full-time training with Belfast Celtic trainer Joe Devlin for the final, only to meet with massive disappointment when they had to field without their captain and inter-provincial star Peter Campbell, whose father died on the morning of the game. Cavan won easily, 3-9 to 0-5. Few Cavan supporters travelled to the final in Armagh as it was difficult to go north without identification during the war. Yet the gate of £525-13-8 was twice the 1940 figure.

For the first time in nine years of the Connacht championship, the 1941 final wasn't a Galway-Mayo affair. When the old rivals met in the semi-final before 15,000 spectators at Tuam, Galway came from behind to beat Mayo 0-10 to 1-5, thanks to a superb save from goalkeeper Jim McGauran in the dying minutes.

Avoiding Galway and Mayo in the Connacht semi-final helped Roscommon's case. The 1940 junior champions were on the way up. Clearly no respecters of reputations, they were to add a 1941 minor title to that of 1939.

Galway scraped through by a single point in the final, 0-8 to 1-4, when Eamonn Boland scored a late goal for Roscommon. Hugh Gibbons, later a

Fianna Fáil TD, had another Roscommon goal disallowed in the first half.

Galway defeated Cavan in the All-Ireland semi-final 1-12 to 1-4, but fared no better against Kerry in the final than they had in 1940 as they went down by four points, 1-8 to 0-7. According to P. D. Mehigan, 'Kerry were outmanoeuvred by Galway's grand team for fully twenty minutes of the first half and it was a miracle that Galway weren't goals in front.'

Again Galway lost the lead, as Kerry had trailed by two points, four minutes into the second half. Six minutes later came a turning-point goal from Tom 'Gega' O'Connor, and with the game getting steadily rougher, Kerry secured their three in a row with two Murt Kelly points. 'It was one tremendous finish where hard knocks were taken as they came and the thud of men's eager bodies left many prone again and again as herculean athletes heaved their weight and unbeaten spirit into the mighty fray.'

Emergency restrictions affected the attendance. Some 45,512 spectators paid £3,540 in receipts, with 11,000 coming by turf-fired train and two hardy Kerry men arriving by tandem from Killarney.

Brawn more than brain characterised the Kerry three-in-a-row team. They are certainly not recalled with affection by lovers of the game in the manner of the 1929–32 team. Dan O'Keeffe still held the goalkeeper's spot he had taken from Johnny Riordan in a last-minute dressing room reshuffle nine years earlier; the full back line consisted of Bill Myers, Joe Keohane (it was said of army officer Joe that you would have to have a written permit before he would let you approach the parallelogram) and Tim Healy; the half back line of team captain Bill Dillon, Bill Casey and Eddie Walsh could also handle themselves in a skirmish. Seán Brosnan and Paddy Kennedy were the classy midfielders with a simple high-catching approach to the game; half-forwards Johnny Walsh, Tom O'Connor and Paddy 'Bawn' Brosnan, skipper of the fishing smack 'Rory', were also known for a solid shoulder; while Jim O'Gorman, Murt Kelly and Charlie O'Sullivan were lighter and more athletic. O'Sullivan once scored a point in a college's final while lying on the flat of his back on the ground.

Brosnan summed up the philosophy of those teams: 'In our day we had a few farmers, a few fishermen and a college boy to take the frees.'

20 SEPTEMBER 1942. DUBLIN 1-10, GALWAY 1-8, CROKE PARK

> 'The match ended on an unpleasant note. Joe Duggan, of the Galway team, was attacked by a number of the Dublin team and was struck by fists.'
>
> *Connacht Tribune*, 26 September 1942

Despite the failures, it was Galway who put a stop to Kerry's quest for another four in a row a decade after the first had been accomplished. Only a fumbled 50 KO'd Kerry. Taken by Galway's Dan Kavanagh, it was tipped to the Kerry net by an unsure back, and Kerry bowed out in the semi-final by 1-3 to 0-3 before 20,420 astonished spectators.

A Kerry players' strike may have helped Galway. After Seán Brosnan was dropped for the semi-final, he persuaded Dingle team mates Bill Casey and Bawn Brosnan not to travel.

Meanwhile, Dublin were growing in confidence, a new threat to Galway's breakthrough. In the first round they were lucky as McGoey missed an open goal for Longford when they drew with Dublin at Mullingar, and a late Banks free forced the match into a replay which Dublin won with an O'Connor goal early in the second half. After beating Longford 2-15 to 1-3, Dublin ousted their principal rivals Meath 3-5 to 1-10, and points from Banks and Joy clinched victory by 0-8 to 0-6 in the Leinster final at Athy after Carlow had equalised near the end. The half-time score was a remarkable two points to nil in favour of Dublin.

Carlow were somewhat lucky to reach their second final in three years: Doyle scored a last-minute equaliser against Offaly in the semi-final. The replay ended in total chaos as the referee accidentally blew for full time ten minutes before time was up. Carlow were leading by 1-9 to 0-6 at the time. When he tried to restart the match, he was threatened by the spectators. Offaly refused to continue and were subsequently suspended for six months. This was not the only bizarre event of the 1942 Leinster championship. Kildare had to recruit players from the sidelines for their first round match against Offaly.

Dundalk staged its third Ulster final, on Down's insistence, as access to venues north of the border was difficult for southern supporters during the war. Down's semi-final with Armagh was ended three minutes early by a crowd invasion, with Down leading 0-7 to 0-6, and forced to a replay which Down won 1-12 to 2-5. The attendance was a large 7,000, paying £430 in receipts, but the final was disappointing. Cavan won 5-11 to 1-3, having weathered fifteen minutes of Down pressure, then switched Tom O'Reilly to centre half forward. They quickly gained control, led 1-8 to 0-2 at half-time as a result of a Donal Morgan goal just before the interval, and then shot four more goals in quick succession after the break, from Paddy Smith, Pat Boylan, Cahill and T. P. O'Reilly.

Wartime restrictions were costing the GAA dear. Only 8,059 watched the All-Ireland semi-final, where another fumbled 50, this time taken by Dublin's Paddy Kennedy, was helped to the Cavan net by a defender. The performance of Dublin's Kerry-born captain Joe FitzGerald and defender Peter O'Reilly decided the game as Dublin came through 1-6 to 1-3.

After depriving Kerry of their four in a row, Galway ended up with three-in-a-row losses of their own, as Dublin won their first All-Ireland since the days of the declaration rule, with the help of a goal from Paddy O'Connor after just ten minutes. As they came back from three points down with a devastating second half performance, Dublin had late points from a Tom Banks 50 and Matt Fletcher. The attendance of 37,105 was the lowest since 1932.

The Galway team had travelled on the Saturday mail train and had difficulty getting on in Ballinasloe. 'Not only was every seat occupied as it left Galway but the corridors were thronged', the *Connacht Tribune* reported.

Dublin had refined their 'native' policy. They could also train a team more cheaply than any of their rivals by bringing them together after work in the evenings. They had Charlie Kelly in goal; Galway-man Bobby Beggs, Paddy Kennedy and Caleb Crone in the full-backs; Paddy Henry, Cavan-man Peter O'Reilly and Brendan Quinn in the half backs; Mick Falvey and team captain, Kerry man Joe Fitzgerald, were at centrefield. A native of Dingle, he had been on the last of the great Garda teams under Killarney inspector P. Cryan. When Garda broke up their club, Joe joined Geraldines where he was later joined by Kerry midfielder Paddy Kennedy. Another Kerry man, Jim Joy from Killorglin, joined Paddy Bermingham and Gerry Fitzgerald in the half forwards; goal-fiend Matt Fletcher, Paddy O'Connor and Tom Banks were the full forwards.

26 SEPTEMBER 1943. ROSCOMMON 1-6, CAVAN 1-6, CROKE PARK
10 OCTOBER 1943. ROSCOMMON 2-7, CAVAN 2-2, CROKE PARK

> 'It is forgotten that not all war-time big games were graceful affairs—indeed the football All-Ireland of 1943 could charitably be described as a thundering disgrace.'
>
> CON HOULIHAN, *The Back Page* (1999)

The clash between Mayo and Galway in the semi-final of the Connacht championship of 1943 brought its lowest attendance in sixteen years—3,000 to Kiltimagh. Galway won easily, 3-6 to 1-5, but times had changed. They had new opponents to worry about.

Firstly, the 1941 provincial junior champions Leitrim had three first half goals from McMurrough when beating Sligo, their first victory in a championship match since 1928. But Leitrim's revival was soundly destroyed, 2-12 to 1-3, in their own Carrick-on-Shannon grounds by Roscommon, who felt their year had come. On 18 July 1943 Roscommon took their long-awaited fourth Connacht title at the third attempt by 2-8 to 0-8 at Roscommon.

Knockcroghery businessman Frank Kinlough and UCD medical student Donal Keenan, from a sparkling hand passing movement midway through the second half, got the historic goals.

Hand passing played its part in the re-emergence of Louth in the Leinster championship. Louth defeated local rivals Meath 2-10 to 1-8 with the help of a doubtful goal from Fanning, and another from substitute Keogh, in Drogheda before a £323 crowd that was a sign of things to come. Then they stopped Dublin's run by 1-6 to 1-5 at the same venue. Coyle's second half goal gave them a relatively narrow 1-9 to 2-3 win over Offaly in the semi-final. In the final against Laois, Louth recovered from an early Harkins goal setback. Goals from Coyle and Corr (who scored 1-7) brought them success by 3-16 to 2-4 after nine years of near misses.

Earlier, Kilkenny forced back into the senior championship when the junior championship was abolished, earned the distinction of being the last team that failed to score in a championship match when they went out to Wexford 3-6 to nil.

But when the breakthrough teams met, Louth's hand passing tactics came unstuck in their semi-final against Roscommon as Frankie Kinlough timed two vital goals for the opening and closing minutes of the game, and Roscommon won 3-10 to 3-6.

Amid all the surprises in the championship, Kerry's exit was probably the most remarkable. In 1942 Kerry's half-time lead against Clare in the semi-final was an unimpressive two points, but they still went on to win 1-8 to 0-2, and hammered Cork 3-7 to 0-8 with second half goals from Murt Kelly, J. Gorman and Bawn Brosnan for seven in a row. Going for eight in 1943, they were foiled by a late goal in the Munster semi-final at Cork and went out to Cork 1-5 to 1-4 after a pre-emptive 2-3 to 0-9 draw at the same venue. In the drawn match, Cork had made most of the running before a late Murt Kelly point saved Kerry. In the replay, Kerry led 1-5 to 1-3 when a Kerry back made a mistake in fielding the ball. Eamonn Casey smashed it into the net, then followed up with two points for Cork's first victory over the ould enemy for 36 years as Kerry's defence fell into disarray.

Kerry had not been beaten in Munster since 1928. Had they not opted out in 1935, they might have been chasing fifteen in a row. They could blame Munster's convention, which decided to make the same draws for hurling and football. Cork went on to beat Tipperary 1-7 to 1-4 in the Munster final at Fermoy.

Cavan too had a case for the monopoly commission. They beat Tyrone (by a colossal 4-10 to 1-3) and Monaghan (by four points, 2-3 to 1-5) to win yet another Ulster title. In the final, Cavan trailed 0-4 to nil during the first half, and seemed to badly miss absentees John Joe O'Reilly and Donal Morgan. But they came back with a T. P. O'Reilly goal before half-time, and took control of the second half with a second goal from Joe Stafford. Morgan came on as a substitute and was back for an exciting one-point win over Cork in the All-Ireland semi-final 1-8 to 1-7. Joe Stafford got the vital Cavan goal fourteen minutes after half-time.

The final was one of the great occasions of wartime Ireland. Before a record 68,023 spectators, Cavan led 1-4 to 0-3 at half-time, thanks to a great Stafford goal, but a spectacular reply by Jimmy Murray two minutes into the second half started Roscommon's comeback. Cavan regained control by bringing Tom O'Reilly to midfield and John Joe to centre half forward and forced a draw, 1-6 each. The referee asked the teams to play extra time, but they refused.

In the replay, Roscommon completed their sudden rise from junior obscurity to put a new name on the Sam Maguire Cup. Cavan's resistance was eventually broken with goals by Frank Kinlough after ten minutes and Jack McQuillan after twelve minutes, but finally with a Phelim Murray point after Cavan had fought back to two points behind.

Roscommon went on to win 2-7 to 2-2. Annoyed Cavan men tried to prevent the umpire signalling the winning score, the crowd rushed the field as a Cavan player felled the referee with a blow, and the trouble took several minutes to clear up.

The sending off of Cavan's semi-final and final goalscorer, Joe Stafford, for a blow on Roscommon's Owensie Hoare ten minutes into the second half started the row. The referee was attacked again after the match and two players were subsequently suspended for life by the Central Council. It was a sad end to a great series.

All around neutral Ireland, sports competition had ground to a halt as Europe worried about more serious matters. Missing from the VIP section of the stand for the first time since 1941 was Italian envoy Signor Bernardis as Mussolini's government had been defeated. German minister Eduard Hempel and British minister John Maffey sat a few seats apart in the Cusack Stand.

24 SEPTEMBER 1944. ROSCOMMON 1-9, KERRY 2-4, CROKE PARK

'A fireman asked me if the ball was safe.'

Roscommon player JIMMY MURRAY, after his pub was burned down, destroying the football used in the 1944 All-Ireland final

Connacht was once more offering an intriguing provincial championship, this time with three contenders for the first time in 30 years. Roscommon took no chances, went into full-time training early, and became the first team to spend over £1,000 defending their All-Ireland title.

Mayo came back from their four-year doldrums to take on Roscommon in 1944—an early Joe Gilvarry goal had helped them beat Galway 1-11 to 1-3 in Castlebar. Sligo too promised a return to the big-time. In the semi-final, Aenghus McMorrow, later to play full back on the Irish rugby team against Wales in 1951, scored a surprise equaliser that forced the new All-Ireland champions to a replay. Second time out Sligo took the lead at half-time and only the wisdom of the Roscommon mentors, who sent on John Joe Nerney for Frank Kinlough, helped Roscommon win in the end 0-13 to 1-6. In the Connacht final at Tuam, Roscommon surprised the begrudgers by holding on to their title by a convincing 2-11 to Mayo's 1-6. They led by just one point at half-time but won by eight, thanks to Hugh Gibbons and Jimmy Murray goals in the second half, while team captain Jimmy Murray thrilled the crowd with his hand-to-toe runs. Liam Gilmartin was man of the match.

Monaghan continued to give Cavan a run for their money in Ulster. Cavan trailed 0-4 to 1-2 at half-time when the Ulster final was played before 10,000 spectators at the not yet officially opened St Tiernach's Park in Clones, a few hundred yards from the border. D. McGrath gave Monaghan an early three-point lead. Tony Tighe started the revival, T. P. O'Reilly shot a goal and three points, and Cavan went on to win by three points, 1-9 to 1-6. Gaelic football was allocated just twenty footballs by the Belfast Ministry of Supplies under wartime regulations. The smuggling of balls kept the game going in the North. The repeat of the All-Ireland final had none of the previous year's ugliness or uncertainty as Roscommon won by 5-8 to 1-3. Frank Kinlough started Roscommon's goal-rush and was joined by Hugh Gibbons (2), Jackie McQuillan and John Joe Nerney. But Roscommon had the most traditional rivals of all to face in the All-Ireland semi-final.

When Tipperary ousted Cork by 1-9 to 1-3 in the Munster semi-final, Kerry gathered strength and won back the title with a strong defensive display, 1-6 to 0-5. Tipperary should have kept the ball on the ground, according to reports, where they had Kerry on the run. Instead Paddy Kennedy got Kerry's vital first half goal, Murt Kelly and Paddy Brosnan picked off the points, and Kerry's defence held firm in atrocious conditions.

Kerry had new semi-final opponents. Carlow defeated Kildare, Laois and Wexford in an impressive run to the final, then celebrated a monumental breakthrough with two goals from Jimma Rea and John Doyle. Carlow came back from 0-1 to 0-5 down to beat Dublin 2-6 to 1-6 and win their sole Leinster championship in Athy. 'What a change in the last half did the minutes unroll,' went the local ballad, 'The boys from the Barrow were swarming the goal / It was blue in and odd spot, but red, gold and green, / Were the colours that rallied the Carlow fifteen.' In the previous four years they had suffered near misses in two finals and a semi-final. But the difference between Carlow in 1944 and their previous teams in 1941 and 42 was centrefield: the Kelly-Morris midfield combination gave Carlow a valuable advantage.

Longford too, inspired by the success of next door neighbours Roscommon, made a brave bid to reach the final: beating Offaly and taking a 1-3 to 1-1 lead against Dublin at half-time, only to succumb by 2-2 to 1-4 to a second half goal from Paddy O'Connor. O'Connor got the goal in lost time that helped Dublin depose champions Louth 2-10 to 3-6 in the Leinster quarter-final. But nobody at that stage expected Carlow to make it to the big-time.

By the time the All-Ireland semi-final came around, the 40,727 who turned out to see them play Kerry were not so sure that Carlow were out of their depth. Carlow celebrated by going two points up, but conceded an unfortunate penalty goal to Murt Kelly just before half-time. When Paddy Bawn Brosnan scored Kerry's third goal ten minutes into the second half, it looked all over. But Doyle and Moore helped Carlow back to a respectable score, 3-3 to 0-10, just two points behind.

That left the test to Roscommon. How good were they? Could they rise to the task of beating the county that had won nine of the previous sixteen All-Ireland titles in an All-Ireland final, and show they were really entitled to the status of champions?

A record 79,245 watched Roscommon succeed by 1-9 to 2-4. Frankie Kinlough scored the vital goal from Nerney's pass after eleven minutes. Then things went wrong. The Roscommon defenders got in each other's way as Kerry's Eddie Dunne landed a goal eleven minutes into the second half. With Roscommon two points in arrears, Donal Keenan took over. He scored two points to equalise with five minutes to go. Kinlough and Keenan slotted over two winning points, and Roscommon bonfires were ablaze.

23 SEPTEMBER 1945. CORK 2-5, CAVAN 0-7, CROKE PARK

> 'The southern invasion reminded me of old times. The driver of one train must have had a bet on the match, for he made the journey from Glanmire to Kingsbridge in four and a half hours. The Hogan Stand was streaked with red and white favours. Genial Mickey Roche shouted at me when I stood up in my press seat. Sit down oura that, Paddy M.'
>
> P. D. MEHIGAN, *Carbery's Annual*, 1945

Two generations of Cork footballers had waited in the wings. In 1945 Cork struck back, won their revenge over Tipperary 1-7 to 1-6, and beat Kerry for the second time in three years. An attendance of 7,384 turned out to see them beat the home team 1-11 to 1-6 at Killarney. Eamonn 'Togher' Casey did the damage again with an early goal, and Cork led 1-6 to 1-2 at half-time. Jim Cronin got their Munster semi-final goal against Tipperary, when the side looked far from All-Ireland championship material.

The Cork team went into full-time training after winning the Munster championship under renowned hurling trainer Jim Barry, first in Clonakilty and then in Cork city.

Pint-sized Derry Beckett gave Cork the start they needed with a goal after eight minutes of the All-Ireland semi-final against Galway, and added four valuable points in the second half. Cavan kicked twelve wides in the second half of their semi-final against Wexford and had to rely on a Joe Stafford goal to pull them through.

Roscommon were going for three All-Irelands in a row when they came a cropper in the Connacht semi-final against Mayo. Mayo led 0-4 to 0-3 at half-time. Billy Kenny and Mulvey both scored Mayo goals in the third quarter, and Eamonn Boland's goal for Roscommon at the tail end of the game succeeded only in cutting the margin to a more respectable four points, 2-8 to 1-7.

Mayo and Galway went to Roscommon to play the final. Galway held out for an exciting two-point victory, 2-6 to 1-7, as a final twenty-minute siege on the Galway goal thrilled the 8,000 crowd. Pierce Thornton's goal gave Galway a half-time lead of 1-4 to 0-1. Then Kilroy and Co. arrived to pick off Mayo points.

Galway goalkeeper Eamonn Mulholland was charged to the net, but no goal was given. Eamonn Mongey eventually scored the goal Mayo needed, but it was too late. Seán Thornton had got one at the other end for Galway.

By now Leinster had the most open championship of them all. A trend was started at Navan when Meath beat Louth 2-9 to 2-7 with a Willie Halfpenny goal. Louth were soon to replace Carlow as Meath's great championship rivals. Carlow failed to Kildare by 2-13 to 2-10. Longford's hopefuls went out to Offaly. Meath needed extra time to dispose of Dublin, 2-16 to 1-10, after a 3-6 to 4-3 draw: Snow got their winning goal in the first period of extra time, and Culhane scored the equalising goal for Dublin a minute from the end of the first match. But a poor start to the semi-final saw them fail to Offaly by 1-8 to 0-5.

The eventual champions, for the last time in their football history, were Wexford, who beat Kildare 5-5 to 0-6, Laois by 4-5 to 1-11, and Offaly by 1-9 to 1-4 in an unusual Leinster final that drew a 9,873 attendance to Portlaoise.

In the final, Wexford timed their winning move well. Joe O'Connor scored a vital goal just before half-time as Offaly were trying to run the ball out of defence. Offaly were leading by three points at the time, thanks to a J. Byrne goal, and dreaming of their first title. But stars such as Bill Goodison and a teenage full forward called Nicky Rackard, who fought a thrilling duel with Offaly full back J. Kelly, put an end to that. Rackard had got two out of four goals against Laois and J. O'Connor two out of five against Kildare.

They had seen off aspiring Antrim 2-11 to 2-3 in the first round, and new challengers, Fermanagh, with an early goal in the Ulster final from their own star newcomer, Peter Donoghue from Crosserlough. Others followed from Joe Stafford, P. A. O'Reilly and P. J. Duke in the second half for a 4-10 to 1-4 victory. Cavan's hand passing style was leading to an increased number of fouls, and occasional bouts of fisticuffs kept spirits high, but their control at centrefield meant the issue was never in doubt.

Fermanagh's rise from junior success in 1943 to the Ulster final was completed when Durnin and Breslin goals gave them a one-point victory over Armagh. Their forward B. Lunny, a 1943 colleges star with St Pat's of Cavan, was the hero of their championship bid.

The Central Council, disagreeing with the hand pass and the effect it was having on the game, took matters into their own hands. They banned the hand pass at a council meeting, an extraordinary decision for which there was no justification under the constitution of the GAA. Cavan were hampered by this decision. They needed a great save from goalkeeper Brendan Kelly to beat Wexford narrowly by 1-4 to 0-5 in the All-Ireland semi-final, having shot twelve wides in the second half. It now appeared that Cavan might have a chance of their third All-Ireland title after ten years.

Cork completed their happy ending after 34 years in the wilderness with a 2-5 to 0-7 win over Cavan in the All-Ireland final, and gave Jack Lynch the fifth of six All-Ireland medals in succession (the others were in hurling). P. D. Mehigan complained: 'The crossing wind put perfect football out of the question; there was much misfielding and wild shooting for a classic game, and the highlight from a spectator's point of view was the stern passage near the three quarter way when Cavan forced the pace and stormed in on Cork's tall backs in one of the finest rallies in many years.'

Clare man Mick Tubridy sent a rising, thundering shot that hit the lower edge of the crossbar and rebounded to the net after six minutes, and Derry Beckett, one minute from the end, got the victory goals. But despite the margin, they were assured of victory only after Cavan had come back to one point behind—'against the wind in the second half they tore in waves and shook Cork backs to their foundations'—and jittery Cork had missed three scoring chances.

Derry Beckett made the issue safe with a goal 29 minutes into the second half. Jack Lynch and Eamonn Young managed to beat the ball out to his corner. He fielded, slipped around Barney Cully and let fly a rising ball to the net. P. D. Mehigan quoted from *The Man with the Velour Hat* in his account of the game: 'What Cavan man could score dat goal of Derry Beckett an' he not the size uv a sod o' turf, wit big Tom Riley and Barney Cully tryin' to drive him down tru' the groun'. An' what about Weesh Murphy of Beare Island—me sonny boy, de Cork full back dat pulled de whole side of a boat agin four strong men in Bantry Bay regatta.'

Cavan corner back 'Big Tom' Riley was now a TD. Trained in the debate of the GAA council halls, he was elected as an Independent in 1944 with a remarkable vote of exactly 5,000, when Fianna Fáil transfers helped him oust former Unionist John J. Cole. He joined Fine Gael before the 1948 election and lost two-thirds of his vote and his seat. Cork's Jack Lynch had more luck. He turned down an offer to stand in the 1946 Cork by-election, turned down another from Clann na Poblachta before opting to stand for Fianna Fáil in the 1948 general election, came in second place, and went on to become Taoiseach between 1966 and 1973.

The character of the Cork team was goalkeeper Moll Driscoll. On the night before the final he offered Mick Finn a shilling for a song, and nineteen to stop. A crowd of 60,000 greeted the Cork team's return to the city, the greatest welcome in football history. One speaker demanded that Dublin Corporation take down Nelson's pillar and put up a new one to Cork trainer Jim Barry.

The hand pass might have helped Cavan win in 1945. The issue of palmed passing would just not go away.

6 OCTOBER 1946. KERRY 2-4, ROSCOMMON 1-7, CROKE PARK
27 OCTOBER 1946. KERRY 2-8, ROSCOMMON 0-10, CROKE PARK

> 'In the 1946 All-Ireland, Jimmy Murray went off injured with about ten minutes to go. Those attending his facial injury were careful to wash away all the blood so that he would look well and presentable when he went up to receive the cup.'
>
> GERRY O'MALLEY, Roscommon footballer from the 1960s, quoted by Brendan Fullam (1994)

Hand passing is as old as the GAA itself. The hand pass was not invented. It evolved from a looseness in the old rule which stated: 'The ball, when off the ground, may be struck with the hand.'

It was used by early teams: Dundalk Young Irelands in the 1887 All-Ireland final, Erin's Hope in the 1887 Dublin championship, Clane in the 1888 Kildare and Leinster championships, and Monaghan in the 1888 Ulster championship. The 1903 Kildare team are said to have 'hand passed the leather along the ground'. Dublin used a short hand pass, involving two or three men, successfully against Kerry in 1923 and 1924. Kildare took it up, used a longer and more frequently used hand pass against Kerry in 1926, and in 1928 Kildare man Paddy Loughlin threw the ball illegally into the Cavan net for a vital goal in the All-Ireland final. Mayo used it from 1936 on in the National League and championship campaigns. Full forward Paddy Moclair moved outfield and slung the ball to either wing as the forwards came forward. Cavan used the short pass even more frequently, and critics claimed that many of their movements broke down through over-elaboration.

A 1939 commission, reporting on the rules of Gaelic football, recommended that it be abolished or 'alternatively that the player receiving the ball from a hand pass be forced to kick the ball'. Michael Ó Ruairc of Kerry was among those who argued at the 1940 congress that 'hand passing gives rise to rough play and makes the task of the referee more difficult'. The motions to abolish it were short of the two-thirds majority by just one vote.

Then came the 1941 Railway Cup final between Munster and Ulster. Ulster further developed the Mayo technique, using the centre forward, Alf Murray of Armagh, instead of the full forward as a pivot of the hand passing movement, 'a mixture of basketball and rugby', as horrified *Kerryman* writer Paddy Foley described it. Ulster soared 1-6 to 0-1 ahead without kicking a single score. Munster came back to draw and won the replay. But Ulster stuck to the new hand pass technique, and when Murray was joined by another hand pass master, Simon Deignan of Cavan at full forward, they came back to win the cup from Munster in 1942 and beat Leinster by a point in a 1943 final that is still remembered as the best ever.

A Kerry motion to the congress of 1945 got a simple majority, but not the necessary two-thirds majority to abolish the hand pass. In August 1945, however, the Central Council conferred with referees and ruled that the ball must be struck with the fist only.

That move, of doubtful legality, may have cost Cavan an All-Ireland, but when it was forced back on to the rule book by an Antrim motion to the 1946 congress, at least the issue was cleared up once and for all.

Antrim had been masters of the tactic 35 years before. Well beaten by Cavan in 1944 and 1945, their Belfast-based players in particular had perfected the technique for the 1946 Ulster championship. Antrim beat Down and Armagh to become Cavan's fifth new final opponents in six years.

The Ulster council benefited from the excitement that Antrim brought to their championship, earning a record £1,051 from 15,000 spectators at Clones. They seemed to have their work cut out for them. Cavan, seeking eight in a row, hit Tyrone with seven first half goals in Omagh, and won 8-13 to 2-4 in the Ulster quarter-final.

But in the Ulster final, Antrim, with Kevin Armstrong acting as their hand pass 'pivot', showed they meant business with three scores in the first three minutes. The third was a goal from Joe McCallin, who also added a second five minutes before half-time, and Antrim had only to defend their 2-5 to 0-4 lead in the second half. When sub Tom O'Reilly got a Cavan goal and had another disallowed, Harry O'Neill moved into the backs to relieve the siege, and Antrim won 2-8 to 1-7.

Kerry had no time for such niceties. They deposed All-Ireland champions Cork 1-6 to 0-7 in the first round of the Munster championship at Ennis, with the help of an own goal from a Cork defender at the start of the second half. It was the last time Munster's great football rivals would meet outside the final. Clare put in a strong challenge in the semi-final against the eventual champions. Denny Lyne's second half goal sent Kerry through by 1-6 to 0-7. In the final, Kerry's 2-16 to 2-1 rout of Waterford was largely due to Tom O'Connor, who scored all of the first half points that sent Kerry 0-6 to 1-1 ahead. There to throw in the ball was former Kerry player Redmond 'Mundy' Prendiville, who had sneaked out of the seminary to play in the 1924 All-Ireland final and became the Church's youngest ever archbishop when he was appointed at the age of 31 (a stand in the football stadium of his diocesan capital, Perth, is named after him).

Jim Clifford, who was born in Kerry but played on the beaten Galway team in the 1942 All-Ireland final, was now stationed in Cork. He played for Kerry in 1943 and 44. Now he had declared for Cork, only to end up on the losing team again.

The clash of styles between Antrim and Kerry in the All-Ireland semi-final was the horror story of a football generation. Still smarting from the memory of the 1942 defeat of a Munster team that contained fourteen Kerry men by Ulster hand passers in the Railway Cup final, Kerry devised an unashamed tactic to short-circuit Antrim's mobile hand passing style: 'Never mind the man in possession, hit the man in position to take the pass.' Two players, Kerry's Bill Casey and Antrim's Harry O'Neill, were sent off. Radio commentator Micheál O'Hehir diplomatically ignored the warfare, despite a chorus of boohs from most of the 30,051 spectators which almost drowned him out.

Within seconds of the throw-in, Antrim were in the midst of a weaving hand pass movement when Bill Casey halted Kevin Armstrong in his stride. Willy O'Donnell sent a low ball to the net for Kerry after 90 seconds. A late Batt Garvey goal sent Kerry through, 2-7 to 0-10. 'Antrim's short passing and swerving methods were hampered by the weather, the greasy topped sod and a slippery ball,' P. D. Mehigan mentioned, and later added: 'Antrim's movements broke down on Kerry's stonewall defence. O'Keeffe and his six backs in front were determined not to let those flashing speed merchants through. As Armstrong was swerving away on a solo run, Casey had him down; O'Neill rushed in and there was a brief ruggy—over in a flash, but Casey and O'Neill were marched off. Casey's loss at this stage almost cost Kerry the game. But there was no mistaking Kerry's all-round proficiency in skilful, orthodox Gaelic football of the very best kind.'

One *Kerryman* writer recorded: 'The Antrim men stormed through from the centre of the field on dazzling attacks, but they persisted in trying to walk the ball to the net and this was something that just wouldn't work with backs like Joe Keohane, Bill Casey, Teddy O'Connor and Eddie Walsh around.'

Joe Keohane compared the barracking and general condemnation Kerry got after the game with the Nuremberg trials! A unique Antrim objection that Kerry had brought the game of Gaelic football into disrepute with their tactics failed by nineteen votes to ten. The two who were sent off were suspended for two months.

The second semi-final was going to be eventful, with Laois breaking through in Leinster and Roscommon, who had successfully defended a three-point lead throughout the second half against champions Galway to win the Connacht semi-final 0-7 to 0-4 and winning back the Connacht title almost as dramatically as they were to lose the All-Ireland, beating Mayo 1-4 to 0-6.

There was almost another Connacht final riot. Jimmy Murray scored the winning goal entering the fourth quarter, with many spectators speculating that the ball had hit the umpire, with Jimmy chasing it, before he pushed it inside the post for the vital goal. In the confusion, Jimmy raised the green flag himself, just as Brendan Nestor had done for Mayo in 1936. Mayo came back for two points from 17-year-old Pádraig Carney, but it was too late.

Laois had relied on a series of goals, first by Tom Keogh against Dublin to win 1-3 to 0-5, by Connolly just as they trailed by two points in the second half against Offaly, and by Bill Delaney as matters were even worse, 0-1 to 0-8 down at the start of the second half against Louth, to win 1-9 to 0-10. They eventually beat optimistic Kildare 0-11 to 1-6 before 27,353 spectators in a famous final with 0-8 from Tommy Murphy, no longer the 'boy wonder' but a full-grown force to be reckoned with in championship football. Murphy's frees kept Kildare's bid for recovery at bay in the second half after Thomas Ryan got Kildare's goal in the first half.

Kildare's optimism stemmed from the fact that they had beaten reigning champions and hot favourites Wexford 3-3 to 0-10, having trailed by eight points before Bob Martin, Tom Fox and Mick Geraghty got their vital second half goals. Laois were the third county in succession to win a Leinster title that have not won one since.

So the second All-Ireland semi-final not only drew a bigger crowd than Kerry versus Antrim, 51,275 (partly because the interminable 1946 summer rain seemed to break for the day), but it was much better to watch. Tommy Murphy led a storming Laois comeback and Hughes went for the winning goal, shooting narrowly inside the post, only to see Roscommon goalkeeper Gerry Dolan make one of the most spectacular saves ever seen at Croke Park. Roscommon held on to win by two points, 3-5 to 2-6. Surely a great series—with an interruption.

The All-Ireland final was postponed from 19 September because of the 'save the harvest' scheme, designed to prevent crops being ruined after a bad summer and lost to an economy still curtailed by wartime conditions. This enabled the suspended Bill Casey to play in the final. With Kerry and Roscommon back in opposition after two years, it was clearly a case for a new record attendance, now that the transport situation had improved, and 75,771 showed up, paying £6,190 in receipts to a grateful GAA.

They saw Gaelic football's most extraordinary finish. Roscommon led by six points with three minutes to go in the drawn final. They had suffered the loss of star Jimmy Murray fourteen minutes after half-time and seen three Donal Keenan shots rebound off the woodwork.

Then, with Murray's hair combed so he would 'look right' for accepting the cup, Kerry struck. Paddy Burke landed a goal. Two minutes later Gega O'Connor sent an easy goal past a confused defence and Kerry had pulled off a remarkable 2-4 to 1-7 draw.

Kerry made sure in the replay by 2-8 to 0-10. Paddy Burke fielded a long ball from Gega O'Connor and scored a 46th-minute goal for Kerry to come from behind again. Gus Cremin, selected as captain for the drawn match but dropped for the replay, came on to the field fifteen minutes from the end. Cremin scored Kerry's lead point from 50 yards out just as time was up. A sideline ball from Gega O'Connor was held by Gerry Dolan, but he was bundled over the line for Kerry's second goal in a last-minute mêlée. Gus broke his leg before the 1947 All-Ireland final and missed a trip to the Polo Grounds.

14 SEPTEMBER 1947. CAVAN 2-11, KERRY 2-7, POLO GROUNDS, NEW YORK

> 'Three thousand came in on an excursion train from Boston, and large contingents from Detroit, Pittsburgh and Chicago. There were specials from Hartford, Springfield and Newark. Lonely strangers were asking, anyone here from my county? This was much more than a football game. It was a rally of the scattered Irish, seeking friendship, warmth and renewal of the spirit. In a big way it was Galway races, Punchestown, Puck Fair.'
>
> *Irish Press*, 15 September 1947

Getting the 1947 All-Ireland final played in New York's Polo Grounds was one of the great achievements of Canon Michael Hamilton's active career (he had been a radio commentator in 1937).

Almost everyone opposed the idea when he first mooted it. Skilful lobbying eventually convinced a controversial Central Council meeting at Barry's Hotel that it was worth carrying through. The legend has grown since 1947 of how Milton Malbay man Bob Fitzpatrick's speech to congress, complete with tear-stained handkerchief, swung the vote as he read from a bogus 'emigrant's letter'.

Relations with New York had cooled somewhat from the heady days of the 1930s. After the fiasco of the 1927 tour by the Kerry footballers, when the promoter made off with all the money and the team had to be rescued from their hotel, and because of bad feeling over the way the series had been billed 'the championship of the world', the Central Council refused an application to tour from the Kildare footballers. In 1931 Kerry toured again, this time successfully, and a world record attendance for a GAA match was set at Yankee Stadium when 60,000 watched them avenge a 1927 defeat by New York.

Immigration restrictions imposed after the Wall Street Crash meant that New York teams never again achieved a level of dominance over the touring footballers from Ireland that they had in 1927. But the tourists came more and more enthusiastically and often throughout the 1930s.

After Kerry toured successfully in 1931 and came home with enough money to purchase Austin Stack Park in Tralee, Mayo followed in 1932, Kerry again in 1933, Cavan and Galway in 1934, Cavan again in 1935 and 1937, Galway again in 1936, Laois in 1937, and Mayo went over again in 1937 (when Leitrim player Johnny McGoldrick defeated them almost single-handedly and then collapsed in the dressing room with pneumonia). Kerry and Galway travelled together in 1939 and played exhibition games across the United States.

Much of the touring, particularly in Mayo's case, was due to the influence and money of Bill O'Dwyer, the Bohola-born judge. When he was elected Mayor of New York in 1946, the GAA now had the necessary clout to stage an All-Ireland final.

Suddenly the entire championship sprang to life. The trip to New York became a prize in itself. Nowhere was this more apparent than at the Munster final in Cork, where 32,000 spectators turned out to watch Kerry beat Cork 3-8 to 2-6. American fever had helped Kerry give Clare a 33-point Munster semi-final thrashing, 9-10 to 0-4, a score that would not be exceeded for 32 years.

Kerry's passage to New York was helped along by a famous penalty miss by Cork ten minutes from the end. Kerry full back Joe Keohane argued with the referee for two minutes, standing on the ball and sending it deeper and deeper into the sticky Cork Athletic Grounds mud. When Jim Ahearne took the kick, it rolled harmlessly along the ground. Keohane was to claim afterwards: 'All the time I was arguing I could see the skyline of New York getting clearer and clearer.'

Meath too had their eyes on a trip. Leinster spectators turned out in their thousands, 41,631 of them, paying £3,636 to watch Meath beat Laois 3-7 to 1-7. Meath newcomer Bryan Smyth scored a goal before half-time and Peter McDermott got the first and third goals for a rather easy victory in that game. Paddy O'Brien was the hero of an 0-9 to 1-4 semi-final win over Louth, when Meath came from three points behind after a Jim Quigley goal for Louth. Paddy Meegan got the goal to beat a fighting Westmeath 1-8 to 0-5, and McDermott celebrated the first round victory over Wicklow by scoring 4-2.

Ulster too had an attendance record, 34,009 paying £2,268 to see Cavan take on Antrim at Clones. Cavan introduced full-time training for an Ulster final for the first time in preparation for this crunch game. Two soft goals early in the second half had similarly served Cavan in the semi-final against Tyrone. An unconvincing twice-played quarter-final against Monaghan provoked this decision. Cavan were foiled by a saved penalty in the drawn match by the Monaghan goalkeeper, and Monaghan regretted a dramatic last-minute save by Cavan's goalkeeper in the replay that sent Cavan through by 1-11 to 1-9.

In the provincial final Cavan got their title back by 3-4 to 1-6, with three goals inside eleven minutes, and when Antrim lost Kevin Armstrong through injury, the record attendance thought the final was over. But Frank Dunlop got a goal midway through the second half, and only Antrim's over-carrying the ball and a missed chance, when an equalising goal looked on, thwarted their comeback in a rain-drenched thriller. Antrim's downfall started when one of their defenders put the ball into his own net. Peter O'Donoghue scored the second, and Joe Stafford got the third.

That same day Roscommon announced their candidature for New York as well, beating Sligo 2-12 to 1-8 with goals from Jack McQuillan and John Joe Nerney as Sligo eventually made it back into the final after fifteen years: beating Galway 2-6 to 1-6 with the help of Eamonn White's 1-2 near the end. White missed a penalty early in the second half of that semi-final, but when he scored one in the early stages of the final, it failed to inspire his colleagues.

The run of attendance records continued in the semi-finals. When Cavan beat Roscommon 2-4 to 0-6, 60,075 paid £5,448 to see man of the match Tony Tighe score a goal in each half to help end Roscommon's run. The new record lasted just seven days, as the following Sunday 65,939 paid £5,693 into the GAA coffers to watch Teddy O'Connor's midfield performance inspire a Kerry win over Meath by 1-11 to 0-5.

The players travelled the gruelling 29 hour flight from Rineanna to New

York via Santa Maria in the Azores, Gander and Boston, the Monday before the game. Even the take-off was delayed by 24 hours—Kerry's Eddie Dowling reckoned he had 30 glasses of beer before he got on the plane. An advance party of 25 officials and substitutes had already journeyed by ocean liner, the *Mauritania.* A cavalcade of 30 cars, eighteen motorcycle policemen escorting them with sirens screaming, drove the awe-stricken footballers through the streets while Irish Americans gave a scaled-down version of the New York ticker-tape parade. Lord Mayor Bill O'Dwyer received them with a party of 5,000 people at City Hall. On the morning of the game, Cardinal Spellman welcomed the teams from the pulpit in St Patrick's Cathedral and was photographed with the team captains on the cathedral steps afterwards.

This was to become one of the most romantic finals of them all. The New York Police Band played three anthems, 'Amhrán na bhFiann', 'Faith of our Fathers', and 'The Star-Spangled Banner', then Cavan won the famous victory on the playing field, 2-11 to 2-7, in what was described as 'pitiless heat', but nobody was quite prepared to admit what a disaster the whole experience was.

When GAA officials got to New York, they found that the match was poorly publicised and had been fixed for a bumpy pitch that was only 137 yards long by 81 yards wide. A big patch of grass had been worn away by the feet of baseball players. Grass on the remainder was scorched by the blistering sun. The ground was as hard as concrete, with a baseball mound in the middle of what should be the playing field for an All-Ireland final.

This strange cairn proved important in the build-up to two of the goals that came in the first half. Kerry went eight points up after a quarter of an hour with Batt Garvey soloing through the Cavan defence on raid after raid. Garvey and Eddie Dowling scored the goals. Gega O'Connor and Batt Garvey had two more disallowed (Garvey felt afterwards that referee Martin O'Neill was trying to prevent a Kerry rout at this stage). 'I knew we had a battle on our hands, but I noticed the Kerry backs were very jittery', Mick Higgins recalled afterwards. Then a six-man move led to T. P. O'Reilly getting one back for Cavan, and when Mick Higgins struck just before half-time, Cavan were a point ahead.

Four points in each half gave Peter Donohue the kudos of the three mainline American sportswriters (from the *New York Times*, the *Herald Tribune*, and the now-defunct *New York Journal*) who bothered to attend. He was variously described as the Babe Ruth or Dead Eye Dick of Gaelic games, but others wrote of Cavan winning a 'rough Irish game'.

The *New York Times* sports columnist Arthur Daley wrote: 'Considering the fact that Gaelic football is what would technically be described as a non-contact sport, there was more violence than you'd find in a football game between Army and Notre Dame. The busiest man on the field was Thomas G.

Dougherty. He was the official physician.' Eddie Dowling was out cold after landing on the baseball mound.

Commentator Micheál O'Hehir suffered the indignity of appealing over the airwaves to the New York telecommunications people not to cut off the commentary to the ears of excited fans at home. Only Irish influence with the telegraphic unions and an appeal to the Mayor got the radio equipment linked up in the first place.

Lastly, the attendance was only 34,491, fewer than anticipated in the 55,000-capacity stadium. It was not much bigger than the Connacht final of the big matches at home that year.

New York's efforts to bring the 1950 All-Ireland hurling final to the Polo Grounds were unsuccessful. The prize trip to New York was confined to League champions for another 25 years.

Only two journalists travelled, O'Hehir, whose passage was paid for by the GAA, and Michel Cogley of the *Irish Independent.* The Sam Maguire Cup stayed at home and was brought to Dun Laoghaire for the homecoming reception, before the teams went to the Aras to meet President Seán T. Ó Ceallaigh.

As for the Polo Grounds themselves, they are no more. They were sold off for development when the New York Giants upped and moved to San Francisco in 1957.

Cavan did not heed the begrudgers. The event lives on in the folk memory. The winning team was photographed with the stars and stripes. When the team reached home, fifteen bands waited for the bus on the outskirts of Cavan town.

Chapter 4

1948–74: STRONG AND FORTHRIGHT MEN

Gaelic football as the defining ritual in Irish rural life

26 SEPTEMBER 1948. CAVAN 4-5, MAYO 4-4, CROKE PARK

'Cavan brought hand passing to its ultimate perfection and Down, Galway and Dublin later built on their style.'

SEÁN FLANAGAN

When the All-Ireland final came home, it was a pageant. The GAA had big plans for what was increasingly being seen as a celebration of Irish nationhood.

In the 26 counties, after twenty years of Irish government, parliament and civil service, and the triumph of nationalism, the players of Irish games could claim that there was nothing more to accomplish.

In the Six Counties, a new state was constructed to exclude members of the nationalist minority from all aspects of political, economic or cultural life. The GAA and the Stormont regime had tried to ignore each other's existence. When they had to come into contact with each other, in education, broadcasting schedules, or rationed footballs, the contact was brief and terse.

The playing of matches on Sundays, the Irish anthem and the flying of the tricolour were ignored by the unionist authorities after unsuccessful attempts to stop them in the 1920s.

There were problems elsewhere. The drift from the land, the growing practice where towns with bakeries and industries were offering regular jobs to good footballers from rural parts, and the slackening of the old parish rules were creating new pressures.

Parish football was in crisis. In many counties, it was claimed, two or three glamour clubs were getting all the publicity and luring players from the weaker clubs. In most counties clubs found they were only offered half a dozen matches a year and local competitions were running up to four years late.

In 1946 the author of a short GAA history urged the GAA to forget the American tours, the 70,000 crowds at All-Ireland finals, and concentrate instead on the grassroots parish games. 'Only by cultivating the mediocre, by having more people playing the games instead of watching others play, will a general and even standard of excellence be maintained.'

The 1947 New York experience had convinced the GAA that they had a valuable nationalist pageant on their hands. In 1948 and in subsequent years, more effort was expended in cultivating the symbolic importance of All-Ireland day. 'Faith of our Fathers' joined 'Amhrán na bhFiann' as a pre-match hymn after the Polo Grounds final. The presence of a Tyrone team from the 'severed six' in the 1948 minor final proved a good starting point.

The crowds were way beyond what Croke Park could handle. It would be ten years before anyone would think of extending the grounds to handle the new crowds.

Cavan's efforts to become the leading football team of their generation continued in 1948. They suffered the indignity of losing an eight-point lead when they met Cork in the 1948 National League final, and were forced to come back for a draw in injury time from a 45 yard free by Pete Donohue. The replay was delayed until after the championship, and Cavan won easily, 5-8 to 2-8.

By then, Cavan were the Sam Maguire Cup-holders as well, after a frenetic campaign. Alongside Antrim, they had transformed Ulster's football final from an irrelevancy that merited three paragraphs in the national newspapers into a national event.

Clones station could not handle fourteen special trains in the same hour for the 1948 Ulster final, but the new park there was proving such a favourite that an Antrim proposal that the match be held in Croke Park was turned down. When the arguments stopped and the football started, Cavan were stung into action by a second half goal by Antrim's Joe McCallin. Cavan tacked on five points and had a late goal from Pete Donohue for a convincing 2-12 to 2-4 win. Goals had been exchanged in the first half by Edwin Carolan of Cavan and Brian McAleer of Antrim. Tyrone had a new star when they hammered Fermanagh to reach the semi-final—a diminutive player called Iggy Jones.

Leinster was in flux before facing Cavan in the semi-final. Four Leinster semi-finalists all felt they could take the Leinster title in 1948.

A Louth goal from White helped beat neighbours Meath 2-6 to 2-5 in a thriller, while Wexford saw off the last Carlow bid for honours by 3-9 to 4-5 with a Padge Kehoe goal in the very last minute.

Cavan built up a massive first half lead against Louth in the semi-final. They went 1-10 to 0-1 ahead before another series of shocks. Fagan, Mick Hardy and Ray Mooney got three Louth goals in quick succession. Another was disallowed. Ray Mooney was narrowly wide and eventually Hardy got Louth's fourth goal. With Louth needing a goal to draw, Casey tried to fist the ball over Benson's head, only to see the goalkeeper make a dramatic fingertip catch. The 51,117 spectators breathed out, and Cavan went through by 1-14 to 4-2 with the phrase 'by the fingertips' on everybody's mind.

In Connacht, Mayo and Galway served up two and a half finals of the finest quality after Galway newcomer Frankie Stockwell helped see off champions Roscommon with his first championship goal. In that watershed semi-final, E. Keogh got two more and Galway saved a late Roscommon penalty to win 3-4 to 1-4. When they met Mayo in the final, Galway trailed 2-3 to 0-3 at half-time, thanks to Tom Langan and Peter Solan goals for Mayo. Then Canavan started Galway's revival in the second half and Stockwell scored the equalising point to make it 2-4 to 1-7. The replay was coming to a close when Galway's Tom Sullivan, from a penalty, and Mayo's Peter Solan exchanged goals in injury time. The thrills continued in extra time. Seán Mulderrig landed the winning goal for Mayo and Pádraig Carney added a point to make it 2-10 to 2-7.

Ageing Kerry had their lead cut back to two points in the Munster final before 40,000 spectators in Killarney, after J. Ahearne scored a Cork goal in the closing stages. But Maurice O'Connor and Tom O'Connor goals in each half saw them through by 2-9 to 2-6.

Throwing in the ball for the Munster final was clerical war hero Hugh O'Flaherty, the monsignor who used the Vatican to smuggle POW refugees out of fascist Italy during the Second World War, immortalised in J. P. Gallagher's book, *The Scarlet Pimpernel of the Vatican*, and Jerry London's 1983 film, *The Scarlet and the Black.*

Kerry trailed by three points at half-time in their semi-final against Mayo, then collapsed completely in the second half, failed to score and went out 0-13 to 0-3. It was the last appearance in Croke Park of many of the team. Goalkeeper Dan O'Keeffe had won most honours of all, seven All-Ireland medals, and played until he was 41. Born in Fermoy, his family moved to Tralee when he was 9.

The final was a game of two diverse halves, one of the most extraordinary in football history. Cavan allowed Mayo to come back from twelve points down to equalise, then won 4-5 to 4-4 with a late point. Cavan's sharpshooter Peter Donohue suffered an unprecedented attack of the jitters.

Tony Tighe got two goals as Cavan went 3-2 to nil up at half-time. Mick Higgins struck the fourth early in the second half, but by the time John Joe

O'Reilly was carried off with a shoulder injury, Peter Solan had already jolted Mayo into action. Eamonn Mongey got the equalising point, and Cavan watched breathlessly as Peter Donohue missed three scoring chances before landing the winning point. Carney had a miss from a Mayo free. Donohue missed another for Cavan. Carney's penalty goal was the first in a final since the 1940 decision to introduce the goalkeeper v kicker situation.

This was the finest hour of the new Cavan team. Goalkeeper John Dessie Benson had the most valuable fingertips in Gaeldom; full backs Willie Doonan, Brian O'Reilly and Paddy Smith prided themselves on their first half display; half backs P. J. Duke, team captain John Joe O'Reilly and Simon Deignan were the most formidable half line seen to date; Phil 'Gunner' Brady partnered Victor Sherlock at midfield; two-goal Tony Tighe, balding 1930s hero Mick Higgins and John Joe Cassidy were the half forwards; while the front-line marksmen were Joe Stafford, Pete Donohue and Edwin Carolan.

Opposition teams were trying to do it 'the Cavan way'. But successful hand passing needs pacey forwards, and Cavan's were not getting any younger.

25 SEPTEMBER 1949. MEATH 1-10, CAVAN 1-6, CROKE PARK

> 'There has always been an unusual rivalry between these border counties in many things, but particularly in football.'
>
> *Anglo-Celt*, 24 September 1949

Cavan's three-in-a-row dream creaked. Their closest call in many years in Ulster came when they faced an Armagh team bolstered by the near-successful juniors of 1948 in the provincial final. Pete Donohue sent a 14 yard free to the net for a 1-2 to 0-3 half-time lead, then an Armagh comeback was prompted by S. McBreen's goal from a high ball that deceived the goalkeeper. Foxy Cavan held on to win 1-7 to 1-6.

Antrim had tested Cavan's mettle by coming back from eleven points behind to a more respectable 3-7 to 2-6, although even a Brian McAleer goal disallowed near the end for 'whistle gone' would not have given them victory in the end.

Kerry went out of the Munster championship in dramatic circumstances. Clare scored their most spectacular victory in championship history when they beat Kerry in the semi-final at Ennis.

At half-time Clare trailed 0-2 to 0-5 and it seemed to be the same old story over again. But when Kerry had a goal at the start of the second half from Gerald O'Sullivan to go seven points up, it was Clare who ignited. J. Murrihy had a point, T. Kelly sent to Murphy for a goal, Daly came through for a point, and Niall Crowley and Pat Crohan struck for goals to complete the shock.

Thus came to an undignified end a formidable Kerry team. Long-serving goalkeeper Dan O'Keeffe was the one who made the record books. His seven medals went unequalled for 40 years. He famously placed a horseshoe at the back of the net for luck before every big match.

Kerry affections were reserved for Paddy Kennedy of Anascaul, however. In 1984 he was still rated as Kerry's greatest midfielder ever against competition such as Pat 'Aeroplane' O'Shea, Mick O'Connell and contemporary Jack O'Shea. He did not make the 1999 Team of the Millennium, but according to Micheál Ó Muircheartaigh, his son said that Paddy would have been happy to stand aside to make way for the boy wonder from Laois.

Kennedy appeared as a tall, slim Tralee CBS student when Kerry were completing four in a row in 1932. He won two Munster colleges medals, played minor in 1933 and 1934, and also played for the Kerry juniors in 1934. He made his senior debut at 19, but Kerry did not compete in the 1935 championship for political reasons. Initially he had difficulty holding down a place in the half forwards and was dropped for the replay of 1937.

Paddy was just 6 feet tall but looked much taller because he was so slim. In 1939 he came to work for the Gardaí in Dublin and joined several Kerry colleagues on the Dublin Geraldines team. They won three Dublin championships and he continued to play with them through the 1940s. When Gus Cremin was dropped for the 1946 replay, Kennedy took over the captaincy. Despite the name for not being able to handle rough opponents, he dominated midfield in the 1946 replay, earning a reputation that outlasted him.

Munster's other semi-final was hectic for other reasons: the referee had to be escorted by Gardai away from the ground after Cork's four-point win over Tipperary. Cork easily beat Clare 3-6 to 0-7 in the Munster final as Cork's first goal from P. O'Donnell proved the turning point of the game.

As Cavan beat Cork 1-9 to 2-3 in the All-Ireland semi-final, Simon Deignan was the inspiration and Peter Donohue the marksman. Donohue scored five of the Cavan points and J. J. Cassidy the goal at the start of the second half.

Brainwave of the 1949 championship belonged to Kilkenny: they played their second team in the senior championship against Wicklow and their first in the junior championship! What that was supposed to achieve was anybody's guess. They lost the senior tie by sixteen points, a point less than their previous first team to compete in 1945!

Westmeath won their second Leinster final place, also in a replay. Peter Molloy scored seven points as they totally dominated three-quarters of the match against Offaly to win 0-8 to 1-2. Molloy, who later played soccer for Dundalk, Bohemians, Distillery and Notts County, scored 2-2 in the second half of the first game. Smallest man on the field, Johnny Ward, scored three goals when Westmeath gave the first signs of their great run to come. A shock win over Carlow followed, and Ward got the second goal against Laois to reach the semi-final.

But the Leinster cup stayed in Navan. Meath beat Kildare 0-11 to 1-5, Wexford 0-14 to 4-0, and Louth in a thrilling replayed semi-final. The first match resulted in a draw, 1-5 each. A swollen 31,845 attendance watched the replay again being drawn, 2-9 to 3-6, before Meath eventually won 2-5 to 1-7 at the third attempt before a 39,034 attendance, almost 2,000 more than at the Leinster final. The incidents from those games went into football folklore: Meegan's equalising point for Meath in the first drawn match, Louth's dramatic equalising point in the replay, Quigley's goal at the end of the second replay for Louth, and P. O'Connell's lost-time point for Meath when it seemed a third replay would be necessary.

Meath beat Westmeath 4-5 to 0-6 in a disappointing Leinster final, scoring three goals at the start of the second half for an anticlimactic victory.

Matty McDonnell was the star of Meath's 3-10 to 1-10 semi-final win over Mayo, snatching two of his side's three goals in the second half. Mayo's Peter Solan had gone on a scoring spree in Connacht. He scored a record 5-2 against Sligo in the semi-final, and 2-1 as Mayo trounced surprise finalists Leitrim in the final by 4-6 to 0-3. Eugene Boland's three goals helped Leitrim come back from 1-2 to 1-4 down to beat Galway 3-3 to 1-7 in the semi-final before 9,000 spectators at Carrick-on-Shannon.

The final had all the trappings of the new All-Ireland spectacle of the 1950s. A group of supporters in Donegal hired a private plane to come down for the game. Another group flew over from New York with P. J. Grimes, former hurler and organiser of the Flying Gaels tour, complete with banners.

When attention turned to the playing field, Meath stopped the Cavan run in the end, as Bill Halfpenny proved his worth with the second half goal that prevented the three in a row by 1-10 to 1-6 in a poor final. It was his third goal chance. He missed one and hit the side netting with another in the first half as Meath went 0-7 to 0-3 ahead.

Cavan tried to come back after Halfpenny's goal. Mick Higgins got a goal in reply, but nothing was added to Peter Donohue's total of six points, five from frees. Jim Kearney, who had played on the 1939 All-Ireland final team, was brought out of retirement to partner Paddy O'Connell successfully at midfield for this game.

The neighbours met again in the 1950 League final. This time Cavan won 2-8 to 1-6, and Gunner Brady played his greatest game. Shortly before the game, Cavan team member P. J. Duke had died at the age of 25.

24 SEPTEMBER 1950. MAYO 2-5, LOUTH 1-6, CROKE PARK

> 'I like to regard Louth as the team of the year. Whether it is their spirited fight against an early lead—so evident in all their games this year—or their smart togs, there is no mistaking the fact that a certain glamour is attached to the Wee County men.'
>
> *Sunday Independent*, 24 September 1950

The hand pass had been abolished by the Central Council in August 1945 but forced back on to the rule book by an Antrim motion in 1946. They may not have invented it, but it appeared that Antrim had patented the hand pass. Surprisingly, in 1950 an Antrim motion to abolish the hand pass was passed, probably as a result of the abuse the players received at the hands of Kerry in 1946.

Antrim was still regarded as the home of the hand pass at the time they moved to abolish it. Internal power struggles between the rural and urban clubs in the county are blamed for bringing the Antrim motion to congress. Passing with the closed fist was retained, but open-palm passing was banished for 25 years.

The confusion was immense. The 1950 championship was full of instances of hand passes which were ruled illegal. Carlow's Jim Rea forgot the rule and hand passed to the net in the Leinster quarter-final against Louth. The goal was disallowed, Carlow lost 1-7 to 1-6, and shortly afterwards Michael Reynolds scored a soft goal for Louth, leaving Carlow to ponder on what might have been as Louth went to the All-Ireland semi-final. Kildare's P. Lyons was luckier: when he hand passed a goal against Dublin in the first round, this time it was the referee who forgot! Kildare went through 2-11 to 1-9.

Contrary to expectations, specialists Antrim seemed to be unaffected by the ban imposed on the hand pass. In the Ulster semi-final, they narrowed the gap by two points in a great second half comeback against Cavan, only to lose 1-12 to 2-6. Cavan got through to face Armagh, who were lucky to get to the final at all. Cole missed an equalising chance for Down as Armagh beat them 1-8 to 1-7 in the semi-final. When they met in the Ulster final, a match with scarcely a breeze and scarcely a foul provided a great day for 30,000 excited spectators, the *Anglo-Celt* declared.

Armagh stoked the bonfires with their first Ulster title since 1902 on a score of 1-11 to 1-7. Bill McCorry got the goal from a penalty near the end. It provoked one in reply by Cavan's Gunner Brady. But by then it was all over bar the shouting—and there was lots of that, as busloads returned to bonfires all over Armagh.

Another relatively new rivalry, between Louth and Meath, was sprouting into one of the most even matches in the history of the game. In 1950 the whole nation sat up when the neighbours met in the Leinster final. The semi-finals from which they qualified were equally full of drama. Roger Smyth got Louth's winning goal to beat Kildare 1-10 to 1-8, but only after Kildare had equalised. Brian Smyth's early goal for Meath sufficed for a 1-5 to 0-6 victory as Wexford missed several chances of winning the other semi-final.

Crowds of 36,202 and 25,000 turned out on successive Sundays to see the games. With the teams level at 1-3 each, the final whistle was greeted with boohs the first day because only 29 minutes of the second half had been played. McDonnell (Meath) and Reid (Louth) exchanged goals for a result that the referee appeared over-anxious should finish as a draw.

Louth won a crunching physical replay 3-5 to 0-13 with a late point by Roe, the same player who had just got their second goal minutes earlier. Mick and Hugh Reynolds got first half goals as Louth avenged the previous year's defeat, but only by a single point.

Louth followed this up with a great semi-final victory over Kerry, 1-7 to 0-8. Seán Thornton, who had become the first *Irish Independent* Sports Star of the Week following a great display against Kerry in 1950, made a fine first half double save to keep the half-time deficit down to 0-2 to 0-6, and Peadar Smith snatched the goal and Jim McDonnell the point that brought a historic two-point victory.

Kerry were still recovering from the shock of 1949, especially as Clare almost did it again in the 1950 Munster semi-final: two goals in two minutes from Lynch sent them into a 2-2 to 0-4 half-time lead, but they lost it when McMahon scored a Kerry goal in the second half, and Kerry came back for a 1-6 to 2-3 draw. Kerry won the replay 5-6 to 2-4 in Limerick in terrible conditions.

Kerry came from behind to beat Cork 2-5 to 1-5 in the Munster final when Dan Kavanagh struck for goals twice in two minutes, in the tenth and eleventh minutes of the second half. Cork managed to stay in contention until Kerry's last point from Teddy O'Sullivan four minutes into injury time. Denis 'Toots' Kelleher scored Cork's first half goal to take a 1-5 to 0-3 half-time lead.

With nothing but an unsuccessful League final and an unsuccessful Munster final appearance to show for five years of effort, Clare faded back into oblivion.

Mayo were clearly the team to watch with Meath and Cavan's elimination. An easy draw in Connacht gave Mayo the chance to win the Connacht final 1-7 to 0-4 from Galway's conquerors, Roscommon, having led by just 0-3 to 0-2 at half-time. Then a goal by M. Mulderrig and great combination play between Eamonn Mongey and Pádraig Carney saw that one-point lead grow to six during the second half.

Mayo easily outpaced Armagh's Croke Park debutants with goals from Mick Flanagan, Tom Langan and Peter Solan to win a disappointing semi-final 3-9 to 0-6.

Experience won the All-Ireland. Mayo snatched the title 2-5 to 1-6 with the help of a freak goal five minutes from the end. Seán Boyle tried to clear, Mick Flanagan charged the ball down and ran twenty yards to score a goal. Mick Mulderrig added a point and Louth's dreams lay in tatters.

Mayo had waited a long time for their success. Goalkeeper Willie Durkin; full backs John Forde, Paddy Prendergast and team captain Seán Flanagan; half backs Peter Quinn, Henry Dixon and John McAndrew; Pádraig Carney and Eamonn Mongey at midfield; goalscorer Mick Flanagan, Billy Kenny and Joe Gilvarry at half forward; Mick Mulderrig, Tom Langan, and ace scorer Peter Solan the full forwards made up the team that achieved the breakthrough. They wanted more.

23 SEPTEMBER 1951. MAYO 2-8, MEATH 0-9, CROKE PARK

> 'A Meath team that toiled laboriously with its football, a side which might be said to have trundled through the second half, was defeated much more decisively than the score suggests.'
>
> JOHN D. HICKEY, *Irish Independent*, 24 September 1951

Mayo crushed Galway's resistance 4-13 to 2-3 before a 27,000 crowd in Tuam in one of the poorest ever Connacht finals.

As Mayo's Peter Solan scored three goals, Galway's only source of consolation was the performance of Seán Purcell, who had starred for Galway as they overwhelmed Roscommon in the semi-final. He also got Galway's first goal in the final, but to no avail, as Mayo won by sixteen points, their biggest victory over Galway in a final since 1907.

Mayo were still accepted as one of the country's premier teams, if only by virtue of their six League titles and one All-Ireland in the 1930s. They had announced their revival by winning the 1949 League, beating Louth in the final.

Kerry were still struggling to replace their 1940s combination. They squeezed past Cork into the All-Ireland semi-final 1-6 to 0-4 when Dermot Hannafin from Fenagh palmed the ball to the net in the last minute after a long Cork onslaught in search of a winning goal, during which C. Duggan hit the crossbar and Mick Cahill (who scored four goals against Clare) and D. Murray were wide with great chances.

Veteran Paddy 'Bawn' Brosnan had one of his greatest days in defence for Kerry, his legend boosted by the fact that he had survived a shipwreck to take his place on the team. His trawler was wrecked in Brandon Creek early in the summer and his team mates helped raise funds to replace the boat.

The man who once said 'the only training I needed for football is a few days on dry land, borrow some boots and play away', and who was reputed never to have owned a pair of boots of his own, had been given a pair by Paddy O'Donoghue from Dykegate Lane in Dingle.

Kerry came desperately close to ousting reigning All-Ireland champions in a drawn semi-final. Mayo trailed by four points as the game entered injury time. Brosnan's kick-out fell to Eamonn Mongey, who got the ball to Tom Langan, who palmed a snap goal with the full back out of position and goalkeeper Liam Fitzgerald racing out to reach the ball. Irwin added a point a minute later to force a 1-5 each draw and earn a replay.

Kerry went into full-time training for the replay, unusually for a semi-final, but, in the absence of Dr Eamonn O'Sullivan, it was an ill-disciplined affair. 'People were acting the fooleen', Jas Murphy told Joe Ó Muircheartaigh in his comprehensive 2008 account of Kerry football, *Princes of Pigskin*.

Mick Flanagan got Mayo's goals as they won the replay 2-4 to 1-5 before a new record attendance for a semi-final of 57,345. They had spent the intervening weeks training at Gaughan's guesthouse in Ballina working out how they would use the open spaces of Croke Park to their advantage (future Kerry officials would deride the 'blackboard tactics' deployed by their opponents). But Mayo had to sit uneasily on their two-point lead through nine nail-biting minutes of lost time. Bawn Brosnan was among those who didn't pay much heed to blackboards. 'In our day,' he once said, 'we had a few farmers, a few fishermen and a college boy to take the frees.'

Without the benefit of the hand pass, Antrim came through for their last Ulster title. Forde's early goal was enough to beat Cavan 1-7 to 2-3 in the Ulster final, concluded with a difficult Ray Beirne free from 35 yards in injury time. It was Antrim's third close one of the series. Joe McCallin provided the valuable winning point to beat Donegal 1-6 to 1-5 in a quarter-final replay (Brogan's goal and Brennan's equalising point for Donegal brought the teams back for a second meeting). In the Ulster semi-final, McCallin scored 1-4 in a second half burst when Antrim were trailing by four points to beat defending champions Armagh 1-8 to 0-5. But it was unrated Derry who supplied the shock of the series: McCann's goal beating Monaghan 1-3 to 0-5.

Leinster's 'real final' was between Meath and champions Louth in the semi-final, when a Taaffe equaliser forced the match to a replay, the fourth between the teams in three years. The replay, before a record 42,824 spectators, was the best of the entire championship and one of the best matches ever seen in Croke Park. Brian Smith and Paddy Meegan scored the late points that sent Meath through 0-7 to 0-6. Ironically, all but three points from both matches were from frees.

What was technically the 1951 Leinster final had a smaller crowd, 32,484, and few thrills as Meath had their fifth title sewn up at half-time, had two goals before Laois had scored, and eventually won 4-9 to 0-3.

Against Antrim in the semi-final, Meath amassed a 2-6 to 0-2 lead with a goal at either side of half-time from Paddy Meegan and Jim O'Reilly, before Antrim came storming back with five points and a disallowed O'Hara goal, only to lose 2-6 to 1-7. O'Neill was Antrim's goalscorer, too late to save the game.

The All-Ireland final brought fine weather, and also brought Mayo two goals in the first half which left them a nose ahead, 2-3 to Meath's 0-8. But they still needed Pádraig Carney's three points in the last five minutes for a 2-8 to 0-9 victory.

The first Mayo goal came when a Joe Gilvarry pass set Tom Langan off on a double-swerve solo run in the tenth minute to crack the ball high into the corner of the net. The second came before half-time when Mick Mulderrig floated the ball into the square, it broke between Langan and two Meath defenders, and Joe Gilvarry pounced on the ball to drive it home.

Mayo's Mick Flanagan lost control of the ball as he almost careered through for a third at the start of the second half. Paddy Mehigan concluded: 'After Langan's goal in the tenth minute, these nimble men of the West left no doubt whatsoever of their superiority. At times they were really brilliant and in the second half often made Meath look a mediocre side. Their final winning margin of five points hardly represented their marked superiority in every department of the game—defence, midfield and attack.'

28 SEPTEMBER 1952. CAVAN 2-4, MEATH 1-7, CROKE PARK
12 OCTOBER 1952. CAVAN 0-9, MEATH 0-5, CROKE PARK

> 'Higgins, cool and unconcerned, as if he was taking practice kicks, landed them dead and true over the crossbar, to win the championship for Cavan in a most unusual way.'
>
> P. D. MEHIGAN, *Carbery's Annual*, 1952

At Castlebar in July 1952, Mayo's three-in-a-row seekers came unstuck. Under pressure from early on in the game, they succumbed to three Roscommon goals from Shivnan, Brendan Lynch and Scanlon late in the second half, and Roscommon took the title back by 3-5 to 0-6. 'The most surprising feature about the result was the ease with which it was achieved', the *Leitrim Observer* commented. Sligo too had pressurised Mayo in the first half of the semi-final and led 0-5 to 0-2 at half-time, but the champions had recovered in that game to win 0-9 to 0-6.

Kerry too faltered. Cork knew they had what it took to beat their ageing rivals, having done so in the National Football League the previous November and again in March on their way to the league title.

This time they won in style, finishing with three great Con McGrath points to end up 0-11 to 0-2 ahead, their biggest win over the old enemy since 1906. In the semi-final, Waterford too led Kerry at half-time 1-4 to 0-6. But this time the Kerry men pulled away in the last fifteen minutes, and Waterford had to wait five more years for a historic victory.

That left Cavan and Meath. Cavan beat defending Ulster champions Antrim 3-6 to 2-6, and then Edwin Carolan scored the winning goal nine minutes from the end of a close final with Monaghan that saw the teams level five times in all. Monaghan's semi-final win over Armagh had almost been halted by a crowd invasion fifteen minutes from the end, but the pitch was cleared and Monaghan went on to make their last appearance in a final for 27 years. Meath beat old rivals Louth 1-6 to 0-8, with Paddy O'Brien starring and Brian Smyth getting the goal midway through the second half when they trailed by two points.

The neighbours did not stop at that. Mick Higgins, who had probably his best-ever game against Down in the first round of the 1952 Ulster championship, scored three of Cavan's ten points in the semi-final as they passed Cork with five points in the last ten minutes for an 0-10 to 2-3 victory. But first they suffered a setback goal in each half from Tom Moriarty.

Meath too had their problems when they chose to play with a strong first half wind in their semi-final against Roscommon. Only a Mattie McDonnell goal prevented them from trailing at half-time, but Paddy Meegan and Jim O'Reilly saved them in the end with points against the wind to go through 1-6 to 0-7.

It took two All-Ireland finals to send the cup back to Cavan. Cavan earned a 2-4 to 1-7 draw with one of the most bizarre points in GAA history. Edwin Carolan chased a ball that appeared to go over the end line, and kicked it across the goal. It hit the far post and rebounded over the bar. Much to everyone's surprise, the umpire signalled a point: some speculated that Carolan had been merely kicking the ball back for the kick-out.

It had appeared that Peter McDermott's late goal had secured Meath's victory over Cavan at the time. The drawn match was played in a downpour, and one casualty of the wet ground was Cavan's Mick Higgins who slipped as he was taking a free at the start of the second half.

Meath's Jim Reilly and Cavan's Tony Tighe both hit the post from goal chances. Paddy Meegan hit the post with a point shot in the second half, and Paddy O'Brien of Meath missed a 50 at the end of the game.

Despite more rain, Cavan could thank a sure-footed Mick Higgins for a cherished 0-9 to 0-5 replay victory. While Paddy Meegan missed three frees he should have scored, Higgins scored five and another two from play for a four-point win. Meath's Peter McDermott missed a great chance towards the end when he shot wide with only the goalkeeper to beat.

An anomaly of the final: the Maguire brothers played for opposite teams. Liam and Dessie played for Cavan, while Brendan played for Meath. Brendan was to create another record after he emigrated to the United States. In 1986 he was elected sheriff of San Mateo County, California, with an overwhelming 81,769 votes. After the count it was discovered he had died two months earlier!

Cavan's celebrations were tempered with tragedy. On 1 November 1952 recently retired team captain John Joe O'Reilly died at Curragh Military Hospital.

> Through the length and breadth of Breifne
> they are singing one refrain
> God rest you John Joe Reilly,
> the pride of Cornafean.

That was a landmark of sorts. Cavan have not won another All-Ireland since.

27 SEPTEMBER 1953. KERRY 0-13, ARMAGH 1-6, CROKE PARK

> 'Groans arose from the Armagh crowds around me as the ball flashed a yard wide. Armagh's glorious chance was gone and time was now short.'
>
> P. D. MEHIGAN, *Carbery's Annual*, 1953

In general, champions had a bad time in 1953. Louth beat Meath 1-7 to 1-6 with a 47th-minute goal from Jim McDonnell, then won the Leinster final 1-7 to 0-7 against Wexford.

Offaly reached the Leinster semi-final in the strangest of circumstances. Alo Kelly arrived late and breathless in a borrowed car for the quarter-final meeting with Carlow, then scored a first half goal and crowned it with the winning point.

There were other championship incidents. Wexford hurler Nicky Rackard scored Wexford's winning goal in the quarter-final against Laois with a spectacular left-footed shot. In the first round Westmeath had a goal disallowed against Louth because the Louth backs stopped when somebody in the crowd blew a whistle!

Two weeks later Kerry took the Munster title back from Cork by 2-7 to 2-3. Tom Ashe was the name on everybody's lips after he came on as a sub, scored the winning goal, and then got sent off. As he was walking through the crowd, the Bishop of Kerry, Denis Moynihan, shouted at him, 'You were right, Tom, dead right.' And according to Ashe, 'It was like getting absolution there and then.'

When Waterford met Tipperary in the first round of the Munster championship, the crowd had to wait for 30 minutes for the first score of the match. Eventually, Ormonde scored a goal for Waterford!

All-Ireland champions Cavan bowed out. After 40 minutes of the Ulster final in Belfast, Art O'Hagan grabbed a Mel McEvoy free and put it in the net for a 1-6 to 0-5 victory for Armagh over Cavan. The newly opened Casement Park in Andersonstown, west Belfast, was crammed with 30,000 spectators for the occasion. A Cavan goal by Johnny Cusack was disallowed for over-carrying at the tail end of the game.

Armagh's early conquests included Antrim, when an extraordinary total silence greeted Armagh's winning goal in the quarter-final at Lurgan as a Mal McEvoy 50 dropped into the net.

That left Roscommon. After beating Mayo 1-6 to 0-6, they had to survive the last great objection saga in GAA championship history. Mayo had had their fair share of problems that year. Short several players for the semi-final against Sligo, they had to recruit four subs from their junior team, but when they lost a three-point lead in the dying minutes of the Connacht final, they saw red.

Mayo objected that five players: Aidan Brady, Ned Ryan, Regan, Seamus Scanlan and T. P. Cullen were not born in Roscommon. Roscommon counter-objected that Eddy Moriarty had been born in Boyle and had not properly transferred to Mayo, and that five Mayo players were illegal because they had attended foreign games.

Objections were the great bugbear of four generations of GAA followers. A major championship result had not been changed since Galway had a Connacht semi-final win taken from them in 1930 and the Tipperary hurlers were thrown out of the 1938 Munster championship under the foreign games rule.

But at club level the objection was part and parcel of GAA life, especially after a suicidal 1920 decision that all correspondence should be on Irish watermarked paper. All over the country GAA secretaries strained their eyes to see if team lists and objection slips were on Irish watermarked paper, because if they were not, they were invalid.

Some objections were legitimate complaints against clubs importing players from outside areas. Techniques included asking football impostors the name of their local parish priest to see if they were really from the catchment area of the club they had played for. But the objection had become an art form of its own before it disappeared practically without trace in the 1950s. A whole army of GAA amateur lawyers roamed the council chambers, upturning results and frustrating the best efforts of the footballers.

One of the jokes of the era went: 'Are you going to the match? No, I'm waiting for the objection.' It was an example of how GAA followers found a funny side to the most painful thorn in the side of their sports body.

On 5 August 1953, only four days before the Connacht champions were due to play Armagh in the All-Ireland semi-final, the objections were heard in Castlerea. Crowds converged outside the council meeting in the local technical school, the same place where Roscommon players were in full-time training. Close to midnight the objections were settled: some counter-objection points were lost and the rest withdrawn, and Mayo withdrew their objection.

Roscommon were gone within a week, victims of Armagh in the All-Ireland semi-final. Ger O'Neill was Armagh's main scorer as they pulled 0-8 to 0-7 ahead of Roscommon in the second half of the semi-final.

Kerry beat Louth in the second semi-final with three first half goals, two by the ubiquitous Ashe, for a comfortable 3-6 to 0-10 win. 'I thought I had seen everything from James Murphy in the Munster final,' Mick Dunne wrote in the *Irish Press*, 'but this was nothing to yesterday's performance. The 6 feet 1 inch Garda was right back on the programme but he was everywhere in defence when danger threatened.'

Nobody anticipated the gate-breaking interest that Armagh's appearance in the final would arouse. Their followers outnumbered the Kerry supporters, according to one estimate, by five to one. The official attendance of 86,155 counts only those who got through the turnstiles before the gates at the Hill 16 end were forced. When the gates were closed again, some 5,000 more stood outside, listening to the match on the radio or on loudspeaker relays.

Almost all of the 86,155, and even those who were locked outside, were quick to claim afterwards that they were directly behind the goal where Bill McCorry had one of the most famous penalty misses in Gaelic history. McCorry was given the chance because goalkeeper Johnny Foley handled the ball on the ground (illegal until 1960) 24 minutes into the second half. Armagh trailed by two points, 0-10 to 1-5, at the time, and Armagh claimed a goal at first, asserting that Foley had fumbled the ball over the line. But they seemed happy enough when they got a penalty instead. Foley had been given a horseshoe by Dan O'Keeffe before the pre-match parade. He now needed all the luck he could get.

Corner backs Micksie Palmer and Jas Murphy heckled McCorry and pulled his shorts to distract him. McCorry hit the ball left and wide. 'I was one side of the ball and Jas was on the other,' Micksie said. 'I nearly had one finger on the ball when he was kicking it. We gave Bill plenty of chat as well.'

Armagh panicked and went goal-hunting in their remaining attacks, while scores from John Joe Sheehan and Jackie Lyne put a relieved Kerry four points ahead. Brian Seeley took a point back for Armagh, but Sheehan's third point put the margin back to a heart-breaking four points, and the Armagh supporters muttered prayers for McCorry.

Would Kerry have won anyway? John D. Hickey, writing in the *Irish Independent*, reminisced: 'In the light of the fact that Armagh failed to score from a penalty and that subsequently they squandered many golden chances of points, it may seem ungracious to say so but, everything considered, I have no hesitation in putting on record that Kerry deserved their triumph.'

At that stage, Armagh badly needed another boost like Mal McEvoy's goal. It had come from long range, helped to the net by a defender after eighteen minutes of the first half, and gave Armagh a two-point lead which they lost and regained. Armagh lost Seán Quinn from defence through injury and had to play with three different goalkeepers at various stages of the game.

Kerry, who might have run away with the game in the first quarter, had not the Armagh full back line held steady, trailed by two points ten minutes into the second half. Then Tadhgie Lyne started to pick off the points. Jackie Lyne scored another and John Joe Sheehan the rest for a four-point win.

Their late choice of captain was, controversially, Jas Murphy, after his match-winning semi-final performance. The rumour was that he was chosen because his Tralee club mate, Johnny Foley, was deemed too small to march behind the Artane Boys Band.

26 SEPTEMBER 1954. MEATH 1-13, KERRY 1-7, CROKE PARK

'Beating Kerry in an All-Ireland final is worth two titles.'

PETER MCDERMOTT after the 1954 All-Ireland final

Armagh were shaken by the experience but survived a hairy first round tie in the 1954 Ulster championship against Antrim. As they trailed by a point in 'lost time' at Casement Park, Joey Cunningham burst through on a 25 yard run and sent a long 50 yard shot bouncing to the net.

Luck ran out for Armagh in the Ulster final, where they went out to Cavan 2-10 to 2-5, having fallen six points behind in the first eight minutes. A Gerry Keyes centre dropped into the net after just two minutes, and Paddy Carolan shot a second goal through the goalie's legs. Cavan went ten points ahead. Then J. McBreen and Art O'Hagan goals revived Armagh's pride. The crowd invaded the pitch near the end, but play resumed.

Meath also had their lucky breaks defending the Leinster title in the quarter-final against Wicklow. Paddy Meegan scored the winning point in the ninth minute of lost time, Wicklow having led by two points at the end of the 60 minutes. The 'long count' went into Wicklow folklore, and Meath went into a semi-final against Longford, where Kevin Lenehan rallied Meath to overtake Longford's lead early in the second half, after an early Arnold Maher goal put the underdogs on top until early in the second half.

Their Leinster final opponents Offaly where getting a reputation for coming back, especially when they beat Dublin 2-5 to 2-4 with goals from Seán Kinehan and Mick Furlong after the early double setback of goals from Kevin Heffernan and Des Ferguson. Meath beat the Offaly men 4-7 to 2-10 with goals from Moriarty, Meegan and veteran Peter McDermott (who came on at midfield when Tom Duff broke his leg) to barely survive an Offaly rally that almost brought them a first-ever title after Paddy Casey and Seán Kinehan scored goals in the dying minutes. Offaly were left to ponder on might-have-beens, particularly after Paddy Casey's missed penalty in the first half.

It would now be customary for provincial champions to retire to Mount Nugent or Killarney for full-time training at this stage. Except that full-time training had been banned in a controversial decision by congress the previous April. Since Louth had introduced it in 1913, almost every county had gone into full-time training for major games. Counties such as Kerry and Galway, whose teams were separated by vast distances, were most affected by the ban. But within two years the more prevalent motor cars were being utilised for twice-a-week evening training, sustained over a longer period than was previously the case, by even the rural counties.

Meath's lucky run continued in the All-Ireland semi-final. Against Cavan, they came back from three points down at half-time with a Brian Smyth goal early in the second half and hung on to their one-point lead, 1-5 to 0-7, as Brian Gallagher missed a 30 yard free with the last kick of the match.

Galway beat Connacht championship favourites Mayo in the provincial semi-final 2-4 to 1-5 with goals from Halliday and McHugh in a three-minute spell at the end of the first half. Mayo ended Roscommon's reign by 4-9 to 1-7 in the first round with four extraordinary goals from a John Lynch own goal, Mick Flanagan, Peter Solan and Dan O'Neill.

Galway were now expected to canter through a final against Sligo, but when they conceded midfield they almost paid the price. Sligo had an equalising goal disallowed and a free-out awarded instead. Mick Gaffney and Mick Christie goals brought Sligo back into the game in the second half, but Galway held on to win 2-10 to 3-4.

Kerry retained the Munster championship with a 4-9 to 2-3 victory over Cork as Cork's star forward Neilly Duggan was sent off with Kerry full back Ned Roche. They then weathered a Galway comeback to win the All-Ireland semi-final 2-6 to 1-6.

Gerry Kirwan stormed past two defenders, only to miss a great goal chance after 58 minutes. Frank Evers too went for points from close-in frees in the 43rd and 55th minutes. Greaney's goal came in the second minute of injury time, leaving Galway three points behind. Paudie Sheehy and Tadhgie Lyne got Kerry's valuable first half goals.

Houdini team Meath won the final, 1-13 to 1-7. The crowds were less boisterous, and they got a blast of Bryan MacMahon pageantry at half-time to quell their rebellious spirits: 'Eire's Four Beautiful Fields' with Mother Ireland calling her four provinces to a united Ireland.

At that stage Meath trailed by a point, 0-7 to 1-5, but piled on the pressure in the second half, and eventually Tom Moriarty's twentieth-minute goal sealed victory. Michael Grace had a brilliant match for Meath.

J. J. Sheehan got Kerry's first half goal two minutes before half-time when he lashed out with his boot after missing a high ball. Meath deserved their goal in reply. It came when Peter McDermott's shot was saved by the goalkeeper but rebounded for a quick interchange between McDermott and Moriarty before entering the net.

P. D. Mehigan concluded: 'Lack of their usual collective training in camp hurt Kerry. Of that I have no doubt. Some restricted but more controlled training may be introduced. They were too bad to be true. Meath, in my opinion, played the best football in recent years—most deserving winners.'

Kerry lined out in blue, and a little terrier joined their first attack as he chased the play. The Kerry Blue terrier, it was often said, fights best when he is on his back.

25 SEPTEMBER 1955. KERRY 0-12, DUBLIN 1-6, CROKE PARK

> 'No defeat as a manager ever hit me like 1955. That was the first time there. It was Kerry. I had great hopes and so on and so on. That formed a large part of what I became as a person.'
>
> KEVIN HEFFERNAN

Gaelic football was extremely short on instructional literature. Kerry player Dick Fitzgerald wrote the first instructional book on Gaelic football in 1914. This slim volume was the sole work to serve a generation of footballers. Larry Stanley wrote a fascinating instructional manual for Gaelic footballers in the 1940s, but it was only distributed among Garda members. In effect, little changed between the 1913 Fitzgerald tactics and the 1950s.

In the days of full-time training, Kerry's trainer for thirteen All-Ireland victories after 1924 was J. P. O'Sullivan's son, Dr Eamonn, a fourth-placed triple jumper in the 1932 Olympics, and the man whose philosophy summed up the first 30 years of the fifteen-a-side game. Dr Eamonn's way of winning an All-Ireland was to bring the team away for two weeks' sharpening up before the big day. Employers were asked to release players. It sounded suspiciously professional for an all-amateur game. Some counties did it for provincial finals. Kerry waited until the All-Ireland, until the system was abolished in 1954.

Four years later Dr Eamonn produced a book, *The Art and Science of Gaelic Football*, but the game technique he described was becoming outdated. He preached that players should stick rigorously to their field positions, because 'Close adherence to positioning by the forwards opens up play and gives more scope to each player for the development of scoring opportunities. What has been described as machine forward play is based entirely on positioning and is incapable of development when indiscriminate wandering to other sectors leads to bunching.'

Dr Eamonn elaborated on a whole variety of basic skills: follow the centre line of the ball in catching and kicking; follow through a kick; never hesitate; clasp ball to the chest; pass only when necessary; cover opponent's kicks; hop the ball only to gain time; train on the weak foot.

He was sticking to traditional methods as Kerry set out on their 1955 campaign, determined that even without full-time training they could continue their winning streak. They were lucky to get out of Munster. In the provincial final, before 23,403 people in Killarney, Jim Donovan gave Cork a goal start to each half, but his colleagues shot seventeen wides. Kerry, who had just eight wides of their own, survived by 0-14 to 2-6.

In the 1955 Leinster final, Dublin scored five goals against All-Ireland champions Meath. Dublin full forward Kevin Heffernan roved out of position and took Meath's full back Paddy O'Brien with him in one of the most famous instances of the 'roving full forward' tactic. Heffernan scored one goal himself and started the moves for three others, as Dublin ran riot and beat the All-Ireland champions by a record twenty points, even larger than the feted Kerry v Dublin match of 1978. Heffernan was not the first roving full forward, but never had a legendary name in football been so completely outfoxed by such a ploy.

Not since Wexford in 1894 did All-Ireland champions make as dramatic an exit as Meath did in the 1955 Leinster final. Gaelic football was shaken. Indeed Meath had been lucky to survive the Leinster quarter-final. Kildare showed signs of revival and were forced to a replay only by Patsy Ratty's free which came back off the post and was sent to the net by the same player—it should not have been allowed under the rules. The teams were level seven times in all in the replay, before Meath went through 1-9 to 0-11 after extra time. Then Meath had to rely on a late point from Michael Grace to beat minnows

Westmeath 0-10 to 1-6. Mick Scanlon was Westmeath's hero for a beautiful 44th-minute goal, and villain for a last-minute miss that would have put them into the final.

The country was now looking to Mayo to see if the Dublin forward machine would be as efficient again. Youth was not on Mayo's side. Captain Tom Langan was now 33 and Seán Flanagan, also 33, came out of retirement. As Mayo beat Roscommon 3-11 to 1-3 in the Connacht final, Langan got two goals and Seamus O'Donnell scored the other from a defensive mix-up. Roscommon had spent £40 flying Gerry O'Malley home from Denmark.

In Ulster, Cavan's Pete Donohue too came out of a three-year retirement and scored 0-8 to help beat 1953 junior champions Derry in the Ulster final as Charlie 'Chuck' Higgins missed a 28th-minute penalty for Derry.

Both All-Ireland semi-finals were drawn. Veteran Langan got Mayo's goal in their semi-final, 1-4 to 0-7, putting the Dubliners under pressure within 90 seconds of the start of the second half. Mayo shot eight wides, three from easy positions. Forwards were in short supply again in the replay. Jim Curran was the only Mayo player to score, and he missed just one shot while scoring his team's 1-7 against Dublin's 1-8. Freaney scored the 25th-minute goal that sent the Dubliners on their way.

Cavan seemed destined for the final after a Gallagher goal and four Pete Donohue frees before John Cronin launched a high ball which Tadhgie Lyne, whose total of 5-42 for the year was to earn him footballer of the year, battled into the net for a late Kerry goal. 'Tadhgie Lyne is a tall clumsy looking man,' wrote Benedict Kiely in the *Irish Press*, 'but he has an uncanny knack of doing the right thing at the right time and for getting there before anyone else.'

Cavan got back for the point that earned a replay, but went down to four second half goals from John Sheehan, Johnny Culloty and two from Mick Murphy before a record semi-final attendance of 71,504 for the replay double bill.

After the escapes of the semi-final, it is hard to work out why Dublin were such firm favourites. In the final, Kerry shocked a fancied Dublin side by 0-12 to 1-6. Jim Brosnan, who was flown home from New York for the game, scored two crucial points at the start of the second half. But they had to survive a goal from Ollie Freaney five minutes from the end and a desperate four-minute onslaught in search of the equaliser.

Tadhgie Lyne scored six of the Kerry points. Flying fair-haired Jerome O'Shea made two spectacular second half saves. 'Two flying saves in the second half must be treasured in the memory of everyone who has seen the game,' Padraig Puirséil wrote in the *Irish Press*. 'One of the finest saves I ever hope to see was effected by Jerome O'Shea. A hard drive that looked a goal all the way, had beaten the rest of the defence and was flying for the net, just beneath the bar. Jerome came with a tremendous leap to snatch the leather at the last minute and bring off a clearance that was spectacular as it was dramatic.'

Kerry captain John Dowling was so exhausted he couldn't climb the steps for the presentation for a few minutes after the final whistle. He recalled: 'It was one of the most shattering defeats ever inflicted on a team in an All-Ireland final. Dublin could make all the excuses they wanted to afterwards, but the simple fact was that we had proved our football to be superior. We were in peak condition and we were determined that we would break the back of this so-called mighty football machine.'

The old school held sway.

7 OCTOBER 1956. GALWAY 2-13, CORK 3-7, CROKE PARK

> 'I never anticipated such polished and almost classical football from this recently sprung Galway side.'
>
> P. D. MEHIGAN, *Carbery's Annual*, 1956

The clear-out of 1955 champions started on 17 June 1956 when Mayo's team of warriors all grew old together. They crumbled by 5-13 to 2-5 against old rivals Galway. Gerry Kirwan and Frankie Stockwell shared the goals, and Seán Purcell kicked eight points.

Roscommon were left equally humiliated after Kirwan's goal helped send them crashing out by 3-12 to 1-5. Sligo's promise of 1954 had never been fulfilled, but on-form Galway did not offer them an opportunity as Seán Purcell's inspired performance on a slippery sod made him man of the match in the Connacht final.

Cork were upset that they had been left behind as Kerry took another All-Ireland. Convinced that they were the second best team in the country, they ousted the All-Ireland champions at the second attempt, despite their habit of giving away last-minute goals to Kerry.

The first meeting started disastrously for Cork, when their goalkeeper thought a lob from D. O'Shea was going wide until it dropped into the net. Cork led 0-6 to nil at half-time in that game, and it could have been more, had not a goal by Neilly Duggan been adjudged to have been thrown to the net. But they still led by three points with just a minute to go, when Kerry's Jim Brosnan snatched an equalising goal to draw 2-2 to 0-8. Then in the replay Cork were leading by three points when Jack Cronin scored a dramatic equalising goal through a crowded Cork goalmouth, 1-7 each.

It looked like Cork had blown their chance. But there were 30 seconds still remaining, and corner back Paddy Driscoll kicked out to Neilly Fitzgerald, who soloed through to the 21 yard line for the winning point for Cork. Fitzgerald had been a teenage protégé and played for four years on the Cork minors.

The replay was played on the same bill as both the Munster junior finals, and Ardfert player Tom Collins played in all three games! He lined out for Kerry junior hurlers in their historic first-title win over Waterford, for Kerry junior footballers in another win over Waterford, and then came on as a substitute for Mick Murphy towards the end of the senior football final.

As Meath faded out in the first round to Kavanagh's goal for Offaly by 1-14 to 1-5, Louth went out to a Ned Treacy goal for Kildare 1-9 to 0-9, and Dublin followed in the semi-final, goals by John Ryan and Padge Kehoe sending Wexford through 2-7 to 0-7. Leinster had to chose their new champions between Kildare and Wexford.

Kildare won the title 2-11 to 1-8 with a clinching goal five minutes from the end by Ned Loughlin, son of 1928 All-Ireland-winning goalscorer. Ned Treacy got the first after a great solo run ten minutes before half-time, when Kildare looked like losing touch against a rampant Wexford team which had just been triggered into action by Mick Byrne's seventh-minute goal.

Leinster provided the accident of the year. A spectator upset the Dublin-Wicklow quarter-final when he blew a whistle. The crowd thought it was full-time and invaded the pitch. The referee didn't get the ball back to restart the match!

No 'new' county had won an Ulster title since 1900, but it was about to happen three times in four years. Tyrone were through first. They beat Derry 3-7 to 2-4. Jody O'Neill was Tyrone's semi-final star as M. Kerr and F. Higgins's first half goals helped to beat Monaghan 2-9 to 0-7. More traditional counties, Cavan and Armagh, had a player each sent off as their semi-final was fought out in a downpour. Cavan qualified for their eighteenth successive Ulster final by four points.

In the final, Tyrone triumphed in the rain. Jackie Taggart caught the Cavan defence out of position after two minutes, Donal Donnelly had a second half shot fumbled to the net by the goalkeeper, and Iggy Jones saw his shot drop between the goalkeeper's legs. It all came together for a first-ever Ulster title.

A second half downpour didn't help the Croke Park debutants in the All-Ireland semi-final. It came just as Tyrone were overcoming their big-match nerves. Purcell was again the hero of the semi-final, as Galway took a five-point lead and defended it ferociously to win 0-8 to 0-6. Ten of the fourteen scores in that game came from frees, five of Galway's from Purcell, and Tyrone's mainly from Frankie Donnelly.

Cork's 0-9 to 0-5 victory over Kildare was featureless: according to sportswriter John D. Hickey, the worst he had ever seen. Cork kicked 21 wides,

Kildare five, and two great saves from Kildare goalkeeper Dessie Marron were the only saving graces.

A polio epidemic in Cork city caused both All-Ireland finals to be postponed, the hurling for three weeks to 23 September, and the football final by two weeks to 7 October. Because the camogie final was played in between, it meant that Cork lost three All-Ireland senior finals in Croke Park in a three-week period in 1956!

The All-Ireland football final was a vast improvement on the semi-finals, bringing five goals and one of the greatest punch-pass partnerships seen in Croke Park. Galway were using the closed fist as skilfully as any of the 1940s hand passers, and Frankie Stockwell—'the will-o'-the-wisp, waltzing, jinking Stockwell'—emerged as the hero of a 2-13 to 3-7 victory.

He scored 2-5 and had another goal disallowed for a record which was to stand for twenty years. Stockwell was just half the story. His 'terrible twin' Seán Purcell sent in the line ball which allowed him to skip in to sidefoot the first goal, Purcell's punched pass gave him the second, and a third was disallowed before half-time.

But a deflected Cork shot was not held by the defence and was tipped in by Johnny Creedon, another was sent sizzling to the net from twenty yards by Denis 'Toots' Kelleher, and then a low Kelleher shot which had been half-stopped by the goalkeeper trickled across the line for Cork's third second half goal. It inspired Cork back to within a point of Galway and it was left to Purcell and Stockwell to wrap up victory with a point each.

Hickey even forgot that Cork-Kildare semi-final: 'Never, I feel certain, was there an All-Ireland Senior Football Final so completely satisfying as the 1956 decider. The game had just everything. The splendour of the football was inspiring, if not awesome; the tenseness of the closing stages simply beggars description; there were individual displays to rank with the greatest I have seen; and yet, despite the supercharged atmosphere of the combat, the conduct of every one of the contestants was a model of good sportsmanship.'

22 SEPTEMBER 1957. LOUTH 1-9, CORK 1-7, CROKE PARK

> 'We can't exactly remember who played better that day, Dermot O'Brien or his accordion?'
>
> LIAM CAHILL, An Fear Rua website, 12 June 2000

Cork got a clean run into the All-Ireland semi-final almost by default. National League finalists Kerry lost the Munster semi-final to Waterford in one of the most astonishing championship games of them all.

Kerry were under strength. Seán Murphy was taking medical exams; Mick

Murphy and Tom Moriarty were unable to travel; Mixie Palmer was living in Waterford; and goalkeeper Marcus O'Neill was sulking because he was turned down for the captaincy. He was suspended by Kerry for six months for not turning out. Among their call-ups were Mick O'Dwyer.

Contrary to rumour, the hackney driver Tom Cournane did not play. Many of the Kerry team had gone to Waterford the night before, but one of those discovered half an hour before the match that he had left his boots in the hotel. The county board secretary was dispatched to buy a pair for him.

And contrary to another rumour, stand-in goalkeeper Tim Barrett, who had come to the game as a spectator, was no novice. He had Munster minor and colleges medals. His brother John, who had come to cover the game for the *Kerryman*, was drafted in as a substitute. Nevertheless, Kerry led 0-6 to 0-2 at half-time and had gone six points ahead, when Noel Power scored a Waterford goal after 45 minutes. Goalkeeper Tim Barrett was shouldered over the line for a second goal with five minutes to go, and Tom Cunningham struck the winning point in the last minute for Waterford.

It was a breakthrough Waterford had promised since Cork scraped by them with a flukey goal in 1953. A two-year suspension on the two top clubs slowed the progress down.

In the Munster final, Jim Timmons started the scoring with a Waterford point, but Waterford disappeared after that, and failed by a massive 0-16 to 1-2, Cork having to survive a rough-and-tumble second half after leading 0-6 to 0-2 at half-time. Waterford never got into the game after Kerry's Jackie Lyne was selected to referee the final, and did so wearing a green-and-gold Kerry jersey with No. 4 on the back!

Cork avenged their 1956 defeat against impressive Connacht champions Galway in the All-Ireland semi-final. By beating Roscommon 0-13 to 0-7, Galway were afforded the opportunity to stage a gala opening of their new Pearse Stadium in Salthill, where they beat Leitrim 4-8 to 0-4.

In the All-Ireland semi-final, Galway started with four points without reply, but Cork got their own back with goals from Fitzgerald and Duggan in a seven-minute period in the second quarter of play, fell a point behind in the second half, but two late points by Eric Ryan, the first allowed to hop over the bar, gave them a one-point victory, 2-4 to 0-9.

Leinster champions Kildare crashed to Louth in the semi-final by a massive 5-8 to 1-9, thanks to three Jim McDonnell goals and one each by Roe and O'Brien. Louth had trailed by five points at half-time against Wexford in the quarter-final, but were stung into life by a superb Stephen White solo-run goal which ended with him punching 25 yards into the net, and won 1-12 to 0-9.

Wicklow won their first Leinster semi-final place in 60 years. John Timmons starred for Wicklow, scoring two goals against both Laois and

Meath. Dublin ended Wicklow's run with a goal from Conroy, two from Boyle and a successful guard on Timmons. To add insult to injury, the following year Timmons won an All-Ireland medal in the Dublin colours!

Dublin now had unfinished business from 1955 to look after, but Louth took command of the Leinster final in the second half to win 2-9 to 1-7. Dublin's Kevin Heffernan and goalscorer Des Ferguson managed to hit the posts, while Jim McDonnell got a Louth goal in each half. Showband star Dermot O'Brien set up the second, and Louth swept from four points down to a four-point victory.

For the first time since 1938, Cavan missed the Ulster final. Derry got revenge for 1955 in their semi-final against Cavan with a Roddy Gribben goal six minutes into the second half to win 1-10 to 1-9. But Tyrone held off optimistic Derry's challenge in a final that would have been unthinkable five years before, the first between two of the six counties since partition. Frank Higgins got a Tyrone goal midway through the first half. With thirteen minutes to go the scores were level. Jackie Taggart and Frank Donnelly got the points for Tyrone's 1-9 to 0-10 victory.

But Tyrone's second All-Ireland semi-final was no more successful than their first. They went 0-5 to 0-1 up, trailed by just 0-6 to 0-5 at half-time, but lost 0-13 to 0-7 to Louth, who turned on a great second half display, despite a penalty miss by Stephen White.

Louth, Ireland's smallest county, had missed out in 1950 and 53. They were not expected to go the whole way against biggest county Cork in 1957. Their 1-9 to 1-7 victory came thanks to Seán Cunningham's goal five minutes from the end. Kevin Beahan sent in a line ball, placed neatly for Beahan to punch past Liam Power into the net.

Beahan, Jimmy Roe and Cunningham had picked off the scores to bring Louth back from three points down shortly after half-time. A switch between Stephen White and Peadar Smith helped thwart Cork, whose goal had come two minutes before half-time from a long Neil Duggan lob that entered the net, with Tom Furlong and Denis Kelleher harassing the defence. Louth were the cheers!

28 SEPTEMBER 1958. DUBLIN 1-12, DERRY 1-9, CROKE PARK

> 'I have heard many thundering receptions for teams entering the playing pitch at Croke Park, but when these red and white clad athletes from Derry pranced in on Sunday, the roofs on the stands shook with the volume of cheering.'
>
> P. D. MEHIGAN, *History of Gaelic Football* (1941)

Dublin were left wondering where they had gone wrong. Since 1955 they had brought in new techniques, innovative tactics and a new mobility to the game of Gaelic football. Now they were backing that up with a more physical presence.

They showed erratic shooting in the 1958 Leinster quarter-final against declining Meath: one shot hit the corner flag, but Des Foley got the vital goal in the end, and three first half goals saw off surprise semi-finalists Carlow. They defeated Louth in the Leinster final at Navan 1-11 to 1-6 with such ease that they wondered why they had taken so long.

Kevin Heffernan's team augmented their 0-8 to 0-1 half-time lead in driving rain in the second half, and the match was well over before Heffernan scored a clinching goal five minutes from the end. Kevin Beahan got a Louth penalty goal in reply, but only Beahan and McDonnell (and he only once) managed to get scores from the Louth forward sector.

In Connacht, Galway fought off Leitrim's best challenge in 30 years with a rugged, disruptive game. Galway's victory was 2-10 to 1-11 on the scoreboard, but the moral victory belonged to Leitrim. Packie McGarty got a Leitrim equaliser sixteen minutes into the second half. Seán Purcell, Frank Evers and Mattie McDonagh notched Galway frees before Cathal Flynn pulled one back for Leitrim, and Galway held on to win a great final by just two points. Galway had led 2-4 to 0-6 at half-time before the brilliant McGarty inspired Leitrim's revival.

He roamed around the field and caused havoc for his Galway opponents, one of whom ripped his jersey in an outrageous foul. McGarty gave Cathal Flynn the pass for a goal fourteen minutes into the second half, but as Leitrim drew level in the last quarter, it began to rain.

The last alias to play in a provincial final was Mike 'Smith' of Leitrim. His real name was Michael McGowan, a Brother based in Cork who was defying monastic rules by playing. E. 'Dowdican' had played for Sligo in 1956. The Leitrim display removed pretensions of the 'real final' from the Galway-Mayo semi-final, which had been decided by two Seán Purcell goals. In the other semi-final, Cathal Flynn's six points helped Leitrim beat over-confident Roscommon for the first time since 1927.

In Munster, Tipperary tried to do a Waterford, and might have done so after they led 0-4 to 0-2 at half-time on a blustery day but for Kerry newcomer Mick O'Dwyer's display. Two goals from Garry McMahon, son of playwright (and 1954 pageant-writer) Bryan, helped Kerry take the Munster title 2-7 to 0-3 against Cork.

Cavan survived two replays against Monaghan in the quarter-final, the first abandoned in extra time when the crowd invaded the pitch, but their great days were over. Derry put them out of the semi-final by 4-7 to 3-6, Seán

O'Connell (scorer of all but two of Derry's points in 1957) scoring two goals. Tyrone too went out at the semi-final stage, thanks to 1-5 from Down's Paddy Docherty.

Derry eventually became champions by beating up and coming Down 1-11 to 2-4 in the first final since 1890 in which neither team had previously won the Ulster championship. Charlie 'Chuck' Higgins scored a Derry goal at the start of the second half, and Down were far too late when they came back with a goal from Jim McCartan, and another penalty goal from Paddy Docherty, stopped by the goalkeeper but at the wrong side of the line, according to the umpire.

Derry were not expected to go any further, but Seán O'Connell had other ideas. A brilliant display by Jim McKeever in the rain pushed Derry into a three-point lead early in the second half. Kerry equalised. O'Connell put Derry a point ahead, and then Smith sent in a free which O'Connell fielded and smashed to the net. Tadhgie Lyne got a goal back for Kerry, but only to cut Derry's victory margin back to 2-6 to 2-5.

Dublin too scraped through, beating Galway 2-7 to 1-9. Johnny Joyce was Dublin's double goalscorer towards the end of the third quarter of the semi-final. Ollie Freaney kicked the winning point from a free after the referee told him it would be the last kick of the match.

As could be expected, Derry were not up to the task of beating Dublin. They entered the field to the most thunderous reception anyone could remember. Then they lost 1-12 to 1-9. But with twenty minutes to go, Derry had drawn level and were still in the hunt.

Owen Gribben shocked Dublin with a goal after the goalkeeper had saved brilliantly twice. But disaster struck for Derry two minutes later. Des Ferguson's centre hopped 25 yards from goal, the full back slipped, and Paddy Farnan was left with a clear run for goal.

Johnny Joyce got Dublin's second goal at the call of time. It was the closest that Columcille's county got to an All-Ireland. Events in Ulster were soon to overtake Derry too.

27 SEPTEMBER 1959. KERRY 3-7, GALWAY 1-4, CROKE PARK

> 'So dense was the throng seeking admission that the stiles were closed almost an hour before the senior game was due to start and an announcement was made requesting the hundreds left outside to move away from the gates.'
>
> *Irish Independent*, 28 September 1959

After Derry's breakthrough came Down. Down's revolutionary approach was to shake Gaelic football into the modern age, adapting and developing the Dublin game. Even in 1959 they tried to play with six interchangeable forwards and introduced off-the-ball running.

Not that they had it easy in Ulster. Brian Morgan scored a morale-boosting goal just before half-time to help Down beat Tyrone 1-12 to 0-4 in a replay. The first day it was Tyrone who led at half-time, and Jim McCartan's goal with ten minutes to go saved Down. It put Down into the final against traditional champions, Cavan, although Derry's shock conquerors, Armagh, felt they were done an injustice in the other semi-final.

Eddie O'Neill had got the Armagh goal that ousted the champions just before half-time in the first round. Then in an Ulster semi-final replay against Cavan, Phil 'Gunner' Brady struck for a Cavan goal eight minutes from the end, when there were three men in the square and the umpire tried in vain to bring the referee's attention to the breach of the rules. The goal stood and Armagh went out by two points.

Down were leading Cavan by six points to two in the Ulster final, when in a twinkling the scoreline changed to 2-10 to 0-2. Brian Morgan scored a goal, Paddy Docherty lofted over three points, and 90 seconds into the second half Tony Hadden shot a second Down goal. Cavan never recovered, and eventual winners by 2-16 to 0-7, Down, became the seventh county to take an Ulster title and Mourneside supporters' dreams were realised in the sweltering heat of Clones.

Hopes for a shock in Connacht the same afternoon were not realised, despite Leitrim's best efforts. Four weeks earlier Leitrim had their first-ever win over Mayo. In a thrill-packed semi-final at Roscommon, Leitrim went 2-6 to nil up at half-time with the help of a strong wind and two goals from Seamus Brogan and Michael Mullen just before half-time. Packie McGarty gave another outstanding midfield display, and Cathal Flynn notched up seven points.

Leitrim hoped to go one better than 1958, but lost to Galway again in the Connacht final, and this time the margin was eleven points. Galway already had three goals at half-time from Frank Stockwell and Seán Purcell (2). Leitrim brought the margin back to seven points before Joe Young and Michael McDonagh struck twice more. Joe Dolan missed a Leitrim penalty.

Having stopped Leitrim, Galway also de-romanticised Down 1-11 to 1-4 with the help of a crushing Seán Purcell penalty nine minutes after half-time, when Galway already led by four points.

Laois appeared to have Dublin on the rack in the Leinster final. They led by six points at the start of the second half before Ollie Freaney punched the goal that changed the course of the game. Cathal O'Leary was man of the match, and Dublin so dominated the second half, they could afford to kick eight wides despite coming back from 2-6 to 0-7 behind to win 1-18 to 2-8. Noel Delaney and Mick Phelan scored Laois's snap goals before half-time.

There followed one of the best semi-finals of the decade, followed in turn by one of the worst finals. In the semi-final, Kerry beat Dublin 1-10 to 2-5 in a game ranked by Mick O'Connell as one of the fastest, most open and best to watch in his entire career: 'It was no accident that some of the best games of the 1950s and early 1960s were those in which the Dublin team was involved. Their attractive brand of combination football was almost totally constructive and they were never wont to adopt spoiling tactics to beat the other side. This was probably their undoing in not harvesting more championships but it was certainly conducive to open, continuous football.' O'Connell came to prominence for his display in that game, running riot in the first half when Dan McAuliffe got the vital goal. Cathal O'Leary moved to mark Mick O'Connell, Paddy Haughey and Ollie Freaney got goals, but Dublin's revival failed by two points.

Kerry went on to beat Galway in yet another disappointing All-Ireland final, thanks to a great display at centre half back from Seán Murphy and a series of switches at half-time. 'On a day when close marking, keen exchanges and bone-hard ground often reduced even long famed stars into very run-of-the-mill footballers,' Padraig Puirséil wrote in the *Irish Press*, 'the UCD medical student gave us the most outstanding exhibition of high catching, long kicking, clever anticipation and intelligent passing that I have ever seen in an All-Ireland.' Mick Dunne was equally fulsome: 'The brilliance of the 27-year-old native of Camp sparkled unforgettably in a bafflingly disappointing final.' In Kerry they recalled it as 'the Seán Murphy final'.

After five minutes Frank Evers stabbed in the first Galway goal from six yards after he seemed to lose possession running through, and it was 0-5 to 1-2 at half-time. 'So close was the charge and counter-charge that there was little spectacular football,' Paddy Mehigan reported. 'Over-anxiety brought many wides. Yet there were some very fine bouts of football which the critics seem to have forgotten.'

Then came the switches, followed by three Kerry goals. A punched Tom Long ball was forced into the net by Dan McAuliffe, and when goalkeeper Jimmy Farrell caught a long John Dowling shot, McAuliffe thundered in on top of him, forcing him to lose possession and drop the ball on the wrong side of the line. A third followed from substitute Garry McMahon, the hero of the previous year's Munster final, who slipped as he sent to the net five minutes from the end. Man of the match was a Kerry defender, wing back Seán Murphy.

Kerry sharpshooter Tadhgie Lyne was married the previous day. Mick O'Connell left the cup in the dressing room in the excitement.

25 SEPTEMBER 1960. DOWN 2-10, KERRY 0-8, CROKE PARK

'A good job only fifteen of them can play.'

EAMONN YOUNG comments in the *Sunday Independent* on the level of Down support, 25 September 1960

Faster, fitter, first to the ball, that was the football played by twentieth-century Down. Schooled on the Queen's University stylists of 1958, they took a clean Ulster championship in 1960. Nobody could match their finesse, starting with a spiritless 0-14 to 1-4 victory over Antrim, a 2-11 to 0-7 victory over Monaghan which showed just how superior they were in terms of fitness, and a crushing 3-7 to 1-8 victory over Cavan before a 33,000 crowd in Clones.

They owed their success to their blitzkrieg starts. Down dashed away on the off in that final with a Paddy Docherty goal after just 30 seconds, and another from James McCartan before Cavan had settled down. The final, a repeat of the National League final in which Down had beaten Cavan before 49,451 spectators in Croke Park in May, was still full of drama.

Down owed success to their tactical astuteness. When Cavan had recovered, and six minutes into the second half when the sides were level, largely through the efforts of Con Smith, Down started breaking the ball at midfield rather than trying to catch it. Docherty added another goal and Down's lead was restored.

Leinster had its revolution too. Midland minnows did well in 1960. Westmeath had their best run in 30 years. They reached the semi-final with two goals against Laois to win 2-10 to 1-11, and two more against Kildare for a 2-9 to 2-8 victory, all scored by 19-year-old Georgie Kane, and then blew their big chance against Louth. Westmeath took a 1-1 to 0-1 half-time lead, Mick Carley scoring the point from the throw-in and the goal from a penalty after just eight minutes, then kicked thirteen wides in the second half as Louth demolished their lead. Longford too beat Meath for the second year in succession with a late Roger Martin goal.

Dublin's Johnny Joyce was the score-finder of the year. He scored a record 5-3 for Dublin against Longford, forced another goal off a defender, and had a rebound finished by Ferguson, as Dublin won 10-13 to 3-8. Kevin Heffernan got one of the most remarkable goals in championship history when he was lying unmarked in the square. Recovering from an injury, he climbed slowly to his feet, received a pass and shot to the net!

In the end Offaly captured their first Leinster title, having been beaten in one final and ten semi-finals. They trailed by four points at half-time against Louth because a defender picked up the ball in the square. Kevin Beahan goaled the penalty. But team captain Donie O'Hanlon scored a winning point with six minutes to go for a 0-10 to 1-6 success.

Offaly seemed to have a knack of conceding penalties. Against Dublin in the semi-final they gave another away, but it was missed by Kevin Heffernan. Offaly hit back in that game with two Donie Hanlon goals and a third by veteran Paddy Carey to win 3-9 to 0-9.

Down's semi-final matches against Offaly did not show many signs of their impending triumph: when they first met Offaly, they trailed 2-4 to 0-3 at half-time, thanks to Offaly goals from Mick Casey and Seán Brereton. Down's equalising goal was not a clear-cut affair either. Dan McCartan could have been whistled for over-running, but he got a penalty instead and Paddy Docherty sent it to the net eight minutes from the end. An exchange of points left Down with 1-10 to Offaly's 2-7. Peter McDermott of Meath was invited to help coach Down after that match.

In the replay Down came from behind again to win 1-7 to 1-5. Brian Morgan got the vital goal after the goalkeeper parried the ball thirteen minutes into the second half.

For the fourth year in a row Leitrim reached the Connacht final and lost to Galway, this time by 2-5 to 0-5. Frank Kyne scored the first goal after just two minutes. The second was punched into his own net by a beleaguered Leitrim defender as the defence panicked in the last ten minutes. Seán Purcell's shot had seemed destined for a point at the time. The own goal was indicative of Leitrim's jitters. Another ball was punched over the Leitrim bar by a defender.

In the Connacht semi-final against Roscommon, Leitrim went into a 1-4 to nil half-time lead, but needed Liam Foran's goal to kill off a Roscommon comeback. Mayo too started with a flourish and went 1-5 to 0-1 ahead before Galway caught them on the proverbial hop with two Seán Purcell goals.

Waterford did a 1957 to Cork. Cork back Eamonn Sullivan dropped the ball in the square, Donal Hurley tried to belt it clear, the ball hit the post, and Tom Kirwan slapped the rebound into the net.

But when they met Kerry in the Munster final, Waterford got a sixteen-point drubbing, 3-15 to 0-8. Waterford trailed by just one point, 1-5 to 0-7, at half-time in that final. But they had to face the wind in the second half. A goal from a Kerry penalty by Paudie Sheehy, one of three footballing sons of 1926 and 1930 captain John Joe, started the rout. It could have been worse. Kerry shot 27 wides and Waterford goalkeeper Denis Corcoran stopped plenty more goal attempts with a brilliant individual performance.

A fumbling Galway defence let Kerry win the All-Ireland semi-final: Garry McMahon got the ball through a mix-up just before half-time and turned the game in Kerry's favour. Kerry went on to win 1-8 to 0-8.

That left Kerry and Down. The climax was uproarious. When Tadhgie Lyne grabbed Archbishop Morris's throw-in and had to elbow his way through two photographers who had lingered a little too long taking the traditional throw-in shots, the referee awarded a free to Kerry! A record 87,768 had turned out to see Down take on Kerry in the final. Two quick-fire goals in the third quarter brought the cup across the border.

There were emotional scenes as Down's 2-10 to 0-8 victory put a new name on the Sam Maguire Cup. Jim McCartan turned the game around eleven minutes into the second half when he took Kevin Mussen's line ball and sent in a high 40 yard lob. According to Paddy Mehigan: 'Down's fairy godmother must have been flighting around Croke Park. The ball travelled dead but Johnny Culloty covered it with great confidence. The ball dropped just under the bar and Culloty put his hands on it. There were no Down attackers in, but by one of those accidents common in sport the ball dropped from his hands into the corner of the net.' Two minutes later Paddy Docherty was pulled down in the square. He scored the penalty to put Down six points up with eighteen minutes to go.

Kerry supporters blamed the selectors who had sent John Dowling on to the field limping badly with a leg injury. Even in the parade it was evident he would be unable to play, yet he stayed on the field until midway through the second half. There were also a few near misses for Kerry. Early in the second half, soon after Kerry had drawn level, Paudie Sheehy sent a low shot screaming a foot wide of Down's right-hand post.

Down too had chances as they showed the knack of opening wide spaces directly in front of Kerry's goal. Paddy Docherty had a great breakaway chance in the early stages, which he cannoned off the post. In another incident Tony Hadden raced clear of the defenders for a spectacular point.

'They came with a strategy,' Tom Long recalled. 'The most professional crowd that ever hit the field. They had the most constructive forwards I ever saw, but the most destructive backs. Their strategy was to nail the forwards, pull the jerseys off them. That is what they did in 1960. I remember my jersey was torn by Dan McCartan and I turned to the referee, John Dowling, and protested. He said play away.'

Faster, fitter, and first to the ball, the sight of the Down forwards running on to collect the ball with Kerry men in pursuit, was a common one during the match.

24 SEPTEMBER 1961. DOWN 3-6, OFFALY 2-8, CROKE PARK

> 'The fact that only a point separated the teams at the end of an hour's play suggests it was a titanic battle for supremacy. Such was not the case however, as it was a scrappy, dull game, devoid of spectacle or thrill not well befitting its status as an All-Ireland final.'
>
> *Anglo-Celt*, 30 September 1961

Down's open football could be stopped with punch rather than with pace. The 1961 Ulster final ended in a mêlée 30 seconds from the end when the ball appeared to cross the line for an Armagh goal. The referee turned down Armagh's claims for a score and had to be protected from raging Gaels on his way back to the dressing room after Down won 2-10 to 1-10.

It was a close shave for Down. Armagh's M. McQuaid scored a goal that gave his side a valuable lead, 1-7 to 1-2, at half-time. Brian Morgan and Jim McCartan got Down's goals, and Paddy Docherty, Seán O'Neill and P. J. McElroy contributed a total of eight points in the second half that secured victory for Down.

Kerry drew with Cork in the Munster final 0-10 to 1-7. They then won the title so easily that they wondered why they needed a replay in the first place. Worse, that first day, Joe O'Sullivan had sent Cork into a shock lead when he bundled the ball into the net after just five minutes, and Kerry trailed by six points at half-time. But Mick O'Connell completed a great comeback with a carefree equaliser in the last minute of play.

The replay was disappointing. Kerry were well ahead before a punched goal by Gerry Clifford at the end of the first half, and another by Brian Sheehy at the end of the second, turned the victory into one of gargantuan proportions, 2-13 to 1-4. That sent them through to meet Down in a repeat of the 1960 All-Ireland final.

The prospect brought a new record 71,573 attendance for a semi-final, a few dozen more than had attended the 1955 semi-final replay double bill. Again a penalty was at issue. This time Docherty's miskick was easily saved by Johnny Culloty, but Down went through anyway, 1-12 to 0-9, thanks to a Seán O'Neill goal in the very first minute. Midway through the second half, with the score at 1-8 to 0-7 in Down's favour, Kerry dropped five 50s in quick succession into the Down goalmouth, but to no avail.

The no-nonsense approach had also defused Dublin. The Leinster final was fixed for Portlaoise, the last time it was held outside Croke Park. Offaly's chances of retaining their title were increased immensely. It turned out to be a rough game.

Tommy Greene got the clinching goal for Offaly seven minutes before half-time. Mickey Whelan got one back for Dublin ten minutes after half-time, then things started getting out of hand. One of the Dublin players threw a stone into the crowd in one of the most reckless acts by a player in Gaelic history. After the match, a Dublin player struck an Offaly player. And, according to the *Irish Independent*, 'Immediately the pitch was the scene of a hundred battles.'

But Offaly were used to battlefield strategies after a rough survival in the Leinster semi-final. Their match with Kildare was stopped 68 times for frees. Kilkenny reappeared after aspiring to a Leinster junior title, and came close to their first senior first round win in 31 years when Paudge Butler (2) and John Nash scored three goals against Kildare. But they lost 3-8 to 3-4 in the end and still haven't won a Leinster senior tie since 1929.

In Connacht, Roscommon retrieved the title after nine years by shrewdly moving Eamonn Curley to midfield eight minutes after half-time in the final. At the time they trailed 0-5 to 1-6, then Mick Shivnan scored a goal with a low drive. Cyril Dunne replied with one for Galway, and eventually T. Kenny got the winning point in the dying seconds for a 1-11 to 2-7 victory.

Roscommon were a poor match for Offaly in the All-Ireland semi-final. Des and Don Feeley helped them nose 0-6 to 1-2 ahead at half-time, but man of the match Tommy Greene scored two goals, and Harry Donnelly a third, to give Offaly a 3-6 to 0-6 victory.

Croke Park did not really have the capacity to accommodate the 90,556 spectators who paid in to see the final, but thankfully nobody was killed in the crush. The record will never be beaten unless some future GAA authority plans for a 100,000 capacity super stadium to see the light of day.

This time the blitzkrieg start was Offaly's. Their first title seemed on the cards after just six minutes of the All-Ireland final. Mick Casey took a Har Donnelly pass and sent in a dropping ball from twenty yards out that arched into the net, and Peter Daly snatched a second goal from a defensive mistake. But Offaly lost their six-point lead, and had a famous penalty request turned down. Harry Green was apparently dragged to the ground by two Down defenders as he raced into the smaller parallelogram four minutes after half-time.

Down got three goals of their own before half-time, from Jim McCartan (eleventh minute), Seán O'Neill (23rd minute) and Ben Morgan (30th minute). These sent Down 3-3 to 2-3 ahead at half-time. Apart from the non-penalty, Offaly's grievances included Har Donnelly's decision to go for a point from a 21 yard free at the end, when his side clearly needed a goal. Down held on to win 3-6 to 2-8.

23 SEPTEMBER 1962. KERRY 1-12, ROSCOMMON 1-6, CROKE PARK

> 'Undistinguished, unexciting, cheerless and insipid, the worst in living memory.'
>
> JOHN D. HICKEY on the 1962 All-Ireland football final

Down's three-in-a-row ambitions were thwarted by a teenager. Cavan's 19-year-old Raymond Carolan was man of the match in a surprise Ulster final that saw the defending All-Ireland and National League champions go down by 3-6 to 0-5.

Down tried five men on him, but never quite coped. Charlie Gallagher placed Jim Brady for the sixteenth-minute goal that started Down's downfall and foiled their four in a row ambitions (they'd won in 1959, 1960 and 1961). Jim Stafford got two more goals for Cavan, while at the other end Jim McCartan missed Down's best chance. Carolan's concerto meanwhile scuppered Down's centrefield.

In Leinster, Dublin's Wicklow man John Timmons narrowly escaped being sent off, then gave a great semi-final display as they beat Laois. An extraordinary last ten minutes in the other semi-final saw Kildare concede two freak goals to Offaly's Mick Casey (53 minutes) and Tom Furlong (57 minutes) as goalkeeper Kieran Dockery lost his nerve.

A record 59,643 crowd turned out to watch Offaly and Dublin resume their all too volatile hostilities in the Leinster final. Dublin regained the title by 2-8 to 1-7, with an early goal from Tom Delaney and another in the second half from Bob McCrea, after Offaly failed to turn their first-half dominance into scores. It was a thrilling game, despite stoppages for the game's 52 frees.

The splendid memory of Dublin's clash with Kerry in 1959 was still fresh in everyone's mind. But there was bad news from Munster. Kerry's second massive win in successive Munster finals, this time by 4-8 to 0-4, led to bottles being thrown, some cars attacked leaving the ground, and sods thrown at the players. Kerry's Noel Lucey and Cork's Joe Sullivan were sent off near the end. On a positive side, Mick O'Connell showed his genius with a beautiful narrow-angle goal near the end, followed by a beautiful catch from a kick-out and another magnificent point.

And that set the tone for the All-Ireland semi-final, watched live on the new RTÉ television channel all over the country. O'Connell was superb, fielding in masterly fashion and scoring one point direct from the kick-out. 'He was a man-mountain, he could catch aeroplanes if it helped Kerry', John B. Keane wrote.

First half goals from Tom Long and Garry McMahon helped Kerry gain a clear-cut 2-12 to 0-10 victory. It was another classic, which was just as well, considering the mind-numbing nonentity that passed for an All-Ireland final.

Roscommon retained the Connacht final with the help of some shrewd switches when, with fifteen minutes to go, they trailed 1-4 to 2-7 against Galway. They moved Gerry O'Malley to midfield, then Cyril Mahon punched a timely goal, Don Feeley shot to the net for a 60th-minute equaliser, and a romping solo run by 33-year-old O'Malley set Des Feeley up for the winning point in injury time for a 3-7 to 2-9 victory. The only spot of bother in the course of the victory was a delay when Aidan Brady broke the crossbar.

Sligo beat Mayo in a first round replay and, in the semi-final, a 19-year-old newcomer, Michael Kearins, scored 1-7 and should have had a penalty before he went off injured with a gashed forehead.

Roscommon pulled off a surprise when a 25 yard shot from Tony Kenny gave them a winning goal in the All-Ireland semi-final against Cavan, after Don Feeley had a first half penalty saved. That gave them an All-Ireland final against Kerry.

Garret McMahon got Kerry's only goal after 34 seconds, punching to the net after two defenders let a Mick O'Connell free fall to him unmarked at the edge of the small parallelogram. Roscommon, confused and demoralised, eventually lost 1-12 to 1-4. Jim Lucey fielded the kick-out and Timmy O'Sullivan had Kerry's first point within seconds.

By the time a foul on Cyril Mahon allowed Roscommon to get back with a 20th-minute penalty goal from Don Feeley, Kerry had added five points to their total. At half-time it was 1-8 to 1-1 and well nigh over. Seán Óg Sheehy, whose father John Joe captained Kerry in 1926 and 1930, was presented with the cup.

The worst All-Ireland final since 1930 was the first to be seen live on television, and new technology had contributed to that 34-second winning goal. Selector Johnny Walsh had seen the Roscommon back go for a ball that wasn't his in the televised semi-final, and told Garry McMahon: 'That first ball that comes in, just stay back and stand your ground.'

The All-Ireland semi-finals, finals and Railway Cup finals were to be broadcast live under a new agreement (for a nominal £10 fee) with the new Telefís Éireann Head of Sports Micheál O'Hehir. Although attendances at finals would not be affected, within five years those at All-Ireland semi-finals would plummet, and the Railway Cup would be wiped out as a viable competition. Broadcasting came into conflict with Gaelic football for the second time in a long and harmonious existence.

After the state broadcasting service 2RN was started, the GAA entered the electronic age in 1926 when, on the instigation of Minister for Posts and Telegraphs, former GAA official J. J. Walsh, the first director of 2RN Seamus

Clandillon, and hurling supporter and radio director P. S. Ó Héigeartaigh, the All-Ireland hurling semi-final, the second replay of the Munster hurling final, the Tailteann football international and the two All-Ireland finals were all broadcast by Cork sportswriter Paddy Mehigan. The All-Ireland hurling semi-final between Kilkenny and Galway and both All-Ireland finals were also broadcast.

The GAA authorities were suspicious of this innovation and the effect it might have on gate receipts. Radio technicians were refused entry to the 1929 All-Ireland hurling final.

The first GAA match to be televised was a hurling match in Gaelic Park, New York, in 1951. The previous year a Birmingham television crew recorded a match between John Mitchels of Birmingham and Naomh Mhuire of London for showing the following weekend. But the only record of All-Ireland finals during the 1940s and 1950s were poorly edited films with voice-over commentaries compiled by the National Film Institute.

From the 1960s on, television brought Gaelic football into homes where the game was unknown. But it was also bringing soccer into homes where it too was unknown. The days of the ban on foreign games were numbered. Surprisingly, the ban was to survive another decade.

22 SEPTEMBER 1963. DUBLIN 1-9, GALWAY 0-10, CROKE PARK

> 'Special Garda reinforcements were called to O'Connell Street this morning as thousands of people, most of them wearing Dublin and Galway colours, jostled one another in the street. Some of the cafés which closed at midnight had difficulty getting their doors closed. The sellers of Galway and Dublin favours were out of stock by 1 am. Many of the people, young boys and girls, were prepared to spend the night in the open.'
>
> *Sunday Independent*, 22 September 1963

Roscommon went into decline after that humiliating All-Ireland defeat. They lost to lowly Leitrim in the 1963 championship. Leitrim, who were still pondering on their four in a row lost, had already beaten Sligo and ousted Roscommon by 1-8 to 1-5 with the help of a Cathal Flynn penalty and five frees.

In the Connacht final, Galway made short work of Leitrim, winning 4-11 to 1-6. Mattie McDonagh eventually won the duel with his old bogey man of 1957–60, Josie Murray. And when Liam Foran fluffed a Leitrim goal chance after just two minutes, a predictable pattern was emerging. This match was to prove the genesis of greater things to come for Galway.

All-Ireland champions Kerry madly reshuffled their team in Munster.

They trailed by five points, 0-2 to 1-4, at half-time in the provincial final against Cork, but came storming back to win 1-18 to 3-7 with the help of Mayo man Frank O'Leary and former Kildare minor Pat Griffin. The sides were level eleven times in all before Tom Long robbed a Cork defender and laid on the winning goal for Mick O'Dwyer.

Kerry threatened to run Galway off the park in the All-Ireland semi-final. At half-time they had only a four points to one lead, having run up eleven wides. Eight minutes into the second half, Kerry led 0-7 to 0-2. Galway were struggling. They needed a lucky break.

Then a Galway player saw that Pateen Donnellan was unmarked. Donnellan had been having an injury tended in front of the Kerry goal. He lofted the ball upfield, Pateen retrieved, evaded the goalkeeper's tackle and tapped the ball into the empty net. They equalised with two minutes to go, and Seamus Leyden kicked two winning points for a 1-7 to 0-8 victory.

Dublin brought Des Ferguson out of retirement in their bid to retain the Leinster championship. When Offaly star Tommy Greene failed to return from London as expected for the Leinster semi-final, Laois ousted them by 2-7 to 0-9 to bring a new pairing to the Leinster final.

Dublin beat Laois 2-11 to 2-9 with goals from Brian McDonald and Gerry Davey. This gave them an eight-point lead. Suddenly Noel Delaney struck with two goals in the last eight minutes. There were frequent bouts of fisticuffs throughout this final, but no names were taken.

Dublin's opponents in the All-Ireland semi-final were Down, and the prospect brought 70,072 people to Croke Park. Down had had an easy run in Ulster. Defending champions Cavan crashed out of the Ulster semi-final by 4-5 to 0-6, their bid collapsing as Donegal's Harry Laverty scored two goals, hit a third that came off the upright, and Des Houlihan punched the rebound to the net. Then Down ambled to victory in the last Ulster final to be staged at Breffni Park. Donegal failed to score in the first half and lost 2-11 to 1-4. Only the Ballybofey brothers Frankie and Brendan McFeely showed signs of not being overwhelmed by the occasion.

But that was all that Down could expect in 1963. Brian McDonald and Gerry Davey goals dumped them out of the All-Ireland semi-final by 2-11 to 0-7, and Dublin qualified to meet Galway in the last of the huge-attendance All-Ireland finals.

Some 87,106 showed up to see Dublin's 1-9 to 0-10 victory. Gerry Davey got the winning goal nine minutes into the second half. It was an untidy affair. Brian McDonald sent a line ball to the goalmouth. It was touched on by Simon Bohan, and Davey powered it to the net with Noel Fox backing him up. Six defenders and four attackers fought for possession in the parallelogram.

Galway managed to cut the margin back to one point near the end, but John Timmons finished the game with a Dublin point. The game produced 52 frees, and at one stage the referee seemed to award a penalty to Galway, then changed his mind.

Galway went west to plot a comeback.

27 SEPTEMBER 1964. GALWAY 0-15, KERRY 0-10, CROKE PARK

> 'Galway were well drilled and stylish. Years before their time. But not among the greatest. They failed to score a goal against two mediocre Kerry teams in the All-Ireland finals.'
>
> MICK O'DWYER, *Blessed and Obsessed* (2007)

The forward machine malfunctioned. On a pleasant July afternoon in Belfast's Casement Park in 1964, a Cavan substitute, the 20-year-old Peter Pritchard, destroyed Down's defence of the Ulster title. Pritchard struck twice for goals in a four-minute spell late in the game, after one of the most dramatic comebacks in Ulster championship history. Down, the one Ulster team that appeared able to hold their heads in Croke Park, were out of the 1964 championship.

Pritchard disappeared. Dentist Gallagher was one of the finest free-takers of his era. He was taken off the field during the 1969 All-Ireland semi-final, overweight and unfit. If he had been on the field to the end, Cavan might have made the final.

Cavan trailed by four points when Pritchard was placed by a pass from his former teacher, Jim O'Donnell, and right-footed it to the net. Charlie Gallagher added a point, and then Gallagher had a shot redirected to the net by an ecstatic Pritchard.

There had been an omen. Down had been in trouble in the Ulster semi-final too. They scraped through 2-8 to 1-9 against Antrim with the help of a controversial goal. Jim McCartan's punched ball was slammed against the upright by Antrim goalkeeper Pat McKay, but the flag went up anyway.

While Down were being clattered in Clones, 30,000 spectators in Tuam were watching Mayo being swept out of the championship in a four-minute spell that same afternoon. After 33 minutes, Mayo's Mick Ruane had a goal disallowed and in the 36th minute Seanie Cleary rounded the goalkeeper for Galway's first goal. Cyril Dunne got eight points and Tyrrell the second goal in a 2-12 to 1-5 victory.

A week later the news came from Leinster. Meath had beaten Dublin by a convincing 2-12 to 1-7. A goal from Ollie Shanley (after ten minutes) gave them a one-point half-time lead, after which they dominated the second half so completely that they could afford to shoot nine wides to none by Dublin. The championship was up for grabs.

Kerry were convincing Munster champions, and when Tom Long had a goal after four minutes against Cavan in the All-Ireland semi-final, it emerged that they were the most likely candidates for a 1964 All-Ireland championship that would ultimately decide who would dominate Gaelic football through the mid-1960s. Kerry won 2-12 to 0-6.

It seemed that the Galway-Meath semi-final would decide the championship. Before 52,547 spectators, Galway managed to take the lead for the first time in that game from a Mattie McDonagh goal just before half-time. But Meath's Jack Quinn kicked an equaliser with ten minutes to go, and it took two late points from Mick Reynolds and Seán Cleary to send Galway through, 1-8 to 0-9.

It turned out that, as suspected within the county, Kerry's team were not up to the standards of their predecessors. Galway won an unpatterned final 0-15 to 0-10, taking a four-point lead in the first ten minutes and defending it throughout the game.

Cyril Dunne got nine of their fifteen points, Mick O'Connell seven of Kerry's. But despite the free-taking duel, this was an impressive Galway display—the best of the three in a row. Their distinctive punched-pass game, developed from the days of Stockwell and Purcell, led them through the Kerry defence. Four of Galway's points were fisted over the bar.

After John Donnellan collected the cup, he learned his father Mick, captain of the 1933 losing team, had died watching the game in the stand. Mick Donnellan was a pioneer, on and off the field. A player in 1919, 1922 and 1925, he captained Galway unsuccessfully in the 1933 All-Ireland final and Connacht, successfully, in the 1934 Railway Cup final before retiring at the age of 34. In 1938 he founded Clann na Talmhún, was elected to the Dáil in 1943 and was leader of the party for a year. He stayed with Clann na Talmhún until his death, one of the Clann's last two deputies.

John, as All-Ireland captain and son, was an obvious candidate to succeed him. He was invited to stand for Clann na Talmhún, for Fianna Fáil by Brian Lenihan, but eventually stood for Fine Gael at the request of Paddy Cooney. He won the seat and was the first footballer TD since Seán Flanagan in 1951, when he played in the 1965 and 1966 All-Ireland finals.

26 SEPTEMBER 1965. GALWAY 0-12, KERRY 0-9, CROKE PARK

> 'I like playing against Kerry. They play good, hard, clean football and are excellent sportsmen.'
>
> ENDA COLLERAN, *Sunday Independent*, 26 September 1965

Galway's wave almost broke in the north-west. Sligo arrived in the 1965 Connacht final on the crest of a wave after beating Mayo 2-11 to 2-8 at Charlestown.

New Sligo star Michael Kearins scored 1-6 in that historic victory over Mayo, and Bill Shannon's ground shot with ten minutes to go proved the decisive score for Sligo as Mayo were denied a last-minute penalty.

There were high hopes of an upset in the final too, when Mickey Kearins scored Sligo's equaliser with eight minutes to go. As the crowd looked on in anticipation, Cyril Dunne got two points for Galway, and Mattie McDonagh a third, for a 1-12 to 2-6 victory. Sligo made most of the running in the game. Dan McHugh and Mickey Durkan scored goals apiece to give the outsiders a 2-3 to 1-2 half-time lead.

Sligo were not the only ones to come close to upsetting the status quo. Limerick had re-entered the senior championship for the first time since 1952 with trepidation, having lost the first round of the 1964 junior championship. It didn't auger well for their chances until they fired a sixteen-point salvo across Waterford. The semi-final brought an unexpected breakthrough when they beat Cork 2-5 to 0-6. Eamonn Cregan scored both goals against Cork, the first from a Mick Tynan centre. The Limerick duo were to become well known as a result of that 1965 championship. In the Munster final, Limerick got the start they dreamed about. They had goals from Mick Tynan after nine minutes, and a second from Pat Murphy after thirteen minutes. With the breeze, they led 2-5 to 0-6 at half-time and were looking superbly fit and confident, with John Ahearne and David Quirke in control at midfield.

As 16,943 spectators looked on, Kerry switched their team around and drew level with Vincent Lucey and John Joe Barrett points by the 40th minute. When Mick O'Connell sent them ahead, Eamonn Cregan gave Limerick their last taste of the lead with two points. John Joe Barrett's goal didn't kill off Limerick: only some great goalkeeping from Johnny Culloty prevented further goals from Mick Tynan and Eamonn Cregan towards the end. Bernie O'Callaghan's last-minute goal eventually gave Kerry the breathing space they needed, and a comprehensive-looking 2-16 to 2-7 victory.

Limerick's impetus burned out within twelve months. They were the last outsiders to reach the Munster final. Kerry's disorganised team now saw the rest of the 1965 championship as a frantic battle for survival. But in fact they came close to winning it.

And in Leinster, Longford were matching Limerick's exploits. Seán Murray and Bobby Burns were Longford's stars as they rampaged past Offaly by 1-5 to 0-6 (Burns set up Murray for a tenth-minute goal) and beat champions Meath 2-6 to 1-7 in the semi-final. Dublin stopped the run, defeating Longford in the Leinster final 3-6 to 0-9 with two goals in a three-minute spell.

Mick O'Dwyer in action against Galway, to whom Kerry lost All-Ireland finals in 1964 and 1965. The Waterville player and close friend of Mick O'Connell became a reluctant manager of the Kerry team after his career ended. He was to become the most successful team manager in Kerry football history, and then guided Kildare and Laois to subsequent championship success.

Kerry's goalkeeper Johnny Culloty following play in the 1968 All-Ireland final. Clashes between Down and Kerry were seen as representing old values, such as positional marking and rigid catch-and-kick play against the more modern and fluid approach of Down. Culloty's transition from outfield player to goalkeeper was an indication that Kerry too could be innovative in their approach to the game.

Before devoting his career to hurling, Jimmy Barry Murphy exploded on to the football scene in 1973, scoring two goals to beat Galway in the All-Ireland final. Widely anticipated to dominate the 1970s, Cork's talented team were unexpectedly beaten by Dublin in 1974 and then failed to emerge from Munster for nine years.

Dublin folklore has it that Kevin Heffernan was persuaded to call Jimmy Keaveney out of retirement by Terry Jennings, a 7-year-old family friend. Keaveney, who had watched the opening round of the 1974 championship from Hill 16, became one of the most recognised faces of the decade and a hero to a generation of Dublin fans who weren't aware Dublin had a Gaelic football tradition, let alone one in which Keaveney was a Leinster medallist in the 1960s. His 2-6 in the 1977 All-Ireland final beat Frank Stockwell's scoring record of 21 years earlier.

Dublin goalkeeper Paddy Cullen had watched Liam Sammon practise penalties in San Francisco early in 1974, little thinking he would face one in the following September's All-Ireland final. His save was the turning point of a landmark game in football history. Dublin's passage to the final had been fortuitous; the unheard of Leslie Deegan palmed the goal that put holders Offaly out of the Leinster semi-final. They trailed by two points at half time in the final before the penalty award twelve minutes into the second half of an 80-minute match. 'I knew he always placed them to the right, slightly rising the ball off the ground,' said Cullen. 'That's just what he did.' Dublin responded with three points in four minutes and went on to win. (*Sportsfile*)

What is arguably the greatest football team of all time pictured before the 1978 All-Ireland final. Kerry went on to complete four in a row in 1982 and dominated the game like no team before or since. *Back row*: Jack O'Shea, Eoin Liston, Paudie Lynch, Charlie Nelligan, Tim Kennelly, Seán Walsh, Pat Spillane. *Front row*: Mike Sheehy, Páidí Ó Sé, John Egan, Denis 'Ogie' Moran, John O'Keeffe, Ger Power, Mick Spillane, Jim Deenihan.

Drama in the rain: Robbie Kelleher, Brian Mullins, Seán Walsh, Eoin Liston, Seán Doherty, Kevin Moran and Tommy Drumm contest a high ball. The 1978 final was remembered for its pivotal moment rather than the quality of the football. (*Sportsfile*)

The most extraordinary goal in football history. When Paddy Cullen was penalised for an incident with Ger Power shortly before half-time in the 1978 final, he paused to argue with referee Séamus Aldridge. Mikey Sheehy took the opportunity to loft the ball over the goalkeeper's head, leaving Dubliners complaining about the injustice of the original decision and the fact that Sheehy had been allowed to take the quick free. The balance of power in the great rivalry and the lives of Cullen, Sheehy and referee Aldridge were all changed by the incident. 'I'm fed up with Dublin whinging,' the referee said later. 'Seventeen points and they're still blaming Aldridge.' Sheehy's boots were later displayed in Cullen's Dublin pub.

Brian Mullins of Dublin and Seán Walsh of Kerry in contention in the 1979 final, with Dublin goalscorer Jim Roynane and Paudie Lynch awaiting. Dublin were now under the management of Tony Hanahoe, an influential thinker who was to draw up revolutionary new rules in 1989 to speed up the game. The much mythologised matches between Dublin and Kerry were stop-start and often one-sided affairs, as in this eleven-point victory for Kerry.

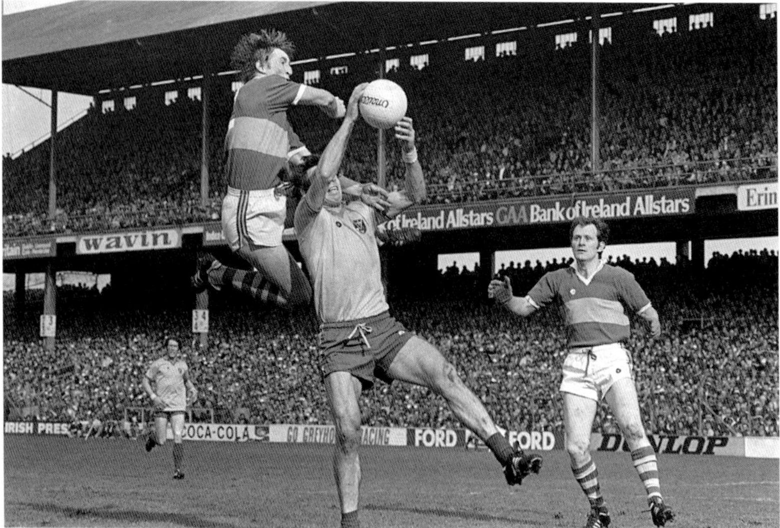

Pat Spillane in action for Kerry against Roscommon in the 1980 final. While the semi-final between Kerry and Offaly was an eight-goal exhibition of the fast hand passing game, derided as 'basketball' by the purists, Roscommon's attempts to close down Kerry in the final led to a torrid and unattractive game. The combination of both matches was to prove fatal for the hand pass, curtailed by a special congress the following year. (*Sportsfile*)

Offaly's Martin Furlong became the second goalkeeper to save a penalty in an All-Ireland final when he charged down Mikey Sheehy's attempt in 1982. By now six penalties had been scored in the final: Pádraig Carney (1948), Paddy Doherty (1960), Don Feeley (1962), Jimmy Keaveney (1976), Paddy Moriarty (1977) and Mikey Sheehy (1979); while Bill McCorry (1953), Liam Sammon (1974) Paddy Moriarty (his second penalty in 1977) and Mikey Sheehy (1982) had all missed.

A light shower preceded Séamus Darby's famous goal which stopped Kerry's dreams of winning an unprecedented five All-Ireland titles in a row, two minutes from the end of the 1982 final. Most of the photographers covering the game from behind the railway goal in Croke Park were changing their lenses, with the exception of veteran *Irish Press* photographer, Colman Doyle, who captured the moment with an iconic sequence of images.

Only one of Dublin's major championship matches in the 1974–95 period was staged outside of Croke Park, giving them virtual home advantage in the Leinster and All-Ireland championships. The exception was a 1983 semi-final replay, when the Dublin team overcame Cork in baking heat. Nobody who was there will forget the atmosphere in the sunshine. Such was the noise that players could not hear their calls on the field of play. The Dublin fans named their temporary home 'Hill 17'.

Barney Rock, the outstanding Dublin forward of the 1980s, set up a famous semi-final replay in Pairc Uí Chaoimh with this equalising goal against Cork. Rock scored the winning goal in an infamous All-Ireland final against Galway, during which Dublin had three players sent off.

Pat Spillane rounds the charismatic Dublin defender Mick Holden during the 1984 All-Ireland final. Spillane recovered from a cruciate injury to complete a record nine All-Star awards and a record equalling eight All-Ireland medals. After being deprived of matches they might otherwise have won by two last-minute goals in 1982 and 1983, Kerry came back for another three in a row. It might have been nine. One of the most popular characters to have played the game, Holden was the only Dublin player who asked for some tablets to help him sleep before the final. He later confessed to manager Heffernan that the tablets were for his mother.

His astonishing commitment to the game, sportsmanship and fielding ability meant that Jack O'Shea became recognised as the outstanding midfielder of the 1980s, collecting seven All-Ireland medals, six All-Star awards and an unprecedented four Texaco Player of the Year awards in a six-year period. No other player has won it more than the twice recorded by James McCartan of Down, Jimmy Keaveney of Dublin and Pat Spillane of Kerry. O'Shea's prominence and enthusiasm was pivotal in re-establishing the international series of test matches between Ireland and Australia. He is the most decorated of four Kerry men considered among the greatest midfielders of all time, the others being Pat O'Shea, Paddy Kennedy and Mick O'Connell.

Three faces of Meath football in 2005: Seán Boylan, the manager who converted from hurling physio to become the outstanding tactician of the 1980s and 1990s; David Beggy, the match-winning wing forward regarded as the fastest man in football; and Colm Coyle whose bounced point earned Meath a replay in 1996. Beggy was a rugby player whose only visit to Croke Park prior to lining out there was for a U2 concert. Coyle later became Meath manager. (*Sportsfile*)

Bounces were big in Meath football in the 1990s. Meath had been outplayed for most of their first round championship match against Dublin in 1991 when P. J. Gillic's shot bounced over the bar to earn a replay. The replay went to four matches, record attendances and TV viewers for a first-round match. It convinced the GAA that live television for matches other than finals, still a new concept, would benefit the game, and it re-established football's place in urban popular culture after soccer's interlude in 1990. (*Sportsfile*)

Keith Barr's missed penalty in the fourth match between Dublin and Meath in 1991 helped boost Meath to a spectacular comeback victory. To Barr's miss in 1991 could be added Charlie Redmond's miss in the last kick of the match in the 1988 Leinster final; Charlie Redmond's early miss in the 1992 All-Ireland final when Dublin were ahead in a match they would eventually lose; Redmond's miss in the final quarter of the 1994 All-Ireland final v Down; and Paul Bealin's hitting the bar with the last kick of the match as Dublin trailed by three points against Meath in 1997. (*Sportsfile*)

The icon of 1995, Dublin's Jason Sherlock, scoring against Cork in the All-Ireland semi-final. Dublin controversially prevented an Ulster five in a row in a near farcical All-Ireland final in which Charlie Redmond was sent off but mistakenly remained on the field for another minute. (*Sportsfile*)

Tyrone player Cormac McAnallen in action in the 2003 All-Ireland quarter-final. The international series trophy was named in honour of the All-Ireland and All-Star award winner after his tragic early death in March 2004 from Sudden Adult Death Syndrome. The death of McAnallen and minor player Paul McGirr in 1997 served as an inspiration to the county's successes of 2005 and 2008. (*Sportsfile*)

History in the making as the Tyrone and Armagh teams parade before the 2003 all Ulster All-Ireland final. The introduction of a second-chance All-Ireland series in 2001, the 'back door' as commentator Micheál Ó Muircheartaigh called it, ended 114 years in which provincial champions played off for the All-Ireland in semi-finals which had been strictly rotated in three-year cycles since 1928, a practice initially introduced to prevent dominance by Munster and Leinster teams. The experiment was enormously successful and Ulster unexpectedly provided five of the eight quarter-finalists and three of the four semi-finalists in 2003. The increased interest in the Ulster championship meant that the final for 2004 was switched to Croke Park. (*Sportsfile*)

Dara Ó Cinnéide scores Kerry's first goal in the 2005 All-Ireland final despite the challenge of Tyrone's Pascal McConnell and Michael McGee. Tyrone won thanks to a classic goal by their six-times All-Star winner Peter Canavan. These high profile victories for Tyrone over Kerry in a six-year period added an edge to what was becoming the defining rivalry of the first decade of the 21st century. (*Sportsfile*)

Outstanding tactician of the 2000s, Tyrone manager Mickey Harte, holding the Sam Maguire cup with his inspirational three-time All-Star winner Brian Dooher. Harte discarded traditional approaches to the game both on and off the field, at one stage scaling down the overloaded collective training schedules for top-class teams. 'We used to train to get fit,' he said. 'Now players have to get fit to train.' (*Sportsfile*)

World cup action in women's football with Mel Crowe from Australia against Orla Smith from London in the 2005 international tournament. Women's football is the sport which has had most success among players outside the Irish ethnic groups abroad. Another unexpected development of recent years has been the growth of Gaelic football among young people in the Brittany region of France. (*Sportsfile*)

The development of ground facilities such as Nemo Rangers in Cork has been one of the success stories of the GAA. A grounds scheme was first put in place by Seán McCarthy in 1927, and by the 1990s over 2,000 clubs owned their own grounds, all vested in the GAA to prevent private interests taking precedence over those of the players. Many of these are used as community centres serving other community interests such as social centres and not-for-profit local societies. Although Dublin is the most populous county, Cork has more GAA clubs, more adult football teams, 442 in Cork as opposed to 236 in Dublin and 181 in Kerry, and more youth football teams, 903 in Cork as opposed to 588 in Dublin and 484 each in Kerry and Tipperary. (*Sportsfile*)

Both goals were inspired by Des Foley, between the 47th and 49th minutes, to kill off a Longford comeback which had just cut the deficit back to a point. Brian McDonald and Jimmy Keaveney were the crucial goalscorers. It had all started going wrong for Longford as early as the seventh minute, when Seán Murray missed a penalty. Two minutes later their goalie misjudged a long ball from Foley and let it slip to the net.

In Ulster, Down secured revenge over Cavan by 3-5 to 1-8, thanks to Jim Fitzsimons's late breakaway goal. Cavan were caught out when Cavan man J. J. O'Reilly had a kick blocked down in midfield and Fitzsimons finished the movement to the net with five minutes to go.

The talk of the 1965 Ulster championship concerned an earlier round. Cavan took two replays to eliminate Donegal in a controversial quarter-final: it was the last serious objection and counter-objection in senior championship history. Donegal had refused to play extra time the second day, and a squabble over the date of the McKenna Cup final was dragged into the argument.

Kerry and Dublin served up their last great game of football for ten years in the 1965 All-Ireland semi-final. Five minutes after half-time, Dublin led by 1-5 to 0-4, but Mick O'Dwyer had come into the game and he sent in the pass for an O'Shea equalising goal after 36 minutes. Bernie O'Callaghan scored a second entering the last quarter, and O'Dwyer scored two himself in the last nine minutes for a 4-8 to 2-6 victory.

Galway and Down could not buy a goal between them in the second semi-final. Galway, who trailed by two points with eleven minutes to go, had a point from Seán Cleary and four from Cyril Dunne without replay to win by 0-10 to 0-7. Pat Donnellan's switch to left half forward in the third minute of the second half was crucial in establishing the trend of the game

Galway struggled to put Kerry away in the All-Ireland final, and had their lead against Kerry cut back to just one point with twenty minutes to go. It could have been worse, had John Joe Barrett scored the probable goal rather than the point he ended up with from a breakaway move five minutes after half-time. But Pat Donnellan curtailed Mick O'Connell, and four points in five minutes from Galway restored order for an 0-12 to 0-9 victory.

Towards the end, Derry O'Shea (Kerry) and John Donnellan (Galway) were sent off, and John O'Shea followed them off minutes later. It was the first time that three players were sent off in a final. The only previous sending-off incidents in an All-Ireland final were an unidentified Dublin footballer in the 1908 final against London and Cavan's Joe Stafford in 1943.

25 SEPTEMBER 1966. GALWAY 1-10, MEATH 0-7, CROKE PARK

> 'The best drilled, best equipped and best trained football machine in the country.'
>
> The *Connacht Sentinel* pays tribute to Galway, 27 September 1966

The fourth county to win three in a row in 1966, Galway found the going got tough as the trio beckoned. Take the Connacht final. A great goal from M. J. Ruddy sent Mayo 1-6 to 0-4 ahead after ten minutes of the second half. Joe Langan was dominating centrefield for Mayo and Galway's reign looked all over. Then Mayo missed three goal chances. Galway sensed the opportunity. They chipped away at the lead, and Liam Sammon scored the winning point in injury time for a narrow 0-12 to 1-8 victory.

Take the All-Ireland semi-final. Cyril Dunne's goal gave Galway a five-point lead against Cork ten minutes after half-time. Niall Fitzgerald was sent on with instructions to get back a goal for Cork. He shot appallingly wide with twelve minutes to go. Then he jinked right through the defence with nine minutes to go, only to produce a distressingly weak shot right in front of the goal. Galway reached the final by 1-11 to 1-9.

West coast championship rivals for both legs of Galway's two in a row, Kerry, ran out of talent just ten minutes short of a record nine in a row in Munster. Two flashes of red in a ninety-second period, ten minutes before the end, gave Cork a 2-7 to 1-7 victory. Jerry Lucey sent to Eric Philpott, who passed to Johnny Carroll for the first. Gene McCarthy tossed in the second. Kerry, reduced to fourteen men when Seamus Fitzgerald was sent off shortly before half-time, were facing a new Cork goalkeeping star in Billy Morgan.

Kildare, the 1965 under-21 All-Ireland champions, were expected to provide a new challenge in Leinster. With the entire population of the country pondering what happened Kildare after their fourth and last All-Ireland in 1928, the usual bar stool solution is that internal power struggles and personality clashes prevented them ever achieving the level of organisation that winners require.

In 1966 Kildare seemed to have found both the players and the balance. They defeated champions Dublin 3-9 to 2-5 with the help of 3-2 from under-21 star Pat Dunny, but ran out of time against Meath in the Leinster final. Another Ollie Shanley goal from a 30 yard solo run gave Meath a 1-9 to 1-8 victory.

Kildare believed they could have drawn. Inspired by a Tom Walshe goal with the third-last kick of the match, they were pressing for an equaliser when the whistle blew for a foul. Kildare protested that time should have been extended to allow Jack Donnelly's late free to be taken, but the referee claimed he had already accidentally overplayed time by five minutes, so even Walshe's goal should not have counted.

Donegal too had high hopes, but went down to Down by 1-7 to 0-8 in the Ulster final at Casement Park. Donegal were unlucky. They presented the opposition with a Seán O'Neill penalty goal after the Donegal full back picked the ball up in the square three minutes from the end. A ragged 57-free match exhibited a dreadful advertisement for the game—especially as it was the first Ulster final to be televised live on BBC. Donegal had objected to the venue too, which was chosen to facilitate the TV cameras.

Meath displayed a soon to become familiar slow start against Down in the All-Ireland semi-final. They got two goals in three minutes from Jack Quinn and tacked on thirteen points for a ten-point win.

Meath's slow start cost them the final. As Galway won 1-10 to 0-7, all was decided in the ten minutes before half-time. A long clearance found Mattie McDonagh unmarked at the edge of the square in the 21st minute and he thundered the ball to the net. At half-time Meath were eight points behind, 1-6 to 0-1. With eight minutes to go, they had cut it back to 1-8 to 0-7, but that was as near as they got.

In conclusion, Galway's three All-Irelands of the 1960s were forgettable affairs.

24 SEPTEMBER 1967. MEATH 1-9, CORK 0-9, CROKE PARK

> 'The attendance was deprived of witnessing an open game by heavy tackling and petty infringements. The game never reached a high standard. We had to wait until five minutes into the second half before any excitement was engendered into the final.'
>
> *Anglo-Celt*, 29 September 1967

Most of the Galway players agree that their team fell in 1967 because of a trip to America. They crashed to Mayo by 3-13 to 1-8 at Pearse Stadium in the 1967 Connacht semi-final, five weeks after a transatlantic hop to play in the National League final. There was no arguing with the defeat when it came. P. J. and Willie Loftus gave Mayo possession at midfield, and Seamus O'Dowd, Johnny Farragher and Mick Ruane the historic goals for Mayo.

As if Connacht had not provided enough talking points, Leitrim caused another upset. They beat Roscommon in remarkable circumstances to reach the final for the last time—thanks to a decision to disallow a bizarre goal from a last-kick fourteen yard free for Roscommon.

The mystery of the disappearing minor had defied Gaelic selectors for over three decades. An All-Ireland under-21 competition was eventually introduced to help clear the matter up in 1964. With a great flush of enthusiasm, the competition that would save the best under-18 players for the senior grade was played out before 10,497 spectators at Croke Park on 13 September 1964. All it supplied was a delusion that an All-Ireland was just around the corner for some of the early champions, Kildare in 1965, Roscommon in 1966, Mayo in 1967 and Derry in 1968.

Hence in 1967 Roscommon fielded five of the previous year's under-21 champion team, who had been promoted en masse in one of those bouts of enthusiasm which accompanied the introduction of the under-21 grade. They would have won the semi-final, had Dermot Earley's goal from a fourteen yard free from the last kick of the game been allowed.

Leitrim goalkeeper Mick McTiernan punched the ball en route to the net and the goal was disallowed as it was not scored direct. Leitrim went on to lose the most one-sided final in Connacht history 4-15 to 0-7, their twenty-point defeat breaking a 60-year-old record. Leitrim got just one point from play. Mayo men like Joe Langan exploited Leitrim's lack of depth with long solo runs, and midfielder Willie Loftus played as an extra half forward, picking up a goal for his trouble.

The argument in Munster ended with Cork retaining their title by a single point, but they had to survive sustained shooting practice from most of the opposition, including the Kerry goalkeeper! Cork started triumphantly by forging 0-6 to 0-1 ahead sixteen minutes into the first half, only to lose the lead 90 seconds after half-time. They eventually nudged ahead again with seven minutes to go. Kerry goalkeeper Eamonn O'Donoghue narrowly missed the equalising point when he was called up to take a free from 35 yards out with three minutes to go. He would later win an All-Ireland medal as a forward.

Cavan beat Down 2-12 to 0-8 in another torrid, mauling final, thanks to a brilliant first half goal from J. J. O'Reilly and a great individual goal from Michael Greenan six minutes after half-time.

But a penalty that Cavan conceded with nine minutes to go, sent to the net by Cork's Denis Coughlan, cost Cavan a place in the All-Ireland final. A goalkeeping error had let Flor Hayes in for a Cork goal in the first half. Cavan still built up and lost a 0-8 to 1-3 lead, and were narrowly ahead 0-11 to 1-7 when they conceded the penalty. Cavan's Charlie Gallagher narrowly failed to equalise with a 55 yard free into the breeze.

In the Leinster final, Meath stopped Offaly's comeback by drafting substitute Frank Duff to midfield. As Meath won 0-8 to 0-6, another sub, Paddy Mulvaney, scored a point, but the referee disallowed it because he had not been informed that Mulvaney was on the field!

Offaly had flown army lieutenant Larry Coughlan back from security duty in Cyprus for the semi-final victory over Longford, but not for the final. Meath went on to beat Mayo comfortably 3-14 to 1-14, thanks to Peter Moore and Tony Brennan goals in the seventeenth and eighteenth minutes of the second half, when they had just taken back the lead, 1-10 to 0-12.

Another slow start almost cost Meath the All-Ireland. Their first half lethargy left them 0-1 to 0-3 behind at half-time. Then from a Matt Kerrigan centre six minutes into the second half, Terry Kearns managed to sneak unnoticed behind the back line to punch the ball to the net from five yards out on the right-hand side.

Some good scoring by Cork's Con O'Sullivan and another last-minute goal bid, pulled up because Con O'Sullivan's short free to Flor Hayes was too short, could not save Cork. It was, on the whole, a forgettable final.

Meath's pride was to be shattered within a month of their triumph by surprise opponents from even further south than Cork, as the GAA grasped a straw of hope for real international competition.

29 OCTOBER 1967. GALAHS 3-16, MEATH 1-10, CROKE PARK

> 'It was a defeat more for Gaelic football at present played than for Meath, who undoubtedly are the best exponents of the game as it has been played here for the past half century.'
>
> *Meath Chronicle*, 4 November 1967

The get-together of Australian and Gaelic football in 1967 was an unusual one. To all intents and purposes, the decision of the Melbourne and Geelong football clubs to replace the round ball used in their Gaelic-style game with the oval ball, had put Australian football beyond the bounds of any international contact with Gaelic football. Australian teams had tried matches against a touring English Rugby Union team under Australian rules in 1896.

Australian Rules had adopted Gaelic-style point posts in 1897, but just thirteen years later the GAA abandoned them. Unlike Gaelic, point posts were a success down under. Scores rocketed to 150 or 200 points per match, and the crowds loved it. They rose to high-catching heroes. In 1914, ANZAC troops at Gallipoli had a battle cry, 'Up there, Cazaly', after a tall Tazmanian ruckman called Roy Cazaly.

Professionalism crept in in a way that it never had in Gaelic football, but it was never possible for anyone but the most accomplished players to make a living from the game.

An 18-year-old player, Haydn Burton, was banned for a year in 1929 when Fitzroy were discovered to have offered him a pair of boots as an inducement to sign. Undeterred, Burton went on to become the game's most elegant and subtle star of the 1930s. Just as famous was Jack 'Captain Blood' Dyer of Richmond, a legendary figure said to have broken the collar-bones of a dozen opponents. Goal-scoring hero was Ken Farmer of South Australia. By 1938 these star players had pushed the attendance at the Victoria Football League grand final at Melbourne Cricket Ground to 96,834. Twenty years later, until seat reservation was introduced in 1957, fans were prepared to camp for a week outside the ground to get seats for the final. In 1970, when Carlton came from behind to beat Collingwood (known around Melbourne as the traditionally Irish 'Fenian' team), a record 121,696 showed up.

Just as Alf Murray, Kevin Armstrong and Simon Deignan had brought the hand pass to perfection in the 1950s, Australian rules at the same time saw the introduction of a new technique by the part-aboriginal ruckman, Graeme 'Polly' Farmer. Until Farmer's day 'hand-balling' was a defensive measure used in desperation when a clean catch was impossible. He turned the hand pass into a devastating tactical weapon. When the punch-pass was brought into more prevalent use by Down and Galway in the 1960s, the Australian and Gaelic codes were looking more alike than at any time since the 1890s.

The explosion of jingoism that followed England's soccer World Cup triumph in 1966, watched on television in Ireland, left the GAA longing for a world competition of their own. Gaelic competitions between Irish and American teams were hastily renamed 'the World Cup', but the only real possibility of a world cup lay in the Australian game.

Australian football had long been looking for an international outlet too (its only international match was staged between North Queensland and Papua in 1957). In the 1960s Australian Rules games were staged in Tokyo, Honolulu, San Francisco and Bucharest. In the autumn of 1967, Harry Beitzel brought a selected Victorian Football League side to Ireland.

The term 'Galahs' was originally applied to them as a taunt, comparing the manner with which they wore their 'digger' hats with a rather vain parrot-like Australian bird. The name caught on, and the Galahs dumbfounded an attendance of 23,149 by beating All-Ireland champions Meath 3-16 to 1-10 and Mayo 2-12 to 1-5 (before a 20,121 attendance for a first-ever Saturday afternoon fixture in Croke Park) in Gaelic football matches. The only concession in the rules was that Australian players could pick the ball directly from the ground. The only solace to Gaelic football was a victory by an over-robust New York team in Gaelic Park by 4-8 to 0-5. Aussie star Ron Barrassi had his nose broken. Hassa Mann was so badly injured that six Victorian clubs refused to release players for future matches against Gaelic teams. 'Not only did we lose the match,' Beitzel commented, 'but we lost the fight as well.'

Irish pride was restored by Meath the following spring when they beat Victoria's semi-professionals 3-7 to 0-9 in front of a 26,425 crowd in

Melbourne. In 1970 Kerry followed this with a world tour, and beat the Victorian selection in a Gaelic game. In Adelaide, Kerry agreed to play half the game with an oval ball. The theory was that at half-time the Australians would be so far ahead that it would make no difference. In fact, the match was a draw at half-time, Kerry 2-2, South Australia 1-5, and Kerry took over when the round ball was introduced in the second half and won 7-13 to 3-5. Talk began immediately about devising a compromise set of rules, but it was another fourteen years before this would come to fruition.

22 SEPTEMBER 1968. DOWN 2-12, KERRY 1-13, CROKE PARK

> Kruschev backs down—newspaper headline during 1963 Cuban missile crisis. 'Why wouldn't he? Aren't they going to win?'
>
> Down supporter quoted in TOMMY SANDS' biography, *The Song Man*

The revolutionary year of 1968 brought new provincial champions in Leinster.

Longford had come close for several years. Roger Martin scored their winning point to beat Meath in 1960. They had almost repeated the trick when they whittled back a six-point lead against Meath in 1961. But heavy defeats put a stop to their gallop against Laois in 1962, Offaly in 1963 and Westmeath in 1964. However, they had beaten Meath en route to the 1965 provincial final, won the National League home final (but lost to Louth in the championship) in 1966, and beaten Kildare in 1967 to reach the provincial semi-final.

When they went all the way in 1968, it was at the expense of Dublin, beaten 1-12 to 0-12 at Tullamore (Jackie Devine scored the crucial penalty three minutes before half-time), Meath, who were back from their Australian conquests, by 0-12 to 0-7, and Laois by 3-9 to 1-4.

Jackie Devine orchestrated two goals in the last six minutes to beat Laois in an unusual Leinster final: Seán Donnelly and Jim Hannify were the scorers. Longford became the tenth of the twelve Leinster counties to win the provincial championship. Only Westmeath and Wicklow remain waiting in the wings for their first title.

The team got a hero's welcome home to Longford. Jimmy Hannify and Mick Hopkins starred in Laois's semi-final win against Offaly, having earlier dumped optimistic League finalists Kildare from the quarter-finals with three goals between the eighteenth and 22nd minutes of the first half from Lalor, Fennell and Dunne.

Then Longford almost added Kerry to their list of scalps. In winning back the Munster championship, Kerry had found a new star as they beat Cork 1-21 to 3-8. A 19-year-old converted goalkeeper, UCC player Brendan Lynch, notched four points from as many kicks at goal. Cork too had a new star. Debutant Ray Cummins got their first goal. Old stars helped too. Mick O'Dwyer and Mick O'Connell had both been coaxed out of retirement after the shock of seeing Wicklow almost beat Kerry in a National League match!

Longford showed no respect for tradition, and took the lead against Kerry by one point with ten minutes to go. This they did by switching Jimmy Hannify to midfield. Then Tom Mulvihill, and Jackie Devine from a penalty, put Longford a point up. Kerry recovered to win by two points, 2-13 to 2-11. It was not a bad showing for Longford, considering what Kerry had done in the first half, racing 2-7 to 0-6 ahead with goals from Pat Griffin and Dom O'Donnell.

In a drawn Connacht semi-final against Roscommon, Galway stuttered again. Cyril Dunne missed a penalty and a couple of goalkeeping errors kept them within reach of Roscommon, for whom George Geraghty scored a frenzied equaliser in the nick of time. Galway won the replay 2-8 to 1-9 and got their title back by a solitary point, 2-10 to 2-9. Midfielder Keenan kicked seven points, three from 50 yards out, and a goal from a free 55 yards out after just nine minutes. Mattie McDonagh added another Galway goal to contain Mayo's comeback when Joe Langan landed an inspirational 50 in the net eight minutes from the end.

Six points without reply between the 40th and 47th minutes helped Down secure their seventh Ulster title in eleven years. They beat Cavan in Casement Park 0-16 to 1-8, despite a Charlie Gallagher goal for Cavan two minutes from the end of the final. This was another match spoiled completely by grappling and dragging.

Bad as it was, it was an improvement on the first round tie between Down and Derry. Four players were sent off, and several other incidents shocked the spectators. Down were awarded 28 frees and Derry fifteen in what became known as the 'Battle of Ballinascreen' and became the subject of an Ulster council investigation.

Victors over Galway in an All-Ireland semi-final of swaying fortunes, Down had to rely on a Seán O'Neill 50th-minute goal to reach the final. The cause of the problem was Galway's two goals from Jimmy Duggan and Cyril Dunne (from a penalty rebound six minutes into the second half). At that stage Down had built up a comfortable 1-5 to 0-3 lead.

Down kept their 100 per cent record in All-Ireland finals when they beat Kerry 2-12 to 1-13, thanks to a dramatic two-goal start.

After six minutes Seán O'Neill got the inside of his boot to a rebounding ball after Rooney hit the post. Two minutes later John Murphy got another goal, following confusion in the Kerry goalmouth.

Kerry recovered admirably in the early stages of the second half, but their goal came too late in the 59th minute from a Brendan Lynch close-in free. Down's Brian Morgan played with a fractured jaw. Down, it appeared, could do no wrong on All-Ireland final day.

28 SEPTEMBER 1969. KERRY 0-10, OFFALY 0-7, CROKE PARK

> And if Sam Maguire goes wandering
> 'Tis oft he's inclined to roam
> We'll open wide our happy doors.
> Dear Sam, you're welcome home.
>
> BRENDAN KENNELLY

Alas, for Down, the same did not hold for the Ulster final. A massive 45,000 turned out to see them defend their Ulster title in 1969 against Cavan in Casement Park.

Cavan had the game well in hand long before Gene Cusack's 22nd-minute left-footed goal secured their 37th (and, extraordinarily, their last) Ulster title. Down replied with goals from Paddy Docherty and Mickey Cole in the second half, but they were a beaten side.

Offaly were big winners over Kildare in the Leinster final, 3-7 to 1-8. Kildare's defensive problems were evident after only four minutes when the goalie was bundled to the net by Mick O'Rourke, but the goal was disallowed and a free-out was awarded instead. The rules were changed to protect the goalkeeper in 1970. O'Rourke later scored the first legitimate goal after eleven minutes, Pat Keenan scored the second and Pat Monaghan first-timed to the net after the goalkeeper parried a Tony McTague shot five minutes into the second half.

Cork missed two penalties in the first quarter of the Munster final at Cork Athletic Grounds, and Kerry went on to win by nine points, 0-16 to 1-4. Denis Coughlan bounced the first penalty off the post. Donal Hunt lobbed the second at Kerry's goalkeeper. As if a reminder was needed that these were changing times, the last 60-minute Munster final took place on the day Neil Armstrong became the first man to step on to the moon.

The Connacht final went to a replay. Galway presented Mayo with a second chance, courtesy of one of the most remarkable blocks in GAA history. Liam Sammon saved Mayo when he slipped on the ball. While trying to make sure Donnellan's shot went over the goal-line, he had actually prevented a Galway goal!

In the replay, Mayo had their lead whittled back to one point with four minutes to go before they won another thrilling battle in what was becoming a great series between the two rivals. Nealon's goal sent them 1-6 to 0-4 ahead at half-time, but Liam Sammon got a goal back for Galway seven minutes into the second half to make the final score 1-11 to 1-8.

The All-Ireland semi-final was drawn as well. Tony McTague scored ten of Offaly's twelve points, and McInerney the Cavan goal in an 0-12 to 1-9 draw the first day. Seán Evans, Paddy Keenan and Kilroy got goals to break the deadlock and give Offaly a 3-8 to 1-10 victory in a broken, 62-free replay.

The other All-Ireland semi-final between Kerry and Mayo was close but extremely boring, until a 50th-minute Des Griffith goal. Mayo's O'Dowd and P. J. Loftus both missed equalising chances as Kerry scraped through 0-14 to 1-10.

There was doubt over Mick O'Connell's participation right up to the start of the 1969 All-Ireland final. The team entered the field without him, wearing the blue jerseys of Munster, and then, to a huge roar, O'Connell appeared, wearing his own personal blue jersey, and inspired Kerry to beat Offaly 0-10 to 0-7.

Kerry's converted goalkeeper (after a cartilage operation ended his career as a forward) Johnny Culloty starred with two great first half saves and another even more spectacular stop at the start of the second half.

Meanwhile, Kerry's forwards were less than impressive, turning over 0-5 to 0-2 ahead with a strong wind. But a Crowley/Prendergast half-time switch helped stabilise matters, and their three-point lead was preserved when Offaly sharpshooter Tony McTague hit the post twice. Kerry too hit the post near the end.

Offaly learned from the experience.

17 MARCH 1969. CONNACHT 1-12, LEINSTER 0-6, CROKE PARK

> 'Next time they should leave the players at home and give us the Bishop Kearney High School band for two hours or so.'
>
> ANDY CROKE on the Railway Cup finals, *Sunday Independent*, 22 March 1970

In the 1950s, the Railway Cup, played at Croke Park every St Patrick's Day, was one of the strongest of the many GAA traditions. By the end of the 1960s it was in danger of disappearing down a siding.

The great crowds dwindled away with alarming speed. In times when the opportunity to see the great Gaelic football personalities was limited to a few big matches a year, the St Patrick's Day outing had an attraction of its own. Now, thanks to television, nobody wanted to go to Croke Park on St Patrick's Day any more.

The popularity of football and hurling personalities grew for three decades. The first final in 1927 was attended by an estimated 10,000 people.

The attendance had climbed to 30,000 by the mid-1930s and 35,170 in 1946. It had reached 40,000 by 1949 and peaked at 49,023 in 1954. The football final alone in 1955 attracted 40,280. Even semi-finals between Munster and Ulster attracted attendances of 18,527 in 1953, 20,200 in 1954 and 20,000 in 1955. By the end of the 1950s attendances had passed over the hump. In 1956 it was 46,278, in 1957 it was 43,805, in 1958 it was 36,637, and the football final on its own attracted 35,002 on St Patrick's Day 1959. Even as late as 1960, 40,473 attended.

The Railway Cup was also a forum for players from weaker counties. It brought players into the limelight like Noel Crowley of Clare, who scored three goals to give Munster victory in the 1949 football final replay. Packie McGarty of Leitrim scored the winning goal for Connacht in the 1957 Railway Cup final, where he struck up a combination with Galway's terrible twins Seán Purcell and Frankie Stockwell. Outstanding Wicklow player Gerry O'Reilly was a goalscorer in the 1952 final. When P. T. Treacy of Fermanagh won the first of four medals in 1963, it now meant that a player from all 32 counties had won an inter-provincial medal.

By then the decline of the Railway Cups had become one of the talking points of Gaelic games. Live television arrived in 1962.

In 1969, just four years after a crowd of 30,734 had cheered Ulster to their first three in a row, the attendance at Connacht versus Munster was down to 9,166, and the competition was described as 'on its last legs'.

After a promising 20,306 attendance at Ulster v Connacht in 1971 (coinciding with a major promotion of Dublin's St Patrick's Day parade), the GAA turned to contingency plans to restore some glamour to the competition. The Combined Universities entered the Railway Cups on an experimental basis in 1972. Although the footballers won the title in 1973 and beat Munster footballers in 1974, and the hurlers beat Ulster in 1972, the experiment was not renewed. Four of the Combined Universities team went on to win Railway Cup medals with their provinces, John O'Keeffe and Brendan Lynch (Kerry), Dave McCarthy (Cork) and Paddy Moriarty (Armagh).

In 1976 sideshows such as Irish dancing and athletic competitions lifted the attendance to 10,647 for one last gasp, but just two years later, 1,900 people turned up at Croke Park on St Patrick's Day, 1978.

That was the death-knell. The competition received a temporary boost when it was moved to provincial venues from 1980 on, to Ennis in 1981 and 1984, Tullamore in 1982 and Cavan in 1983. In 1987 it was moved to the autumn and the St Patrick's Day connection was finally broken.

By then Gaelic football had changed utterly. While the Railway Cup was imprisoned in the 1950s, and all that it stood for, a series of unexpected changes had put a new glamour into Gaelic football that bewildered officials and aficionados alike.

27 SEPTEMBER 1970. KERRY 2-19, MEATH 0-18, CROKE PARK

'Tis a Kerryman's clear understanding
That, when to those colours he's true
He's wearing a mantle demanding
The best that a mortal can do.

JOSEPH SMYTH

Unannounced and unheralded, football had changed inconceivably over a three-year period. The old leather football, which became unplayable in wet weather, was replaced with a ball that was coated in plastic. The old boots were getting lighter. Even small rural clubs were appointing team coaches. Now the playing time of major games was to be extended by twenty minutes.

The idea was not original, but it had taken 43 years to become a reality. A motion had been passed at the 1927 congress stipulating that All-Ireland finals and semi-finals should be lengthened to 80 minutes. But under the rules at the time, changes were not to be implemented for five years. This particular rule change was never implemented, apparently forgotten, until another group of zealots came along with the same proposal in 1970.

While the Australians had a game that engrossed spectators for two hours, even top-class Gaelic games were only an hour long. Referees sometimes stopped the watch often enough to extend playing time to 40 minutes or so. Compared with soccer (90 minutes) and rugby (80 minutes), Gaelic appeared to be offering spectators bad value for money.

The 1970 decision that top games would be increased from 60 to 80 minutes applied only to provincial finals, All-Ireland semi-finals and All-Ireland finals. All other matches were to remain at 60 minutes.

And if the 80-minute game needed any justification, Meath and Offaly provided it in the Leinster final. Their flowing, action-packed match never seemed to let up, before Meath eventually won by a single point, 2-22 to 5-12. Meath went five points up before Offaly scored. Offaly hit back with four goals and led 4-7 to 0-9 at half-time. Then two goals from Mick Fay and a point from Mick Mellett equalised. Offaly took the lead again. Meath took a three-point lead. Offaly equalised with four minutes to go, and Tony Brennan got the winning point two minutes from the end. Nothing like it had ever been seen before. Those that longed for a game like the Australians had shown them in 1967, licked their lips. Earlier in the year the Meath centre forward created his own bit of history by saving a penalty from Carlow full back Pat McNally. The goalkeeper was injured at the time!

All-Ireland champions Kerry had their doubts about how to handle their first 80-minute match, when they played the Munster final in Killarney. Cork cut back Kerry's half-time lead from fourteen points to six. Mick O'Dwyer improved spectacularly in the second half. Spectators wondered had he been holding himself in reserve! Barney O'Neill fielded magnificently for Cork, but eight points from Mick O'Dwyer and six from Mick O'Connell sent Kerry further and further ahead for a 2-22 to 2-9 victory.

Star of Antrim's under-21 success in 1969, Aidan Hamill, proved to be the find of the Ulster championship. The 20-year old scored two goals against Monaghan to earn Antrim's place in the final. There, Antrim lost to Derry 2-13 to 1-12, and Hamill sent a late penalty rebounding off the post. Instead Derry won their second-ever title thanks to two first half goals from Seamus Lagan and 1958 veteran Seán O'Connell. Derry's midfield lost control in the second half, but they held on to win by four elusive points.

Derry missed two penalties themselves as they went down by thirteen points to Kerry in the semi-final, 0-23 to 0-10. Kerry were slow to start. While masseur Owen McCrohan tended the thigh of injured Mick O'Connell on the sideline, Derry raced into a four-point lead, but things started going wrong. Seán O'Connell missed the first penalty after 21 minutes, then ignored requests to take the second when he was pulled down after 48 minutes. Instead Seamus Lagan took it and sent it wide.

Sligo transferred the venue of the Connacht semi-final against Galway from the decaying Markievicz Park to Charlestown 'because of insurance problems'. A freak goal helped Galway beat Sligo in that semi-final, the ball bouncing awkwardly as the goalkeeper advanced to meet it.

Galway beat Roscommon 2-15 to 1-8 in the Connacht final when they managed to eclipse Dermot Earley at midfield, while Pat Donnellan had the game of his life. Then Galway's Liam Sammon hit the post twice as they went out to Meath, 0-15 to 0-11, in the All-Ireland semi-final.

The public wanted to see how Meath's panache would fare against traditional Kerry catch-and-kick in the All-Ireland final. According to the programme for the game:

> It is not so very long ago, since the very knowledgeable people were shaking their heads and dishevelling their hair over what they pronounced the corpse of Kerry football. Kerry, they said, had paid the penalty for being too rigid and tradition bound. The game had passed them out. Failure to adapt to new ideas and new methods had found Kerry lagging behind. And while Down and Galway and others were dividing the spoils between them, the funeral of Kerry football was being well attended by those who could hardly catch and only kicked when no alternative appeared. This team is a most interesting one: plenty of traditional Kerry style, yet plenty of the best in the modern game incorporated into a basically sound pattern. It is the

> integrated work of the forwards which has given Kerry a new dimension. Most of the six could easily be outmatched individually from the lists of Kerry forwards past: but when they use their talents in combination they are exciting to watch and direct in their intention. The pass and the solo are used as they were ever intended to be used—as means subordinated to an end, rather than ends in themselves. The approach of Kerry in attack suggests a new high point in football forward play: they pass or solo and drive on with an eye on the goal chance every time, but if the opening does not occur they cut their losses in time, and take a point.

It was a victory for old-time football. In what Kerry team manager Tadhgie Lyne called 'our answer to the Gormanston professors, and their blackboard tactics', Kerry defeated Meath 2-19 to 0-18, but Kerry had to sweat out the last twelve minutes as their eight-point lead was cut back to three.

Meath pressed for an equalising goal, but Mick Mellett was hopelessly wide. Then came Kerry's final rally, which was finished by a classic Din Joe Crowley goal just four minutes from the end. Crowley, a Garda who had failed at full forward before striking up a great midfield combination with Mick O'Connell after switching to the position in the 1968 All-Ireland semi-final, soloed through for 40 yards before giving Meath goalkeeper Seán McCormack no chance with a spectacular shot. Legend has it that Jackie Lyne had his name on a slip of paper, ready to substitute him at the time.

Kerry led from the fourth minute to the end of the game. Four times Kerry were deprived of goals by the goalkeeper or goalpost. Crowley had a stormer and John O'Keeffe and Mick Gleeson were switched to midfield to thwart the Meath comeback. It had been a close game until eighteen minutes after half-time when Mick Gleeson had a simple goal for Kerry from a left-footed ground shot which went under the goalkeeper's body.

Lyne was aware of the significance of the changes: 'Football was a very different game, even in the 1970s. The game has changed completely over the last generation. The weight of the boots and the weight of the football has changed. Gone is the day when the working man could play football at top level. Now the players are virtually professionals.'

12 APRIL 1971. ECUMENISM (WALKOVER); THE BAN (SCRATCHED)

> 'Let there be no sounding of trumpets as the rule disappears. Nor should there be talk of defeat. If victory there be, let it be victory for the Association.'
>
> PAT FANNING, at the 1971 Congress as the ban was removed by unanimous agreement

One of the extraordinary things about the GAA's ban on foreign games is how it survived on the rule book for so long.

For three generations the GAA sounded a note of triumphalist nationalism that embarrassed even the most triumphant nationalists. The same speeches were revived every five years for the quintennial 'ban' debate. Staying with the ban was staying with 'the spirit that made us strong'. Appeals to make the same uncompromising stand as the stand of 'Pearse, Emmet and Tone' were often emotional enough to change the minds of mandated delegates when it came to a vote. The 1930s, 40s and 50s are full of instances of delegates defying their voting instructions because of one impassioned speech. At one Kerry convention in the 1960s, an anti-ban motion was greeted with such ire that even the proposer and seconder voted against it, and it was defeated by 71 votes to nil! Motions from players who wanted to play or attend rival codes were met by other motions with the opposite message, such as one from Tyrone before the 1947 Congress that the GAA should: 'Not even entertain a motion relating to foreign games until the national flag flies over the 32 counties of a free and undivided Ireland.'

Even Fianna Fáil's Seán MacEntee was to declare in 1931: 'I would like every Irishman to play the game that most appeals to him and I have no sympathy with the policy of exclusion pursued by the Gaelic Athletic Association.'

The 'policy of exclusion' had its origins in the 1885 ban on a rival athletic association, the Irish Amateur Athletic Association (IAAA), as both bodies battled for survival. Within a month, the two had assumed entrenched positions, the GAA as nationalists, the IAAA as unionists, in which they would remain until 1922. In 1887, rugby and soccer were proscribed on the suggestion of a former rugby and soccer player Maurice Davin, who had drawn up the rules of Gaelic football, and RIC members were debarred because they had been shadowing GAA members and joining clubs to spy on their activities. When Cork's Tom Irwin appealed against a suspension for playing rugby in 1896, however, the GAA executive ruled that members could play any games they liked. The ban was thrown out at the 1896 congress through the efforts of Dick Blake.

For a decade, dual players made quite an impact. The brothers Jack and Mick Ryan from Rockwell in Tipperary helped Ireland win successive triple crowns on the rugby field in 1898 and 1899. Dublin All-Ireland footballers Val Harris, Jack Ledwidge, Pat McCann and Jack Kirwan won 48 Irish soccer caps between them.

Within ten years the ban was back. First in 1901, Kerry man T. F. O'Sullivan called: 'on the young men of Ireland not to identify themselves with rugby or Association football or any other form of imported sport, but to support those games which the GAA provides for self-respecting Irishmen who have no desire to ape foreign manners and customs'.

In 1902 a motion was carried from one of the counties which benefited most from the relaxation of the ban, Dublin, where the rivals of clubs such as Dolphins pushed the ban through. It proposed that anyone who played rugby or Association football be automatically suspended. The ban was made optional for county committees in 1903, but restored as a compulsory ban in 1904. Police, soldiers, sailors and militiamen were also banned in 1902.

In 1922 many felt that the ban was no longer necessary, but moves to get rid of it were defeated by 21 votes to 12 in 1922, 50 votes to 12 in 1923, 54 votes to 32 in 1924, 69 votes to 23 in 1925, 80 votes to 23 in 1926, and eventually a motion allowing the ban to be debated only every third year was passed by 72 votes to 23 in 1927. According to Brendan Mac Lua, most of the ban debates were a direct reflection of the treaty debate in the years after the Civil War: if you were anti-treaty you were pro-ban; if you were pro-treaty you were anti-ban.

In 1938 the GAA expelled its patron, Dr Douglas Hyde, the man who had delivered the de-Anglicising lecture of 1892, for attending an international soccer match in his capacity as the President of Ireland.

In 1947 an attempt to allow GAA members to attend (but not to play) sports which were banned was defeated by 188 votes to sixteen. Even a move in 1962 to set up a commission to enquire into reasons for retaining the ban was defeated by 180 votes to 40 after a rousing speech by former GAA president Dan O'Rourke of Roscommon: 'It is that sense of allegiance to something permanent and enduring that has always been our strength. Our rules derive not only from a desire to organise health giving exercise but from a determination to defend national values, traditions and aims. That is what has given an enduring vitality to the work of the Gaelic Athletic Association. This is the force which has forged the links that bind our members. At all times we shall continue to guard our pastimes that have enriched the national life.'

In 1965, before another defeat, it was suggested by Séamus Ó Riain that traditional values provided 'ballast in an era of aimlessness and disillusionment'. But televised soccer was now being beamed into areas where a match had never been seen. Many of these players looked decidedly unBritish. One, Edson Arantes de Nascimento, rejoiced in a nickname that sounded appropriately close to the Irish for football: Pele. Eventually a commission was set up to report to the 1971 congress asking what reason there was that the ban might be retained in the 1970s. The case for removal was not, as yet, clear-cut. The chairman of congress, Pat Fanning, was in favour of the ban. He told delegates: 'The motion [to remove the ban] is not a proposal to rescind a rule but rather a proposition to alter the fundamental structure of the Association and to open the ranks to those who never accepted us for what we are.' But when 30 of the 32 counties voted to change the rule at grassroots level, the debate came to a quiet end.

Taking down barriers reflected the spirit of the times. The ban on Catholics entering Protestant churches had just been removed, and Jack Lynch and Terence O'Neill had embraced each other at cross-border meetings.

At the 1971 congress in Belfast, the ban was taken from the GAA rule books without discussion. The rule prohibiting members playing 'foreign' games such as hockey, rugby, cricket and soccer (but not tennis, basketball, American football or boxing), was clearly an embarrassment—outdated, outmoded and sectarian. Fanning now commented: 'Let there be no sounding of trumpets as the rule disappears. Nor should there be talk of defeat. If victory there be, let it be victory for the Association.'

The second section of the ban, that on British soldiers and policemen, was also up for removal, but the motion was inexplicably withdrawn. Perhaps the proponents felt that that was enough revolution for one day. It was a decision that was to haunt the association over the next three decades as several further efforts to remove the ban on British soldiers and RUC men failed, most spectacularly during a Special Congress in the aftermath of the peace process in 1998. Reform of the Northern Ireland police force, when the RUC evolved to become the PSNI, eventually enabled a long overdue removal of a rule which had its roots in the shadowing of GAA members by the colonial police force of 1886. Official GAA feeling is that a motion to let them in should come from the six northern counties. They say that the RUC are not interested in joining GAA clubs anyway. Only half a dozen RUC men have ever pulled on a GAA jersey, whereas legions of soccer players defied the foreign games rule.

Soccer-playing was now legal. In Sligo the football selectors sat up. Within two months of the ban's removal, Sligo Rovers soccer players Gerry Mitchell and David Pugh became the first soccer players to play inter-county GAA. They almost collected provincial championship medals in their first season.

26 SEPTEMBER 1971. OFFALY 1-14, GALWAY 2-8, CROKE PARK

> 'How long can a team continue to make mistakes and get away with them?'
>
> *Connacht Sentinel*, 28 September 1971

Sligo had been in the hunt for a Connacht championship since the mid-1960s. Gaelic politics in Sligo reflected that of comparable garrison towns such as Waterford and Athlone. The country played Gaelic; soccer was the sport in the town. With a revamped team, Sligo beat Roscommon 0-10 to 1-5 in the Connacht semi-final at Roscommon.

Sligo's Mickey Kearins, now at peak form, scored 1-8 as his side drew with Galway, 2-15 each, in the Connacht final. Pugh got Sligo's first goal that day, and former goalkeeper Peter Brennan, the second. This was the closest Sligo came to a title in a decade of 'almost' years.

A gift goal from a Seamus Leyden lob after five minutes of the replay gave Galway the start they wanted. But Mickey Kearins gave Sligo the lead two minutes after half-time. Galway got the lead back, only to see another goal from Sligo's soccer convert David Pugh. At the final whistle Galway were just a point ahead, 1-17 to 3-10. The fifth-minute fluke had saved them.

Kerry's three-in-a-row bid came to an abrupt halt at Cork Athletic Grounds. Having dropped Denis Coughlan for the final, at half-time Cork were 0-7 to 0-11 behind and clearly in real trouble. Their opponents were left waiting on the field at half-time as they stole an extra five minutes to plan their second half strategy. When they re-emerged, late and fired up, and with Coughlan on the team, it took just six minutes for them to equalise. Coughlan scored ten points in a historic 0-23 to 0-14 victory, a record for a substitute.

But that was as far as Cork got. Offaly had another big win over Kildare, 2-14 to 0-6, in the Leinster final, and Tony McTague scored nine points from frees as Offaly defeated Cork 1-16 to 1-11 in a tame semi-final.

Down's old-timers beat Derry's youngsters 4-15 to 4-11 in a refreshing Ulster final. Seán O'Neill laid on goals for John Murphy and Michael Cunningham in the first half. Michael Cunningham and Donal Davey struck twice more in the second half, and then Mickey Niblock brought Derry storming back with left and right-footed goals. It was a tremendous spectacle, played in Casement Park, in the middle of Northern Ireland's most troubled year. This was to be Belfast's last final.

Galway's 3-11 to 2-7 semi-final win over Down was also eminently forgettable, as Down missed a penalty and had a goal disallowed five minutes before half-time.

For the first time in eleven years, a new name went on the Sam Maguire Cup. Offaly lost a fierce midfield battle against Galway in the first half, trailed 0-4 to 1-6 at half-time, then switched Nicholas Clavin in to partner Willie Bryan six minutes after half-time.

A 21st-minute goal from Murt Connor gave Offaly the lead. Despite Seamus Leyden's equalising second goal for Galway, Offaly got three more points for a famous victory, 1-14 to 2-8. Colour television was there for the first time. Viewers saw the players lose control of their vertical hold. Galway shot fifteen wides to Offaly's eight, twelve of these in the first half.

24 SEPTEMBER 1972. OFFALY 1-13, KERRY 1-13, CROKE PARK
15 OCTOBER 1972. OFFALY 1-19, KERRY 0-13, CROKE PARK

> 'On the morning of the match the scene outside the hotel resembled Croke Park. It was just too much for the players and it caused much irritation to officials.'
>
> Kerry official explains why Kerry went to a secret location before the replay of the All-Ireland final

For the third time in four years, Offaly inflicted a humiliating defeat on Kildare in the Leinster final. They were proving better and better prepared for the 80-minute game on each occasion. Kildare were still preparing for provincial finals on a haphazard basis. Offaly won the 1972 final 1-18 to 2-8 with a thirteenth-minute goal from John Cooney, who forced the goalkeeper over the line with the ball.

Ulster had new champions. Donegal became the eighth county to take the Ulster title when they beat Tyrone 2-13 to 1-11 with one of the most dramatic finishes Clones has seen. They drew level with seven minutes to go. Seamus Bonner sent a 60 yard lob to the goal area; the goalkeeper let it slip through his fingers under the crossbar and they set the heather ablaze in the Rosses. Roscommon beat Mayo 5-8 to 3-10, despite kicking an incredible 23 wides in the final. Mick Freyne, Dermot Earley, Johnny Kelly (2) and Mick Finnegan scored the goals. Mayo stopped Sligo in extra time after a replayed semi-final. Then Roscommon stopped Galway by 1-8 to 0-7.

In the All-Ireland semi-final, Offaly beat newcomers Donegal by four points, 1-17 to 2-10, having trailed 0-5 to 1-4 at half-time. A Dan Kavanagh goal after six minutes of the other semi-final gave Kerry a lead they never lost against Roscommon. Kerry went through by 1-22 to 1-12.

Kerry's old-timers knew 1972 was the final fling. Although John O'Keeffe, Paud Lynch and Brendan Lynch were to be there in future battles, this was Kerry's last team of short-back-and-sides, rural footballers. One of the biggest crowds since seating was installed under the Cusack Stand in 1966 turned up, 72,032. Midway through the second half of the drawn match, Johnny Cooney (Offaly) and Brendan Lynch (Kerry) exchanged goals to avoid Offaly stretching their two-point lead, and Mick O'Dwyer eventually equalised with five minutes to go to make it 1-13 each.

Offaly eventually broke down Kerry's resistance with a goal after 48 minutes of the replay when Pat Fenning's long speculative ball hopped over the line without a Kerry defender touching it. Kerry plunged from a two-point lead to their heaviest All-Ireland defeat ever, 1-19 to 0-13, as a result of this slip-up. McTague scored ten points in the replay and six in the drawn match as he captained Offaly to victory.

As things started to go wrong in the second half, Kerry selector Joe Keohane looked around at the substitutes on the bench. They included 1970 minors Ger Power, Mickey O'Sullivan and John Egan. 'Who have we got to send on,' he asked. 'This crowd of garsúns?'

20 JUNE 1971. KERRY 0-11, MAYO 0-8, CROKE PARK
14 MAY 1972. KERRY 2-11, MAYO 1-9, CROKE PARK
6 MAY 1973. KERRY 2-12, OFFALY 0-14, CROKE PARK
12 MAY 1974. KERRY 1-6, ROSCOMMON 0-9, CROKE PARK
26 MAY 1974. KERRY 0-14, ROSCOMMON 0-8, CROKE PARK

> 'There was a need to concentrate on the league then to earn money. The team had come back from Australia and the board lost a lot of money so the league raised finance. You'd hear people say there was no football in Kerry in those years but that's not the case. They say football was redundant then. It wasn't. Just look at our league record.'
>
> JOHNNY CULLOTY interview with T. J. Flynn in *Princes of Pigskin* (2008)

By the early 1960s the National League had become a major event in its own right. When Dublin played Down in the 1964 'home' final, a crowd of 70,148 showed up.

By the 1970s it was almost dead. The drawn final between Kerry and Roscommon in 1974 attracted a crowd of 12,541. It reflected the strange ambivalence with which Gaelic football administrators, players and supporters have had with their second most important competition.

Winning the competition is important in the development of county teams or in boosting football in a county, as with Derry in 1947 and 92 (they won again in 95, 96, 2000 and 08), Down in 1960 (they won again in 1962, 68 and 83), Longford in 1966, Meath in 1975, Roscommon in 1979, Galway in 1981, Monaghan in 1985, Laois in 1926 and 86, Offaly in 1998, Mayo in 2001, Tyrone in 2002–3 and Donegal in 2007. Semi-final spots could also boost a county, as with Donegal in 1965, 66, 67 and 69, Sligo in 1968, 73 and 74, Westmeath in 1969 and 94, Derry in 1970, 71 and 72, Antrim in 1976, Tyrone in 1985, Clare in 1993, and Laois three times in the 1990s.

Some of the indignities visited on the competition bordered on the farcical. The winter of 1946–47 was so bad that some teams had not played a single match by April, so the organisers invited the four group leaders to play in the semi-finals. Derry beat Clare in the final, while Longford and Wicklow were the beaten semi-finalists.

After an exhaustive series of relegation and promotion play-offs in 1992 and 97, the leagues were completely abandoned and restructured with four random divisions. In 1999 Cork beat Meath by six points to three in a semi-final.

The four-division structure survived until the 1960s when, after a number of experiments, a new first division north and south and a second division north and south was tried. At one stage there were six divisions, northern and southern versions of Divisions 1, 2A and 2B.

The ambivalence remained through the history of the competition. When Dublin beat Kildare in the 1991 League final, a match that was to define the relationship between the teams for years to come, the attendance was 44,000. When the 'forgotten' League final of 1999 was played in Pairc Uí Chaoimh, just 8,794 people turned up.

'You get more contact in an old-time waltz at the old folks home than in a National League final', television pundit Pat Spillane declared in a late 1990s television programme. 'The fact is that the competitions were damaged by ourselves and it is up to us to give them the status that they deserve', GAA general secretary Liam Mulvihill declared in 2000.

One of the anomalies of the National League throughout its history was the ability of even inconsequential ordinary group matches to draw large crowds. The group match between Dublin and Kerry in Croke Park in October 1977, the first since the famous semi-final between the teams, attracted an attendance of 25,227, not that far short of the 39,623 that attended the final of the competition the following April.

With the installation of floodlights at Croke Park in 2007, the opening match of the National League staged in February became a pageant, attracting a crowd of 81,678, far greater than the finals of the competition three months later. This scale of attendance repeated in the years afterwards. The crucial advantage of the League was that it generated revenue for the counties, not for the provincial and Central councils, as the championship did.

D. J. Crowley recalls how, when Jackie Lyne took over the Kerry football team in 1968 and brought them training for seven successive nights, the players asked Dr Jim Brosnan for something more than sandwiches. He offered them steak and chips. 'The only problem is ye will have to win the League to pay for it.' Over the next five years they went on to win four National League titles. Kerry have won eighteen titles in all, well ahead of the eleven that Mayo won. What did the league do for Kerry in the early 1970s? It kept them winning. It is something that Dublin and Ulster teams were to turn to their advantage in the 1990s.

When the Kerry team played their replay against Roscommon on the last Sunday in May, Jimmy Keaveney watched from Hill 16. The curtain-raiser was a Leinster championship game. Dublin, managed by Keaveney's club mate

Kevin Heffernan, were playing Wexford.

23 SEPTEMBER 1973. CORK 3-17, GALWAY 2-13, CROKE PARK

> 'One of the most honest and most wholesome games I have ever seen.'
>
> JOHN D. HICKEY, *Irish Independent*, 23 September 1973

After a smell of success in 1971, Cork were yearning for something more. In 1973 they seemed to have the material. No county had enjoyed anything like the crop of underage successes these players had. They were used to winning. Brian Murphy had won dual All-Ireland medals at under-18 (minor football in 1969 and hurling in 1969 and 1970), and under-21 (football in 1971, hurling in 1973) levels. Jimmy Barry-Murphy, the darling of the side with a distinctive shaved head, was only 19 and had missed the 1971 under-21 success, but had dual minor and under-21 hurling medals already. The team was laden with confidence, enthusiasm and talent. Four of them, including Brian and Jimmy Barry-Murphy, would add 1976 hurling medals to the football medals they won in 1973.

First they trounced Kerry. The Munster final in Cork was an extraordinary affair, as Cork flashed five past a startled Kerry in the first 25 minutes: after four minutes Declan Barron fisted in a long Denis Long free; after eleven minutes John Barrett landed a long pass in the net; after 21 minutes Billy Field scored a penalty; a minute later Jimmy Barry-Murphy finished McCarthy's rebound; and after 25 minutes Barrett fisted a ball to the net when it seemed to be going wide.

Dave McCarthy gave a brilliant display. Kerry's ageing team had no answer. Nobody had ever scored five goals against Kerry in a championship match before, or since.

In the All-Ireland semi-final, Tyrone too got mauled by Cork, 5-10 to 2-4. Ray Cummins and Declan Barron scored first, then Cork snatched 3-1 in the last ten minutes after Tyrone's King and John Earley had goals of their own. Jimmy Barry-Murphy scored two of those goals and laid on the last for substitute Seamus Coughlan.

Tyrone had won their first Ulster title in seventeen years when they defeated Donegal 0-12 to 1-7 with fourteen players in the first round, Fermanagh by 1-15 to 0-11, and Down by 3-13 to 1-11. In the final they were ignited by their own defensive mistake. One of their corner backs picked the ball up in his own square, and Down's Dan McCartan landed a goal from the resulting penalty. Tyrone responded ruthlessly. Two minutes later Kevin Teague had the ball in the Down net. Brendan Donnelly sent the ball back downfield and Seán McElhatton had a second Tyrone goal a minute later, and scored a third seven minutes from the end.

With Kildare having failed miserably and going out to Offaly yet again in the Leinster semi-final 1-15 to 2-6, Meath re-presented themselves as likely rivals to Offaly in Leinster. Offaly retained the title by 3-21 to 2-12, but their twelve-point win disguised their having trailed 1-5 to 1-7 at half-time, coming back when Kevin Kilmurray fisted a 57th-minute goal over the goalie's head. Meath's full back was boohed throughout the second half of the Offaly match for striking Offaly star Tony McTague (scorer of 0-22 in the championship) seven minutes after half-time.

Galway got their revenge over Roscommon, 1-13 to 1-8, and beat Mayo in the Connacht final 1-17 to 2-12 with a goal by Michael Rooney after a great passing movement shortly after half-time. They had a 1-14 to 0-9 lead 30 minutes from the end, but it crumpled as Mayo moved Seán O'Grady to centre half forward. Substitute Mick Gaffney scored a goal and Garda hero John Morley, later to die on active service during a bank raid, scored the second. In the All-Ireland semi-final, Johnny Tobin scored eight of Galway's sixteen points against Offaly. Second half goals from Tony McTague and Seán Evans could not prevent the double champions going out by 0-16 to 2-8 and Galway's revenge for 1972.

The question about the All-Ireland final was whether Galway would follow up that victory over Offaly with another championship, or whether they would come out the wrong end of another five-goal Cork special. A crowd of 73,308 saw teenager Jimmy Barry-Murphy score two goals and Jimmy Barrett the third in a sparkling 3-17 to 2-13 Cork win.

Barry-Murphy's first, after two minutes, meant Cork took the initiative and never gave it away. Barrett's seventeenth-minute switch to left half forward got the Cork attack moving. The result was a 1-10 to 0-6 half-time lead. Galway's goals came from Liam Sammon and Johnny Hughes. Cork looked unbeatable.

Jimmy Keaveney and Seán Docherty were on Hill 16 acting as stewards. Brian Mullins was selling programmes outside the ground.

Chapter 5 ~

1974–84: URBAN REALISM AND RURAL REACTION

Dublin, Kerry and the reinvention of the Gaelic code

22 SEPTEMBER 1974. DUBLIN 0-14, GALWAY 1-6, CROKE PARK

'If there was a fellow up in Mountjoy doing life for stabbing his wife and Heffernan thought he could help win an All-Ireland for us, then he'd bust him out.'

JIMMY KEAVENEY

Everybody got wet at the 1974 Munster final. The Kerry men were the most miserable at the end of the drenching, losers by 1-11 to 0-7, as Mick O'Dwyer ended a distinguished seventeen-year playing career, first as a half back from 1957 to 1964, then as the highest scoring forward in Kerry's history. The man who was humiliatingly dropped off the panel and did not even tog out with the minor subs for the 1955 All-Ireland final, had already left a lasting impression on football in the county. As the scenic McGillycuddy mist turned into wet Reeks rain on the sidelines in Killarney that day, they were talking about him as Kerry's next trainer-selector.

Cork's match-winning goal came from Dave McCarthy after 57 minutes of struggle against vicious rain and cold. Kerry led 0-6 to 0-4 at half-time, and it was nine minutes into the second half before Cork took the lead. Kerry's only point in the second half came from Mickey O'Sullivan 90 seconds from the end.

Donegal re-emerged in Ulster, drawing the provincial final 1-14 to 2-11 with Down, when Neilly Gallagher's extraordinary equaliser ten seconds from the end went unnoticed by Down's Cathal Rigney. He thought Down had won by a point and started celebrating!

Donegal then won the replay 3-9 to 1-12, thanks to two controversial goals. Was Gerry McElwee outside the square when he was fouled midway through the second half? Donegal's Seamus Bonner tucked away the penalty anyway. Was Joe Winston in the square when he passed to Kevin Keeney with a minute and a half to go? Keeney punched the high ball to the net for a clinching Donegal goal. Tyrone went out in the first round. The tragic death of 1973 Ulster final hero Brendan Dolan and the loss of Frank McGuigan to America scuppered their chances.

But things were stirring in Leinster. Dublin had a new manager, Kevin Heffernan. His appointment in 1973, for a second innings as team manager, went unnoticed at first. Then came a string of victories.

The team were first named the Dubs by the followers who flocked with their sky blue scarves to Hill 16. Until then it was rather draughty up there due to a shortage of Dubs supporters, a total of 60 for one second division League game.

One who watched the opening round match from Hill 16 was Heffernan's club colleague Jimmy Keaveney. He was called out of retirement at the age of 29 and his sharpshooting helped Dublin come back from 0-6 to 1-5 down to win the Leinster final 1-14 to 1-9. Keaveney was to claim, 'It wasn't so much a question of being asked to come out of retirement. You know he'll make you do it anyway.'

That final started disastrously. Mick Fay had a Meath goal in less than a minute. But their five-point victory convinced the supporters to come back for a semi-final against the hitherto unstoppable Cork. In that semi-final, Dublin's 2-11 to 1-8 victory confirmed that, at last, here was a team to be taken seriously.

The match was not without its peculiarities. Cork had sixteen men on the field when Martin Doherty was fouled in the square (Ned Kirby, the man he replaced, had not yet left the field). Jimmy Barry-Murphy lashed the penalty into the net, but Anton O'Toole and Brian Mullins, from another penalty, got Dublin goals back for victory.

While Dublin's wave was gathering force, Donegal's had already broken. Donegal returned to Croke Park for the second time in three years, but prolonged attacking play in the last nine minutes could not reduce Galway's winning semi-final margin from nine points to five, 3-13 to 1-14. Johnny Tobin's 2-6 and a Colin McDonagh goal had already done the damage.

The final was a poor game but a great breakthrough for Gaelic football. The game was urbanised in a twinkling. Dublin canonised goalkeeper Paddy Cullen after their 0-14 to 1-6 victory. Cullen saved Liam Sammon's 52nd-minute penalty (the first goalkeeper to save a penalty in an All-Ireland final) after Sammon was fouled going through for what would have been Galway's second goal.

Sammon was a bit of a penalty specialist. He had scored one in the Connacht semi-final when Galway beat Sligo in a replay, and two more when they beat Roscommon 2-14 to 0-8 in the Connacht final. His shot to Cullen's left was a carbon-copy of those in the Connacht final, but Cullen diverted it around the post.

At the end of the game Dublin's Ashford-born captain, Seán Doherty, was presented with the Sam Maguire Cup. When the cup was presented to Billy Morgan in 1973, Doherty was a steward on Hill 16.

Galway should still have won. They led 1-4 to 0-5 at half-time through a punched goal from the edge of the parallelogram by Michael Rooney, who beat off a defender to latch on to Liam Sammon's high cross. Their lead should have been greater than two points. But Galway failed to last the pace after Dublin took the lead seventeen minutes into the second half. Judging by the bitter debate that followed the game, it was just as well that a Dublin penalty claim, after Anton O'Toole was fouled early in the second half, was not significant.

Why had the game in Dublin, a force between 1955 and 1965, declined? Maybe it was because televised soccer swept the city in the aftermath of the 1966 Soccer World Cup, but Dublin was a GAA wasteland by the end of the 1960s. City life had changed faster than the old-style GAA could handle. Gaelic football in Dublin had been played by immigrants to the city, immigrants such as those who arrived to jobs in the civil service and the Garda Síochána, but rarely by workers in the manufacturing industries.

Interest had turned to neighbouring cross-channel cities, Manchester and Liverpool, for sporting inspiration. Shay Brennan played on Manchester United's team that won the European Cup in 1968. *Match of the Day* was viewed in public house television sets every Saturday night on the new colour televisions. Apart from selected areas, almost exclusively on the northside and most notably the St Vincent's base in Marino, Gaelic was a culchie sport.

Westmeath in 1967 (admittedly with a goal two minutes from the end), Longford in 1968 and 70, Laois in 1971 and Louth in 1973 dumped Dublin out of the Leinster championship and kept the attendances down on Hill 16. After the 1973 defeat, an incensed Kevin Heffernan announced in the dressing room he would get a team that was going to win.

Dublin reappointed him as the new manager in 1974 after a brief innings between 1970 and 1972. A forward of the 1955–65 revolutionary era, Heffernan was still remembered as an innovator in the far too stagnant 1950s. Against highly rated full back Paddy O'Brien, he took Meath's defence apart in the 1955 Leinster final with his roving game.

Heffernan had learned how to change his mind on the sportsfield. The roaming full forward tactic had succeeded against Meath's Paddy O'Brien in the Leinster final of 1955. But he changed to a more orthodox role after the tactic failed in the All-Ireland final.

Heffernan got the job without anybody paying much notice. County secretary Jimmy Grey instigated the move to pass control of Dublin football to a three-man hard-core group of football thinkers who had a three-year target to get Dublin back into All-Ireland contention. The seconder of the motion was Eugene McGee, later a man to face Heffernan in successive Leinster finals. The Three Wise Men were to be Donal Colfer, Lorcan Redmond and Kevin Heffernan. Heffernan was appointed manager when a group of reformers at Dublin's 1973 convention felt the game in the city needed a father-figure to work with the team and take tough decisions. Their first effort went awry, as Dublin crashed out of the Leinster championship in the second round to lowly Louth. In Castlerea the following September, a group of unsmiling supporters watched Dublin dive to a 3-7 to 0-11 defeat against Roscommon and descend to the second division of the National Football League.

Heffernan came to the job with the clear idea that players needed just two things: basic skills, nothing very fancy, and the temperament for the game. He searched the county for 'ability that would fit into a team. Players who would react to the rest of the team and the team would react to him. A two-way system.' But as opponents were to find out over the next eight years, strength, physique and physical fitness were also to rate in Heffernan's check-list. 'None of us would have even thought of doing it for anyone except Heffo,' Keaveney recalled. The players became unpaid professionals, with little or no private life.

Heffernan's revival had occurred just when the great Dublin soccer team of the 1960s, Shamrock Rovers, were at their lowest ebb. Supporters wanted a chance to imitate the Stretford End of Manchester United's Old Trafford. In despair afterwards, Shamrock Rovers, doyen of Dublin soccer clubs, switched their League of Ireland matches to Sunday mornings after breakfast to avoid bankruptcy. Even in winter time the crowds were going northside to Hill 16 instead.

The transformation would not have been possible without the increased media coverage. Two evening papers generated daily stories about the young Dublin players in a town where celebrities were in short supply. The players became increasingly resentful of what they regarded as an intrusion into the lives of amateur sportsmen, and even grew suspicious of team members who co-operated with the press, such as Gay O'Driscoll. Too much coverage invariably chased too few stories. Heffernan shared the distrust. He remembered how the press made Dublin red-hot favourites for the 1955 All-Ireland final.

The Dubs' approach was based on a professionalism that was alien to Gaelic ways. Heffernan was responsible for most of it. When the hand pass was revived in 1975, Heffo had called upon Simon Deignan of Cavan, referee and chairman of the committee which recommended that the hand pass be reintroduced, to demonstrate the hand pass and how it should be used. He recruited Tiernan McBride, later chairman of the Association of Independent Film Producers, to video the games. The videos, along with some obtained from RTÉ, were studied at length to find flaws in the game. Players were encouraged to criticise each other's play at the meetings.

Heffernan's crew were an unlikely bunch of champions, successors to Manchester United on the city teenagers' walls. Paddy Cullen had first played for Dublin in 1966, and stayed on as Dublin's best known player despite an offer to play soccer with Shelbourne. He had been an All-Star replacement in 1973. He had left school at 15, worked as an electrician, a sales rep, personnel officer and now he owns a pub in Ballsbridge.

Gay O'Driscoll had been one of St Vincents' best dual players, and had played in an All-Ireland under-21 hurling final. He had worked in office supplies until setting up his own company after the 1974 All-Ireland final.

Much was made of the fact that team captain Seán Doherty was born in Wicklow. He played hurling for Wicklow, even after the family moved to Ballsbridge. Then in 1969 he was called up to the county team and appointed captain by Heffernan for the 1974 campaign, but was replaced by Hanahoe after the 1975 final. He had been a plumber, and went out on his own in 1972.

Robbie Kelleher was from Glasnevin and played for Scoil Uí Chonaill. He was one of the quiet boys on the team, and got off the bus in 1974 to mingle with the crowd after the 1974 All-Ireland final. After football he went on to become one of the country's top economists.

Two players who had first played in 1972, Paddy Reilly from St Margaret's and bearded Alan Larkin from Raheny, together with Leinster player George Wilson from Balbriggan, formed a half back line that was replaced in 1975, but Larkin kept up the fight to win back his place until 1980.

Brian Mullins attended Coláiste Mhuire. A nephew of 1940s Kerry star Bill Casey, he was studying physical education in Thomond College at the time of the All-Ireland. After graduation he went to teach in Greendale. He played under-19 rugby for Leinster and was a good cricket player. Most outstanding of all was his ability to recover from a terrible car accident injury which almost ended his career at the age of 25.

Stephen Rooney had been on the team since he was 19, seven years previously. At the start of the 1974 campaign he used to hitch from Balbriggan to training every Tuesday and Thursday night.

Bobby Doyle from Coolock, long hair flowing and sideburns sprouting, was the darling of the denim brigade. He was also the only true Dub on the team, both parents being from the city, but ironically Coolock was surrounded by farmland when he grew up. Captain in 1973, he was dropped in 1975, but came back to restore his reputation as a constantly running, rampaging forward.

Tony Hanahoe had almost made it on Dublin teams in 1964 and 65. He played between 1970 and 72, and was recalled by old friend and colleague Heffernan in 1974. A year later Heffernan made him captain. He later became manager in 1977 when Heffernan retired.

David Hickey came from Portmarnock and had been on the Dublin team since he was 18. Yet four years later, in 1973, he was concentrating on rugby with UCD. When UCD were knocked out of the 1974 Leinster Cup, Heffernan was on the phone asking him to come back to the team.

Hickey's close friend John McCarthy was the Garda on a team full of college boys and sales representatives. Recruited for the 1973 replay against Louth in the Sunnybank Hotel after the drawn match, he kept his place until 1984.

Jimmy Keaveney, a veteran of the 1966 Leinster final, had been restored to the team because Heffernan's 7-year-old son had suggested it to his dad after the first round championship match against Wexford. He was large and slow, but they say that, over ten yards, Keaveney was one of the quickest on the panel. In the final he scored eight points and won a Texaco player of the year award and was on the threshold of a whole new career.

The fifteenth man was Anton O'Toole, who had failed to make the Synge Street school team. From the age of 18 he began to grow, made the Dublin team in 1972 and was still there for the 1983 All-Ireland, after a brief retirement. By then the Dubs were regarded as the second-best team in Gaelic history.

13 JULY 1975. KERRY 1-14, CORK 0-7, KILLARNEY

> 'Ger McKenna gave me a free rein with the team. Do it your way, he said. I told him we had great potential, perhaps we would win the All-Ireland in three years. It came straightaway. There'll never be another 1975.'
>
> MICK O'DWYER, *Blessed and Obsessed* (2007)

Every generation believes that the changes they innovate are all-sweeping. The young Ireland of the 1890s probably believed it. Dick Fitzgerald talked of introducing science into the football of his time. The 1920s Kildare men thought their hand pass and the 1930s Mayo men their toe to hand were revolutions. Dublin of the 1950s imagined the game would never be the same after they disrupted old man-marking tactics. The 1960s Down team thought they too had changed football for ever.

The generation of the 1970s believed it too. 'The old concepts and maxims went by the board,' Tony Hanahoe told Raymond Smith in 1984. 'What we thought were static formations in defence, with corner backs never venturing beyond the half-way line, were completely overturned. New ideas were introduced into attacking play. Counties that had not moved with the times discovered that they were heading nowhere by adhering to outmoded concepts.'

So, no longer nobodies, Dublin went to the other extreme. They looked invincible. Every county in Leinster called for the appointment of Heffernan-style all-powerful team managers, while traditionalists poured cold water on this 'import from soccer'. Meanwhile, the Dublin team that had claimed one representative on the Leinster team in 1974 (the about-to-be-dropped George Wilson) destroyed all opposition. They devastated Wexford 4-17 to 3-10, Louth by 3-14 to 4-7 and tore Kildare's defence open in the 1975 Leinster final by 3-13 to 0-8.

A set of rule changes helped them. The hand pass was back, and on Simon Deignan's advice Dublin perfected the technique that had won the 1942 and 43 Railway Cup for Ulster. They used both a wandering centre half forward and a roaming full forward. Tony Hanahoe and Jimmy Keaveney would both stray out to the sideline, which permitted Brian Mullins and Bernard Brogan to run freely along what Kildare manager Eamonn O'Donoghue described as 'a dual carriageway right through the heart of Kildare's defence'. Mullins popped in two goals in the eighteenth and 33rd minutes, and Hickey found the net with a tremendous shot in the second half.

A bad-tempered clash with Wexford in Carlow was the only blemish on the Dubs' great run, and a little horseplay from the 44,182 spectators at the Leinster final. The occupants of Hill 16 demolished a fence while they were waiting for the match to start. The new urban followers were turning violent.

The removal of the ban had released a new generation of players to the game. Wicklow had future rugby international Paul McNaughton in action alongside Moses Coffey at midfield when they met Louth in the first round. One of the cities worst hit by the ban had been Derry. Since 1970 they had been threatening to break through, with 1958 All-Ireland final veteran Seán O'Connell still on board. Derry made it after seventeen years, just when it appeared that Down might re-emerge. A superb third-minute goal from boxer cum soccer star cum Gaelic footballer Gerry McElhinney gave Derry a 1-16 to 2-6 victory over Down in the Ulster final.

McElhinney, who was all of 18, was set up by 1958 veteran Seán O'Connell. That sent Derry 1-5 to 1-3 ahead at half-time, but when Dan McCartan missed a Down penalty, Mickey Lynch and O'Connell scored five points each, while

Down's two goals by Willie Walsh came too late to make a difference and Derry's youthful team won a surprise Ulster title.

Derry's previous appearances in Croke Park had been marred by violence. With Dublin and Derry's followers set to come together, the GAA braced itself for the worst. There was a storm of controversy, a few fights and a few bottles thrown, but no serious repercussions.

Derry went out in the semi-final by a surprisingly respectable 3-13 to 3-8. Derry seized a surprise 2-2 to 0-6 lead, but crumpled. Veteran Seán O'Connell, O'Leary and Brendan Kelly three minutes from the end, were their goalscorers. Anton O'Toole (33rd and 63rd minute) and Tony Hanahoe (46th) notched Dublin's winning goals. On the other side of the fence, many felt that Derry's breakthrough had come too late to achieve anything.

Just like Sligo's. Sligo won a title they had threatened to take for a decade in Connacht. But they failed so dismally in the All-Ireland semi-final that all the sideline sages agreed that 1971 was the year they should have got the breakthrough.

Luck was on Sligo's side for a change. In the drawn Connacht final, Mayo's J. P. Kean had a shot miraculously scrambled clear by the Sligo defenders when he hit the crossbar. Des Kearins and teenager Frank Henry scored Sligo's drawn-match goals for a 2-10 to 1-13 result. The teams went back to Castlebar, where Sligo, too old and past their best to make any impact in the All-Ireland championship, got their second Connacht title at last. Mickey Kearins, now in his fourteenth championship campaign, scored a vital penalty that put them back in the game after half-time when they trailed 0-7 to 0-9. Then he laid on the pass for Des Kearins's 56th-minute winning goal for a historic 2-10 to 0-15 victory.

London re-entered the senior championship after 65 years, this time in the Connacht section, amid much hullabaloo, and lost 4-12 to 1-12 to Sligo in Castlebar.

The All-Ireland semi-final was a disaster. Sligo looked overweight and under-confident. The players waved to their friends in the crowd as the parade passed around the ground. Then they collapsed by 3-13 to 0-5. The new-look Kerry team were not impressive winners. They fumbled and overcarried in the face of inept opposition.

Mickey Kearins missed a Sligo penalty, and Kerry led 0-7 to 0-2 at half-time. Sligo decided to bring their full back to midfield after 55 minutes. That was a mistake. The floodgates opened. John Egan, Pat Spillane and Egan again harvested goals. There was a new force to challenge Dublin, but the Dublin players in Croke Park that afternoon did not really rate their new opposition, as they lectured embarrassed Sligo men on how Kerry should have been beaten.

28 SEPTEMBER 1975. KERRY 2-12, DUBLIN 0-11, CROKE PARK

The flags of Heffo's Army now,
How limp they hang and lean,
Their bearers stunned by dire defeat
By Kerry's young machine
The Dubs' young blood to silence hushed
By our gallant gold and green.

KERRY BALLAD (1975)

Those who had watched Kerry's 1973 under-21s beat Cork on a rainy day in Skibbereen knew there was more to this bunch than happy-go-lucky hand passing. They had an average age of 21½, the youngest Kerry team in 37 years, and had slightly sullied their reputation as a result of a poor performance in the League quarter-final against Meath. That slip-up was timed impeccably. The young team decided to answer the critics and went on to win eight All-Irelands in twelve years!

Yet it might never have happened. Kerry would not have won the 1975 Munster senior final, had not a nervous Cork full back, Martin O'Doherty, dropped the ball into the net after just thirteen minutes and Cork's quest for a first ever three in a row disappeared in the panic that ensued.

Kerry won 1-14 to 0-7 and gave the first display of the 'long pass, run, stop, draw the man, pass' game that was to serve them for a decade. Kerry were more traditional in their structure than their Dublin rivals. There was a reluctance in the county to abandon the old catch-and-kick principles that had won 22 All-Irelands. They were by no means as badly off as the reports of the 1975 League quarter-final would suggest. The *Kerryman* suggested: 'I don't think anybody in their right senses should say that the Kerry team as presently constituted is going to win an All-Ireland this year or in the immediate future.' Yet any team manager in the country would gladly have accepted the produce of the 1970 minor and 1973 under-21 All-Ireland teams to build on.

Fate decreed that the man who got the opportunity was trainer-selector Mick O'Dwyer, the player who had retired less than twelve months beforehand with a pedigree that was respected all over the country, a non-smoker, a non-drinker, and a fitness fanatic.

O'Dwyer was the first selector elected at the 1975 Kerry convention, but was not yet manager. Mick O'Connell and Kerry captain Mickey Ned O'Sullivan were considered. Frank King wanted O'Sullivan to go on a coaching course in Gormanston. O'Sullivan brought O'Dwyer, which he did reluctantly, and pressed on him the need to have a trainer for the team. O'Dwyer was appointed trainer on 22 March 1975, the day before Kerry lost to

Meath in a National League quarter-final, and exit a competition they had dominated for four of the previous five years.

'In the run-up to the 1975 Munster championship we trained like no team had ever trained before,' O'Dwyer said in his 2007 biography, *Blessed and Obsessed*. 'It was crazy stuff but they were young enough to take it and, anyway, I believed it was the right thing to do because Dublin had raised the fitness bar and I knew that if we were to match them we would have to be better prepared than them. Had I kept all the older lads on the panel they would not have been able for the training, and even if they were they probably would have revolted.'

Despite the horrendous distances the team was forced to travel to train (Dwyer himself faced a 102-mile round trip from Waterville), O'Dwyer brought his charges into Killarney for 27 sessions in a row. According to Joe O'Muircheartaigh's *Princes of Pigskin*, Tadhg Crowley said midway through the ordeal: 'horse nor hound nor man will not stick that', a reference to Bryan MacMahon's 'Who can beat the Kingdom sweet, at horse or hound or man?' In the six weeks between the All-Ireland semi-final and final, they trained five times a week, 35 times in all. Heffernan brought Dublin into training six times a week in the run-up to the final. In their final trial game, Kerry's firsts beat their reserves 7-9 to 2-5. Tom Woulfe commented that here at last was a match that 'would be decided by the head rather than the hip'.

According to O'Dwyer:

> We rowed along with the notion that we were wide-eyed innocents taking our chances against the slick city masters. We played on that as only Kerry men could. We reckoned Dublin had a poor enough All-Ireland in 1974. Their return from the wilderness complete with songs about Heffo's Army, Hill 16 and so forth, had been hyped to the heavens by a Dublin based media. Dublin had given Gaelic football a fresh impetus when it was badly needed. However, it didn't alter the reality that Cork's arrogance had undermined them in the 1974 semi-final, while Galway, who were edgy after losing finals in 1971 and 1973, completely lost their nerve in the final.

In their separate dressing rooms before the 1975 All-Ireland final, both were making speeches that would have got them convicted under the Race Relations Act. O'Dwyer was thumping the table with a lucozade bottle, imploring Kerry to do it for him, for themselves, for Kerry. Heffernan was goading his players, terrifying them, asking them who would be the Judas on the team, who would betray his colleagues in the moment of truth.

'Prepare yourself for probably the greatest game of running football ever seen in Croke Park', *Kerryman* writer John Barry said in his preview. Luck largely decided the day. John Egan and substitute Ger O'Driscoll got the goals. The defence slipped to let Egan in after three minutes. Egan and O'Driscoll could have had a second goal each; Ger O'Driscoll blazed wide from a great position before his goal; and Egan beat Cullen with a punched ball only to see it come back from the crossbar.

The Dublin team returned to their Croke Park dressing room to find there was a problem with the showers. But there was a man with a hose offering 'to hose down any of the players that wanted it'.

Paudie O'Mahoney from Spa, near Killarney, had been on the 1970 minors and 1973 under-21s and would become part of a goalkeeping battle with Charlie Nelligan, the young goalkeeper who played in the curtain-raiser to the 1975 final.

Ger O'Keeffe was a 1975-style footballer, one of the fastest backs in the business. He started at full back but ended up at corner back for the championship and most of his career. He earned the nickname Gidacha after a Polish winger in the 1974 World Cup.

John O'Keeffe had been a teenage protégé, captain of St Brendan's in an All-Ireland colleges final, a senior club midfielder at 16, a minor on the 1969 senior panel and a player in 1970. His clashes with Jimmy Keaveney caused great heart-break. O'Keeffe was taken out of position regularly by Keaveney's wanderings, until the 1978 All-Ireland final.

Jim Deenihan, honoured with the position of 23rd sub in 1972, had studied as a physical education student in London and Limerick's Thomond College. He had tamed Jimmy Barry-Murphy in the Munster by fair means and foul.

Paudie O'Shea, a 20-year-old trainee Garda from Ventry, had marked Mick O'Dwyer in a Kerry championship match. Three years a minor, he won his place in the team with a great display against Dublin in the League the previous November. He would later change his name to Páidí Ó Sé after 1984.

Tim Kennelly was the only farmer on the team of teachers and professionals, in fact a farmer's son waiting to inherit both farm and pub. He did not sleep a wink before the final.

Ger Power was the son of a Limerick All-Ireland hurler, Jackie, who was transferred to Tralee by the CIÉ. He had saved Kerry in the 1974 drawn League final. A pasting from Anton O'Toole in the 1977 All-Ireland semi-final lost him his place on the team, then he returned as one of the country's top forwards and won All-Stars in his new position.

Paud Lynch was one of the most skilful players on the team, a solicitor who played at midfield and among the backs before his career ended prematurely. They said that under another regime he would have played until his mid-30s.

Pat McCarthy was an unexpected success in the 1975 final. Called up after the League disaster against Meath, he came from hurling territory, Churchill, and his grandfather had an 1891 All-Ireland hurling medal.

At 26, Brendan Lynch was the oldest on the team, a team member since he was 18, and played in the 1968 final. Denis 'Ogie' Moran was Limerick born, but had starred with Ballybunion teams since he was 12. Two years earlier he had won a colleges medal with Gormanston. He was now 19, and star of the final.

Michael O'Sullivan captained the team, but he did not know the result of the game until he woke up in hospital after four Dublin players sandwiched him. John Egan put down his goal to 'a defensive mistake' but was to enjoy a lot of goal-making throughout the 1975 championship.

Mike Sheehy had practised free-taking at the corner of his street in Tralee, sending the ball through the narrow angle between his house and the one next door. His accuracy had let him down during the 1974 National League final, but he was to keep the touch for ten years and he turned down an offer to play professional soccer with Southampton.

Pat Spillane from Templenoe, near Kenmare, had three uncles, the Lyne brothers, with All-Ireland medals. He also had two younger brothers who would join him on the medals list. In 1975 he was the second youngest on the team, six weeks older than 'Ogie' Moran and not yet 20.

Ger O'Driscoll from Valentia had been tried at midfield and missed selection by a single vote. When he came on as a substitute, he answered his critics with a goal.

O'Dwyer says that his remark in the dressing room that this was the best Kerry team of all time might have been a slight exaggeration as they were still in their formative years. 'What I really meant was that they were going to be the best Kerry team of all time which they most assuredly were.'

26 SEPTEMBER 1976. DUBLIN 3-8, KERRY 0-10, CROKE PARK

> 'I've waited twenty years for this.'
>
> KEVIN HEFFERNAN, after Dublin beat Kerry in 1976

Dublin regrouped. Things had gone badly wrong for them ever since a shock defeat in the 1975 League final by Meath, who had already ousted Kerry in the quarter-final.

In 1976 they took the League title by beating Derry, then defeated Meath in the Leinster final 2-8 to 1-9, with a superb goal from Hanahoe after a hand passing movement, soon after Meath had taken the lead early in the second half. With midfielders Joe Cassells and Derry Rennicks, Meath appeared to have the beating of Dublin, but Colm O'Rourke sent their best chance, a 53rd-minute penalty, wide.

Connacht surprise packets Leitrim faced three championship matches in successive weeks. They beat Mayo with one of the most remarkable comebacks in GAA history, making their way back from ten points down. Michael Martin missed a penalty along the way. The following week Martin scored a dramatic last-minute equaliser from 60 yards to force a draw with Mayo. In the replay Mayo-born Eddie McHale helped Leitrim to a 2-8 to 0-10 victory, a win that was only their second championship victory in thirteen years.

Galway allowed a six-point lead to be swallowed up by Roscommon for yet another drawn Connacht final, 1-8 each. To make matters worse, Harry Keegan missed a Roscommon penalty, but Galway made no mistake when they ensured the margin was never less than six points in the replay. Billy Joyce dominated midfield and Pat Lindsay tipped the ball over the goalkeeper's head for the winning goal, 1-14 to 0-9.

Dublin beat Galway 1-8 to 0-8 in a pedestrian All-Ireland semi-final, thanks to a Jimmy Keaveney goal sixteen minutes into the second half. It was a poor 67-free game on a greasy surface in which five players were booked and frequent outbursts of fisticuffs marred the play.

The grand opening of Cork's new stadium, Páirc Uí Chaoimh, went drastically wrong. Confused spectators milled around the entrances. When they got inside, stewarding was non-existent. The event degenerated into a shambles with some of the 40,600 spectators spilling on to the field, two gates being broken down, and between 5,000 and 10,000 getting in without paying.

Events on the field were almost incidental. The players found it difficult to concentrate. Dave McCarthy had another brilliant performance as Cork and Kerry drew the Munster final, 0-10 each. Mike Sheehy missed a Kerry penalty, and 63 frees spoiled the continuity of play.

A larger crowd at the replay, 45,235, saw one of the most spectacular Munster finals of all time. A more successful replay helped appease the Páirc's critics. But over the next five years it turned into a major headache for Cork's County Board as the outstanding debt on the modern stadium doubled before it was paid off.

Kerry won the 1976 Munster championship 3-20 to 2-19. Super-sub Seanie Walsh scored the turning-point goal five minutes from the end, the umpire judging that Brian Murphy had caught the ball on the wrong side of the line. Cork had been leading by four points until then. Cork had a punched goal at the other end from Colman Corrigan almost immediately, but it was disallowed. Then Cork watched in disbelief as Kerry outran them in the second period of extra time.

Ulster's final was drawn too. Derry's John O'Leary and Cavan's Steve Duggan exchanged goals the first day for a 1-8 each draw, after Duggan got the equalising point for Cavan.

Derry outlasted Cavan in an endurance test in the replay. Brendan Kelly, Johnny O'Leary and Mickey Lynch got the points in the closing stages of extra time, after an enthralling encounter that contrasted with the earlier rugged draw between the teams. In the semi-final, Derry, strangely enough, were leading Kerry at half-time 0-9 to 0-8. In the end, Kerry were using their corner forwards to draw the opposing team's corner backs away from goal and getting somebody into the space created. The final score was 5-14 to 1-10. 'That's the trouble with easy wins in semi-finals. They create a false impression,' O'Dwyer recalled.

A massive crowd of 73,588 attended the final. Dublin started explosively and won handsomely 3-8 to 0-10. From the throw-in Kevin Moran careered through the Kerry defence, took a return pass from Bernard Brogan and sent a shot screaming narrowly wide. John McCarthy finished a five-man move for their first goal after fifteen minutes.

Jimmy Keaveney sent a penalty into the top corner at the start of the second half, and Brian Mullins side-footed the third goal with twelve minutes to go. Kerry had cut the gap to two points when Dublin moved Mullins to centre forward and sprang the fresher Fran Ryder at midfield.

Dwyer reminisced that he played Jimmy Deenihan and Ger O'Keeffe despite the fact that they were suffering from ankle injuries which restricted their training. 'They struggled. Kerry lost. It was a bad mistake.'

Dublin's half back line had been renewed. The Dublin selectors had spent the winter of 1975–76 looking for three new half backs, and they found them. Tommy Drumm had been a team mate of Liam Brady on St Aidan's school soccer teams and had played soccer for the Irish universities. He was just 20 when he became Dublin's first Trinity student All-Ireland medallist. Kevin Moran arrived on a motor bike at a Dublin training session in early 1976. He would last just two years before he got snapped up by Manchester United.

Doctor Pat O'Neill used to tell his team mates to hit opponents as hard as they liked, because he could look after them in hospital the following week. He came with a poor reference, having been sent off in the 1968 All-Ireland minor semi-final for an off-the-ball punch.

Bernard Brogan also restored his reputation after a poor 1975 performance. He was to kick one of the most memorable goals in Gaelic football against Kerry the following year.

21 AUGUST 1977. DUBLIN 3-12, KERRY 1-13, CROKE PARK

'Twenty nine minutes still remaining in this game. Alleluia!'

MICHEÁL O'HEHIR commentating on the 1977 All-Ireland semi-final

Television reruns have not been kind to the pretensions of the All-Ireland semi-final of 1977 as the greatest football match since television, and possibly the greatest ever. Tony Hanahoe conjured up two late goals from David Hickey with six minutes to go, and substitute Bernard Brogan with three to go for Dublin to win.

During the second half the sides were level five times. Then came the closing stages. Kerry went two points ahead, 1-13 to 1-11. 'Maybe Sam will be coming to the O'Keeffe house', captain Ger O'Keeffe recalls thinking.

Anton O'Toole's pass downfield for Dublin was going nowhere in particular, and then it dangled just that pace too far away from John O'Keeffe. O'Keeffe lunged forward, half-falling and instead of catching or breaking the ball away, he turned it awkwardly slightly off-course and into the hands of a surprised Tony Hanahoe. Married three weeks beforehand with not a whisper to his team mates, Hanahoe was the most organised of the Dublin attack in the frenetic heat of the moment. 'You could always rely on him to do the right thing', Heffernan used to say. And he did. He had Dave Hickey on his right, and found him with a short hand pass. Hickey raced away alone under the blue of Hill 16 with lots of space, took just long enough to evade the defensive efforts of Jim Deenihan and Denis Moran, and shot diagonally across the goalmouth.

Nobody believed that Kerry would fail to come back at least to equalise. Ogie Moran floated a ball into the Dublin goalmouth, Seán Docherty retrieved it, fell in a relieved heap, then realised his task was not yet complete and launched a 50 yard kick back downfield.

Out of chaos came the follow-up goal. The ball was juggled around among five players before a poke by Pat O'Neill helped Bobby Doyle win possession at midfield, a hand pass to David Hickey, a long, accurate, booted pass to Hanahoe, who turned around to look behind him, then slung the ball to Bernard Brogan, careering through at full speed four paces ahead of Paudie O'Shea. Brogan took one bounce, one toe-to-hand, twelve paces in full flight, and a measured shot inside Nelligan's left-hand post.

'Tony just slipped it to me and I couldn't miss. At that moment the goal seemed so big,' Hickey recalled in Tom Humphries' book, *Dublin v Kerry*. 'People look back and say the football wasn't that great but the context and intensity made it different from any other game,' Jim Brogan recalled. 'They were two teams at the absolute limit. For both teams that was the moment they were at their best.'

'Up and down the field 1977 was the all action game,' John O'Keeffe wrote. 'It was rated a tremendous game in every aspect of football. It was for Dublin and for the neutrals; it was not for us.'

Robbie Kelleher too had been married a week before the match in San

Francisco. He was back for a fitness test on Wednesday. His wife flew in to a celebrity reception the day before the game.

25 SEPTEMBER 1977. DUBLIN 5-12, ARMAGH 3-6, CROKE PARK

> 'I went from being a quiz question to a statistic.'
>
> JIMMY SMYTH, 1977 Armagh captain, on how the 1977 team was affected by the county's victory in 2002

Even the excitement of a draw in the other semi-final could not compare with it. Armagh supporters had taken over Hill 16 to watch their team come back from seven points down to draw with Roscommon. Jimmy Smyth kicked the equalising point with two minutes to go for a 3-9 to 2-12 draw. Armagh weathered Roscommon's comeback from three points down to win the replay by a single point, 0-15 to 0-14.

It was an anticlimactic final, all-ticket for the first time as a result of the fear of trouble. Dublin got all the room they needed for a total annihilation of Armagh.

Jimmy Keaveney set a new individual scoring record of 2-6. His first goal came after just 90 seconds, the second two minutes into the second half, and four of the points were from frees. Bobby Doyle (thirteen minutes), John McCarthy (33 minutes) and Doyle again (60 minutes) were Dublin's other goalscorers. For Armagh, Paddy Moriarty scored from the first of his two penalties, seven minutes into the match. Joe Kernan scored two Armagh goals (in the 46th and 51st minutes). But when Armagh needed goals badly, Seán Devlin hit the post and Moriarty missed a second penalty. The 66,542 who got the scarce tickets were disappointed.

Armagh had taken back the Ulster title after 24 years when they stunned Derry with two spectacular goals in a 60-second spell before half-time. Paddy Moriarty and Noel Marley were the scorers, and Jimmy Kearins wrapped up the argument eight minutes into the second half for a 3-10 to 1-5 victory.

Two notable events occurred in Connacht. A year after beating Mayo, Leitrim were humble victims of London's first-ever victory in a senior football championship match by 0-9 to 0-6. London had two Leitrim men in action against their native county. The other notable item was the emergence of Roscommon, this time to stay. They had suffered three defeats to Galway in the previous eight years, but got it right at last, by a single point, 1-12 to 2-8, before 18,000 spectators in Roscommon.

It was the sixth time in sixteen years that a solitary point separated the teams at the end of the Connacht final—a period when four more finals had been drawn! There were only five one-point wins in the 60 years prior to that.

The 46,087 spectators who turned out to watch the Munster final in Killarney expected a closer game than Kerry's 3-15 to 0-9 victory. Cork's last score from play came after ten minutes of the first half, and they scored only one solitary point against the wind in the second half. A gale force wind had helped Cork go 0-7 to 0-1 up after sixteen minutes!

Leinster was closer. Dublin eventually beat Meath in a tense and much-criticised stop-start game 1-9 to 0-8 with a goal from Anton O'Toole. The Dublin goal may have been thrown to the net. Meath had two shots which beat the goalkeeper but were scrambled away by defenders, and they also hit a hatful of wides.

Kildare had given Dublin a scare in Navan on their return from the All-Stars trip to the United States, but Bernard Brogan struck back in reply to Tommy Carew's second goal for Kildare, and won by three points. Kildare pondered that 1977 near miss in Navan for a long time.

24 SEPTEMBER 1978. KERRY 5-11, DUBLIN 0-9, CROKE PARK

> 'In front of 70,000 people when things are going wrong there is nothing in the manual.'
>
> TONY HANAHOE

Kildare's misconceptions were quickly straightened out in the 1978 Leinster final. Kildare fans in the Nally Stand had bottles thrown at them from Hill 16. But that was nothing compared with the 1-17 to 1-6 defeat that was thrown at the players on the field. Kildare had Dave Hyland sent off as their hopes crumbled.

There was more trouble in the All-Ireland semi-final. Keaveney started Down's downfall with an eighteenth-minute goal for Dublin. When Down's Cathal Digney was sent off, a steward was cut by a flying bottle.

Ulster champions were beginning to despair of a breakthrough at Croke Park. They had a new theory: that it was only after a second successive provincial title that an Ulster team could achieve anything in an All-Ireland semi-final. All-Ireland finalists Armagh crashed out in the first round to Cavan by 0-16 to 0-9, and Derry followed by 1-14 to 2-8 in the semi-final. That left Down and Cavan to fight out the Ulster title. Down won 2-19 to 2-12, using their powerful new centrefield combination of 30-year-old six-foot Colm McAlarney, and 20-year-old 6' 3" Liam Austin.

Kerry's new full forward finished scoreless as Kerry beat Cork 3-14 to 3-7 in the Munster final. Eoin Liston, a converted midfielder from Ballybunion, earned the nickname 'Bomber' on the local beach from the time the lads used to ape 1974 soccer heroes in low-tide soccer games. He had been too heavy and unfit to make it at minor, but had been spotted by O'Dwyer at an under-21 club match in Gneeveguila. For the Munster semi-final match against Waterford, Liston was selected at midfield and Seanie Walsh at full forward, but once their positions were reversed, Kerry found the winning formula.

Roscommon recaptured the Connacht title by 2-7 to 0-9, but came a cropper in the All-Ireland semi-final. Kerry asserted their superiority over Roscommon after 26 minutes with a Spillane goal. Ger Power and Packie O'Mahoney got the others in the second half.

O'Dwyer always held that Dublin's weakness was their inability to score long-range points, so if Kerry could stop them getting closer than 30 yards from the goal, the rest would be simple.

This time 71,503 came to watch. In 1976 and 77 John O'Keeffe had been taken out of the full back position by a wandering Jimmy Keaveney. In 1978 it was decided to let Keaveney go as far as he liked, where he could score points, but O'Keeffe would stay back to mind the square and keep that all-important first goal out.

The first goal had been of the utmost importance for Dublin in Dublin-Kerry matches in 1975, 76 and 77, as well as in League and under-21 clashes between the teams. Yet the O'Keeffe plan, the plan that won Kerry the 1978 All-Ireland, almost backfired. In those opening minutes Keaveney punished Kerry for the freedom he was given. 'We had them. The Kerry defence were arguing among themselves,' Keaveney recalls. 'Then we lost the plot.'

The second of the five Kerry goals that day was to become one of the most famous in football history, though the first goal may have been more important. Jack O'Shea, who made his reputation that day, scored a point before the first goal that may have been more important again.

John Egan struck after 24 minutes. Mickey Sheehy became the scorer of the most famous goal of all time after 32 minutes, when he sent a free kick over the head of a frantic Paddy Cullen, caught off his line protesting against referee Aldridge's decision.

The newly discovered 6' 3" full forward Eoin Liston unveiled his fist for three second half goals. Arguments that he was in the square for the fifth goal were overruled, while near by Hill 16 yelped at the referee. Kerry won by seventeen points, 5-11 to 0-9.

Who was to blame? Earlier, Ger Power late-tackled Paddy Cullen as he ran twenty yards out from the goal to clear the ball. Cullen retaliated by tripping Power as he was clearing. Aldridge was watching them when they jostled again three minutes before half-time. When the whistle sounded, Cullen automatically assumed it was a free to Dublin. He strayed off the goal-line initially because he was preparing to take the free. 'It was nothing serious, but the free should have been out.' Pat O'Neill too put the ball down, assuming it was a Dublin free.

The free-in, Cullen knew, would almost certainly result in a score, and Cullen stood protesting his innocence. 'This has to be a free out,' he said. Aldridge stood silently, facing Cullen, his back to the ball and the kicker. 'There's no foul,' said Cullen. 'It has to be a free out.' The referee was having none of it. To the horror of watching defenders, Robbie Kelleher helpfully handed the ball to Mikey Sheehy with Cullen still off his line. And Sheehy popped the ball into the Dublin net.

Cullen said he retaliated because Power had earlier 'stuck an elbow in my face'. He feels that Aldridge punished him for an earlier incident when he definitely fouled Power. 'I came out in a similar situation and picked up the ball and hand passed it out. He followed through and when I was running back to the goal I tipped his ankle. He fell over. About 25,000 people saw the incident and everytime I touched the ball in the intermittent period between that and the goal, they boohed me. The referee knew something had happened. As it turned out, he penalised me for the earlier incident when I had committed no foul.'

Cullen complained afterwards: 'There was no whistle. It is unusual that there would be no whistle for a free from that distance. And the referee had his back to the kicker. The ball could have been kicked from the hands. It could have been thrown into the net. It was a lot of egg on my face.'

Con Houlihan's description of the incident is possibly the most famous passage in the entire canon of Irish sportswriting history:

> Paddy put on a show of righteous indignation that would get him a card from Equity, throwing up his hands to heaven as the referee kept pointing to the goal. And while all of this was going on, Mike Sheehy came running up to take the kick—and suddenly Paddy dashes back like a woman who smells a cake burning. The ball won the race and it curled inside the near post as Paddy crashed into the outside of the net and lay against it like a fireman who had returned to find his station ablaze. Sometime Noel Pearson may make a musical of this final—and as the green flag goes up for that crazy goal he will have a banshee's voice crooning: 'And that was the end of poor Molly Malone.' So it was. A few minutes later came the tea-break. Kerry went in to a frenzy of green and gold and a tumult of acclaim. The champions looked like men who had worked hard and seen their savings plundered by bandits. The great train robbers were out on to the field for Act Two.

16 SEPTEMBER 1979. KERRY 3-13, DUBLIN 1-8, CROKE PARK

> 'There was a special bond, something that people would not understand unless they were playing on that team. There were special understandings built up. Words hadn't to be said. People understood each other. It came just spontaneously to us. It was intuitive. It was within us.'
>
> JIM DEENIHAN, Oration at the funeral of Tim Kennelly

A dollop of Dubs had threatened to retire if they won the three in a row in 1978. Paddy Cullen, Seán Docherty, Tony Hanahoe, Jimmy Keaveny, Gay O'Driscoll and Pat O'Neill would almost certainly have gone. But as Kerry players would find out half a decade later, the Dubs found it difficult to retire gracefully in defeat.

They stayed on, which was a mistake, because the Dublin team was brought to a humiliating end in 1979. Kerry crushed their opponents, stylishly winning with a shattering Mike Sheehy goal after ten minutes, another Sheehy penalty after 56 minutes, and a third from John Egan eight minutes from the end for a 3-13 to 1-8 victory.

Starting without Ger Power, losing John O'Keeffe and having Páidí Ó Sé sent off, did not deter them. Jim Ronayne's controversial 46th-minute hand passed goal was Dublin's only reward for a spirited comeback attempt in the second half.

Pretenders everywhere had waited for the duopoly to crack. League champions Roscommon almost made the All-Ireland final. Roscommon beat Mayo 3-15 to 2-10 in the Connacht final. They went out of the championship by 0-14 to 1-10 at the hands of Dublin, only because Michael Hickey scored Dublin's winning point against them four minutes from the end of a tense semi-final, minutes after a dramatic equalising goal from Roscommon's Michael Finneran. Hickey scored nine points in that semi-final, yet was taken off early in the final when he missed two 50s. The subs were not finding it easy to win a place among the Dubs.

Monaghan beat Donegal 1-15 to 0-11 to recapture the Ulster title after 41 years, and after a false start. Donegal in fact had scored an opening point. But the referee suddenly realised that the band was still on the field waiting to play the national anthem. Play was stopped and the point was scratched, 'Amhrán na bhFiann' was sounded and the ceremony of the throw-in to start the game was repeated! A second time, Monaghan took control immediately with a Kieran Finlay goal (Finlay added nine points), led 1-9 to 0-2 before Donegal got moving, and never relinquished the lead.

Monaghan brought their colourful supporters to Croke Park on the crest of a drumlin. But their noisy welcome for their heroes was silenced as Ger

Power slammed in two goals in the first fifteen minutes for Kerry. Mikey Sheehy collected a record score of 3-5, and Liston and Spillane had goals disallowed as Kerry won 5-14 to 0-7.

Kerry may have been at their very best in 1979. Certainly Ger Power was, scoring 2-4 as Kerry beat Cork 2-14 to 2-4 in the Munster final. Cork missed two penalties. Clare fared worse, the wrong end of a record 9-21 to 1-9 hammering in Miltown Malbay. The Kerry 1978–79 League campaign included victories of 7-8 to 0-7 against Kildare, whose goalkeeper Ollie Crinnigan had just had an All-Star award announced the previous Friday, and 6-11 to nil against Laois.

One team alone was threatening to break the Dublin-Kerry axis. Dublin beat Offaly by a close-call 1-8 to 0-10 before 52,348 spectators in the Leinster final with the help of a controversial goal two minutes from full-time. When Brian Mullins was fouled, he flung the ball at an opponent in retaliation. Instead of a Dublin free, the referee decided to throw in the ball between the two players, then threw the ball directly to Mullins. He cantered off in the direction of the Offaly goal, leaving Bernard Brogan to finish the score for Dublin's six in a row. A well-worked goal by Jim Ronayne was earlier disallowed, and Jimmy Keaveney was sent off in a dramatic and often bad-tempered final. Offaly's ire was raised.

21 SEPTEMBER 1980. KERRY 1-9, ROSCOMMON 1-6, CROKE PARK

> 'Our style was an open book, one we had employed over several seasons, so why would we want to become embroiled in a war of attrition?'
>
> MICK O'DWYER, *Blessed and Obsessed* (2007)

It was the genius of Matt Connor that eventually lifted Offaly out of the shadow of Dublin in 1980.

Matt Connor was the third youngest of a football-mad family of eight, one of whom, Murt, won 1971 and 1972 All-Ireland medals, and another, Richie, was captain of the 1982 Offaly team. Two double cousins, related on both the father and mother's side, Liam and Tomas, were also on the 1982 team. Matt grew up on a farmyard where the kids were served by two ready-made goalposts, the horse door on one side, the supporting walls for the diesel tank on the other. The lads would play there, commentating as they played: 'A point for Laois but back down the field and a goal for Offaly.'

Around the farmyard, Matt brought a football with him on his chores. Leaving a fork or a bucket down, he would pick a target for himself, the small window beside the turf shed, the second rung of the ladder, even the red hen by the cowhouse door, and a ball would go flying in that direction. The pasture at the back was reserved for the 'big men's ball', a much-punctured leather that Uncle John was repeatedly called upon to repair. There the local boys would gather with the Connors for impromptu games.

Matt set records at every level. He helped Walsh Island to six in a row in Offaly, scored a record 5-4 for his club against Dunlavin in a Leinster club championship game, and took over the free-taking for Offaly in 1980. He was Ireland's top scorer for five years. His astounding 1980 year total of 22-135 defeated Mick O'Dwyer's ten-year-old record, and his match average of 11.5 in the 1980 championship may never be beaten.

In the Leinster final, as Offaly dethroned Dublin 1-10 to 1-8 before 50,276 people, Connor scored 1-7, including the vital goal eleven minutes after half-time. He switched from corner to centre forward and restored Offaly's morale just when they seemed to have lost all chance of winning. Dublin hit eleven wides in the first half and might have come back had any injury-time been played. Kevin Moran, now in his second year with Manchester United, lined out in the semi-final for Dublin against Meath. Connor scored 2-8 as Offaly weathered an early Kildare siege in the other semi-final.

The All-Ireland semi-final between Kerry and Offaly was a celebration of the hand pass at its best, a year before the tactic was banned. Both sides let the game open up and Kerry snatched four goals, two from Pat Spillane, the others from Mikey Sheehy and John Egan. Kerry eventually won 4-15 to 4-10. Matt Connor scored 2-9.

The following year's congress banned the hand pass, unimpressed by the eight-goal spectacle. This was reckoned by Kerry manager Mick O'Dwyer to have been one of the best games ever played.

Clare, horrified by their drubbing in 1979, had pushed through a motion at a November 1979 Munster council meeting that Kerry should have a bye into the following year's Munster final. Kerry were angry, and feared that lack of match practice might damage their prospects against Cork, still one of the biggest threats to their ambitions. The fears proved unfounded as Kerry beat Cork 3-13 to 0-12. Tim Kennelly of Kerry scored an extraordinary own point—kicked over his own crossbar from twenty yards out!

Roscommon had a hand pass romp of their own, winning 9-19 to 1-10 in the Connacht championship against London, whose impressive array of warming-up exercises beforehand was the closest they came to entertaining the small crowd.

Ulster too had eight goals to celebrate, as Armagh beat Tyrone 4-10 to 4-7 and took their sixth title with three late points, two from Peter Loughran and another from Jimmy Smyth, to clinch the game after Damien O'Hagan brought Tyrone bursting back into the contest with two goals.

When Armagh met Roscommon in the All-Ireland semi-final,

Roscommon fell 0-7 to 2-6 behind at half-time. Tony McManus then wiped the lead with a 50th-minute goal. Roscommon fell behind again, and Michael Finneran's goal six minutes from the end sent Roscommon through by 2-20 to 3-11.

On this showing, Roscommon were not rated a danger to Kerry's chances. But the 1980 All-Ireland was the one out of Kerry's four in a row that they came closest to losing. Mick O'Dwyer was to reminisce: 'Roscommon squandered a glorious opportunity in 1980. They were strong, experienced and well organised and made a great start but then lost faith and instead of continuing with their positive game became negative. They adopted an over-aggressive approach. It backfired completely.'

In his biography, many years after the event, he is even more forceful: 'There is no point sugar coating anything about the 1980 All-Ireland final. It was a rough, untidy, fractious affair for which Roscommon were solely and totally to blame. Our game was based on quick movement on and off the ball and Roscommon had clearly spent lots of time on the training ground devising ways of stopping us.'

Kerry fell five points behind to Roscommon in the first twelve minutes. Seán Walsh's first free was charged down by Dermot Earley and he delivered to Tony MacManus. Kerry full back John O'Keeffe slipped. Corner back Ger O'Keeffe came across to block McManus, leaving John O'Connor unmarked and in position to take the pass and hand pass to the net after 35 seconds.

A hand passed Mikey Sheehy goal brought Kerry back on level terms at half-time and eventually the Liston-less Kerry won a ragged 64-free final by three points, 1-9 to 1-6. Their lead had been only two points until the 34th minute of the second half, when Finneran late-tackled Spillane, and Sheehy took a gift of a free for the insurance point.

At training on the Tuesday before the final, Eoin Liston asked Mick O'Dwyer to skip press-ups because he had a sharp pain in his side. For a while he stood leaning against the fence in his togs. A doctor gave him a pain-killer, and he drove himself to Tralee to a hospital. Appendicitis was diagnosed. Liston was out of the final.

Mike Sheehy was only 75 per cent fit to play. Ger Power's leg was suspect. He was prodded with pain-killers and sent on to the field only to find, to his horror, that they wore off soon after the national anthem sounded.

Sheehy saved Kerry in the end. He scored six frees, all but three of the Kerry total. His best point was scored from fourteen yards out, near the sideline on the Hogan Stand side. Roscommon tried three free-takers and missed some great chances. John O'Connor and Dermot Earley scored just one free each for Roscommon. Michael Finneran missed two eminently scoreable frees in the second half.

Roscommon missed three great goal chances. John O'Connor misjudged a 30 yard Michael Finneran pass which bounced awkwardly, allowing Nelligan to come out and gather. O'Connor had another shot spectacularly pushed over the bar by Nelligan. And ten minutes from the end, Nelligan blocked down a Michael Finneran shot. Páidí Ó Sé saw Aidan Dooley about to latch on to the rebound and flung himself across the goal for a miraculous save, then held the ball off the ground to avoid conceding a penalty.

There is a theory that short-pass games involve up to five times the amount of physical contact as the catch-and-kick game. Whatever the reason, the Kerry v Roscommon final in 1980 was the most free-ridden since the 80-minute drawn final in 1972. The ball was in play for less than fifteen minutes.

The 64 frees, and the physical aspects of the game, caused controversy. One Roscommon selector claimed: 'You could not look at a Kerry man but there was a free.' County chairman Michael O'Callaghan criticised the referee afterwards, and was deprived of an American trip with the All-Stars.

But O'Dwyer countered for Kerry: 'All-Irelands are not won by physical force. Ways and means to dethrone the present Kerry side are being tried throughout the country and those who have not got the skill must resort to other tactics.'

The most extreme tactic of all to dethrone Kerry was the decision to change the rules of the game.

24 AUGUST 1980. KERRY 4-15, OFFALY 4-10, CROKE PARK

> 'It was a horrifying sight when this Kerry team came forward in droves with the ball and usually ended up hand passing the ball to the net.'
>
> EUGENE MCGEE, Offaly manager, commenting after the 1980 All-Ireland semi-final, a high paced match that eventually led to the removal of the open-hand pass from football

Three separate committees had proposed several sets of rule changes in the 1970s. Those that were ignored included one made up of the Kerry manager Mick O'Dwyer, the Dublin manager Kevin Heffernan, the Kildare manager Eamonn O'Donoghue and Roscommon All-Star Dermot Earley. The proposals were probably the only ones to have been devised completely by coaches and players: curtailment of the solo run; clarification of the mess caused by the personal foul; elimination of the fisted tackle, 'because the man in possession invariably gets bruised and battered'; clarification of the hand pass rule: 'Either get rid of it altogether or define a throw, preferably as the one-handed pitch that one sees in baseball or American football.'

Defining the hand pass was always a problem. The chairman of the referees committee which drew up the rule that made it legal in 1975, Simon Deignan, who taught Dublin how to use the technique, stated:

> For the past twenty years players have used a fisted pass as one of the skills of the game. Today the open palm of the hand may be used in all circumstances. This is the true definition of the hand pass. It is clear to us that the palmed pass may not be extended in its use beyond the boundaries of the fisted pass. A good guide-line is to remember that the ball may not be allowed to rest, even momentarily, in the passing hand. In other words, there should be a clear movement in the striking of the ball off one hand by another.

That 'clear movement' was a talking point for a decade. Critics of the hand pass, seen to great effect in Dublin's defeat of Armagh in 1977 and by Kerry's passing movements that yielded five goals against Dublin in 1978, seven against Kildare and six against Laois in the League, and nine against Clare in the championship, came forward from all parts. Even Kerry had passed a motion calling for the abolition of the hand pass in 1980. The motion was carried by a majority of 40 votes. But it was still considerably short of the two-thirds majority required to change the rule. The hand pass stayed.

Was there a clear movement when Jim Ronayne scored for Dublin against Kerry in the 1979 All-Ireland final, or when Mike Sheehy scored short-range goals against Cork and Monaghan in the same year's championship? Throughout 1981 forces to abolish the hand pass continued to muster. The next chance to get rid of it would not come until 1985. But football legislators were horrified by the events of 1980, the fact that an aggregate of 8-35 was scored in the semi-final by the teams that had apparently disregarded the high fielding and long kicking traditions of the game, and the reduction of the final to rugged chaos by a Roscommon team intent on stopping another scoring spree dominated by the hand pass.

Even where the technique was at its zenith in Kerry, Michael Lyne complained:

> Football is becoming very much akin to basketball, or even rugby—except that forward passing is allowed. No longer do we see the high fielding, the long clearance or the long range points. The catch phrase backs stay back is quickly becoming outdated. Is it not time that the GAA looked again at the contribution of the hand pass to the game? It was said it would speed up play. Does hand passing back to the goalie speed up the play? Can a hand passing movement move the ball faster than a long clearance? Nowadays when possession football is the order of the day, is there any

legal way of dispossessing a player? The GAA must move now before the nauseating feature of holding possession creeps into the game.

He was backed up by other Kerry old-timers. One claimed that, as the rules of Gaelic football are now framed, a team of tall basketballers from Alabama could come over and destroy the All-Ireland champions.' Joe Keohane joined the charge: 'I believe the game is becoming popular in convent schools and reverend mothers are losing their minds about it.'

The hue and cry against the hand pass had grown so much that a special congress was announced, purportedly to examine the hand pass, the solo run and the personal foul. The event was to become a public execution of the hand pass.

A committee was asked to report to the special congress. It decided that the hand pass had four advantages: it eliminated pulling and mauling from the game; it gave the player plenty of options in a tight situation; it helped the less physical player; and it speeded up the game for spectators. The committee listed two disadvantages of the hand pass: that it changed the character of Gaelic football from a kicking game to a running game; and that it was virtually impossible to manage for referees, claiming (without much foundation) that 60 per cent of all hand passes were in fact foul passes.

It produced a slim but influential 24-page report. Future GAA president and referee Mick Loftus chaired the committee. It was top-heavy with officials, Jim Roche, Ciaran O'Neill, Gerry Fagan, Jim McKeever and director general Liam Mulvihill. There were two players appointed, but Dermot Earley pulled out and Jack O'Shea was unable to attend any of the meetings.

Their decision to recommend that scores from the hand pass be abolished was made on such improbable grounds as: it 'was a poor ending to a good movement', that it was 'too simple, there is not much skill involved', and it was 'not in full keeping with the game of football', alongside more credible reasons such as 'the hand pass disadvantages the defence too much', and that it was 'too difficult for a referee to determine the legality of a hand pass where an important score was involved'.

A tiny sample were asked their views on the hand pass, 59 people in all. Of these, twelve were players, fifteen were coaches, fourteen were referees, and eighteen were spectators and administrators. Only 45 replied.

The special congress, held at Na Fianna clubhouse, Mobhi Road, on 9 May 1981, decided it wanted to retain the hand pass with scores by the hand allowed. Kerry's motion 'that the hand pass in play be retained' was passed on a 77/40 vote.

It was decided to define the hand pass: 'There must be a visible striking of the ball by the hand, and where the striking action is not visible the referee shall deem the pass as being a foul', according to a proposal from Cork and Louth. A revival of the old 'If a player receives the ball by hand pass, he must kick it' rule was lost. Congress then decided that scores be allowed with the fist only.

The satisfied delegates adjourned to lunch. Then some of them began to realise the mess they had created. Allowing only fisted scores would create havoc when it came to a referee having to come to a decision in a tense junior B match surrounded by 30 footballers and the goalie's granny.

They had to reverse the morning's decision by a two-thirds majority when they returned. They decided to outlaw all scores with the hand unless the ball is already in flight. It was a vital definition that would allow Pat Spillane to score a goal against Tyrone in the 1986 All-Ireland final.

The hand pass had been retained in play but its new definition was, to say the least, vague. It 'had to have a visible striking movement'. Referees began to enforce this new 'definition', whatever it meant, rigidly. The most influential managers in the country, Kevin Heffernan and Mick O'Dwyer, were both reasonably happy with the redefined hand pass, but they were astonished and disappointed when they saw how the new rule was being interpreted by referees.

O'Dwyer maintained: 'The speedy transfer of the ball that was part and parcel of 1970s football may have helped the game. The punched pass is slower to execute, slows down play and brings about untidy play.'

20 SEPTEMBER 1981. KERRY 1-12, OFFALY 0-8, CROKE PARK

And it's up the gallant Kingdom
And up the great O'Dwyer
The Kingdom's greatest trainer
Whose skills we all admire
We'll toast our Kerry heroes
Who brought our county fame
And thank them for their victory
In this very sporting game.

KERRY SUPPORTERS' BALLAD (1981)

Roscommon crumbled after their near miss. Their Connacht championship five-in-a-row bid came unstuck in the semi-final at Markievicz Park. They went down to Sligo by 2-9 to 1-8. Sligo's Martin McCarrick established a firm base at midfield and J. Kearins scored both goals.

Meanwhile Mayo had their eye on the crown. Their championship campaign started at London board headquarters at leafy Ruislip before 5,000

London-Irish supporters. Galway succumbed in the semi-final by 2-8 to 1-9 to a spectacular Mayo goal by Jim Bourke (seventeen minutes) and another by Jim Lyons (55 minutes).

In the Connacht final at Castlebar, Mayo couldn't even get the ball into the Sligo half for the first ten minutes. When they eventually did, it hardly ever came out again. Mayo scored six points without reply, as Sligo missed chance after chance, and won by 0-12 to 0-4.

Munster provided the poorest provincial final in nineteen years. Mikey Sheehy scored the only goal in the match for Kerry after 58 minutes and Cork were confined to just a single point from play, scored by Dave Barry. Cork's tactic of switching the six backs around at intervals had no effect whatsoever on Kerry's attack. The score was a paltry two points to one at half-time. The change in the hand pass rule seemed to have reduced the whole game to a shambles.

Kerry were held by Mayo for 49 minutes of the semi-final. Eddie McHale scored a splendid goal, sandwiched between two by Power and Liston, for Mayo to trail 2-7 to 1-6 at half-time. Then came utter devastation as Mayo failed to score in the second half and eventually went down to a 2-19 to 1-6 defeat. The semi-finals represented Kerry at their best, combining their preparation and skill with none of the tension of an All-Ireland final.

In Ulster, Down wrapped up their tenth title in 22 years with two goals from John McCartan in the final five minutes to beat Armagh 3-12 to 1-10. It finished an Armagh fight back. Armagh had equalised at the three-quarter stage with a disputed Brian Hughes goal.

Teenager Greg Blayney got the game off to a tremendous start by scoring a goal with his first touch of the ball in the final. It was a time of turmoil in Ulster. An H Block protest was held on the field at half-time.

Laois shocked Dublin by 2-9 to 0-11 in the Leinster semi-final with a great performance from John Costelloe, who shared the goals with Tom Prendergast.

Wexford too had a few moments of inspiration in beating hopefuls Meath 2-9 to 1-11 in the quarter-final. Meath man Eddie Mahon kicked six points against his native county, and John Wright landed a Wexford goal just seconds after Eamonn Barry missed a penalty for Meath. Tom Prendergast's three goals helped Laois oust Kildare. Mahon was not the only one to defy his native county: Wicklow-born John O'Leary produced a last-minute save which stopped a major Wicklow breakthrough, 0-10 to 0-8, in the quarter-final, leaving Moses Coffey and Pat Baker without a Leinster final appearance to their name.

Annual failures, Kilkenny, started excellently against Wexford when Paudie Lannon and Seán Fennelly scored first half goals, but two Ger Howlin fisted goals put them out by 2-11 to 2-4.

Laois did better in the final than most people expected. Offaly trailed 0-3 to 2-2 after twenty minutes of the final, but Johnny Mooney and Tomas Connor took control at midfield, Brendan Lowry extracted two great saves from the Laois goalkeeper Tom Scully and struck the goal that started Offaly's comeback for a 1-18 to 3-9 victory. Missed chances prevented Offaly winning by more.

Offaly shook off Down in the second half of their 56-free semi-final, Down being held scoreless for the final sixteen minutes to go down 0-12 to 0-6.

The All-Ireland final was played at something less than the terrific pace of the previous year's semi-final. But it was still an open game. Although there were 31 stoppages, this was the least free-ridden final since 1966.

Kerry were missing Pat Spillane. Offaly too had a real injury worry. Both midfielders were badly hit. Tomas Connor had not trained for a week and was obviously carrying an injury throughout the match. Then Johnny Mooney fell off a turf trailer and injured his shoulder.

Although, after 61 training sessions, the team was fighting fit, Kerry's combination passing went into history with the hand pass. They opted instead for the high ball into the Offaly square. It was 0-5 each at half-time. Offaly's best chance came in the second half when Gerry Carroll hit the post.

Kerry struck for four in a row with three minutes to go. Seven players were involved in the move. Kerry corner back Jim Deenihan cleared, Tim Kennelly gathered and passed to Tommy Doyle; Eoin Liston was found near the left-hand touchline; he gave a quick short pass to John Egan, who gave another short pass to Mike Sheehy; Offaly back Charlie Conroy advanced to take on Sheehy and left Jack O'Shea unmarked. O'Shea took the pass in full flight and crashed his shot to the net from fourteen yards. The game finished 1-12 to 0-8 soon afterwards. Only 61,489 showed up, the lowest attendance at a final since 1947.

19 SEPTEMBER 1982. OFFALY 1-15, KERRY 0-17, CROKE PARK

> 'If it was a push, a traditional corner back would have been ready for it. Tommy Doyle played very natural football and played like a wing back would. That's no criticism of him. It just happened. Nobody could make the switch.'
>
> SEÁN WALSH

Two years after his Fiat 127 had collided with a lamp post, smashing his femur and apparently bringing a fabulous football career to an end at the age of 25, Dublin's Brian Mullins completed a remarkable comeback in 1982. He was the dominant figure in Dublin's ugly victory over Kildare that saw Kildare's John Crofton sent off.

Laois played a thrilling semi-final with Offaly, going down by 3-13 to 1-15, after they were spurred on by a goal twelve minutes into the second half, but allowed Gerry Carroll and John Guinan to run free for two goals. When Brendan Lowry got a third for Offaly, it was all over.

Offaly and Dublin met again in the Leinster final, but it was a disappointment. Offaly led Dublin at half-time by eight points and eventually won by nine, 1-16 to 1-7. A veteran from the 1972 All-Ireland, Seamus Darby, was recalled to the team after two years and his shrewd positional play made his comeback a success. Darby scored the winning goal in the second minute of play. Ironically, this was to be the direct inverse of his goal in the All-Ireland final of a year later, two minutes from the end of play.

In the All-Ireland semi-final, Galway proved to be better than most people anticipated and narrowly missed doing to Offaly what Offaly did to Kerry in the final. Galway took the lead and held it until ten minutes from the end, thanks to a Tom Naughton goal midway through the first half.

Gay McManus was soundly apportioned blame for Galway's failure. He missed two scoring-range frees in the dying minutes of the match and Offaly stole through to the final by 1-12 to 1-11. McManus will never forget the scene as he drove past the Aisling Hotel the following day, the car window open, amid the jibes of disappointed Galway supporters. 'Is he still taking frees?' a Galway man roared.

Offaly had a new hero. Johnny Mooney was playing instead of the injured Seamus Darby. He was flown home from America for the semi-final amid an embarrassing amount of publicity for an illegal immigrant. Brendan Lowry scored their goal five minutes before half-time and also scored a winning point.

The only county waiting for an Ulster title, Fermanagh, had a rare championship run in the north. A goal from debutant Arthur Mulligan helped them beat Derry 1-9 to 1-8 in the first round. In the second round 19-year-old Dom Corrigan scored 1-3, and towering midfielder Peter McGinnity 0-5, as they ousted Tyrone 1-8 to 0-10.

McGinnity was one of Ulster's outstanding midfielders at the time, despite Fermanagh's lack of success. He provided one of the best moments in the Ulster final when he ran for about 40 yards with the ball before launching a superb left-foot 25 yard shot for the only goal of the game.

But it was a futile gesture. Armagh shot twenty wides in one of the poorest ever finals, but won their seventh title anyway as Fran McMahon and Colm McKinstry took control of midfield and ended any hopes of a Fermanagh breakthrough.

Kerry were looking not too invincible at all, as they stuttered on the way to their eighth Munster title. Ger Power missed the chance of victory as Cork held them to a draw, 0-9 each, but Jack O'Shea, a car crash victim the Friday before the drawn final, had recovered sufficiently to inspire a great replay victory by 2-18 to 0-12. Mikey Sheehy also came to the rescue with scores, 2-4 in all.

Kerry's full forward line of Liston, Egan and Sheehy scored the requisite three goals to beat Armagh 3-15 to 1-11 with another brilliant All-Ireland semi-final performance. Only 17,523 showed up.

That left Kerry and Offaly to fight out the championship. The prospect of a record five-in-a-row All-Ireland titles came up again and again to haunt Kerry. 'Five in a row, five in a row. It's hard to believe we've won five in a row' sang the group Galleon in a £5,000 single that was prepared for release the day after the game in anticipation of history. Advance copies went out the week before the game. Eugene McGee recited a verse to the Offaly team before the match. He talked about smashing records, and the players all knew what he meant.

Offaly's resources were scarce, hardly comparable to the riches that Kerry enjoyed. But the team destined to stop the five in a row had been built around a few players who could kick a ball 40 or 50 yards accurately with the side of the foot on the run. In the post-hand pass game, that was important.

Kerry were using the hand pass as the first option, and kicking as a last resort. The Offaly formula was to deny these free-flying hand passers the opportunity to catch the ball, and kick the ball themselves, leaving the hands free.

At the same time that Eugene McGee was considering Darby's recall, before the championship had even begun, Jim Deenihan knocked the ball out of John O'Keeffe's hand during a Kerry training session. Deenihan went to boot it on the ground and John Egan, Deenihan's marker, came thundering in to block down the shot. The two collided and were tossed over each other. As Egan fell on top of Deenihan there was an almighty crack. Egan's leg was broken.

In contrast to 1981, in the 1982 All-Ireland final, Richie Connor overcame Tim Kennelly and Liam O'Connor kept Eoin Liston under control. Tomas Connor, missing in 1980 and 1981, was back in full flight. Pádraig Dunne, a discovery of 1981, blossomed in 1982. Pat Fitzgerald, an average footballer, played out of his skin.

Offaly got everything right. The story of how they smashed the five-in-a-row dream with two minutes to go comes with at least four 'what might have happened if' addenda.

Offaly had built up a lead of three points five minutes before half-time, after a breathless first half. At half-time, Kerry official Seamus Mac Gearailt enthused, 'If you blinked you'd have missed a score.'

Rain had fallen in the morning, then cleared, then fell again at half-time. The ball and the sod were slippery. Eoin Liston fell when he was chasing a loose ball that might have ended in the Offaly net.

Mick O'Dwyer emphasises in his biography the period when Kerry were four points up with six minutes remaining. 'I have always believed that referees are unconsciously susceptible to what I would term the underdog influence. It becomes easier for the underdogs to win frees when they've fallen behind, not because the referee is biased, but because he is human.'

'Their points came from frees. You would have to say that two of them were dubious calls,' John Egan reflected.

'As we defended our four-point lead, Seán Lowry won a free and to this day I have no idea why it was awarded', O'Dwyer wrote. Matt Connor pointed another free and the lead went back to two. 'There's no doubt that we became nervous. Instead of holding our shape and taking the game on, we funnelled back in an attempt to protect the lead.'

Substitute Seamus Darby, a replacement for John Guinan, had entered the play almost unnoticed, and had yet to touch the ball. He moved to corner forward and Guinan's marker, wing back Tommy Doyle, followed him. Kerry's wing back was now playing corner back and vice versa.

Liam O'Connor delivered a pass towards Darby. Doyle got ahead of him, jumped early, over-committing himself, but was about to collect the ball when Darby appeared to nudge him on the back. Doyle fell forward in a bundle, Darby gathered unimpeded, ran four paces and blasted a goal past stranded goalkeeper Nelligan.

Was it a push? 'I held him, and as I took the ball I arsed him out,' Darby told Michael Foley in 2007 for his award-winning book about the game, *Kings of September*. 'People say to me, even to this day, I saw your hands on his back. But my hands weren't on the man's back.'

O'Dwyer wrote: 'Ask yourself this, why would Doyle totally misjudge the flight of the ball so badly that he didn't make any contact? Would he really have got it so wrong that the ball would drop gently into Darby's arms? That's not the Doyle I knew.'

The referee, P. J. McGrath, told Foley: 'I had a clear view of it. My only worry was whether or not it was a goal. And it was. There was no one talking to me about the alleged push that evening. I spoke to the umpires about it but none of them saw anything that would warrant any sort of a free. If you look at Darby's hands in the frame, he didn't touch Tommy Doyle at all with his hands. He never pushed him. He pushed out his backside and Doyle backed into him. He never touched him with his hands.'

'It would have made a beautiful point,' Kerry goalkeeper Charlie Nelligan said. 'He just stuck it. I was so close to getting it I felt the breeze on my fingers as the ball flashed by. When I got up off the ground and was going back to pick up the ball, the spray from the net was hitting me on the head.' Nelligan was in such a daze he placed the ball on the fourteen yard line instead of the 21 for the kick-out.

Kerry in disarray could not organise their counter-attack, so Offaly won their third title 1-15 to 0-17. The Kerry players did not complain. They left Croke Park dazed. No one suggested robbery. 'We definitely could have equalised but you don't blame anyone,' Kerry team captain John Egan said in *Princes of Pigskin* 26 years later. 'We could have been calmer. You don't like losing but the manner of the defeat was devastating. It was very hard to recover from it.'

'I was told by 25,000 people,' Tom Spillane says, 'why didn't you look up? There was someone on the edge of the square. I don't know what I did. I went for a point or something and didn't score. That was it.'

Kerry's supporters had plenty to speculate about. What might have happened, they asked, if Darby's push on Doyle had resulted in a free out? If Deenihan had been there? If corner back Ger O'Keeffe had taken over the marking of Darby? If even the bench had seen what was going on and sent on appropriate instructions? If two doubtful frees had not been presented to Matt Connor just before the whistle, one when Paud Lynch punched the ball clear, another when Seán Lowry seemed to fall with three Kerry men around him? If the Kerry forwards and Jack O'Shea had not flocked to the defence in those closing minutes? If Tom Spillane had kept his head and passed the ball across the field in that fateful last counter-attack? Above all, if the five in a row and immortality was not at issue, would Kerry players have concentrated on keeping possession and not panicked?

Martin Furlong did his part—saving a dramatic penalty seventeen minutes into the second half by advancing from his goal and charging down Mikey Sheehy's shot.

Penalties were always a problem for Kerry. The final Tuesday before the big match at a training session in Killarney's Fitzgerald Stadium, Sheehy took twenty penalties against Charlie Nelligan. He worked out that Furlong's weak side was to the goalie's left. Penalty after penalty was sent hurtling past Nelligan, many of them to the top corner, all to the goalkeeper's left. Nelligan was impressed.

But when it came to the real thing, Sheehy changed his mind at the moment he was kicking the ball and decided to kick to Furlong's right side. Furlong had guessed that was where he would place it. According to Sheehy: 'Hitting it wasn't the problem. It was just that I hit it to Furlong's better side.

I still think that penalty was the turning point in the game. I felt it immediately when he saved it that the five in a row was not on. All sorts of fears went through my head.'

Seamus Darby was later to say that, sometimes, he regretted that goal that turned him into a celebrity.

17 JULY 1983. CORK 3-10, KERRY 3-9, PÁIRC UÍ CHAOIMH

> 'As time passed, I began to think that maybe it was a good thing for some of the players that they didn't win the five in a row. The celebrations would have taken a heavy toll on anybody who wasn't prepared for them. Instead, we all had to face up to the reality that nobody is immune from disappointment.'
>
> MICK O'DWYER, *Blessed and Obsessed* (2007)

They thought last-minute lightning would only strike Kerry once. But in 1983 Kerry lost to another tail-end goal. Kerry were two points ahead and 30 seconds away from a nine in a row in Munster, when Tadhg Murphy took a high free which was struck to the net off the post by Tadhg Murphy for a winning goal for Cork.

A rainstorm early in the day set the scene. By the time the minor final began at 12.45 the pitch was a sheet of water. The provincial junior final was also played in spilling rain. The rain only stopped just before the senior final. Brave spectators, 17,000 of them, began to arrive to face this torrent in the last few minutes before the senior match was due to begin.

The sides were level five times before that dramatic finish. Kerry captain Jack O'Shea scored two goals and Mike Sheehy what looked like a winner in the 60th minute. But the backs rambled out of position and it all began to go wrong.

Tadhg Murphy, the bandit-in-chief, had made his name as an opportunist when still at school. Under the experimental thirteen-a-side colleges hurling rules of the early 1970s, the tiny four foot, 15-year-old Murphy came on as a substitute and scored a last-minute winning goal for St Finbarrs, Farranferris, against St Kierans, Kilkenny, in the 1972 All-Ireland Colleges hurling final.

This time he was dispatched to hang in around the goalmouth, Darby-like, in the closing minutes of the 1983 Munster final. Kerry's defence had been slightly dislocated. Regular full back John O'Keeffe was missing, retired injured at half-time, and Paudie Lynch had moved to take his place. Referee John Moloney was looking at his watch. Denis Allen was fouled some way from the Kerry posts. Allen appeared to want to take the kick. He hesitated. John Cleary also started a run, but changed his mind. Tadhg O'Reilly took responsibility. He sent the ball soaring in over the heads of the Kerry backs and it dropped into the hands of Tadhg Murphy. Murphy recalls how he caught and turned and shot the ball low. It ricocheted back in from the left post, behind the stranded goalkeeper: 'I think the kick into the square was longer than Dave Barry anticipated. When I realised I was inside everybody except Charlie Nelligan I only had one thought on my mind. I went up, caught it cleanly, and turned to bring the ball to my right foot as I landed. I had just two seconds to gather my thoughts and put everything into my shot. When I fell I was looking directly at Charlie Nelligan. I concentrated on putting the ball out of his reach, sending it low into the corner of the goal. That's where it went, only into the wrong corner—it hit the post and rebounded into the far corner of the net.'

'Next time we are on the same team together,' Paud Lynch said to Páidí Ó Sé, walking off the field, 'it will be for the Jimmy Magee All-Stars.'

Time had been up for 90 seconds. Mick O'Dwyer could not remember a single stoppage during the second half. The referee had blown 35 seconds beyond the 70 minutes in 1982, when there seemed to be a lot of stoppages. Now another referee had extended time just long enough to beat Kerry.

'It was a blessing in disguise,' Páidí Ó Sé wrote afterwards. 'We were flat. Our hunger would not be sufficient to match Dublin. We needed a period to recharge, take stock of the situation, ask ourselves a few hard questions.'

18 SEPTEMBER 1983. DUBLIN 1-10, GALWAY 1-8, CROKE PARK

'You never know what might happen in the tunnel . . .'

EOIN LISTON before the 1984 All-Ireland final

That should have been enough drama for the year. But in Leinster two sun-soaked matches between Dublin and Meath in the quarter-final provided more thrills—for everyone except the Meath goalkeepers involved.

A goalkeeping mistake and an own goal gave Dublin a 2-8 each draw they hardly deserved the first day. Five minutes into the replay, the new goalkeeper smothered the ball but allowed it to escape and trickle over his line for a goal! Dublin won 3-9 to 0-16 in extra time with an Anton O'Toole goal after yet another mistake. Neither team looked like potential All-Ireland champions at the time.

Two well-fashioned goals in a three-minute spell before half-time did the damage against All-Ireland champions Offaly, who tamely opted out in the Leinster final before a poor 36,912 attendance, and Dublin came through by 2-13 to 1-11. Spectators spilled on to the field near the end of the game and attacked Offaly player Mick Fitzgerald after he made a wild lunge at Ciaran Duff.

Fitzgerald was beaten up by Dublin supporters, then sent off by the referee.

As summer temperatures soared, the on-field drama was growing in stature, timing and grandeur. In the Dublin v Cork All-Ireland semi-final, Barney Rock snatched as dramatic an equaliser as Croke Park has ever seen when he got a goal with 30 seconds to go. Brian Mullins saw Ray Hazley free to the left and sent him a well-placed pass. Hazley sent to Rock. Another split-second decision brought results: 'It was the only ball that bounced properly for me all day. Everything else went totally against me. The only place I could put the shot was low along the ground. The keeper came flying out. I just put the shot low and it went under him. If I'd kicked it a little bit higher the keeper would have got it.' That goal equalised the game 2-11 each, after Dinny Allen's two goals had given Cork a 2-6 to 1-6 half-time lead.

When the match was replayed in the bright sunshine of Páirc Uí Chaoimh, the players could not hear each other's calls because of the noise of the crowd. However, any fears of a riot proved without foundation.

A goal almost straightaway for Dublin ensured things would not be close. Mullins (from a penalty), Ciaran Duff, Barney Rock (when a replacement for him had been asked to warm up on the sideline) and Joe McNally got four goals for Dublin's 4-15 to 2-10 win. 'Hill 17', they called the Dublin supporters who descended to colourful Páirc Uí Chaoimh to a good-humoured, good-natured and memorable semi-final, probably the most atmospheric game in Gaelic football history.

Ulster had a good year. National League finalists Down and Armagh ended up training within five miles of each other in the week before the National League final: Down in Newry and Armagh (awaiting clearance on whether Cliftonville's Mickey MacDonald would play) in Killeavy. An Ambrose Rodgers goal gave Down victory.

But neither county made it when it came to the Ulster championship itself. Instead, with new manager Brian McEniffe at the helm, Donegal won a thriller against champions Armagh by 1-10 to 0-7.

The same teams had been level eight times during the 1982 championship encounter and Donegal had failed only to a late point from Mickey McDonald. Since then Donegal took six of their 1982 All-Ireland under-21 champions on board and shook champions Armagh with a third-minute Charlie Mulgrew goal.

For the Ulster final, McEniffe switched wing backs to prevent a repeat of Derek McDonnell's runaway fourth-minute goal for Cavan. The 1974 veteran Seamus Bonner marshalled the forwards and sent a first half penalty to the net, then bravely opted for the point from a second penalty 90 seconds from the end. At that stage Donegal still led by just two points, and they won 1-14 to 1-11.

The Galway-Mayo battle was re-enacted again in July when Galway won 1-13 to 1-10, largely by default, in the Connacht final at Castlebar. Galway's twelfth-minute goal, shot to the net by Val Daly after a back fumbled his pick-up, proved vital when Mayo's Martin Carney struck back in the 25th minute. Mayo claimed they should have been awarded a penalty. They had been awarded one in the first round against Roscommon and missed it. A great winning point by 19-year-old debutant Brian Kilkelly ousted Roscommon.

In the All-Ireland semi-final, Kieran Keeney's fifteenth-minute goal gave Donegal the lead against Galway. But a miskicked free let Val Daly through for Galway's clinching goal and fortunate 1-12 to 1-11 victory five minutes from the end.

Dublin showed their text-book composure throughout the game. Team manager Kevin Heffernan was tending to an injured Dublin player in the square in front of the goalkeeper. The goalkeeper miscued his kick-out, and Barney Rock fielded and sent it straight back to the unguarded net. Rock indicated after the game that Heffernan's presence contributed to the goal. 'I was hardly going to check to see if my mother was looking in the stand first.' But the composure was most needed when they were reduced to twelve players. Outbreaks of fisticuffs and a kicking incident diminished Dublin's numbers. Their remaining twelve men fell back into defence, abandoned traditional positioning and crowded out the Galway attack by bringing both corner forwards back to midfield.

Dublin's victory in 1983 bore no resemblance to what had gone before. 'What Kevin Heffernan did with the 1983 team was deserving of the highest praise,' Tommy Drumm told David Walsh in the 'Goodbye to the Hill' feature in *Magill* magazine in 1989. 'During the seventies he gave the orders and the lads got on with it. Cold and clinical. That was not going to work with the 83 team and Kevin changed his style. He cajoled them; he spoke with individuals outside of the group discussions and did many things completely different to the methods he used in the seventies. I would not have believed he had the capacity to change but I saw how he did.'

The performance received a mixed reaction from an aghast public and officialdom. Brian Mullins, Ray Hazley and Ciaran Duff of Dublin and Tomas Tierney of Galway were all sent off, a record for an All-Ireland final, and bitterness remained for months afterwards throughout a long sequel of disciplinary hearings which never established exactly who had given Galway midfielder Brian Talty a black eye in the tunnel on the way to the dressing room.

Mick Holden of Dublin confessed afterwards that he had not realised that Dublin had a third man sent off until after the final whistle: 'If I had known that I would probably have given up altogether.'

Holden had been the only respondent to Kevin Heffernan's offer to the Dublin footballers of sleeping pills for the night before the match. When Heffo expressed surprise that Holden would have trouble sleeping he replied, 'It's not for me. It's for my mother.'

23 SEPTEMBER 1984. KERRY 0-14, DUBLIN 1-6, CROKE PARK

> 'I've just watched the All-Ireland and if Dublin can win it with twelve men, I'd back us with fifteen.'
>
> MICK O'DWYER, team talk with Kerry players, Red Cliff Hotel, Ballybunion, October 1983

> 'Kerry are past it.'
>
> *Irish Independent*, 22 September 1984

Kerry found a new midfield partner for Jack O'Shea in 1984: Gneeveguila player and new captain Ambrose O'Donovan. 'I have to live next door to these Cork men in Gneeveguila' was his inaugural speech before the Munster final, holding a football in his giant hands. The speech seemed to work. Kerry won their Munster title back.

Galway beat Mayo 2-13 to 2-9 in Connacht. They were in trouble midway through the second half when two goals in four minutes from Brian Talty and Stephen Joyce swept them into the lead. Kevin McStay, the slightly built Mayo player, basketball star and Universities soccer international, scored 1-7 and had a goal disallowed, which might have given Mayo a five-point lead. Mayo resorted to a series of bewildering switches in the end—to no avail.

Ulster had a change of champions yet again. Tyrone overcame favourites Armagh by 0-15 to 1-7 to win their fourth title. The week before the Ulster final, the local paper criticised Tyrone's Frank McGuigan for scoring only three points: 'That was from centrefield. Nobody scores eleven points from midfield.' He responded by scoring a remarkable eleven points, three from his right foot, seven with his left, and one with his fist, all of them from play. 'I figure if you get a couple early on it settles you down a wee bit. It's easy to get eleven points really—if you get the ball.'

The 19-year-old Gerard Houlihan, a goalkeeper's son, scored Armagh's only goal in the first-round game against Donegal and the semi-final winner against Monaghan, and the second half goal for Armagh in the final.

Others to score included the thieves who seized the semi-final takings at gunpoint from Casement Park, Belfast. Specially for the centenary, the Ulster council had decided to use Casement Park for its first major fixture in thirteen years.

Meath felt they were the heirs to Dublin's crown in Leinster, but in the semi-final battling Laois gave Meath a fright, and led by two points with fifteen minutes to go, 3-9 to 1-13, before Colm O'Rourke and Ben Tansey goals brought Meath through. Laois would give Meath a bigger fright the following year.

Offaly supplied the human interest angle of the series in the quarter-final: they trailed Longford by eight points, equalised eight minutes into the second half, and when they came back to a replay, their hero was the substitute goalkeeper, an under-21 player recruited from the stands, called by the papers, 'Lazarus' (in fact, Lazarene) Molloy.

Dublin v Meath was the Leinster final everybody wanted, and 56,051 showed up to watch it. Pádraig Lyons missed a Meath penalty early in the game to set Dublin on course for a 2-10 to 1-9 victory on the hottest day in 1984. Meath had felt they needed only a goalkeeper to beat Dublin. When Mickey Lyons missed the match through injury, they knew they needed much more. Ben Tansey got their goal as they struggled to come back against Dublin's fourteen men (John Caffrey was sent off in controversial circumstances).

Dublin's tactic of playing John Kearns as a third midfielder worked in the All-Ireland semi-final, although they hit eleven wides as they kept Tyrone scoreless for the first 28 minutes of the game. Meanwhile they picked up victory goals from Barney Rock and Joe McNally.

Highlight of the pre-match build-up was a battle for the Hill 16 goal, where two goalkeepers and 56 players all held their kick-around at the same end for several hilarious minutes.

Kerry easily defeated Galway in the other semi-final. Galway's four pre-match casualties were augmented by an injury to Gay MacManus during the match. Jack O'Shea had an outstanding game, and Sheehy and Egan took the goals.

Sheehy was missing from the final with an achilles tendon injury. Instead, John Kennedy took the frees for Kerry—three months earlier he was not even a free-taker with his club in Ballylongford.

When Kerry gathered in the Grand Hotel in Malahide the night before the All-Ireland, O'Dwyer had newspaper headlines pasted on to the wall of the room where the final team talk was given, 'Kerry Team Over The Hill', 'End of the Line'.

Kerry were in control throughout the centenary final, the second ever final to be all-ticket, and won 0-14 to 1-6. Only two Dublin forwards scored, and Barney Rock's 43rd-minute goal for Dublin was the only goal of the match. If Dublin were inspired by that goal, so was Pat Spillane. At the end of seven minutes of frantic, post-goal play, he dispossessed Dublin's centre half back, slid the ball away from the grasp of four Dublin defenders, and Ger Power was able to place Ogie Moran for a Kerry point. Goalkeepers were largely redundant as both teams opted for points.

For Barney Rock it was another in an extraordinary sequence of big match goals, against Meath, Offaly, Cork and Galway in 1983, and against Wexford, Meath, Tyrone and Kerry in 1984. For Kerry it was a relief not to be chasing a record for a change. 'Now we are going for one in a row,' said Eoin Liston before the final.

22 SEPTEMBER 1985. KERRY 2-12, DUBLIN 2-8, CROKE PARK

> 'There was a kind of modesty about the Kerry team of the 1970s and 1980s. Our motivation was compact. We kind of played for ourselves. Sure we were inspired by the jersey, the county, the wonderful tradition, the supporters. But we never once thought about standing back and admiring our achievements.'
>
> PÁIDÍ Ó SÉ, *Páidí* (2001)

Heads rolled early in the 1985 season. In the Leinster championship, Laois made amends for their near miss in 1984 by shocking Meath 2-11 to 0-7 in the 1985 Leinster semi-final at Tullamore. They did it with two goals in the sixteenth minute.

Paschal Doran scored the first, and when John Costelloe returned the kick-out, with the defence hopelessly out of place, Willie Brennan scored the second. So ended Meath's All-Ireland aspirations.

Tommy Conroy and Joe McNally (in the last minute) scored Dublin's goals against an Offaly side unsettled by the absence of Matt Connor, a car crash victim the previous December. But Dublin took control of a tough final in the last twenty minutes as rain lashed Croke Park in revenge for the previous year's sunshine, and won 0-9 to 0-4.

Kerry defeated Cork 2-11 to 0-11, as Ambrose O'Donovan was stretchered off bleeding after an off-the-ball incident that nobody saw and which went unpunished.

Early in 1985 Derry suffered a revolt by five disenchanted players and an open draw competition defeat against Limerick, yet came back to beat Ulster champions Tyrone with a controversial Declan McNicholl penalty goal—a decision that led to an assault on referee Greenan by Tyrone fans after the game. Derry followed this up with an impressive four-point win over Cavan to reach the Ulster final.

There the run ended. Midway through the first half of the final, Eamonn McEneaney fisted the first of his two goals and Monaghan went on to beat

Derry 2-9 to 0-8. McEneaney had a good goal-scoring run in 1985. He also scored the third-minute goal in a semi-final replay to beat Armagh 1-11 to 2-7.

A Monaghan-Armagh match in the championship had the distinction of being played with two referees: Michael Greenan (Cavan) had to take over from the limping Damien Campbell (Fermanagh) at half-time.

Both All-Ireland semi-finals were drawn. Kerry and Monaghan played an intriguing 1-12 to 2-9 draw when Eamonn McEneaney kicked a tense equaliser from a free, out near the sideline. McEneaney was haunted by people who recalled where they were when that free was taken: watching on television, listening on the radio, or howling in Croke Park—a moment to mark one's career by.

Mayo came back from six points down to draw the other semi-final 1-13 each with Dublin: Billy FitzPatrick and T. J. Kilgallon kicked the equalising points in the last 45 seconds. A superb Pádraig Brogan goal could not save Mayo in the replay. Ciaran Duff struck twice as Dublin won easily 2-12 to 1-7 after trailing by a point at half-time.

Kerry faced a younger than ever Dublin team in the final. Joe McNally celebrated his 21st birthday the week before the match. Dave Synnott and Tommy Conroy were also 21, Charlie Redmond was 22, and John O'Leary, Gerry Hargan, Pat Canavan, Barney Rock and Ciaran Duff all 24. Yet it was the older Kerry who seized the initiative with a Jack O'Shea penalty goal after eleven minutes. They led by nine points, 1-8 to 0-2, at half-time. But when Dublin came storming back in the second half, they relied on a perfectly finished Timmy O'Dowd breakaway goal thirteen minutes after half-time. That secured victory by 2-12 to 2-8.

Dublin's comeback was spurred by two goals from Joe McNally, a 52nd-minute shot off the crossbar that hopped over the line and a 64th-minute goal punched under the bar. Dublin disputed the Kerry penalty and complained that two claims of their own were not allowed: for a Jack O'Shea pick-up in the square in the second half, and another technical foul by Tom Spillane.

'Dublin didn't pick the right team until half-time', one observer commented. In the first half, Dublin had crowded midfield and Jack O'Shea roamed free on the wings, slotting over three points. In the second half it was Roynane who roamed.

'Experience, nothing more, got us through that second half,' sighed Kerry chairman Frank King.

21 SEPTEMBER 1986. KERRY 2-15, TYRONE 1-10, CROKE PARK

> 'If you walk with a swagger, people always assume you know where you are going.'
>
> MICK O'DWYER, *Blessed and Obsessed* (2007)

There was a shock wave across Gaelic football when a third division team, Laois, won the 1986 National League. Midfielders John Costelloe and Liam Irwin made amends for their defeat in the 1985 Leinster final by beating Monaghan 2-6 to 2-5.

Laois's championship opponents, Wicklow, were storing up a surprise. As they filed off the pitch after a morale-boosting victory in a pre-season tournament, they discovered that the referee had blown the whistle five minutes early at the end of their O'Byrne Cup final. They held on to win anyway.

Then Wicklow shocked League champions Laois by 2-10 to 1-9 in Aughrim in controversial circumstances. The first argument between the teams arose over whether the venue was suitable. Then came the sending-off spree. Wicklow were reduced to fourteen men and Laois to thirteen. Wicklow teenager Kevin O'Brien, a Railway Cup star before he had made his championship debut, scored two goals.

The 1986 Leinster championship heralded a breakthrough for a new team. Meath selected Joe Cassells at corner back, and when Dublin tried the third midfielder tactic, Cassells cleaned up in the centre. They beat Dublin 0-9 to 0-7. Dublin crucially had sharpshooter Barney Rock injured in a collision with Liam Harnan just before half-time. Joe Cassells successfully roved around on the heels of Dublin's wandering Tommy Carr, and the ghosts of 1983 and 84 were finally banished. Meath's David Beggy had been in Croke Park just twice before—for a school tour and a U2 concert!

Kerry seemed to have more problems in 1986 as Cork's debutant full back Denis Walsh curbed Eoin Liston. Kerry nevertheless took a six-point half-time lead and went on to win 0-12 to 0-8. Cork twice cut the lead to three points but could come no closer. Liston starred against Tipperary as Pat Spillane took time to sign autographs while an injured player was being tended!

Kerry struggled to beat Meath 2-13 to 0-12 in the semi-final. A defensive mistake let Ger Power through for Kerry's first goal. Willie Maher scored the second.

Mayo were to travel on Knock Airport's inaugural flight to London for a Connacht championship tie but, as one official surmised afterwards, 'We'd have been quicker walking.' The flight was delayed by bad weather and eventually diverted via Shannon. Leitrim took a half-time lead in the semi-final against Galway with two penalty goals from Michael Martin, but Galway hit back with five points in the first ten minutes of the second half.

Galway waited until the last minute to beat Roscommon 1-8 to 1-5 in the provincial final with a dramatic winning goal from substitute Stephen Joyce, which came at the end of a dreadfully boring and pedestrian final.

Much more spectacular than Meath's long-anticipated breakthrough was that of Tyrone in the north. They owe their 1-11 to 0-10 victory over Down in the Ulster final to a freak goal from Plunkett Donaghy, awarded when Down goalkeeper Pat Donnan stepped back over the line. Donnan denied it was over the line and one of the umpires agreed with him: 'My feet were firmly on the ground, and I even felt my elbow touch the post.' Donaghy had the distinction of making his senior club debut at 16—because his club, Moy, had only fourteen players when it was founded, one of them his 54-year-old father.

In the All-Ireland semi-final, Kevin McCabe got things right from the penalty spot: five minutes from the end of the match with Galway he tucked away the penalty that set Tyrone alight and set up a 1-12 to 1-9 victory. 'Come on Tyrone! Come on Tyrone! We're going to take the Sam Maguire home', the supporters' song went. It was a big ask.

Kerry won majestically by 2-15 to 0-10 in an All-Ireland final where everybody wanted Tyrone to win. Kerry scored nine points from all angles as Tyrone tired. But by then they had suffered a fright.

Eugene McKenna was dominant as Tyrone went 0-7 to 0-4 up at half-time. Just 45 seconds into the second half, Plunkett Donaghy controlled a difficult ground pass, got the ball in to Damien O'Hagan, who sent Paudge Quinn in for a goal. That left Tyrone six points clear, and a miskicked penalty from Kevin McCabe three minutes later left them seven ahead.

Two years beforehand, Eugene McKenna had missed a penalty at the same goal. 'Keep the ball low, or it will take off,' he told McCabe before the final. McCabe put the ball into a hollow, took seven steps in the run, but still hit the ball over the bar. 'I think the ball was lighter than normal, but I was glad of the point. It would have been a big blow if we had missed it.'

Between that and the finish, Kerry outscored Tyrone 2-11 to 0-2. Man of the match Pat Spillane ran 50 yards for a hand passed goal (diverted to the net) in the 41st minute, and Ger Power cantered through to give Mike Sheehy a second goal after 49 minutes. 'That's the thing about instinctive finishers. The greater the pressure the more they thrive', Mick O'Dwyer wrote afterwards. Tyrone eventually failed by eight points, claiming with some justification that Ger Power fouled Donaghy in the run-in to the second Kerry goal.

Timmy O'Dowd restored the midfield dominance that Donaghy had demolished, while unlucky Tyrone lost Eugene McKenna and John Lynch through injury within minutes of each other.

Tyrone won the hearts of a nation. 'We had to beat 31 and a half counties,' Mick O'Dwyer said afterwards. 'We didn't beat them, but we had the beating of them,' Tyrone manager Art McRory concluded.

There was also a theory abounding that, to beat Kerry, you had to do what Cork did in 1983, or Offaly in 1982, which was to stick with them point for point, not allowing the pace to get too fast or the game to get too torrid, and hit them with a hammer blow in the end, like Tadhg Murphy or Seamus Darby did, with a goal.

'You keep going,' Pat Spillane said, 'not for some mythical three in a row or five in a row, but basically because of the fascination to see if you can do the same again.'

But Kerry could not do the same again. 'Kingdom come' had arrived for the greatest team in Gaelic football.

Chapter 6 ~

1987–2000: INSIDE THE MIND OF THE CHAMPION

Dublin, Meath and the new psychology of Gaelic football

20 SEPTEMBER 1987. MEATH 1-14, CORK 0-11, CROKE PARK

'There was an edge between Meath and Cork at that time. In a sense, it was unfortunate that both teams peaked around the same time.'

SEÁN BOYLAN, *The Will to Win* (2006)

For eighteen months in 1987–88 Meath were the best team in the country, the most dominant force since Kerry. Then they fell out of favour—especially in Cork, who coveted the position as much as Meath ever did, but did not earn the reward for one of the strangest years in their history.

First the bizarre. By refusing to turn out for extra time in the National League quarter-final, Cork allowed Dublin to conduct the most extraordinary ceremony in a century of competitive football. Dublin's Declan Bolger took the ball from a farcical throw-in at the start of extra time, passed the ball to Barney Rock, who kicked it into the Cork net. Cork were meanwhile packing for the train home. They protested.

Most supporters wanted to know what would have happened had Rock missed. Dublin were awarded the match anyway. The final score was 0-10 to 1-7, not 1-10 to 1-7, after extra time. With newcomers such as David De Lappe and Glen O'Neill, Dublin went on to win a classic League final (now bearing a sponsor's name for the first time, Ford) against Kerry by 1-11 to 0-11, thanks to a first-minute goal from Ciaran Duff.

Then the unprecedented. On 2 August 1987 Cork brought Kerry's greatest era crashing to an end. Kerry were lucky to get a second shot at the title: Mike Sheehy managed to slip through for a late goal, and it was left to Larry Tompkins, Cork's Kildare migrant, who came from an eighteen-month stint in New York to live in Castlehaven, to score the equalising point from a free.

That made the score 1-10 for Cork, 2-7 for Kerry, and 49,358 gathered in Killarney the following Sunday to see Kerry's last stand. 'Kerry were slipping in 1987 but still would have beaten Cork if they didn't have Tompkins and Fahy', O'Dwyer wrote in his biography.

O'Dwyer called up Vincent O'Connor to rejoin the panel after four years, and sent him on for the last two minutes of the replay. The greatest team in football history went down together in the replay, 0-13 to 1-5. Newcomer Dermot Hanafin scored Kerry's goal. It took 33 minutes to score Kerry's first point. 'If drug testing were in place in the GAA at the time we would have had the entire squad tested', O'Dwyer wrote. He was criticised afterwards for staying in the dug-out, but retorted 'Everybody could see how flat the team was and there was no point in showboating on the sideline.'

Kerry captain Mike Sheehy missed several frees in what was to be his last big match appearance for Kerry. It later emerged that his boots had been split open at the end of the drawn match and the replacement pair didn't suit. 'The circus is over, it's time for a new act,' Kerry full forward Eoin Liston said. When Liston attempted a free in the second half, Sheehy commented, 'He didn't even get a good wide.'

It was Tompkins's year. He landed a pressure-kick point from 50 yards to earn Cork a replay with Galway, 1-11 each. Galway had shown a long-lost spirit to come back from four points down with ten minutes to go. Right corner back John Fallon put Galway ahead with three minutes to go before Tompkins landed a point that repeated his Munster final replay-earner and earned him the nickname 'Equaliser' after a popular television show. Tompkins went on to score eleven points in the replay as Galway foundered.

The first round of the Connacht championship against Roscommon seemed to be the same old sad story for Sligo when they trailed 0-4 to 0-9 at half-time. Then a fine opportunist goal by Anthony Brennan started a revival and a goal from a penalty with two minutes to go from Mick Laffey, the only survivor of the 1975 victorious campaign, gave them a shock 2-8 to 0-12 victory. As Leitrim beat London, London's Brian Grealish, brother of soccer international Tony, fired a penalty straight at the goalkeeper.

Galway midfielder Brian Talty secured his side's victory in a poor Connacht final against Mayo, 0-8 to 0-7. Mayo failed to score for three-quarters of an hour, having led 0-6 to 0-2 at half-time.

Derry led 0-10 to 0-3 against Armagh with twenty minutes to go in the Ulster final, but Armagh's fourteen men (Vincent Loughran was sent off in the seventeenth minute) launched a comeback when subs Jim McKerr and Joe Kernan were brought into the game, and the final score was a minimal 0-11 to 0-9. Tony Scullion roamed successfully as the loose man for Derry. In the semi-final Paul Kealey, just 18, won Derry their final place with a last-minute goal against Cavan after he had come on as a sub in the replay after a lucky 2-7 to 1-10 draw. Derry had plummeted from the first to the third division of the League in successive seasons, and were offered 14/1 against winning the Ulster championship the previous year!

Derry stole a replay from Cavan in the semi-final, but they were not the only thieves in Omagh. An armed gang made off with the gate receipts.

In the end it was Meath who were to make the podium as the last holders of the old Sam Maguire Cup, and the first holders of the new one. Their ascent to the 1987 title began at hard-frosted Kells when they beat Kerry 1-12 to 0-4 in a League match. They lost the League quarter-final at bogey venue Portlaoise. But the long evenings on the sand dunes at the beach between Mornington and Bettystown in cold and foggy April concentrated their minds. They went back to Portlaoise to beat Laois by three paltry points.

With twelve minutes to go against Laois in that quarter-final, they were in trouble. Colm Browne's long shot skidded to the net to leave the sides level, but Laois never managed to take the lead and were left instead regretting a missed goal chance in the first minute as they went down 1-11 to 2-5.

Their 0-15 to 0-9 semi-final victory over Kildare was interrupted by an injury to referee Joe Woods, who pulled a calf muscle and had to be replaced by linesman Tomas Ó Reachtara. Meath's staying power ousted Kildare after they failed to take the lead until twelve minutes after half-time.

The Leinster final against Dublin was tough and tense. According to Colm O'Rourke: 'Like boxing, whoever was able to stay up and slog it out the longest was going to win.' Meath won 1-13 to 0-12. Mattie McCabe snatched a goal after thirteen minutes and they kept their heads when they fell behind at half-time, when both sides had been reduced to fourteen men.

'Meath teams had succumbed to Dublin teams almost dutifully, as if we were born to lose to them,' Liam Hayes reminisced afterwards. 'Our football lives may just as easily have been contained in a stately home in an earlier century. We knew our place in that home, and that place was generally below ground level, making some noise, but seldom seen. That same order, that subservience, has now been erased.'

Derry brought a sizeable number of the 40,285 spectators to Croke Park for the All-Ireland semi-final, but left their skills behind. Star forward Dermot McNicholl showed obvious signs of an injury, having aggravated a hamstring in the kickabout before the match. Meath scored two points in the first minute and the final score was 0-15 to 0-10. It took Derry 68 minutes to score their first point from play.

Meath beat Cork 1-14 to 0-11 in an unspectacular final. Long-serving Colm O'Rourke deservedly got the winning goal ten minutes before half-time, his half-blocked shot rolling into the net.

Seven minutes earlier Cork had their goal chance blocked by Mick Lyons, when Jimmy Kerrigan seemed through for a goal: 'Kerrigan did not kick the ball with conviction, and we conceded a goal that should not have happened at all,' Cork manager Billy Morgan said afterwards.

The goal would have put Cork seven points ahead. Instead it was Meath who led 1-6 to 0-8 at half-time, and they went eight points ahead as Larry Tompkins, the Cork super-shooter, sent six of his eight free kicks wide in the second half. A Meath banner read, 'Meath's midfield pair to leave Teddy bear.' Meath midfielder Liam Hayes was awarded man of the match.

18 SEPTEMBER 1988. MEATH 0-12, CORK 1-9, CROKE PARK
9 OCTOBER 1988. MEATH 0-13, CORK 0-12, CROKE PARK

> 'In The Heat Of Battle—Nice Guys Finish Last.'
>
> Headline on article by COLM O'ROURKE in the *Sunday Tribune*, 20 October 1988

Meath completed their first-ever three in a row in Leinster in 1988, but only because Charlie Redmond missed a last-second penalty for Dublin.

Redmond sent over the bar and fell face down on the field while Gerry McEntee slapped his back in congratulation. He had never before missed a penalty, and was only appointed kicker because Mick Kennedy was injured. Dublin's Dave Synnott was sent off, in the recurring tradition of Dublin-Meath encounters. Mattie McCabe and P. J. Gillic scored Meath's goals in the seventh and fifteenth minutes of the first half. Dublin came back to equalise midway through the second half, but points from Liam Hayes and Gillic, free-taking in the absence of injured Brian Stafford, put Meath back in front.

Monaghan beat Tyrone 1-10 to 0-11 to take their fourteenth Ulster title when a mistake by the goalkeeper let Nudie Hughes dash in for a 27th-minute goal, the unfortunate keeper having failed to clear a long Donal Hughes ball. To add to their woes, Tyrone then had a penalty claim turned down in the very last minute of play, as Noel McGinn shot wide, having been bustled in front of goal.

Mayo brought 36-year-old Martin Carney, the Donegal-born schoolteacher who had first declared for them in 1979, out of retirement to score four great points in their victory by 1-12 to 0-8 against Roscommon.

Cork surprisingly struggled against rapidly improving Limerick, and trailed 0-4 to 1-3 at half-time after Eoin Sheehan set up Chris McGuinness for an eleventh-minute goal. Cork eventually took the lead from a Larry Tompkins point six minutes from the end. It was not the stuff of champions.

Cork brought 35-year-old Denis Allen and soccer exile Dave Barry back for the Munster final. Allen ended up scoring the goal that beat Kerry by a single point, 1-14 to 0-16. 'Take Tompkins and Fahy out of the equation and we would have certainly won,' Mick O'Dwyer recalled. 'The spell had been broken and it was time for a reassessment. I didn't quit because I was still enjoying it and, ever the optimist, I reckoned we could recover. I was wrong.'

The match erupted into a fracas near the end, and although only four players were booked by referee Pat Lane, eight were further disciplined after the game by the Munster council and both counties fined £500 each. Pat Spillane scored just one point five minutes from the end, but 19-year-old newcomer Maurice Fitzgerald scored ten points for Kerry, three from play.

In the All-Ireland semi-final, Meath escaped a Mayo comeback when they went ten points up, then relaxed suddenly to eventually get in by 0-16 to 2-5. Liam McHale struck for a goal in the 48th minute, Anthony Finnerty added a second, and then McHale had the ball in the net again, only to see it disallowed. The match yielded 52 frees and until the 21st minute the sides scored just one point each.

Cork, meanwhile, won a 54-free semi-final against Monaghan 1-14 to 0-6 with a controversial goal. Brendan Murray was sandwiched in a tackle just before Barry Coffey passed to Dave Barry and he drove in a great twenty yard goal.

Cork scored the only goal of two All-Ireland final meetings with Meath after three minutes of the drawn final, when Teddy McCarthy finished a Dinny Allen-Paul McGrath move by sending to the net through the goalkeeper's legs. Meath came back to lead 0-6 to 1-2 at half-time, and then Cork failed to convert their second half domination into scores, ending up with fifteen wides as against Meath's seven.

The Cork backs insisted that Meath's rugby-playing half forward, David 'Jinksy' Beggy took a dive when a vital fourteen yard free was awarded against them 30 seconds from the end. Brian Stafford converted for the equalising point, 0-12 to 1-9, and it was back for a controversial replay. 'Cork should have won the first day in 1988 but they didn't,' Seán Boylan reminisced. 'The folklore will grow over the years about Jinksy winning the last minute free, but it still had to be converted.'

Meath players were convinced that the All-Ireland final replay would be played in the wet. It rained for the week coming up to the game. The training session on Saturday night in Dalgan Park, near Navan, was reduced to a mushy, messy quagmire. Croke Park should have been the same on All-Ireland Sunday.

So the players took precautions. Bernard Flynn got studs fitted on his boots that were the maximum permitted length. Liam Hayes spent Saturday night getting long studs fitted for his boots. All the players could think of was holding their feet in the promised rain at Croke Park. Meath started the day at the beach in Malahide, with ten balls being kicked from player to player. Selector Pat Reynolds's sons were sent into the waves to retrieve the bobbing balls.

But what the Meath players saw of the London-Meath curtain-raiser alarmed them. The groundsman had kept up Con O'Leary's good work and all the rain had passed through the topsoil. The pitch was bone dry.

Brian Stafford brought two pairs of boots on to the field with him. He wore his multi-studded wet weather boots, and gave his normal pair to selector Tony Brennan. When Meath ran on to the field for a pre-match kickaround, Stafford tried a few frees. His multi-studded boots were hurting and uncomfortable. Flynn's long studs were jarring his sole. Colm Coyle had the longest steel studs permissible. Hayes's feet were coming up in blisters soon after the second half started.

Meanwhile the photographers were objecting that Meath had not waited long enough to allow the team picture to be taken. Two officials started to move the bench, but a photographer sat on it and refused to budge. At each match that year, the Meath players were breaking earlier and earlier as the team picture was being taken. First Robbie O'Malley and then the rest of the back line would start racing back to the goalmouth. After three seconds the team was broken up and some of the photographers hadn't even focused. Their protests were in vain. Meath were not going to regroup.

By the time of the parade, Brian Stafford had had enough of his cogs. When the parade was passing the Meath dug-out, Stafford skipped in to Brennan and changed his boots. Most of the Meath players never even noticed he was gone. After four minutes of play Stafford sent a 50 sailing over the bar with his first kick of the match. The new boots worked. Stafford scored seven.

The match was tough. When Meath's Gerry McEntee was sent off for a blow on Niall Cahalane after six minutes, Meath did not even have a team-talk. Automatically, P. J. Gillic moved to McEntee's midfield spot, and the midfielders and half forwards fell back into their own half of the field. It worked. Meath crowded and fouled the Cork forwards, kept the score down to 0-5 to 0-6 at half-time, and eventually harried themselves into a three-point lead at the three-quarter stage.

Eleven players competed against twelve when the ball entered the Meath half of the field. It was not a pretty sight. When Meath went in at half-time, there was no mention of the fact that this was fourteen men against fifteen. Seán Boylan talked about the game as if it was normal.

Bernard Flynn swapped his long-cog boots with substitute Liam Smith at half-time. He had never before worn Smith's boots, but the shorter studs helped him. Fourteen minutes into the second half, Martin O'Connell sent a long clearance down, which Flynn grasped, turned and sent over for a point that gave Meath the lead for the first time. Two great blocks by Liam Hayes and some cool defending by Robbie O'Malley and man of the match Martin O'Connell secured the two in a row. After the victory, Colm O'Rourke tossed his jersey over the fence to the gathered Meath supporters on Hill 16.

Meath had employed similar tactics in the replay of the League final against Dublin, when they won despite having a man sent off early in the first half. They had come back to beat Armagh in the League, despite the fact that they trailed when they had a man sent off. They had drawn with Kildare in the League three years before, despite having two men sent off and playing with thirteen men against fifteen.

Afterwards, Colm O'Rourke explained Meath's tactics of controlled aggression in a controversial *Sunday Tribune* article headlined (he did not write the headline) 'In The Heat Of Battle—Nice Guys Finish Last.' Dinny Allen responded that Meath 'gloried in intimidating Cork and resorting to fouling to retain their title'. Seán Boylan said that his team 'had resolved that we would not be pushed around as in the drawn match'. The arguments lasted for months, and in January 1989 both teams turned up together in the Canary Islands for squad holidays at the same time.

Meath players Gerry McEntee and Liam Harnan refused to accept their medals from GAA president John Dowling over critical comments he had made. Dowling replied in his speech to the 1990 All-Ireland final lunch. 'If we all had our lives to live over again.'

Boylan mused in his biography, 'Things might be different to the way they turned out on that night.'

17 SEPTEMBER 1989. CORK 0-17, MAYO 1-11, CROKE PARK

> 'Football badly needs a good game.'
>
> Mayo manager JOHN O'MAHONEY before the 1989 All-Ireland final

Mayo reached the 1989 All-Ireland final by default. The four strongest teams, Cork, Kerry, Dublin and Meath all ended up in the same half of the draw. Things went predictably in both Munster and Leinster. Meath defeated Louth with a spectacular solo-run goal from Liam Hayes, then trailed Offaly by a point at half-time before crushing them 3-11 to 0-9. Dublin defeated Kildare with the help of a freak goal when Ciaran Duff's sideline ball went straight to the net, then easily dismissed Wicklow.

Meath's reputation for winning matches with fourteen men ran out of luck in the Leinster final. Colm Coyle was sent off seven minutes into the second half. Dublin, leading through a Ciaran Duff goal at the time, experienced a few moments of panic after a Mattie McCabe goal for Meath, but came back to win with another Vinnie Murphy goal, sent in with the outside of the boot as the Meath backs anticipated he would shoot to the other side.

Cork too had a moment or two of panic. An early opportunist goal when Barry Coffey sent a quick chip to John O'Driscoll helped them to a lead of 1-11 to 0-6 with eleven minutes to go in the Munster final. Kerry came storming back to lose by only three points, 1-12 to 1-9.

The All-Ireland semi-final was another fraught affair between Dublin and Cork. Dublin led 1-4 to nil before referee Michael Kearins awarded two controversial penalties to Cork, both converted by John Cleary, and sent off Dublin's Keith Barr, who was carted off to hospital with a broken jaw which he had sustained a few minutes beforehand in an off-the-ball incident. Play was stopped for 29 frees in the first half. After half-time the 60,168 spectators watched referee Michael Kearins bring both teams together in a huddle to warn them to clean up the game or there would be more sendings-off. The game improved and Cork went through to the final 2-10 to 1-9.

Gaelic football had been licking wounds to its image from the start of the season, when a Cork footballer was badly injured by what team mates claimed was a deliberate kick by a New York player in the National League final in New York.

In Ulster, an Armagh supporter struck Tyrone footballer John Lynch as he left the field at half-time in an Ulster championship match. Lynch took no further part in the action, but incensed Tyrone gave Armagh an eight-point lead, then came back to win the game 1-11 to 2-7.

Four players were sent off and six booked as Tyrone beat Down in the next round. Tyrone eventually won the Ulster final with a Stephen Conway equaliser to force a second meeting with Donegal, and goals from Conway and Damien O'Hagan to win the replay.

Two were sent off and six booked as Mayo beat Galway in a replayed Connacht semi-final after Gay MacManus had brought the teams back with a last-gasp goal the first day. Mayo and Roscommon played a mercifully clean 170 minutes in the Connacht final. In extra time Roscommon first took the lead with a Tony MacManus penalty, then Anthony Finnerty and Jimmy Burke scored Mayo goals to put them into the All-Ireland semi-final. Burke did so by default, missing his kick completely, falling, and somehow propelling the ball over the line in the process.

With the 48,177 spectators at the semi-final talking of unfinished business, Tyrone's from 1986, Mayo's from 1985, it was Mayo who came through. Eugene McKenna scored a Tyrone goal at the end of the third quarter. Tyrone failed to score again while Mayo tacked on six points and went through to their first final in 38 years by 0-12 to 1-6.

Mayo flew to Dublin from Monsignor Horan's new airport in Knock the day before the game. Four local country and western bands brought out records commemorating their achievement and armies of supporters to the All-Ireland final. Their optimism proved well founded, while Cork worried about the prospect of losing three in a row. 'The population of this county will drop by 35 if we are beaten by Mayo,' Cork team doctor Con Murphy said before the game.

On the field too Cork huffed a little before winning 0-17 to 1-11. The three-point margin was as much as they were allowed, although the knowledgeable who had been talking about Cork's inability to kill teams off commented that Cork could not succeed in getting four points ahead.

Mayo substitute Anthony Finnerty fired in the goal four minutes into the second half, and blazed another shot wide minutes later. Seven different Cork players scored. 'The colour of the occasion was spectacular and matched by some of the football served up', one sportswriter commented. There was a sigh of relief that so few frees—44 in all—were awarded. The total was in fact higher than the 1986 and 1987 finals. But it was an improvement on the battle of 1988.

16 SEPTEMBER 1990. CORK 0-11, MEATH 0-9, CROKE PARK

> 'Right from the start I thought I was taking part in a boxing match rather than the All-Ireland final.'
>
> COLM COYLE who was sent off in the 1990 All-Ireland final

Castleblayney was the unlikely location of the start of a new TV revolution for football. It began with a match between Monaghan and Antrim on 13 May 1990. The BBC had just won the rights to cover the Ulster championship and when Jerome Quinn and his crew pulled in with their armoury of cameras, they brought TV coverage and the profile of the GAA in the north to unprecedented and unexpected levels. Northerners were treated to the thrills and spills of the new games, with frees and sideline kicks taken from the hands, sunshine football, big crowds and articulate post-match interviewees.

Donegal's Anthony Molloy found out the extent of the TV revolution when his off-the-ball punch on a Cavan man was spotted by an overhead camera in the first round seven days later and he was suspended.

The viewers got a chance to see one of the great comebacks in championship history when John Treanor's lost-time point hauled Down back from eight points down in the last ten minutes of the semi-final against Armagh, but Armagh won the replay and then lost the Ulster final to Donegal by a point.

There are those who claim that the new profile boosted Ulster teams and inspired their victories in the next four All-Ireland championships. In 1990 Donegal promised much but failed to deliver. They then drew level, 1-6 each, early in the second half of their semi-final against Meath, but scored only once again before the finish, Martin McHugh having miskicked a goal chance that would have given them the lead.

In Munster, Cork beat Kerry by their biggest margin of the age, fifteen points, despite fielding without six key players. 'Players didn't want to come back out at half-time,' Charlie Nelligan recalled. The Cork goals came from Michael McCarthy and Danny Culloty. Kerry were a pale shadow of their former selves, scoring just one point from play when playing with the wind in the first half, and relying on veterans Jack O'Shea and substitute Pat Spillane to maintain any contact with the eventual All-Ireland champions.

Connacht was less eventful. Sligo had beaten Galway to deny them promotion in the National League in November, so the revenge was a 32-point hammering, 6-18 to 0-4, in the first round of the championship on an afternoon when Sligo lost two players through injury and had another sent off. Galway then ousted champions Mayo, but Roscommon beat Galway in the Connacht final and were trailing Cork by just two points, eight minutes from the end of their All-Ireland semi-final, when Paul Earley's punched effort from Tom Grehan's 45 was narrowly wide. Cork switched Shay Fahy from full forward to midfield at the start of the second half to take command and qualify for another final with a seven-point margin to spare.

In Leinster, Mick O'Dwyer's Kildare were beaten spectacularly by Wicklow at Aughrim, where Kevin O'Brien's rib injury did not prevent him from scoring a crucial goal for Wicklow with eleven minutes to go, and adding the winning point for good measure. Wicklow were heavily beaten by Dublin, so setting up the fifth successive Meath-Dublin Leinster final.

Bernard Flynn's burst of two goals and two points in the Leinster semi-final against Laois turned what one writer called 'a mismatch into a travesty' and gave Meath a 4-14 to 0-6 victory.

Colm O'Rourke scored the goal which won the 1990 Leinster title after just 30 seconds, beating John O'Leary to punch Colm Brady's high ball to the net. Dublin trailed 1-10 to 0-5, five minutes into the second half, but climbed back to two points before sub Gerry McEntee intervened to set up a point eventually scored by Brian Stafford.

So Meath faced Cork for the third final in four years, and this time Cork won, goalkeeper John Kerins providing the turning point of the 1990 All-Ireland final with a 37th-minute save from Brian Stafford.

Larry Tompkins, who needed two pain-killing injections to play in this stop-start 69-free final, scored four frees in all. Shay Fahy took control of midfield and Teddy McCarthy became the first player to win All-Ireland hurling and football medals in the same year.

Cork had seven wides as against thirteen for Meath, and had Colm O'Neill sent off four minutes before half-time to reverse the situation of 1988. 'Billy Morgan had chosen his team well to do the job,' Boylan wrote. 'They totally smothered us and we could not break them down.'

The two points after half-time, Billy Morgan said, convinced him that Cork were going to win. He had waited for the moment, and savoured it.

2 JUNE 1991. MEATH 1-12, DUBLIN 1-12, CROKE PARK
9 JUNE 1991. MEATH 1-11, DUBLIN 1-11, CROKE PARK
23 JUNE 1991. MEATH 2-11, DUBLIN 1-14, CROKE PARK
6 JULY 1991. MEATH 2-11, DUBLIN 0-15, CROKE PARK

> 'This was, undoubtedly, our poorest performance of the four. We led 0-4 to 0-2 after sixteen minutes. We trailed 0-5 to 0-7 at half-time, and 0-6 to 0-12 after 50 minutes. But there are good reasons why we managed to cling to Dublin and finally beat them this afternoon. We had our share of good luck (though we also had a few unlucky breaks). We remained calm all through. We knew what it was like to beat Dublin. We hate losing to them. We hate them. We believe they dislike us too and we honestly believe that they're not good enough to beat us.'
>
> LIAM HAYES, *Out of Our Skins* (1992)

Meath's Leinster championship of 1991 was the hardest earned in history, a title that took eight matches plus an hour of extra time and a score of 11-89 to win. A decision to reintroduce the open draw the previous year had unexpected results. Three preliminary rounds were needed to reduce the field to eight. Dublin and Meath came out of the hat. According to Seán Boylan, 'The implications were obvious—to be ready for the Dubs in a preliminary round we would need a level of fitness that we would normally need for a Leinster final.'

Most of that was in the four-match drama against Dublin, witnessed by then record crowds and an incredible TV audience of 611,000 for the most viewed of the matches. Both the total attendance of 400,577 and the average attendance in the competition, 26,705, were the highest in the history of any GAA provincial championship.

The games caught the public imagination to an extent not seen since the height of Dublin-Kerry rivalry in the 1970s. And it was timely. Ireland's performance in the World Cup of 1990 had gripped the public imagination and raised the profile of soccer to levels that only Gaelic football had ever enjoyed before. The viewing figures for a European championship qualifier between Ireland and England, 1,307,000, was one of four to exceed the highest for a Gaelic football game in 1991, the All-Ireland final at 749,000.

Between the third and fourth matches in the series, Seán Boylan brought his team and partners to the tranquil village of Drymen, close by the shores of Loch Lomond, allowing everybody to freshen up. They stayed up in the hotel bar until 4 am, singing and drinking.

'We'd been playing badly against Dublin and we needed to take time away from them,' team captain Liam Hayes wrote in his biography, 'view them from a distance.' Hayes said it was important to 'wake up and not find the Dublin struggle on our doorsteps each morning'.

Did it make a difference? No. Meath started the game well, leading 0-4 to 0-2 after sixteen minutes, but it was Dublin who took control, held an 0-7 to 0-5 lead at half-time, and had increased that to 0-12 to 0-6 by the 50th minute.

The series turned on as dramatic a goal as we have seen in 125 years of football. Seán Boylan says it resulted from a move that was practised on the village soccer pitch at Drymen, on an uneven and sloping piece of ground. Boylan says he told Hayes to instruct the players to 'throw the ball around like we did in Scotland'.

They did. In the final minute of the game Martin O'Connell retrieved the ball which was about to go over the Meath end line. O'Connell had one foot out of play, but got his pass away to Mick Lyons. Eleven passes later, the unlikeliest goalscorer, Kevin Foley, was kicking the ball past John O'Leary for the equalising score of the game. Foley, a corner back, had been instructed by Mattie McCabe to follow the play the length of the field as Dublin's cover would not expect him to crop up at the end of the move. 'It was like watching a car crash,' Colm O'Rourke commented afterwards.

'I'm deadly from two yards,' Kevin joked. Team mates said they hadn't seen him score a goal before, even in training.

From the kick-out Mattie McCabe won possession, and fed Liam Hayes, who made ground on the left wing, turned inside and found P. J. O'Connell in space. He passed to Dave Beggy, who scored the winning point. 'And there was nothing Dublin could do about it,' Hayes recalled.

It had all started badly for Meath. Twenty minutes before Meath took the field, Terry Ferguson pulled a muscle in his back as he was removing his slacks, and he went into spasm. He was lifted on to the table in the centre of the room. Anne Bourton and Gerry McEntee worked on him to get him fit, but he was never going to play.

When the game did begin, Pádraig Lyons, Ferguson's replacement, collapsed after ten minutes. When Meath were six points down, Bernard Flynn hobbled off with a calf injury. There were few physical encounters.

'Handbags at three paces,' Charlie Redmond described the one incident that arose.

According to Hayes, there seemed no way back. 'The game was Dublin's. Keith Barr had uprooted the green flag that accompanies one of the goalposts, nine minutes from the end, when his penalty kick went inches wide. But by then we looked disorganised, and every one of us felt disheartened.' Then Brian Stafford scored a goal. A few minutes from the end, Paddy Cullen took off Charlie Redmond, who had been one of his best forwards. Keith Barr took a Dublin penalty, and missed, partially due to the distraction of Mick Lyons illegally accompanying him on his run. 'Their names should be etched in stone for what they did for Gaelic football,' Taoiseach Bertie Aherne said later.

Meath still had a Leinster semi-final and final to go through. Brian Stafford's tenth-minute goal failed to shake Wicklow, who came back from two points down in the last five minutes to draw. Fifteen seconds of injury time had elapsed when Brian Stafford placed Bernard Flynn for a would-be winning score that the referee called back as full-time had elapsed—the reverse of the long count of 1954.

'If Wicklow had taken all their chances we would have been wiped out,' Seán Boylan said. Pat Baker brought Wicklow back level with a goal before half-time in the replay, on a day both captains were sent off, Liam Hayes of Meath and Hugh Kenny of Wicklow, Kenny for an off-the-ball incident with Meath's thirteenth-minute goalscorer Bernard Flynn. Elsewhere, two Stefan White goals helped Louth come back from six points down to stun fancied Kildare, who had appointed Mick O'Dwyer as manager the previous September.

Then Louth kicked seventeen wides to draw against Laois the week before the leader of their attack, Brendan Kearns, got married. That mini saga ended in an ugly four-minute brawl at the close of the semi-final for which no player was cautioned, Mick Lawlor scoring 2-3 as Laois progressed.

Louth and Longford had produced a splendid first round tie, during which the teams were level seven times in 60 minutes followed by a sparkling finish during which Ciaran Fox of Longford and Ciaran O'Hanlon of Louth exchanged goals and Fox missed a would-be equaliser.

Laois snuck into the lead just before half-time in the Leinster final, despite Tommy Smith becoming the second man in three weeks to be sent off for hitting Bernard Flynn—as he celebrated David Beggy's championship-winning goal. The only Laois score of the second half came from a free in the 32nd minute.

15 SEPTEMBER 1991. DOWN 1-16, MEATH 1-14, CROKE PARK

> 'Walking away from Croke Park I found myself crying, and I felt ashamed and angry. I quickly stopped. We had lost a damn game of football, and nothing more.'
>
> LIAM HAYES, *Out of Our Skins* (1992)

Another broadcast revolution was taking place. Local radio stations springing up the length and breadth of the country were bringing new sophistication to the coverage of matches everywhere. And when Roscommon's 19-year-old corner forward Des Duggan stepped up to take a 65 yard free kick at the end of the 1991 Connacht final, Shannonside commentator Seamus McHugh told listeners he would never get it over the bar. Duggan did, and Roscommon won the replay on a day Paul Earley made a match-saving clearance and McHugh had a story to tell.

Meath's semi-final victory over Roscommon by a single point was the best game of the championship. Roscommon led for 65 of the 70 minutes. Highlights included Derek Duggan's goal a minute before half-time and Gay Sheerin's save from Liam Hayes in the 58th minute. 'Our forwards were playing with crumbs,' Hayes recalled, 'and they weren't even using them very well. . . . In the final twenty minutes of the game we had totally outplayed the same team which had agonisingly toyed with us for the first 50 minutes. Don't ask me how that happened, or why. I can only guess.'

Munster had reintroduced the open draw as a result of a motion from Clare, bringing to an end 25 successive years of Cork-Kerry finals. In the Munster semi-final, Kerry avenged the previous year's massive defeat against Cork. John Cronin scored a goal sixteen minutes into the second half, and Maurice Fitzgerald pointed two winning frees during the tumultuous closing stages after Danny Culloty had equalised with eleven minutes to go.

Then Kerry were pushed all the way by John O'Keeffe's surprising Limerick team, who scored three magnificent goals. A James O'Donovan penalty after just 50 seconds set the trend. A second from Seán Kelly before the break left it 2-8 to 0-10 at half-time. Seven Kerry points without reply were followed by another Seán Kelly goal thirteen minutes into the second half, and Kerry had to rely on veterans Ambrose O'Donovan, Jack O'Shea, Pat Spillane and twelve points from Maurice Fitzgerald to secure their first Munster title since 1986.

There was no hint that 1991 was going to be Down's year as they faltered through to the final, beating Armagh with a Mickey Linden penalty in a shambolic first round in which eight players were booked.

Derry's first round victory over newly crowned under-21 champions

Tyrone, thanks to a late Damien Cassidy goal, was the game of the Ulster championship. Derry then forced Down to a replay after they had fallen four points behind early in the second half of another shambolic drawn semi-final, with two sent off, eight booked, a free every 80 seconds, and more wides than scores from play.

Only one Derry player kept his original position for the replay. 'They confused themselves more than they did us,' Down's Mickey Linden said afterwards. 'Once we got through those two matches, for me that was the turning point in Down's fortunes, not just because Derry were such a big obstacle, but the way we played over those two games. It was fantastic football. Both teams played fantastic football, but the scores, the support play, the commitment—all the ingredients for a great football team were there. I think we knew then what the team was capable of.'

In the Ulster final against Donegal, Down's Mickey Linden gathered a lengthy Greg Blaney pass for an early goal and a surprisingly easy victory, Brian McEniff's first championship defeat as the Donegal manager.

As 1960s style momentum gathered behind Down, Peter Withnell scored in the tenth and 58th minutes to give Down a memorable semi-final victory over Kerry, holding them to just one point in the second half. Down led from the twentieth minute and won with a 50th-minute goal from Barry Breen.

So to the final against Meath, playing their tenth match in the championship campaign. Down went eleven points ahead before Meath rallied in the final eight minutes, only to run out of time as referee Seamus Prior blew on the stroke of 70 minutes.

Colm O'Rourke, suffering from a virus, came into the game ten minutes into the second half to rally Meath, just as full back Mick Lyons retired injured midway through the second half. Then they nearly caught up again with the help of a spectacular Liam Hayes solo-run goal, before losing by two points.

A Down fan who had climbed on to the roof of the Nally Stand almost fell off when Hayes scored, Seán McConnell reported in *The Irish Times*.

'They didn't walk on to the field like a team who knew it has an All-Ireland title within its reach,' a grieving Liam Hayes mused. 'They didn't start the game as a team which held that knowledge within it. At least when I looked at them it was never visible.'

19 JULY 1992. CLARE 2-10, KERRY 0-12, LIMERICK

'There won't be a cow milked in Clare tonight.'

RTÉ commentator MARTY MORRISSEY

Something seismic was taking place at the Gaelic Grounds in Limerick. Clare beat Kerry in the Munster final with second half goals from Martin Daly (48 minutes) and Colm Clancy (51 minutes). Clare goalkeeper James Hanrahan saved from Pa Laide at the other end to complete the heroics.

At half-time it had looked less hopeful: Clare led by just one point, 0-7 to 0-6, having played with the wind, missed a penalty and kicked seven wides against one.

Kerry's 34-year-old Jack O'Shea, by now the same age as the Clare manager John Maughan, retired after the match. It was a far cry from Kerry's first round display against their fancied Cork rivals, which had spectators comparing Kerry's 1992 team with Mick O'Dwyer's 1975 team, according to Paddy Downey in *The Irish Times.* Cork missed two second half penalties, their only wides of the half, as their golden age came to an end in Páirc Uí Chaoimh.

Kerry's inflated expectations were quickly revised as Limerick, still inspired by their 1991 display, came within a point of Kerry, four minutes from the end of the Munster semi-final, despite trailing 1-7 to 0-4 at half-time on a day Karl O'Dwyer made his championship debut. Limerick's late call-up at corner forward, Chris McGuinness, scored 1-6, including a second half penalty.

The shocks continued in Leinster where Richie Connor's Laois team shocked provincial champions Meath, with Leaving Cert student Hugh Emerson among their stars. The sending off of Joe Nolan entering the third quarter left Laois a man down facing Meath for the third year in a row in a first round game that came complete with a brawl and the settling of personal grievances throughout the pitch, having lost by twenty points to Meath in 1990 and six points in 1991. A Mick Turley goal gave Laois the lead for the first time with thirteen minutes to go. Tommy Dowd's goal with six to go might have revived Meath, but the hero of 1991, Kevin Foley, fouled Seán Dempsey, and Laois goalkeeper Tony MacMahon ran the length of the field to score the penalty. Liam Hayes was sent off for the second year in succession, as the game degenerated in the final minutes. 'One of those days that catches up on every side in the end,' Seán Boylan said.

In their absence, Dublin won the title, beating Kildare by six points. Keith Barr scored the decisive goal in the twentieth minute. They then went ten points ahead early in the second half, then weathered the storm as Kildare came back within four points. One brawl in what was a stormy affair held up play for three minutes.

Clare arrived in Croke Park for the All-Ireland semi-final with a huge support, and no fear of their highly rated opponents, cutting Dublin's lead from five points to two in the third quarter and from eight back to four in the final stages of the semi-final. Pádraig Conway's goal was controversially disallowed (Con Houlihan described him as having 'picked Paddy Cullen's pocket') after nineteen minutes, despite being uncannily similar to one by Colm O'Rourke in the 1990 Leinster final, which was allowed.

Gerry Killeen contrived to score a 53rd-minute goal from a penalty that was initially saved, then conceded a goal ten seconds later as Vinny Murphy punched past Clare goalkeeper James Hanrahan. Mick Galvin scored Dublin's third goal, Pádraig Conway scoring in reply for Clare. There the adventure ended.

The memory of Clare's breakthrough proved an inspiration to little counties for years to come. After the quintessential suburban club Erin's Isle won a 1998 club semi-final, their quick-witted forward Keith Barr declared: 'There won't be a cow milked in Finglas tonight.'

20 SEPTEMBER 1992. DONEGAL 0-18, DUBLIN 0-14, CROKE PARK

> 'When I began playing football for Donegal, even the cows in the field would turn their backs when Donegal came to play.'
>
> BRIAN MCENIFF, *The Irish Times*, 19 September 1992

Occasionally a provincial newspaper sportswriter gains a national following. Sometimes a columnist plays a part in a county's All-Ireland campaign. We shall never know what part Cormac McGill, who wrote for the *Donegal Democrat* under the name, the 'Follower', played in his county's All-Ireland triumph of 1992 with what Seamus McRory has called his 'rousing weekly diet of hope'. McGill, originally from Donegal, was a schoolteacher based in Dromod in Leitrim, but the campaign he mounted after the county's under-21 success in 1987 fired up their spirits when it was most needed.

Even before Donegal started getting it together, 1992 was an eventful year for the newly energised Ulster championship. James McCartan's first half goal helped Down become the first team to win a championship match at the Armagh Athletic Grounds since 1969.

Monaghan and Cavan both forged unexpected first round draws. Monaghan scored just one point in the dying seconds of the first half against ten-point National League champions Derry, then came rattling back with goals from Steven McGinnerty, Raymond McCarron and Kevin Hughes to lead by two points. Declan Bateson replied with a Derry goal. Damien O'Reilly forced Cavan's replay with a tense point three minutes into injury time, a game distinguished by two acrobatic points from Damien O'Reilly for Cavan and Martin McHugh for Donegal. Donegal's superior fitness told in the replay.

The match against Fermanagh in the Ulster semi-final, Anthony Molloy said, 'was the defining moment in our team's football careers. I had just played 100 competitive games for Donegal and I knew, like many others, that our careers were coming to an end.'

Against Derry in the Ulster final, Donegal fell behind to a Henry Downey goal with twenty minutes to go, but recovered to win despite having John Cunningham harshly sent off. They changed their game plan and began using the short ball to great effect. 'The sending off forced us to do what they were good at, possession football,' Molloy recalled.

Martin McHugh took over in the dressing room at the break and said, 'The one thing we couldn't do was give the ball away in the second half. We have to keep possession.'

'The team was very fit,' Tony Boyle said, 'and when you're playing that type of game you need to be fit because you have to have two or three runners going alongside the man in possession and taking the ball at pace.'

Mayo's Raymond Dempsey scored the match-winning goal in the Connacht final against Roscommon, when the full back let the ball slip from his grasp. The crossbar was broken by Mayo goalkeeper Enon Gavin when he swung from it early in the second half, as if in a 30-year tribute to Aidan Brady's adventure of 1962.

Donegal kicked seventeen wides in their semi-final against Mayo. Martin McHugh had the luxury of tapping a penalty over the bar. Mayo's Liam McHale struck the best goal chance of the game against the crossbar in the eighteenth minute, but his county had just one score from play in the second half.

Thus the storm gathered. Martin Rushford, the Aer Lingus man in Glasgow, said he could fill fifteen Jumbos with Donegal followers returning home for the match.

Donegal had sent a man in disguise to watch Dublin's training sessions in advance of the final. Dublin threatened to overwhelm Donegal in the first twelve minutes, during which Charlie Redmond missed a ninth-minute Dublin penalty. Donegal moved their half forward line back towards midfield, creating space for Manus Boyle to pop over nine of Donegal's eighteen points, and contribute to several others scored from frees by Tony Boyle when he was fouled.

James McHugh had a shot rebound off the crossbar for Donegal. Vinny Murphy's despairing shot for a goal in the 67th minute was diverted out for a 45. 'We played well and then just stopped,' Dublin manager Paddy Cullen said.

19 SEPTEMBER 1993. DERRY 1-14, CORK 2-8, CROKE PARK

> 'I remember at half-time seeing Coleman and thinking that he was resigned to it. The game was lost. He just lost his temper. He shouted and roared. He could see that we could do it. He could sense the Dublin defence was flakey.'
>
> JOE BROLLY

Derry had won an Ulster title in one of the wettest summers on record in 1958. They did it again on another wet summer in 1993. Derry moved Dermot Heaney to full forward on a sodden day to devastate Down in the first round, Heaney's goal being joined by Eamon Burns and Richard Ferris, as Derry set out the intent that was to carry them to a first All-Ireland.

Donegal's recovery in the last five minutes of the semi-final against Armagh was described as 'miraculous' by Paddy Downey: points from Seamus Bonner, Manus Boyle and Duffy earning a replay in which they killed Armagh off by racing into a 2-5 to nil lead in the first thirteen minutes.

Exhausted Armagh had replayed each of the three rounds they played, Ger Houlihan's goal with five minutes to go beating Tyrone, after John Toner's late equaliser had earned a second chance. Fermanagh had a new star, Raymond Gallagher, as they flirted with victory over Armagh twice. They led by nine points against fourteen-man Armagh with five minutes of normal time to go in the replay, before leaking 2-1 from Denis Hollywood and an unlikely last gasp goal from centre half back John Grimley. 'Logic defying' wrote Desmond Fahy in *The Irish Times*.

The first day, a 46th-minute Colm McCreesh goal and John Reihill and Fergal McCann's deft breaking down of midfield ball seemed to be working, only for Fermanagh to lose both midfielders to injury and a sending off, and their lead to a late John Rafferty point. Ger Houlihan's blown kiss after scoring an Armagh goal in the drawn match started a trend in the province.

'Conditions more appropriate to water polo', Tom Humphries wrote of the final in the newly refurbished St Tiarnach's Park, when Derry came from 5-4 down at half-time to beat champions Donegal by eight points to six in the final, mainly through the exertions of Anthony Tohill.

In Connacht, Leitrim had their first win over Galway since 1949, and Mayo's Ray Dempsey almost lobbed the Roscommon goalkeeper when he spotted him off the goal-line, then scored the only goal of the final from a Dermot Flanagan pass.

In Leinster, Charlie Redmond's goal and Jack Sheedy's injury time winning point helped Dublin dispatch Meath in the semi-final, having endured a *déjà vu* scare as Meath fought back from five points down for Colm O'Rourke to equalise at full time. 'You could see the fright in their eyes,' Liam Hayes recalled. A tunnel brawl erupted at half-time in the Leinster final in which the Dubs sorted out the fancied Kildare players. Kildare scored just seven points in the final, three of them from play in the final fifteen minutes.

Derry captain Henry Downey was the star of the semi-final as Derry edged out Dublin, bursting forward from centre back to score two inspirational points. It was a day for the backs. Right half back John McGurk kicked their winning point with two minutes of normal time to go. Derry outscored Dublin 5-2 in the final nineteen minutes. Derry joker Joe Brolly claimed McGurk sold the match-winning left boot several times over at impromptu auctions in the US. McGurk's retort is that he still has the boot, and he has Pat Gilroy's jersey. 'He gave it to me and I suppose he thought I was entitled to it—I'd been grabbing it all day long.'

'The place was heaving,' Brolly recalled. 'In the second half you couldn't hear anything. Just roaring and screaming. The last ten minutes, just people screaming. It must have been a terribly exciting match. I remember on the Hill one of the Dubs had a blow-up doll and as the game went on the doll began to sag. I meant to look to see how she was at the end.'

Cork beat Mayo by twenty points in the other semi-final, scoring 3-3 in the last four minutes to run up the most one-sided margin since Kerry's 22-point massacre of Monaghan in 1979.

Back after 35 years, Derry won a rugged All-Ireland final amid much jubilation. Seamus Downey scored what turned out to be the winning goal after fifteen minutes, timing his run perfectly to take Damien Cassidy's lob. Cork's Tony Davis was harshly sent off, the first foul after Niall Cahalane had floored Derry's Enda Gormley.

Cork regained the lead with John O'Driscoll's goal ten minutes into the second half, but Derry finished strongly with points from Anthony Tohill, John McGurk and Gormley.

18 SEPTEMBER 1994. DOWN 1-12, DUBLIN 0-13, CROKE PARK

'Does Charlie Redmond have a penalty clause in his contract?'

RTÉ broadcaster JOE DUFFY

The defining match of the nineties was played in the tight confines of Celtic Park in Derry in May. 'When we came away from Celtic Park that day, we knew we were going to win the All-Ireland,' said McGrath. 'We didn't say it, but the players knew there was nothing out there to beat us.'

Derry surrendered their Ulster and All-Ireland titles. Joe Brolly passed to Fergal McCusker for the Derry goal and a 1-11 to 0-12 lead after seventeen minutes of the second half. Derry subsequently scored just one point while Down substitute Ciaran McCabe scored what proved to be the winning goal with six minutes to go. Much of the subsequent reputation earned by this game is down to the second half tension. 'If we see a better match in 1994, the cheering will shatter the rafters', *The Irish Times* correspondent Paddy Downey wrote.

What made the 1994 match so memorable, apart from the second half tension? It could be the successful use of the tackle by the winning team. Against Derry in 1994, Down had 30 successful tackles. In the 1977 semi-final, acclaimed as 'the greatest ever' by a previous generation, there were just fourteen successful tackles by both teams.

Down fans were ecstatic. They chanted 'Ooh Aah Pete McGrath' after a Ross Carr penalty won them the Ulster title against Tyrone

Aidan Farrell was set up by Mickey Linden for Down's semi-final goal against Cork, Linden drawing the goalkeeper so that Farrell could punch to an empty net after twenty minutes. Down led 1-12 to 0-7 at the end of a storming third quarter, and won by five points.

In Leinster, Dublin came back from eight points down against Kildare to draw a quarter-final, played on Saturday and televised live, and then won the replay by a comfortable five points. At half-time in the replay they led by nine points. 'It was like seniors against juniors,' Mick O'Dwyer was to recall. 'After winning the 1991 League final, a very good Dublin grabbed Kildare in a psychological headlock and held them there.' Charlie Redmond scored the crucial goal to win the replay from a 48th-minute penalty. Kildare goalkeeper Kit Byrne made a great save from Brian Stynes immediately afterwards.

It put Dublin back into the final against Meath, which they won by a point. Charlie Redmond scored the crucial goal seven minutes from time, his free kick squirming through the grasp of Meath goalkeeper Mick McQuillan. 'There's only one Packie Bonner' the Dublin fans sang, cruelly, after McQuillan's calamity. Redmond then went round to his team mates with his fists clenched saying 'Remember 91' a minute later when Dublin went six points up. He had a point. Graham Geraghty retrieved a goal and Meath cut the lead to one point. P. J. Gillic's last attempt from 55 yards dropped short.

In Connacht, Leitrim bridged a 67-year gap by winning the Connacht title. Leitrim manager John O'Mahoney was an enthusiastic user of the new parentage rule, which allowed players to declare for the county of either parent, enlisting Jarlath Ward and launching a search for other eligible players the previous October.

Declan Darcy kicked the winning point from a 45 against Roscommon that started the journey. Darcy then kicked the equaliser against Galway in the semi-final after three minutes of injury time. McNamara saved a penalty from

George Dugdale in the replay.

Jack O'Shea's Mayo team scored a bizarre goal after just eighteen seconds of the final, when Pat Fallon's lob slipped through the fingers of three players before crossing the line. It was the only score of the first half for Mayo, who trailed 0-6 to 1-0 at the break on a drizzly day.

Leitrim's huge support went home disappointed from their first All-Ireland semi-final since 1927, leaving Dublin to face Down in the final.

Down's winning goal in the All-Ireland final came from James MacCartan after seventeen minutes as Dublin's slow start left them with too much to do, four points behind at half-time and six points down fifteen minutes from the end of the match. Although Down failed to add to their tally after the fifteenth minute of the second half, they still led by just three points eight minutes from the end, when Neil Collins saved a Charlie Redmond penalty and eventually won by two points.

It was Redmond's third penalty miss on a big occasion (after the 1988 Leinster and 1992 All-Ireland finals), and to make matters worse, he was impeded by club mate Johnny Barr as he ran on to the rebound, which resulted in him putting the ball narrowly wide. Redmond went straight home from Croke Park without showering or changing.

Dublin finished with twelve wides as against six by Down. The penalty miss caused Dublin to hunt for goals when precious points were there for the taking.

Down had now played five All-Ireland finals and won them all. 'The players weren't conditioned by me,' said McGrath. 'They were conditioned by what they were told when they were younger, by their parents or their uncles or people who knew. It's a process of conditioning that takes place over a long period of time.'

17 SEPTEMBER 1995. DUBLIN 1-10, TYRONE 0-12, CROKE PARK

> 'Winning the All-Ireland was like getting a donkey off our backs.'
>
> KEITH BARR

Jason Sherlock was 7 years old when Dublin won their previous All-Ireland in 1983. Then came 1995. The time was ripe for the creation of a new GAA personality, and Sherlock was the right man at the right time. His football skills, but most of all his boyish good looks, captivated the media and popular culture of the city.

Jason's bootless goal against Laois, taking Jim Gavin's pass for the winning goal with fourteen minutes to go; Jason's plucking Keith Barr's controversial free from the hands and sticking it into the corner of the net for the decisive goal against Cork in the All-Ireland semi-final; Jason's pass to Charlie Redmond ('I couldn't miss from three yards') in the 25th minute of the All-Ireland final for the winning goal; Jason's advertising campaign for Penney's; Jason's TV appearances (Marty Morrissey: 'Is there a lady in your life?' Jason: 'I know you with the girls, Marty'); Jason on the Pat Kenny TV show; Jason's spat with GAA president Jack Boothman; and the rise of a Jason cult that was to result in his presenting a TV show of his own in 1998.

Sherlock had won a Leinster minor medal in 1994. His championship debut against Louth was a revelation. He was hauled down for a penalty immediately when he got his first touch of the ball. New *Irish Times* sportswriter Tom Humphries described Jason bringing 'the sort of flair which Dublin have pined for since the end of the seventies'.

Dublin then laid a few ghosts with their ten-point victory over Meath in the Leinster final. 'In terms of the work rate and ability to stick to formations,' manager Pat O'Neill said, 'it was the best performance ever.' Dessie Farrell commented: 'The ball was introduced and dutifully ignored, as was the case in most Meath-Dublin clashes.' Debutant Evan Kelly's 42nd-minute equalising goal for Meath bore 'an uncanny resemblance to Kevin Foley's 1991 goal,' Liam Horan recalled. Colm O'Rourke, now 37 and already a media commentator, retired.

Far from the big city, Carlow's winning point against Laois by Mick Turley at Cullen Park was quite clearly seen to be wide from video evidence. Laois sportingly offered a replay, the first time since 1903 that the Leinster council overruled a referee's decision.

Sligo held Galway to a draw in Connacht. Declan McGoldrick missed a first half penalty, then redeemed himself by kicking an equalising point in lost time from an acute angle into an errant wind. Galway then came back from two points down to end profligate Leitrim's brief reign with scores from Ja Fallon, Seán de Paor, and Niall Finnegan in injury time. Mayo shot seventeen wides in winning the Connacht semi-final, and eighteen wides in losing a thoroughly forgettable final. Galway led 0-8 to 0-3 at half-time and went on to win by seven points—it would have been ten only for Ray Dempsey's goal in the 70th minute.

Martin McHugh's Cavan had a good run in Ulster, winning Division 3 of the League and squeezing out Monaghan in the provincial semi-final with a Fintan Cahill goal that came back off the inside of the post. Peter Canavan's eight points helped Tyrone to a startling Ulster semi-final victory against Derry, despite being down to thirteen men and three points behind at half-time. Tyrone then won the Ulster final less convincingly than they had suggested by a 2-13 to 0-10 scoreline against Cavan with goals from Stephen McGleenan and Adrian Cush in the closing stages of a tumultuous final.

Cork pulled away in the last twenty minutes of their Munster final against Kerry to complete three in a row after falling behind twice by three points, but fell under Jayo's spell in the All-Ireland semi-final.

Peter Canavan was the counter-star to Dublin's Jayo, reeling in Galway's lead in the All-Ireland semi-final with 1-7, the goal coming in the first half when he knocked Ronan McGarrity's high ball to the net, and scoring three of their five points in the spell that decided the game between the 48th and 55th minute.

Canavan, scorer of eleven points for Tyrone in the final, was penalised for playing the ball off the ground to Seán Kavanagh, who scored a disallowed equalising point. According to Canavan, the ball was marginally off the ground. 'When I punched the ball, I slightly elevated it. It would have been very hard to do that if the ball was flat on the ground.' Referee Paddy Russell was in a good position to see it, and had no doubt that he made the correct call. According to Canavan, 'Nine referees out of ten would have been waiting on a chance to make a draw out of the game.' Canavan had had a rough handling. 'When he did get the ball, we more or less fouled the shit out of him,' Dessie Farrell wrote in his biography, *Tangled up in Blue.*

The final was marred by an embarrassing fiasco over the sending-off of Charlie Redmond for allegedly head-butting Fergal Lohan eight minutes after half-time, after which Redmond failed to leave the field for a minute after he was sent off.

Redmond spiced up the story after the incident. According to Redmond, the famous exchange with referee Paddy Russell—'You shouldn't be here' and 'I know, I failed a fitness test earlier on'—was made up. Redmond had been a doubt about starting at all, as he was recovering from a torn muscle. Pat O'Neill refused to give him a pain-killing injection and he couldn't get a pre-match kick off the ground. Having scored what turned out to be the winning goal, he went into history for all the wrong reasons.

According to Redmond, 'I remember coming out for the ball when Paul Devlin fouled me from behind. I was lying on the ground and a few seconds after the whistle had gone, Fergal Lohan came up and fell into the back of my neck with his elbow. I took exception to that and charged at him. I could have made contact, but I didn't,' Redmond told Tom Humphries. 'If I had, he would have gone down with a broken nose. He sent me off then he changed his mind and told me to stay on, and then he rechanged his mind two minutes later and put me off.'

Russell's 2008 biography confirmed that Lohan would have been sent off as well only the linesman had not been able to see his number. When Russell asked the linesman if he had seen Lohan's number, he replied no, and Redmond assumed the no was an answer to another question, whether

Redmond had head-butted Lohan. 'Redmond was bould. He was chancing his arm,' O'Mahony said.

'I was following play when I saw Redmond throwing his head at Fergal Lohan', Russell wrote in his biography, *Final Whistle*. 'I consulted with my linesman, Willie O'Mahony, who confirmed Redmond had aimed a head butt. It was a definite sending off offence. You're off, I told Redmond, pointing to the line. It was the normal way I would send off a player. Redmond knew he was off, but he continued to argue.' Russell restarted play by throwing the ball in, and claimed afterwards he did not see Redmond even though he was standing right in front of him as he restarted play. Nineteen seconds after the restart, Redmond delivered the ball downfield. Russell consulted with O'Mahony again to see if Redmond had gone off. And so it came to pass that Charlie Redmond became the first player ever to be sent off twice in an All-Ireland final.

At the end of the match, Dublin manager Pat O'Neill did not realise the team had won. He thought Seán Cavanagh's disallowed point had been allowed to stand and there would be a replay. There was relief amid the celebration, that the capital had its long-awaited All-Ireland success. 'The city is safe for Gaelic games again', Tom Humphries wrote in *The Irish Times*. Not everyone agreed. 'We knew the GAA wanted Dublin to win an All-Ireland, but I hadn't realised they wanted it that badly,' Tyrone manager Art McRory complained.

Redmond's goal-scoring boot, one stud missing ('I don't know how that happened. I certainly didn't go into the final with one stud missing'), was later sold for a few thousand pounds.

21 JULY 1996. KERRY 0-14, CORK 0-11, PÁIRC UÍ CHAOIMH

> 'You could have blasted a fog horn into Maurice's ear that day he was so focused. There was this long kick into the wind and you're wondering is he going to do it. I remember seeing it float over and that's when I knew we had it.'
>
> STEPHEN STACK

In Munster, John O'Keeffe's Clare forced a semi-final draw with Cork when Aidan O'Keeffe kicked an injury time 45. Mark O'Sullivan scored what looked like the decisive goal in the 52nd minute of a tight match after a free by Colin Corkery found John O'Driscoll in space.

Cork led 1-8 to 0-4 at half-time in the replay, thanks to a Don Davis goal, then Martin Daly set up Ger Keane for an equalising goal thirteen minutes into the second half. The match went to extra time and John Buckley's goal, four minutes into the second period of extra time, secured Cork's place in the final, where the Kerry team under new manager Páidí Ó Sé were waiting for them. Páidí was a revivalist, using the jersey again as a motivational device, pleading with supporters to travel to the match. Dara Ó Cinnéide recalls that the Kerry fans at the final were singing the English Euro 96 soccer anthem, 'Football's Coming Home.'

Kerry eventually killed off the Cork challenge in the dying minutes of the Munster final with a few breaks from Clare referee Kevin Walsh and a couple of points from frees by Maurice Fitzgerald, who kicked more reliably than Cork's Colin Corkery, one from 60 yards into the Cork fans.

By August it was beginning to look like Mayo's year. Colm McMenamon was deployed as a third midfielder and James Horan scored a 67th-minute goal from a long-range lob to give John Maughan's Mayo a six-point semi-final win over Kerry. A Kerry newspaper had published a photograph of the Kerry players celebrating their Munster final success (their second in nine years) in Páidí Ó Sé's pub in Ceann Trá. 'I couldn't get Cork out of my mind,' Páidí Ó Sé admitted in his biography. 'When we beat them I let rip. I didn't keep a tight rein on discipline, especially my own discipline.'

15 SEPTEMBER 1996. MEATH 0-12, MAYO 1-9, CROKE PARK
29 SEPTEMBER 1996. MEATH 2-9, MAYO 1-11, CROKE PARK

> 'Gaelic football is personal. It's not a kick around in the park early on a Sunday morning. It's not a run out for the boys.'
>
> LIAM HAYES, *The Title*, 5 January 1997

By 1996 Meath's ability to win matches they should have lost was at its peak. 'We are good at learning from defeat, Laois in 1985, Dublin in 1995, and the teams that we beat, they learn from it as well', Seán Boylan wrote in his biography. Meath came from losing the Leinster final of 1995 by ten points to winning the All-Ireland in 1996, but had few friends at the end of it all.

Meath had four unanswered points at the end of the Leinster final to come from two points down to win their first Leinster title in five years. Dublin's cult hero Charlie Redmond had a miserable afternoon, missing four quite straightforward free kicks.

Tyrone became the first county to retain the Ulster title since Derry in 1976, thanks to Peter Canavan's 37th-minute goal. Donegal debutant Dessie MacNamara was sent off after a record fifteen seconds of the first round encounter for an off-the-ball foul on Michael Magill of Down. To add to Donegal's woes, goalkeeper Gary Walsh stepped back over his own line after saving Conor Deegan's hopeful long-range shot.

Meath kicked just four wides in their All-Ireland semi-final victory over Tyrone. Peter Canavan had his best goal chance blocked down in the 58th minute, probably the turning point of the match. Goals at the end of either half from Graham Geraghty and O'Callaghan, and seven unanswered points in a row between the 50th and 63rd minutes, secured their place in the All-Ireland final, but it was the manner in which they had smothered Tyrone's inventiveness, and an alleged stamping incident by Martin O'Connell (the Meath management maintained it was accidental), that dominated the reports and airwaves afterwards. The image of the game was not helped by the fact that two Tyrone players re-emerged after half-time with bandaged heads.

'When Meath put it up to us physically, we should have taken them on at their own game,' Ciaran McBride, one of the bandaged players, said afterwards. 'If that meant having a row, so be it. Instead, we looked to the referee for protection. We allowed ourselves to be divided, and then picked off. Afterwards, we should have retreated, said nothing, licked our wounds, learned from our mistakes and stayed together to set the record straight in 1997. Instead, the team fell apart.'

Mayo beat Galway in a Connacht final for the first time since 1969 with Ray Dempsey's late goal. Galway's rivalries with Leitrim and Sligo were meanwhile taking on a life of their own. John O'Mahoney resigned as Leitrim manager after his team's two-point defeat to Galway in the semi-final, insisting that a Leitrim penalty refusal for a 21st-minute foul on Declan Darcy was the turning point in the game.

Galway held an eight-point lead before Leitrim had two superb goals in the last five minutes from substitute Jason Ward and Declan Darcy. Ward even got the margin back to one at the end of normal time.

Sligo led Galway by five points to three at half-time in Markievicz Park, but had to rely on Paul Taylor for their late equalising free. Goals were exchanged by Galway's Niall Finnegan and Sligo's Paul Taylor, after Paul Durcan's shot had been parried by Cathal McGinley.

James Nallen scored a 31st-minute goal for Mayo, but Seán Burke took possession from the kick-out for Kerry and launched a long shot from the middle of the field that landed in the net, apparently as the goalkeeper John Madden was distracted by the replay shown on the new big screen at Croke Park. The RTÉ television cameras missed the goal. Seán Boylan mused that Mayo showed strength and spirit they hadn't shown for years.

Mayo now had a final to prepare for, with their best prospects of winning since 1951, when they had beaten Meath. They objected to the appointment of Pat McEneaney as the match referee for the All-Ireland final because of McEneaney's Meath business contacts. He had been awarded the match ahead of Paddy Russell on the casting vote of Games Activities committee chairman Dan McCartan of Down.

It was not to be. Mayo led Meath by six points nine minutes into the second half after Ray Dempsey scored their goal, only for Meath's Colm Coyle to score a slapstick equaliser. Coyle's long ball dropped between two Mayo and two Meath players. All four missed it. Then, bizarrely, it bounced over the bar in an echo of P. J. Gillic's equalising point in the first drawn match between Dublin and Meath in 1991. Meath players recalled that Colm Coyle had said the night before the game, 'Don't believe what you read in the papers. At the end of the match there will only be the hop of a ball in it.' Having drawn a match they should have won, Mayo then lost a replay they might have drawn.

The match became infamous for the chaotic 27-second punch-up which led to Liam McHale and Colm Coyle being sent off. Subsequently, six Mayo and eight Meath players were suspended.

Meath trailed from the tenth minute and first took the lead with nine minutes to go. Meath's goals came from Trevor Giles (34th-minute penalty) and Tommy Dowd from a quick free in the 60th minute, on a day that Eamonn McEneaney called back almost every other quick free. Mayo's James Horan scored a 66th-minute equaliser. A magnificent shoulder charge by Trevor Giles won possession leading to Brendan Reilly's winning point for Meath in the 70th minute.

After the fracas came farce. Meath captain Tommy Dowd and manager Seán Boylan were refused admission to a Monday function in Croke Park by a Dublin security guard, despite the fact that Dowd was carrying the Sam Maguire Cup. The GAA's PR officer Danny Lynch commented that the two should have had their tickets, and the security guard a bit more common sense.

Liam McHale and John McDermott had a verbal exchange at the post-match function. Officialdom was unimpressed. GAA president Jack Boothman mused about the violence in society being responsible for the punch-up.

The recriminations that followed Meath led to a passionate defence by former team captain Liam Hayes in his new sports newspaper in January 1997: 'Meath players are decent, honest-to-God young men playing a particular brand of football which demands from them bravery and courage and ruthlessness', he wrote.

'It is quite difficult for young players, even with natural talent, to achieve something like that,' Seán Boylan wrote. 'They were a different breed to the 1987–88 teams, playing a different brand of football.'

28 SEPTEMBER 1997. KERRY 0-13, MAYO 1-7, CROKE PARK

> 'The difference between the top teams in Gaelic football was narrowing by the year. Any advantage which could be squeezed out of a situation needed to be grabbed.'
>
> PÁIDÍ Ó SÉ, *Páidí* (2001)

The prevailing wind seemed to be coming from the west. Sligo, with the wind from Ben Bulben at their backs, came back from five points down against Roscommon with the help of a 24th-minute goal from Dessie Sloyane. Roscommon were left to rue the fifteen wides they ran up in the second half.

Mayo beat Galway in Tuam for the first time since 1951 on the day Galway discovered a new star, 19-year-old Michael Donnellan. A Leitrim player put Mayo manager John Maughan on the seat of his shorts, when he entered the field during a stormy second semi-final.

Back in the Connacht final for the first time since 1975, Sligo whittled back a six-point lead with a late Brian Walsh goal, followed by a Paul Durcan point in the final two minutes, only to lose by one. Sligo manager, Mickey Moran from Derry, was among those who bemoaned the fact that referee Michael Curley allowed a mere fifteen seconds of added time at the end.

Under a new team manager, Tommy Lyons, Offaly were on a roll. They started their Leinster championship poorly and were forced to stage a late comeback to earn a second crack at Barney Rock's Westmeath. But Leinster in 1997 was soon gripped by a new rivalry and a three-match saga between Meath and Kildare. Kildare with thirteen men produced one of their best championship performances to run out four-point winners over Laois. Mick O'Dwyer described it in his biography: 'It may have been the greatest victory I ever presided over in my many years as manager.'

Kildare hadn't won a first round championship match in a few seasons and were up against a Laois team that had beaten them comfortably a year earlier. If that weren't enough to leave Kildare feeling brittle, they were dealt a shocking blow in the first few minutes when both Martin Lynch and Johnny McDonald were sent off. Kildare manager Mick O'Dwyer commented later: 'If Kildare had lost that game, there would have been no Leinster titles for them in 1998 and 2000.'

They then drew with Meath before a famous replay in which Jody Devine turned in one of the most famous extra time performances of all time with four points when he came on as a substitute. Meath hauled in a six-point deficit and took a one-point lead before Kildare substitute Paul McCormack touched a hopeful centre over the bar for another equaliser. Devine was the star in a game that was forever after identified as 'Jody Devine's match', but he was still not picked to start in the third match.

The second replay turned ugly. Four players were sent off, two from Meath (Mark O'Reilly and Darren Fay) and two from Kildare (Davy Dalton and Brian Murphy). Another Meath player, John McDermott, was fortunate to stay on the field after flattening Martin Lynch, who required six stitches to a facial wound after the game. To add insult to injury, literally, Lynch had just scored a would-be Kildare goal that was disallowed for over-carrying, and Murphy's goal followed within a minute.

Suspensions, and the loss of Martin O'Connell through a back injury before the throw-in, eventually proved too much for Meath in their Saturday afternoon Leinster final against Offaly. Roy Malone scored two well-taken goals, the second the result of a 50 metre dash to secure the Leinster title.

When Jimmy McGuinness's goal brought Meath back to four points with four minutes remaining, Offaly pulled away with four points of their own, a performance one pundit described as 'the rebirth of Gaelic football'.

Mayo beat Offaly in the All-Ireland semi-final, despite kicking nineteen wides, nine of them and six points, before Offaly got their first score. Offaly did manage to haul the margin back to four points with three minutes to go, but lost by six. Their seven points was the lowest score by a semi-finalist since Monaghan in 1988.

There was a joke doing the rounds in Ulster: what have Cavan and the British Army got in common? Neither of them have got out of Ulster since 1969. In 1997 that changed. Cavan's Jason Reilly scored the winning goal in the Ulster final, shooting low to the net with ten minutes to go, just after Kieran McKeever had nosed Derry in front for the first time. Goalkeeper and medieval scholar Paul O'Dowd was a hero of the championship encounters with Fermanagh, whom they beat in a first round replay, and against Derry when, memorably, he cursed a penalty-taker in old English before making a save.

The Cavan team enjoyed a tumultuous reception for their first All-Ireland semi-final win. Fintan Cahill scored a goal just before half-time to give them a 1-7 to 0-9 lead, but they lost by seven points as Kerry's 19-year-old sub Michael Francis Russell scored the winning goal in the 66th minute.

Mayo started badly in the final but scored 1-2 in two minutes, including Kieran McDonald's 48th-minute penalty, and cut the margin from 1-7 to 0-4 back to one point, 1-7 to 0-11, by the 51st minute. Then it all went wrong. They failed to score in the last twenty minutes of the match and finished with thirteen wides against nine for Kerry.

There was no mistaking the Kerry hero. Maurice Fitzgerald scored nine points to earn a man of the match and player of the year award. 'We had our anxious moments in the second half after conceding a penalty,' Páidí Ó Sé wrote. 'Then there was Maurice, and Maurice again. This was his stage. He was absolutely magnificent.'

'The Kingdom are back and there is no disputing who is king', Seán Moran wrote in *The Irish Times.*

Páidí Ó Sé spent what he described as the most enjoyable hours of his football career discussing the game with Mick O'Dwyer in the Burlington Hotel in the early hours of the following morning, little knowing that the two would come face to face in the following year's All-Ireland semi-final.

27 SEPTEMBER 1998. GALWAY 1-14, KILDARE 1-10, CROKE PARK

> 'Hype, hype hooray.'
> *Irish Independent* colour writer MIRIAM LORD on Kildare's 1998 campaign

Double All-Ireland finalists Mayo bowed out tamely from the 1998 championship, despite two goals from Kieran McDonald from Crossmolina. A spectacular Derek Savage goal gave Galway half-time parity, which they extended for a four-point win.

It was the first of several tales of the unexpected from the west. Sligo held a seven-point lead going into the last quarter of the semi-final with Roscommon, but conceded two swift goals from Eddie Lohan (who had earlier missed a penalty) and Nigel Dineen. Sligo had to rely on a last-gasp equaliser from a 45 by Brian Walsh. Tommy Grehan's 30th-minute goal propelled Roscommon to victory in the replay, Paul Taylor reducing the margin to one point just at the end.

The final was drawn, Galway kicking seventeen wides to Roscommon's four. Roscommon wondered why Gary Fahy was given a free in the drawn match, although he appeared to have earlier lifted the ball from the ground, and Galway quickly moved the ball the length of the field for Niall Finnegan to kick the equaliser.

Galway then kicked twenty wides over the 100 minutes of the replay, but were presented with their winning goal two minutes into the second period of extra time when Roscommon goalkeeper Derek Thompson lost control of the ball, and Michael Donnellan booted it first-time to the net to open up a five-point lead.

Derry won their Ulster final against Donegal dramatically in the 69th minute, Geoffrey McGonigle feeding Joe Brolly to round Donegal goalkeeper Tony Blake for the winning goal. Gary Coleman's penalty goal came too late to make any impact on the All-Ireland semi-final.

Kerry faced down Cork in the Munster semi-final. Alan O'Regan's 56th-minute goal sent Cork two points clear in the semi-final, before Maurice

Fitzgerald scored the goal which undermined the Cork challenge. Kerry then held on to win against a brave Tipp fightback, for whom James Williams's 62nd-minute goal cut their winning margin to three points.

Long-sidelined Louth might have drawn with Meath in Leinster. Wexford referee Brian White overruled his umpire and awarded Graham Geraghty a point for Meath in the tenth minute of the semi-final against Louth. In the end it proved the difference between the rivals as Louth failed to capitalise on Stefan White's first half goal.

Kildare might have had two penalties in their drawn quarter-final encounter with Dublin. 'To scrape a draw Kildare need to be four points a better team', Liam Horan wrote in the *Irish Independent.* Dublin finished with thirteen men in the replay. Dessie Farrell had been sent off and Paul Galvin was injured after all three subs had been used up. Kildare led by four points until Declan Darcy's goal with the last kick, the first time in the game a Dublin forward scored from play.

Against Meath in the Leinster final, Kildare's Brian Murphy expertly finished off a move that brought the ball the length of the field for a goal in injury time. Meath full forward and team captain Brendan Reilly was sent off for a high tackle on Kildare centre forward Declan Kerrigan, who was stretchered off with a suspected fractured jaw. After just three minutes, Brendan Reilly had his shot for goal brilliantly smothered by goalkeeper Christy Byrne.

Kildare's first Leinster title since 1956 meant that their manager Mick O'Dwyer came up against his former protégé, Páidí Ó Sé, in the semi-final. 'If anyone else had been managing Kildare we would have beaten them seven or eight points,' Ó Sé maintained. Denis Dwyer had a late fisted goal disallowed for Kerry, and two late Maurice Fitzgerald frees cut the margin back to one point with time running out. 'When I retired from the game I thought that's the end of Mick O'Dwyer,' Páidí Ó Sé said in the Kildare dressing room afterwards. 'Little did I think that ten years down the road he'd come back to haunt me.'

It became famous as the purist's final, with just 27 frees in total. Galway took the Sam Maguire Cup, thanks to Pádraig Joyce's goal and some magnificent finishing by Ja Fallon.

Kildare lost full back Ronan Quinn before the start and Brian Lacey and Glen Ryan weren't fully fit, but Dermot Earley had scored a seventeenth-minute goal to give them a 1-5 to 0-5 half-time lead.

Glen Ryan put in a long ball, Martin Lynch read the flight better than Tomas Mannion; he fisted back to the onrushing Willie McCreery, whose pass put the ball over Martin McNamara's head for Earley to palm to the net. The climax came as a result of first-time, direct, kicking football that was celebrated by the commentators. John Divilly kicked long to Michael Donnellan, who laid it off to Joyce for the match-turning goal in the 39th minute.

'Galway's All-Ireland victory will convince many that transferring the ball quickly and accurately by foot should be the principal method of moving the ball,' Colm O'Rourke enthused. 'The GAA should get down on their knees and give thanks for John O'Mahony and his gallant Galway players,' former Offaly manager Eugene McGee wrote in the *Irish Independent*. 'They reinvented the great old game of Gaelic football. After years of the short-game mania by many other counties they reverted to the game's original great skills and triumphed. Marvellous high catching, brilliant long range points and, above all, moving the ball with the foot rather than the hand, these are the skills which saw Galway steamroll Kildare into a comprehensive defeat. And if Galway's example is followed by others then maybe Gaelic football will regain its former greatness.'

It wasn't as simple as that, as analyst Gerry McDermott pointed out. Appearances can deceive. Of the six kicked passes that occurred in the lead-up to scores, two occurred at the end of the move. Two were in the first half and four in the second half. But two were in the final minute of the game. Most notably, after 70 minutes there were two kicked passes leading to Seán Óg de Paor's final point of the match.

Kildare had 59 per cent accuracy with foot passing, almost 50 per cent higher than Galway. The longest foot pass in the lead-up to a score by Galway was 27 metres. Another was twenty metres, one was fifteen metres, one seven metres and one three metres. The two players most clearly identified with Galway's success, Ja Fallon and Michael Donnellan, did not kick the ball in the lead-up to any score from play.

Galway's score of 1-10 from play involved a total of 29 passes in the lead-up to the team's eleven scores. Of these, 23 were hand passes. Galway used the hand pass 86 times, 80 of which were accurate, a 96 per cent success rate.

26 SEPTEMBER 1999. MEATH 1-11, CORK 1-8, CROKE PARK

> 'We had a better image and I was pleased that the 1996 lads were belatedly getting credit for their achievements.'
>
> SEÁN BOYLAN, *The Will to Win* (2006)

Meath had cleaned up their act. Just one player was sent off in their 1999 campaign, in a year that started with the greatest spree of sendings off in championship history.

The referee of a preliminary round tie between Carlow and Westmeath sent off four players from Carlow and two from Westmeath, gave out a record fourteen yellow cards, and for the first time in championship history a team finished with eleven players. After the usual furore, the new disciplinary code was quietly and quickly abandoned.

Laois had the beating of Dublin in the Leinster semi-final, but Dublin scored six points without reply and came from four points down in the last two minutes to draw the match. Ian Robertson scored Dublin's goal and a controversial point that he appeared to pick from the ground. Robertson excelled as Dublin then led the replay by eight points, with Laois down to fourteen men, but Laois were helped back to two behind with a Chris Crowley penalty in injury time. Dublin's forwards managed just two points, both from Jim Gavin, from play in the Leinster final, as Meath strolled to a five-point win.

Oisín McConville and Diarmuid Marsden scored 3-9 between them as Armagh convincingly beat Down to recapture the Ulster title they last held in 1982. Marsden snatched the winning point in injury time to defeat Derry in the semi-final. But not before Paul McFlynn missed a would-be equaliser for Derry, who kicked twelve wides as against Armagh's four.

Cavan and Derry played out the best Ulster championship match in years. Joe Brolly emerged from his sick bed with scarlet fever to score an equalising point, five minutes into injury time of the quarter-final, Cavan having dramatically wiped out a five-point deficit with two goals from the penalty spot by Ronan Carolan and Dermot McCabe, who rose above everyone else to box in a Ray Cunningham centre in a crowded goal area.

Meath lost their habitual goal-scorer of the age, Ollie Murphy, through injury after 22 minutes of their All-Ireland semi-final against Armagh. Armagh crowded out the midfield, creating enough space for two well-taken goals by Diarmuid Marsden in the fifteenth minute and Kieran Hughes in the 25th minute, while Marsden had a close-run thing for what would have been a third just before half-time. Ger Reid, Armagh's full back, was sent off at the start of the second half.

Cork conceded two goals in the second quarter from Aodhán MacGearailt, then scored two of their own in the final twenty minutes to regain the title with a six-point winning margin over Kerry. Kerry goalkeeper Declan O'Keeffe failed to hold a dropping ball from a Podsy O'Mahony free in the 51st minute. Substitute Fionán Murray scored Cork's second in the 62nd minute, after which Seán Óg Ó hAilpín denied Billy O'Shea a certain goal. Philip Clifford scored 1-4 in Cork's All-Ireland semi-final victory over Mayo, the Connacht champions, by virtue of a great second half performance and a four-point win over Galway. Galway were in trouble through most of their Connacht semi-final clash with Sligo, for whom Brian Walsh scored three goals. Galway needed a last-minute point from a free by Pádraig Joyce to force the semi-final to a replay,

The Cork-Meath final bore no resemblance to those of 1988–90. Richie Kealy came on as a substitute for Nigel Nestor. He changed the course of the game when he went for a ball he should not have gone for, won it, was fouled, and won a crucial free.

Trevor Giles launched a ball in on the square, where Graham Geraghty broke it down to Ollie Murphy for a trademark winning goal in the 25th minute. It spoiled Cork's hopes of another double. Meath held their nerve as Graham Geraghty was fouled and Trevor Giles missed a penalty at the start of the second half. Joe Kavanagh responded with a goal that gave Cork a brief lead. Injured Tommy Dowd came on in the last minute.

The GAA moved the Sam Maguire Cup presentation ceremony to a platform in the middle of the pitch. Enda McManus's shins were so sore he couldn't climb the platform. He had almost missed the match, having lain down in the team hotel, fallen asleep and missed the team bus. A taxi got him there with the help of a Garda squad car.

Meath players won seven All-Star awards. Martin O'Connell even found his way on to the team of the millennium. They went to Boston for an exhibition game, something that had been denied the bad boys of old. An over-zealous security official wouldn't let them into the ground, as the team bus had already arrived. It turned out that a busload of supporters from New York had been waved through instead.

All was forgiven in the spirit of the new millennium.

Chapter 7 ~

MORE MATCHES, MORE WATCHERS

Gaelic football becomes an industry

'It's only a game of football. There are more important things in life.'

PADDY CULLEN after the 1992 All-Ireland final

In 1983 it was clear that Croke Park was no longer adequate for the demands of the Association. Unknown to the public at large, there was serious crowding and crushing on Hill 16. A gate was forced and people were squashed. Tragedy was narrowly averted.

The day after the match, the GAA went into emergency session. Six years before the same conclusion was forced on the soccer world, they decided a nineteenth-century stadium design couldn't stage a modern sporting occasion. Croke Park would have to come down.

Croke Park became the fourth biggest stadium in Europe. The first part to be replaced was Hill 16, which had been rebuilt in 1988. But in the course of that exercise the GAA looked at American stadiums, especially Giants Stadium in New York and Joe Robbie Stadium (later Dolphin Stadium) in Miami, and began to rethink the landscape of their home.

They devised plans for a three-tier horseshoe stadium, with Hill 16 retained as a standing area. Two tiers of corporate boxes, the first at an Irish sports facility, would be sold to corporate clients.

Progress would depend on financing, and was not dependent on government grants, although three tranches of aid were later made available by successive Irish governments.

The old Cusack Stand was demolished after the 1993 All-Ireland, and the new stand was finished for the 1996 All-Ireland. By 2000, the Canal end had been completed, and by 2003 the Hogan Stand. Floodlights were installed in 2007. The whole exercise cost in the region of €250 m and included escalators, new players' lounges, first aid and security facilities, an executive level and a museum where the story of the ancient games could be told.

A hotel was added in 2007. For the first time the GAA's income was no longer wholly dependent on gate receipts.

24 SEPTEMBER 2000. KERRY 0-14, GALWAY 0-14, CROKE PARK
7 OCTOBER 2000. KERRY 0-17, GALWAY 1-10, CROKE PARK

> 'All the top teams were striving for the edge. Everything was scrutinised. If a team was working the ball one way, then the other would match it, outdo it, do it faster. When I studied a video in 1997 I would pick out the man who missed the ball, missed the tackle, misdirected a kick, hit a chance wide. Three years later I would source the original pass, trace the difficulty back, query why another option wasn't chosen, why the ball wasn't worked a different way. It's like snooker. You have to think five or six shots ahead.'
>
> PÁIDÍ Ó SÉ, *Páidí* (2001)

Leitrim were back in the Connacht final in 2000. Their comeback in the Connacht semi-final against Roscommon was dramatic: they trailed by seven points (3-3 to 0-5) after 26 minutes and conceded two goals within a minute from John Gillooly and Frankie Dolan, but Leitrim equalised when Dermot Reynolds fisted the ball to the net on 47 minutes and captain Seamus Quinn kicked the winning point. Leitrim's wing back Colin Regan, a member of the Church of Ireland, reacted to a sectarian remark by punching his Roscommon opponent Frankie Grehan, and was caught on video.

Sligo stormed ahead of Mayo in the first round through a Ken Killeen goal and scarcely looked back. James Horan, Mayo's potent distance kicker, was sent off in the second half.

Galway took command in the thirteenth minute of the final when Kieran Joyce was fouled and Derek Savage scored the resultant penalty. They led 1-8 to 0-2 after 39 minutes, and Leitrim's tentative comeback never threatened them.

Leinster was developing a new rivalry in 2000, Kildare against Dublin. The Leinster final turned on Kildare's two goals in 90 seconds immediately after half-time. Thirty seconds into the second half, Dermot Earley slipped the cover and rolled the ball under Dublin goalkeeper David Byrne. Brian Murphy sent in Tadgh Fennin for the second goal immediately afterwards. Dublin could have had two goals in a similar spell before the break. Jason Sherlock fired a goal opportunity over the bar and Brian Stynes dropped a scoring chance into Kildare goalkeeper Christy Byrne's hands. It took fifteen nervous minutes before Kildare took the lead as they held Dublin to one point in the second half.

Kildare might not have made it that far. Donie Ryan's last-minute goal earned Offaly a draw against Kildare in the Leinster semi-final, and Offaly had two chances to win in injury time, first with another Donie Ryan run at goal and then a later free. Up came goalkeeper Padraig Kelly for the 55 metre shot and, while he found the distance, he couldn't find the direction. Offaly failed to register a score for 32 minutes of the replay, while Kildare shot nine points without reply after half-time to cancel the advantage from Colm Quinn and Ciaran McManus's first half goals.

The Leinster council organised a round robin for four 'weaker' counties for the first time since 1939.

Dara Ó Cinnéide's two penalty goals helped Kerry beat Cork in the Munster semi-final, despite a storming second half comeback from Cork. Cork manager Larry Tompkins caused a stand-off in the second half by refusing to retreat to the dugout on the referee's orders.

Clare were back in the Munster final and seemed to be getting a grip on it, until Liam Hassett scored a goal against the run of play before half-time and precipitated a Clare collapse in the second half. Aodhán MacGearailt and Mike Francis Russell added Kerry's goals in the second half.

Rory Gallagher scored a 26th-minute goal as Fermanagh overcame Donegal in Ballybofey with fourteen men in the second half. Tony Boyle missed a penalty and Donegal manager Declan Bonner announced his resignation afterwards.

It might have been an Antrim-Fermanagh Ulster final. A gigantic leap by the 6' 6" Derry midfielder Anthony Tohill prevented a winning point for Antrim in the semi-final, and Derry won the replay. Fermanagh had a great first half against Armagh and led by a point at half-time in the other semi-final. Fermanagh slipped into a three-point deficit, but the Gallagher brothers, Ray and Rory, kept their heads and cut the lead back to a point and missed a couple of chances to draw. Antrim ended eighteen years without a championship victory, despite a fortuitous penalty scored by Gregory McCartan.

Armagh then retained the Ulster title amid great drama, when Derry's Anthony Tohill missed a would-be equaliser. Steven McDonnell's fourteenth-minute goal overturned Derry's early lead. Derry manager Eamonn Coleman, who had been banned from the sideline, complained he was 'bitter at how you get treated in GAA circles by people who never played football but sit up and lay down the law'.

Galway overturned a four-point deficit to lead 1-2 to 0-4 at half-time in the semi-final against Kildare. Martin Lynch's high ball found Brian Murphy, who placed Tadgh Fennin for the goal after thirteen minutes, but Galway came from behind with four unanswered points in the closing minutes. Fennin set up Murphy for a diving, fisted second goal after 45 minutes. John Finn was sent off with four minutes to go. The inspirational Michael Donnellan drove over a 50 metre free in the last minute to extend the lead to two points. 'The talented Tribesmen reminded us why the game is called football,' Eamonn Sweeney wrote in the *Irish Examiner*. 'Kildare were an unholy genetic cross between basketball and athletics.'

There was another problem—the absence of a Hogan Stand. Páidí Ó Sé commented that the majority of the play seemed to be drawn towards the Cusack Stand side of the field 'probably because of the absence of a defined barrier on the far side'. Graham Geraghty had commented after Meath's exit: 'Who wants to win an All-Ireland on a building site?' Ó Sé was determined the same thing would not happen in Kerry's semi-final against Armagh.

The match was a draw. Kerry raced into a 1-3 to nil lead after five minutes with the help of a Dara Ó Cinnéide penalty. 'I knew it was only a matter of time,' Páidí Ó Sé wrote. 'They packed the middle, put a powerful squeeze on us, clawed us back, turned the tables.' Barry O'Hagan responded with Armagh's first goal in the ninth minute. Kerry substitute Maurice Fitzgerald set Kerry up for a win with a goal. Twice more Kerry opened a four-point lead, but Armagh drew them back. Andrew McCann scored a sensational equalising goal for Armagh in the 70th minute and snaked ahead. Then, four minutes into injury time, Fitzgerald stepped up to score an equalising free. 'The winning of that year was that moment against Armagh when we hung on to the game,' Mike Hassett recalled.

The replay took extra time, Mike Francis Russell finishing with 2-3, his first goal saving Kerry in ordinary time and his second setting up the extra-time victory. Oisin McConville scored Armagh's goal and had an extra-time shot smothered by Declan O'Keeffe when the margin was two points. According to Páidí Ó Sé, the strain of the Maurice Fitzgerald debate (should he be in the starting fifteen?) was beginning to tell on the Kerry team in the run-up to the final. 'I could sense the tension on the train to Dublin,' but he was relieved when Fitzgerald confounded the team with an inspirational speech at the team meeting.

Galway came from seven points down to draw the All-Ireland final as both sides missed easy chances. 'We stuck to our plan, everything seemed to be going right, and the wheels fell off,' Páidí Ó Sé said. Kerry then won the replay, controversially played on a Saturday for the first time in GAA history to avoid clashing with an Australian Rules international. 'With our homework done the replay went like a dream', Páidí Ó Sé wrote.

A disputed free meant Kerry took the lead with seventeen minutes to go. Galway worked the ball the length of the field for Declan Meehan's memorable seventh-minute goal, arguably the best in the history of All-

Ireland finals. It started in Galway's goalmouth. Dara Ó Cinnéide's 45 was blocked down by Walsh. John Divilly collected and raced out to initiate an eight-pass movement down the left flank. Padraig Joyce moved the ball into the centre, where Paul Clancy gathered and fired a brilliant pass over the defence and into the arms of the advancing Meehan. Galway then lost Kevin Walsh to injury after nineteen minutes.

23 SEPTEMBER 2001. GALWAY 0-17, MEATH 0-8, CROKE PARK

> 'If you get over one or two rounds, people get behind you. It's a whole new ball game.'
>
> SEÁN BOYLAN describing his team's run in the 2001 football championship

In the All-Ireland championship, Galway did not even play in the provincial final. After a series of disappointing Connacht finals, 2001 was a classic.

Roscommon's Gerry Lohan scored the winning goal three minutes into injury time, described by Keith Duggan in *The Irish Times* as the match 'around which this 2001 GAA summer will revolve'. The match ended, Duggan wrote, 'as a rhapsody, as an entity beyond analysis'.

Mayo celebrated a last-minute goal of their own, from David Nestor, to go ahead just on full time. Then came Roscommon's enchanting winning goal, the ball passing from Alan Nolan's sideline kick to Jonathan Dunning to Denis Gavin to Gerry Lohan. Roscommon's Cliff McDonald and Mayo's Ray Connelly were sent off as the game gathered pace in the second half.

Mayo barely squeezed by Sligo by a point in the Connacht semi-final. Sligo had a perfect start when Seán Davey's first-minute ball ended up in the net. Stephen Carolan scored Mayo's winning point against Sligo, for whom Paul Taylor missed a penalty. Dessie Sloyane scored Sligo's goal. Kieran McDonald demanded a fresh ball from the sideline before firing an extravagant wide on to the terrace in front of the bacon factory.

New York did not exactly come close to winning their first Connacht championship match. They lost to Roscommon in Hyde Park by ten points. However, they managed to reduce a commanding Roscommon lead to a mere two points midway through the second half, but had both their wing half backs P. J. Lanigan and Niall McCready sent off within ten minutes of each other.

Kildare were missing four players from their 2000 team, including the entire half back line. They lost their provincial title as Kildare's Karl O'Dwyer went off with concussion after half an hour of the semi-final. Meath's Trevor Giles scored a 56th-minute penalty, and Meath held their nerve when substitute Killian Brennan fisted a goal to revive Kildare's hopes briefly in the 66th minute. Meath's Paddy Reynolds and Kildare's Ken Doyle were sent off.

It was back to Dublin v Meath in the Leinster final. Meath led from start to finish. Goals from Graham Geraghty in the fifth minute and Richie Kealy in the 56th minute secured victory as Dublin kicked twice as many wides as Meath.

In Munster, Kerry came back from six points down to beat Cork by three. They took the lead with a Donal Kelleher point in the 46th minute. Cork might have had a penalty shortly afterwards when Seán Óg Ó hAilpín was grounded in the square by the advancing Kerry keeper. 'This is the second year in a row we have been on the wrong end of a number of ridiculous refereeing decisions,' Cork manager Larry Tompkins said.

Fermanagh beat Donegal again with a goal in the last minute of play. Raymond Johnston's free hopped into the path of Fermanagh substitute Mark O'Donnell, who calmly toe-poked the winning goal. The whistle was then blown 30 seconds prematurely by referee Brian White.

Tyrone's 19-year-old Owen Mulligan scored one of the quickest goals in championship history in the Ulster quarter-final against Armagh. Tyrone trailed Cavan by three points at half-time in the Ulster final and took the lead in the third quarter as Cavan kicked five wides. Tyrone's Cormac McAnallen and Jason Reilly exchanged goals. Reilly tried for another from a 14 yard free that went wide with fifteen minutes to go.

It was all change for the 113-year-old championship as a qualifier series was introduced. The new system delivered a back-door champion in its very first year. It also provided the score of the year from Kerry's Maurice Fitzgerald with a point from a line ball to draw the quarter-final in Thurles on a day 30,000 fans had not taken their seats with ten minutes to the throw-in. Dublin fans who departed on the journey south got caught in traffic jams at still un-bypassed Kildare.

Vinny Murphy, a former Dub-in-exile who couldn't get his place on the Kerry team, propelled the Dublin comeback from an eight-point deficit with the first goal. Corner forward Johnny Crowley contributed 2-2, as Kerry won the replay.

Westmeath gave the new system its imprimatur. 'The new system has to be seen as the most significant development for the GAA in its history,' former All-Ireland manager Eugene McGee wrote, 'and certainly the one that has brought it more goodwill from the public than anything else it ever did. What Westmeath's progress this year has shown above all is the travesty that was the old-style championship for over 100 years. Thankfully, things will never be the same again.'

First half goals from Paul Conway, Michael Ennis and Dessie Dolan gave

Westmeath a 3-7 to 1-6 half-time lead against rivals Meath. Ollie Murphy snatched a draw with his second Meath goal in the last minute of normal time. A Paddy Bradley goal twelve minutes into the second half set Derry on the way to victory over Tyrone. Westmeath had twelve wides in the replay compared to just three for Meath, who progressed through goals by Graham Geraghty and substitute Raymond Magee.

Dessie Sloyane scored eight points as a fourteen-man Sligo team defeated Kildare in their first championship match at Croke Park since 1975. 'Even the qualifier system's most ardent advocates could hardly have anticipated the damburst of happiness released by this new format', Seán Moran wrote in *The Irish Times.*

In the All-Ireland semi-final, Galway scored seven unanswered scores to come back from five points down against a Derry side that had dominated the game.

Meath completed an astonishing fifteen-point demolition of Kerry in the All-Ireland semi-final, led by 1-6 to 0-4, thanks to a 25th-minute goal from veteran John McDermott, and went on to beat Kerry, John Cullinane scoring a second goal with six minutes to go.

In the All-Ireland final, Galway's Pádraig Joyce scored eight points in a row as Galway became the first back-door champions, overwhelming Meath in the second half after Nigel Nestor was sent off.

22 SEPTEMBER 2002. ARMAGH 1-12, KERRY 0-14, CROKE PARK

> 'I want to play for Armagh. I want to score the winning goal in the All-Ireland final. I want to lift Sam Maguire.'
>
> OISÍN MCCONVILLE's school essay for his teacher, Miss Cassidy, at age 8

All-Ireland champions Galway won back the 2002 Connacht title, thanks to a Derek Savage penalty, a five-point to one scoring spree at the start, and a strong third quarter on a wind and rain-swept day.

Sligo beat Leitrim 2-13 to 2-4 in the semi-final. Leitrim's Adrian Charles was sent off, and Leitrim conceded 1-10 during what young Leitrim manager Declan Rowley described as 'ten minutes of madness in the third quarter'.

Galway conceded a goal from Mayo's Michael Moyle after just sixteen seconds. Séamus Quinn, one of three survivors of the historic Connacht championship side of 1995, shot Leitrim's first goal after eight minutes.

Kildare needed extra time to see off Offaly in a replayed Leinster semi-final, goals from Eddie McCormack, Ronan Sweeney and Dermot Earley keeping them ahead. Ciaran McManus scored a penalty for Offaly shortly after the restart. The game remained scoreless for the last eighteen minutes before Kildare prevailed in extra time.

Only half of the allotted four minutes of added time were played as Offaly forced a draw on the first day, with a late Ciarán McManus penalty and a Vinnie Claffey point. The match was moved to 4.45 pm to avoid a clash with Ireland's World Cup match with Spain.

Dublin got their revenge for 2000 with two goals in the space of a minute in the Leinster final from Alan Brogan and Ray Cosgrove. Stephen Cluxton saved brilliantly from a Tadhg Fennin snapshot in injury time. Fennin scored both Kildare's goals earlier in the game.

Meath's All-Star goalkeeper Cormac Sullivan was caught twice for Ray Cosgrove goals in the semi-final, in the sixteenth minute and at the end of the match. Meath were missing Ollie Murphy and lost John Cullinane, their star at midfield against Westmeath, with a head injury just after the semi-final started.

Colin Corkery missed a penalty as Cork beat Kerry in the Munster semi-final, despite Darragh Ó Sé's goal at the start of the second half. Brendan Jer O'Sullivan missed the chance of a winning score in the last minute.

Tipperary footballers forced a surprise draw with Cork in the Munster final, when corner back Niall Kelly popped up to clinch an equaliser in the second minute of injury time. Two goals from Brendan Jer O'Sullivan gave Cork a five-point lead, and substitute Benny Hickey scored Tipperary's goal eleven minutes after the restart. Cork took an eight-point lead against Tipp in the replay, and started the second half with a goal.

The 19-year-old Seán Kavanagh scored an injury time equalising goal for Tyrone as they renewed a famous rivalry with Armagh in the Ulster championship quarter-final. Armagh captain Kieran McGeeney then saved the day, blocking down a shot from Seamus McCallan.

The second half of the Tyrone-Armagh replay was, in Keith Duggan's words, 'awesome, the equivalent of two heavyweights slugging it out'. Steven McDonnell and young substitute Barry Duffy scored Tyrone's goals. John McEntee scored Armagh's goal with the very last kick of the first half.

Armagh then beat Donegal by four points in the Ulster final. Jim McGuinness's deflected would-be equaliser was smothered by Benny Tierney with two minutes to go. John McEntee's second-minute goal was the result of a fumble from Donegal goalkeeper Tony Blake. Donegal recovered to equalise, but succumbed in the third quarter. Kerry's 23-point hammering of Wicklow was a record for the new-style qualifier system.

An August bank holiday Monday was used for the first time for a championship match when Cork played Mayo and Dublin played Donegal. Chrissy Toye's goal three minutes before half-time helped Donegal avenge their huge semi-final defeat to Meath twelve years earlier.

Limerick were another surprise: two late goals in a four-minute spell from sub Johnny Murphy and Conor Mullane defeated Cavan in a replay. They then had goals from Pat Ahern and Micheál Reidy inside the first four minutes of their match with Offaly, led by 2-4 to 0-3 at half-time, and sealed victory with a third goal from Stephen Kelly five minutes from the end. They then led Mayo by 1-5 to 0-5 at half-time in the next round, thanks to a Jason Stokes goal, only to lose by a point after late Mayo points from a James Gill free and substitute David Brady.

Peter Forde's Sligo shocked Tyrone after going six points behind in the first half, Dessie Sloyane's 62nd-minute goal securing victory. They then took Armagh to two matches in the quarter-final. Dessie Sloyane and substitute Pádraig Doohan scored two points each as Sligo came back with fourteen men for Darragh McGarty to punch over a dramatic equalising point in the third minute of injury time. They lost the replay by two points, Armagh teenager Ronan Clarke grabbing the only goal a minute into the second half, as Kieran McGeeney dived full length to block a goal-bound Gerry McGowan effort to end Sligo's dream.

Cork fans threw plastic bottles on to the field and three players were sent off in the second half, as Kerry avenged their Munster final defeat by Cork with a fifteen-point victory in the semi-final. Teenage corner forward Colm 'Gooch' Cooper, Mike Frank Russell and Eoin Brosnan contributed the goals. 'That chip against Fermanagh, that goal against Kildare after three minutes, four points from play against Galway, the Gooch owned the qualifiers', T. J. Flynn wrote in his 2008 history, *Princes of Pigskin.*

Tensions were high before the throw-in, as Kerry GAA officials insisted that they had acted 'properly and fairly' in their decision not to suspend inter-county captain Darragh Ó Sé.

The Gaeltacht midfielder had been was red carded in a county championship game against Austin Stacks. Radio Kerry commentator Liam Higgins abandoned his post, having announced on air, 'Jesus, a Cork man wouldn't do it', and raced out to settle matters with the referee. County chairman Seán Walsh intercepted the commentator before anything happened. The referee admitted in his report that he made a mistake, and Darragh was cleared to play. Seán O'Sullivan and Aodan Mac Gearailt got the Kerry goals in a majestic quarter-final victory over Galway.

Ray Cosgrove was a goalscorer twice in the drawn match, and again in Dublin's replay win over Donegal, after Donegal had come from three points behind with four minutes to play, to draw a thrilling quarter-final that was level on nine occasions.

Armagh achieved their first win in Croke Park since 1977 in the All-Ireland semi-final against Dublin, and it was one of the most dramatic in championship history. Dublin's Ray Cosgrove struck the post with a would-be equalising free in injury time, as Armagh clung on for a one-point victory. Both goals came in the space of a minute, five minutes into the second half. McKeever ran on to a Diarmuid Marsden flick for Armagh's goal, and Ciaran Whelan soloed through from midfield to shoot in off the underside of the crossbar.

So to the All-Ireland final. 'The entire All-Ireland final is a nightmare,' Oisin McConville wrote in his autobiography, *The Gambler*. 'You're there too early and you're on the field with 25 minutes to go before the throw-in. Everything about that day heightens the worst emotions possible and it's why some teams have lost finals. It's more than a test of footballing skill.' It was a day for emotion. McConville's 55th-minute goal gave Armagh their first-ever All-Ireland and victory over Kerry in the new look Croke Park.

The final seemed lost at half-time when Armagh trailed by four points, faced the wind, had lost John McEntee to concussion, and McConville had missed a 34th-minute penalty. 'I put it where I wanted but it should have been harder and O'Keeffe saved it,' McConvile wrote. 'The second the penalty was stopped, I thought of Bill McCorry who missed a penalty in the 1953 final. All people ever said about him was that he cost Armagh the 1953 All-Ireland. It was even mentioned at his funeral. That was his legacy and, although it was wrong, he had to live with this until he died.' McConville says he was inspired by the words of 19-year-old Ronan Clarke, who said to him as they walked off at half-time, 'It'll happen for you.'

Armagh manager Joe Kernan delivered one of the most famous dressing room speeches of all time, producing his runners-up medal from 1977 in the dressing room, the sign of a loser as he called it, and said he was ashamed to show it to his wife and family. He threw it against a wall and sent his team back into play.

McConville described the winning goal: 'I waited and waited. It seemed so long but on video it happened so quickly. I just knew I had time and wasn't going to blast it. The keeper expected me to go for the far post, as anyone would, but I tucked it in the near side.'

Kerry failed to score in the final seventeen minutes. 'Helicopters landing' was how Páidí Ó Sé described the closing stages of the game.

28 SEPTEMBER 2003. TYRONE 0-12, ARMAGH 0-9, CROKE PARK

Now certain folk down South don't like us
They say our game is dour
'Well boys,' I say, 'don't ate the grapes
If you find they are sour.'

PATSY O'HAGAN, the bard of Tyrone (2003)

Laois recruited a new manager in October 2003, Kildare boss Mick O'Dwyer, who had been awaiting a renewal of his contract when it became clear Galway's John O'Mahoney was being approached by Kildare. O'Dwyer joined Laois, and Kildare appointed Padraig Nolan.

Brazilian soccer legend Jairzinho was among the attendance at the quarter-final between Laois and Offaly, when Mick Lawlor's 1-1 in little over a minute saved Laois. Ciarán McManus, having seemingly won the match for Offaly going into injury time, had to convert a last-minute 45 to earn a replay. Beano McDonald's 47th-minute goal brought the hammer down and effectively saw off Offaly in the replay before he got a straight red card in the 68th minute.

Westmeath's Dessie Dolan had the most famous miss of his career in the drawn quarter-final against Meath from a 21 yard free in front of the goal. The miss meant a replay after Westmeath trailed by five at half-time, and led by the same margin with twenty minutes to go. Dolan had scored 1-7 and, minutes earlier, a free from the hands from out on the left touchline which dissected the posts. Meath had a goal from Hank Traynor after just one minute. To add to his discomfiture, he missed a penalty in the replay, and from the kick-out Meath worked the ball through for a David Crimmins goal.

A 1983 and 93 style tunnel incident marred Dublin's defeat to Laois in the semi-final. 'I didn't see anything,' O'Dwyer said afterwards. 'I walked straight into the dressing room. A little scuffle like that, sure there's no harm in it.' Other officials agreed and no action was taken. Laois's victory was epitomised by Padraig Clancy's long-range strike in the 69th minute, which put a safe four points between the teams. Then Kildare shot just six wides in the semi-final in beating Meath.

Laois prevailed when they met Kildare in a sparkling Leinster final, with three late points from Donal Miller, Ian Fitzgerald and Barry Brennan, after the sides were level with eleven minutes to go. Goals from Beano McDonald (Laois) seconds into the second half, Ross Munnelly (Laois) a few minutes later, and Ronan Sweeney's penalty for Kildare set up the grandstand finish. Kildare, who were already without Anthony Rainbow and Dermot Earley, kicked seventeen wides and lost Alan Barry and Mick Wright in harsh sending-off decisions, while Laois lost Kevin Fitzpatrick. Barry's two yellow cards were accumulated in a record ten seconds for an off-the-ball incident with Pauric Clancy and a bad tackle on Tom Kelly. The absurdity was that Laois got fined when Joe Higgins's twins accompanied the team around Croke Park in the pre-match parade for the final.

Limerick beat Cork 0-16 to 0-6 in the 2003 Munster championship, their second time to do so after a 38-year interval. Limerick could have had a late goal after Cork had Fionan Murray red-carded for 'use of the foot'.

Kerry beat Limerick in the 2003 Munster final, benefiting from a Dara Ó Cinnéide goal at the end of the first half and Limerick's inability to deliver in the first quarter when their challenge was strongest. Stephen Kelly almost sneaked in a goal after 35 seconds and was in devastating form on the right wing. Michael Reidy failed to take advantage of an eleventh-minute penalty, won by Jason Stokes; Stephen Kelly was forced off injured, and the title prospects of Liam Kearns's team were long gone when Reidy kicked a second penalty against the crossbar.

One of the great near upsets of the century occurred in the Connacht championship, when Leitrim needed extra time to beat New York, before dramatic late points from Shane Canning and Padraig McLoughlin finally proved decisive in a match in which the sides were level on eight occasions. Galway led Roscommon by six points at half-time at the newly refurbished Pearse Stadium.

Galway's Matthew Clancy scored the winning goal just before half-time in the Connacht final. Stephen Carolan missed a penalty for Mayo, who lost captain Fergal Costello in a clash of heads with Paul Clancy. Sligo's Dessie Sloyane flashed a 73rd-minute shot just over the bar as they tried to retrieve their semi-final.

In Ulster, a fourteen man Fermanagh team shot eight first half wides to leave themselves 0-6 to 0-4 ahead at half-time and beat Donegal for the third time in four years. Derry's Paddy Bradley scored the crucial second half goal in a fiery quarter-final draw with Tyrone, in which Derry lost a four-point lead. Tyrone's Peter Canavan scored eleven points and his former pupil, Owen Mulligan, added four more in a replayed Ulster final. They came back from nine points down, ten minutes into the second half of the drawn match, after a first half goal from Brendan Coulter and two goals in two minutes at the start of the second half from Liam Doyle and Dan Gordon. Gordon got Down's fourth goal before Peter Canavan equalised, and Tyrone missed two injury time chances. Steve McDonnell hit the post as champions Armagh went out to fourteen-man Monaghan.

Dom Corrigan's Fermanagh team showed signs of what was to come in the 2004 qualifiers with wins over Cavan, thanks to four points without reply at the start of the second half, Meath, when Raymond Gallagher started a second half comeback with a goal, and Mayo, when a late goal by Trevor Mortimer set up a gripping finish. Roscommon needed extra time to beat Offaly after a late Finbar Cullen goal brought matters to extra-time in the second round, and again against Kildare, when six points kicked by Frankie Dolan in extra-time saw them through to the quarter-final.

A 45 metre injury-time point from Galway captain Kevin Walsh earned a quarter-final draw against Donegal, then Galway staged a fierce fightback in the replay after falling seven points behind, keeping out three goal attempts in the process. Second half goals from Karol Mannion, Gary Cox and Frankie Dolan kept Roscommon in touch against Kerry, who threatened to run away with 1-1 from Declan O'Sullivan in the first four minutes. Mick O'Dwyer's Laois were level with Armagh on nine different occasions in their quarter-final, seven Oisin McConville points proving the difference between the sides. Armagh's Paddy McKeever and Dublin goalkeeper Stephen Cluxton were both sent off in their quarter-final, won by Armagh's run of six unanswered points in the second half.

The semi-final between Tyrone and Kerry became symbolic of an entire style of football. Tyrone lost Peter Canavan, forced out of the game with a serious ankle injury after just twelve minutes, but their swarm defence strangled Kerry's efforts, hunting in predatory packs and closing their opponents down as they chased a seven-point half-time deficit, having taken a 0-6 to nil lead by the twentieth minute. 'It was like a train ramming into us,' Gooch Cooper recalled. 'It was like we didn't have air to breathe.'

'It was intense, but not one Kerry player had to leave that field injured,' Tyrone manager Mickey Harte said. 'If anything was injured, it was Kerry's pride.' Harte wondered how history would have projected the match if his team and Kerry had served up the greatest spectacle of high-scoring football and Tyrone had lost. 'Then it would have been said that Tyrone are a great footballing team but they can't win. There's no use in us playing flamboyantly and losing.'

All the semi-final flamboyance was shown by Armagh, who shot 21 wides in the semi-final to just four from Donegal, who looked as if they might just hold on for victory with just fourteen men. Normal time had elapsed when Peter Loughran fisted the lead point for Armagh, and Oisin McConville added a penalty before the end. Toye's goal ten minutes before half-time gave Donegal a 1-4 to 0-4 half-time lead.

Tyrone manager Mickey Harte's daughter Michaela had written down a prediction after Tyrone's defeat in the 1997 All-Ireland minor final. It proved prophetic for a nucleus of players that had formed around the tragedy of the death of their team mate Paul McGirr in the run-up to that 1997 final, that Tyrone would win an All-Ireland minor title the following year, the under-21 title in 2000, and the senior title in 2003.

'Maybe, just maybe out there, there's a Paul McGirr factor,' Harte said. 'I think it has been a real basis for the character of these lads that are now in the senior team. They've grown together. They did a lot of growing in a short space of time.'

Brian Dooher played superbly, and Peter Canavan overcame injury to reappear for the last ten minutes of the final and guide his county to their first title. Tyrone had three missed goal chances in a dour match that produced ten yellow cards. Armagh had Diarmaid Marsden sent off in the 56th minute, and Steven McDonnell's goal shot spectacularly blocked by Conor Gormley. 'It'll change our lives forever. Today we're made men,' John Devine of Tyrone commented on the result.

Within months of Tyrone's victory, their young star Cormac McAnallen had died of Sudden Adult Death Syndrome. 'For over 100 years the Sam Maguire Cup had been the holy grail of every Gaelic games supporter in Tyrone,' Ciaran McBride said at the funeral. 'But here, amid such grief, its presence was scarcely noticed.'

26 SEPTEMBER 2004. KERRY 1-20, MAYO 2-9, CROKE PARK

> 'In 2003 we put up or shut up and we got on with it and won 2004. The only unfortunate thing is that we didn't get to meet Tyrone that year.'
>
> DARA Ó CINNÉIDE, interview with Joe Ó Muircheartaigh in *Princes of Pigskin* (2008)

Westmeath dumped the Dubs in the Leinster quarter-final, bursting through with points from Gary Dolan, Joe Fallon and Paul Conway. Dessie Dolan said afterwards, 'There was some bafflement in Westmeath as to why the team couldn't take a big scalp in recent years. They had done so regularly as youngsters coming up through the ranks.'

Dublin imploded to a series of boohs from Hill 16, failing to score after Alan Brogan put Dublin a point ahead with ten minutes of ordinary time and six minutes of added time left. Colm Parkinson scored Laois's match-winning goal as they took the other big scalp, Meath, in another quarter-final. Meath replacement John Cullinane was later sent off for stamping on goalscorer Parkinson. Second half goals from Shane Colleary and Dessie Dolan sent Westmeath into the final against stop-start Wexford. 'When you play champions you have to be six or seven points better than them to beat them, and we weren't,' Seán Boylan said after the Laois match. 'They picked it up in the second half and got all the breaks. That's it.' Mattie Forde scored eight of Wexford's points as they overturned Kildare.

Westmeath reduced the number of counties waiting for their first provincial title to two (Fermanagh and Wicklow) the hard way in Leinster, surviving six minutes of added time and a goal chance from Laois's Kevin Fitzpatrick which went wide. Westmeath manager Páidí Ó Sé, pitted against his old manager Mick O'Dwyer, told his team at half-time: 'We are coming out, and if we have to stay out until six in the morning we aren't coming in without winning the bloody thing.'

Westmeath went scoreless for the opening 23 minutes of the replay, then scored freely after Alan Mangan had opened their account to lead 0-7 to 0-5 at half-time. Referee Pat McEnaney called up the drawn final a minute early at 0-13 each, Laois captain Chris Conway having scored the equalising point. Páidí Ó Sé described it as a 'bit of humanity'.

Limerick led Kerry 1-7 to 1-4 at half-time in the Munster final, Eoin Keating dropping three free kicks just short of the goal before Mike Frank Russell equalised for Kerry. Kerry then won the replay with a 30th-minute goal from Eoin Brosnan, a morale-boosting penalty at the end of the first half from Dara Ó Cinnéide, and a third from Tomas Ó Sé after 43 minutes. Stephen Kelly volleyed Limerick's shock first-minute goal, and Eoin Keating scored the second from a 58th-minute penalty. Limerick left it behind them the first day.

In Ulster, Steve McDonnell hit the post as champions Armagh went out to fourteen-man Monaghan. Fourteen-man Fermanagh shot eight first half wides to leave themselves 0-6 to 0-4 ahead at half-time and beat Donegal for the third time in four years. Derry's Paddy Bradley scored the crucial second half goal in a fiery quarter-final draw with Tyrone, where Derry lost a four-point lead. Tyrone's Peter Canavan scored eleven points, and his former pupil, Owen Mulligan, four points in a replayed Ulster final against Down. They came back from nine points down, ten minutes into the second half of the drawn match, after a first half goal from Brendan Coulter and two goals in two minutes at the start of the second half from Liam Doyle and Dan Gordon. Gordon got Down's fourth goal before Peter Canavan equalised, and Tyrone missed two injury-time chances.

Three penalties decided the Roscommon-Sligo replay in the first round. Roscommon's Ger Heneghan and Sligo's Paul Taylor swapped first half penalties. With Heneghan, scorer of the opening penalty, substituted at half-time and with regular penalty-taker Frankie Dolan harshly sent off, Roscommon goalkeeper Shane Curran ran the length of the field to score the third penalty goal. Roscommon spent the final 27 minutes of the drawn match without a score. After Davey Sloyane's equaliser, Frankie Dolan missed Roscommon's would-be winning free.

Leitrim forced a draw with Roscommon in the Connacht semi-final with a controversial penalty by debutant Michael Foley nine minutes into the second half of the drawn match. John Hanly had Roscommon's semi-final winning goal as Leitrim scored only three points from play in the replay, and for bad measure had John McKeon sent off late in the game.

Mayo's young team breezed past the Roscommon side with goals from Trevor Mortimer after 57 minutes and Austin O'Malley after 70.

Armagh laid the foundation for a thirteen-point victory over Donegal in the 2004 Ulster final, two more than their defeat of Down in 1999, with Diarmuid Marsden's fisted 28th-minute goal in a game controversially moved to Croke Park. Paddy McKeever and Oisin McConville added second half goals as Donegal were left to ponder what might have happened if Colm McFadden's 37th-minute shot on goal had hit the net instead of the crossbar.

Fermanagh's was the story of the 2004 qualifiers. Tipp pulled out of their first round qualifier. Colm Bradley's memorable point from a sideline ball forced their second round match with Meath into extra time, and Bradley starred as they pulled off their first shock. They then thoroughly outclassed Cork after the teams were level 0-6 each at half-time. Meath had hit two early goals from Daithi Regan. Eamon Maguire scored Fermanagh's goal in their extra-time defeat of Donegal, in a game that produced fifteen yellow and two red cards. Fermanagh then knocked out championship favourites, fourteen-man Armagh, in the quarter-final, with Tom Brewster's winning point in the fourth minute of stoppage time. Derry goals from Enda Muldoon and Paddy Bradley in the ten minutes before half-time swept newly crowned Leinster champions Westmeath out of another quarter-final. Mayo stepped up the tempo against Tyrone in response to a Stephen O'Neill equalising goal ten minutes after half-time with points from Trevor Mortimer, Alan Dillon and David Brady. Dublin hit just three scores from play in their quarter-final as Kerry captain Dara Ó Cinneide swept in for a 46th-minute goal.

Fermanagh took Mayo to a replay in the semi-final, substitute James Sherry scoring their goal in the 31st minute and Colm Bradley giving them the lead twice in the second half before Mayo staged a strong finish.

Points from Trevor Mortimer and Austin O'Malley clinched Mayo's two-point victory. A series of Fermanagh wides in the final stages allowed Mayo off the hook the first day, while a goal chance for Ciaran O'Reilly was saved by Peter Burke.

Colm Cooper scored six superb points in Kerry's semi-final victory over Derry and sent Declan O'Sullivan through for a goal four minutes from the end.

Kerry won the 2004 All-Ireland final, thanks to man of the match Gooch Cooper's 25th-minute solo-effort goal, which put the match beyond Mayo's reach. Alan Dillon scored a goal in the first half, and Michael Conroy had a consolation goal for Mayo in injury time.

25 SEPTEMBER 2005. TYRONE 1-16, KERRY 2-10, CROKE PARK

> 'There was never an issue with the Kerry team and northern opposition. Any team you were playing you wanted to beat. If we were playing Kilkenny in the All-Ireland football final it would be the same.'
>
> DARRAGH Ó SÉ

Leinster champions Westmeath bowed out to fourteen-man Kildare, who lost forward Ronan Sweeney to a second yellow card on 20 minutes. Tadhg Fennin punched Kildare's crucial goal against unlucky Wicklow immediately after Wicklow's Thomas Harney had put daylight between the sides with their second goal. Kildare rattled off five more scores without reply.

'Wonderfully combustible' was Tom Humphries' phrase for the quarter-final between Dublin and Meath that was decided by Alan Brogan's seventeenth-minute goal, Mark Vaughan's two nerveless frees late in the match and Brogan's crucial intervention in the square a minute from the end of normal time to thwart a goal chance for Daithí Regan. Humphries paid tribute to Seán Boylan, in his seventeenth and last year as manager. 'Without Trevor Giles, handing debuts to five young fellas and operating to the alleged indifference of most of his countymen, his team led by two points at half-time having splurged with five wides into the bargain.'

The irony of Mick O'Dwyer's Laois slipping a late goal past Offaly in front of the Hill was not lost on those who saw Ross Munnelly's 71st-minute goal decide the quarter-final on a day Offaly kicked twenty wides.

Substitute Jason Sherlock scored Dublin's winning goal in the semi-final against Wexford with just over ten minutes left to play, and Dublin had equalised. Ciarán Whelan was sent off for a second booking just moments after Sherlock's goal.

Dublin's free-taker Tomás Quinn scored a 46 metre free in the 70th minute and a 45 in injury time to beat Laois in an enthralling final. Dublin started better, but Laois came back with the help of two five-point runs with Ross Munnelly centrally involved in many of them. Chris Conway's 63rd-minute point put Laois 0-13 to 0-11 ahead.

London led Roscommon by two points at half-time in their first round Connacht championship match, thanks to a fine twelfth-minute goal by Shane McInerney after a well-judged free kick by man of the match, midfielder Senan Hehir.

'We left ourselves with too much to do after a poor first half performance,' Leitrim manager Dessie Dolan mourned, after bowing out by three points to

Galway in the semi-final. Leitrim trailed by six points at half-time before Leitrim substitute Donal Brennan and Galway's Gareth Phelan exchanged goals.

Galway's Micheál Meehan scored the late point that sealed the title, with new Mayo-born manager Peter Ford stepping in after seven years with John O'Mahony. Mayo went 26 minutes of the first half without landing a point.

Kerry's 42nd-minute goal from Declan O'Sullivan crucially gave them the lead for the first time in the Munster final against Cork, and they went on to win by three points. Cork could only score two more points, from James Masters and substitute Phillip Clifford

Armagh cancelled out Tyrone's four-point lead in the last minute of the Ulster final, when Steven McDonnell took Oisín McConville's floated ball for a goal, then Paul McGrane rose to fetch the kick-out and scored an equaliser. Oisin McConville's two points in injury time won the replay, after Ryan Mellon had hit the post for Tyrone. Peter Canavan entered the field, only to be immediately sent off on a harsh straight red by referee Michael Collins. Stephen O'Neill, scorer of ten points in the drawn match, followed him just five minutes later.

The qualifiers threw up a historic rivalry. Cavan beat Meath with a 22nd-minute goal from Jason O'Reilly. Meath came back to within a point with a 71st-minute penalty from Graham Geraghty, but Finbarr O'Reilly scored a free 50 seconds later to give Cavan an insurance point. Stand-in manager Marty McElkennon saw his goalkeeper James Reilly save Brendan Devenney's late penalty against Donegal. Larry Reilly (Cavan, nineteen minutes) and Brendan Devenney (Donegal, 45 minutes) exchanged goals. Louth surprised Roscommon with an injury-time free from J. P. Rooney. Meath needed extra time to beat Leitrim, Ollie Murphy coming off the bench to score a levelling point in the first minute of injury time after James Glancy scored the Leitrim goal in the 53rd minute.

Owen Mulligan's 50th-minute goal and seven points helped Tyrone beat the Dubs. Stephen O'Neill also scored a first half goal before a late goal from Dessie Farrell helped improve the scoreline. Tomas Quinn rescued the Dubs the first day with a pressure free deep into stoppage time. A goal from Tomas Quinn in stoppage time gave Dublin a five-point half-time lead, but Tyrone hauled them back with Owen Mulligan's goal in the fourteenth minute of the second half.

Peter Canavan was Tyrone's semi-final hero, kicking the winning point in the second minute of stoppage time to avenge defeat by Armagh in the Ulster final. Stephen O'Neill scored a penalty in first half stoppage time for Tyrone. Stephen McDonnell squeezed home a goal eleven minutes from the end for Armagh. Kerry too were in the revenge business, taking command of their semi-final against Munster champions Cork to lead 0-11 to 0-4 at half-time, Eoin Brosnan scoring the only goal of the game nine minutes into the second half.

Tyrone won their second championship in three years, thanks to Peter Canavan's classic goal just before the break, and later on by his outstanding defence, crucial in limiting the threat from Colm Cooper. Tomas Ó Sé's opportunist goal in the 56th minute gave Kerry hope of salvaging their title. Kerry's first goal came after six minutes, when scores were level at 0-2 each, and Colm Cooper's ingenuity and a mistake by left corner back Michael McGee left Dara Ó Cinnéide with the relatively easy task of putting the ball in the net. Cooper then suffered an injury in an off-the-ball incident in the ninth minute.

17 SEPTEMBER 2006. KERRY 4-15, MAYO 3-5, CROKE PARK

> 'The hips were bad on my grandmother, so they brought her in on a wheelchair. Get me an ould goal, she said.'
>
> KIERAN DONAGHY

Cork led 0-7 to 0-1 in the first half of the drawn Munster final against Kerry. Masters scored all but one of Cork's nine points in their semi-final against an impressive Limerick team. In the drawn match he scored seven points, including the equalising free, and had a would-be winning point disallowed as one of the umpires raised a white flag and the other signalled a wide. Cork's James Masters scored the crucial goal after 21 minutes of the replay, and added six points. Kerry hit fifteen wides to Cork's thirteen.

Leitrim's Michael McGuinness, attempting to block, deflected the ball into his own net in the Connacht semi-final against Mayo. Leitrim came from eight points down to fail by one against Mayo, having missed some late chances.

Mayo came from behind to win the Connacht title with Conor Mortimer's left-footed injury-time point. Galway led 0-5 to 0-4 at half-time, before Matthew Clancy beat Mayo goalkeeper John Healy to a bouncing ball with a flick of his hand 25 minutes from the end.

Offaly used six substitutes in the Leinster quarter-final against Kildare, but the DRA ruled the substitution of Pascal Kelleghan by James Coughlan, after the former had been asked to leave the field by the referee, was not what the DRA termed a 'counting substitution' as it was covered by the rules on temporary replacement for a blood injury. Offaly won with goals from Alan McNamee, a Niall McNamee penalty and Thomas Deehan, despite being down to fourteen men for the last 25 minutes. Longford pulled 0-5 to 0-1 ahead of Dublin before Dublin settled. Mark Vaughan snuck in for a goal, although Longford finished strongly, cutting back the margin with points from Peter Foy, David Barden, James Martin and Brian Kavanagh.

Offaly's two-man full forward line, Thomas Deehan and Niall McNamee, scored the first half goals to beat Wexford in the semi-final.

Dublin's 67th-minute goal from Jason Sherlock under Hill 16 killed off Offaly in the Leinster final. Offaly's best chance was when Cathal Daly was brought down by Dublin goalkeeper Cluxton at the end of the first half. Niall McNamee missed the close-in free, reviving memories of his nightmare miss from a similar position in the narrow defeat by Laois a year earlier.

Armagh needed a late free from Oisin McConville to draw with Fermanagh in the semi-final, after Fermanagh goals at the start of each half from Tom Brewster and substitute Ryan Keenan. Fermanagh defender Shane McDermott received a straight red card following a clash with Mackin in the replay, as they went down to a late Armagh flurry, despite a second half goal from Ciaran O'Reilly.

Armagh beat Donegal to win three in a row in Ulster through Paul McGrane's 37th-minute goal.

The qualifiers provided more than their annual quota of surprises. Laois ousted champions Tyrone (memorably described as 'the Taliban of Gaelic football' by television pundit Colm O'Rourke) in a downpour after leading 0-6 to 0-3 at half-time. Westmeath surprised Galway with the help of a Gary Dolan goal midway through the second half.

Mayo needed a stoppage-time equaliser to draw with Laois in a quarter-final that was level on five occasions. Conor Mortimer scored five points in the replay, as Noel Garvan's fisted best goal effort for Laois went inches wide. Cork centre back Ger Spillane scored the stoppage-time winner to beat Donegal. Eoin Brosnan, Kieran Donaghy and Darren O'Sullivan scored Kerry's goals as they came from two points behind to beat Armagh.

Ciaran McDonald's late winner gave Mayo victory over Dublin in a classic semi-final after the sides were level seven times. Conal Keaney scored a 24th-minute goal for Dublin, but Mayo led by a point at half-time. Dublin went six points clear within six minutes of the restart, as Jason Sherlock punched Kevin Bonner's cross to the net. An Andy Moran goal in the 51st minute brought Mayo back to two points and set up the finish. Kerry avenged their Munster final replay defeat against Cork in the other semi-final, with Mike Frank Russell scoring six points.

Kerry then crushed Mayo in the final by thirteen points, having led by the remarkable scoreline of 3-8 to 3-2 at half time. Kerry led by a spirit-crushing 2-4 to nil after thirteen minutes, thanks to two goals in the space of a minute, Declan O'Sullivan playing a one-two with Kieran Donaghy to score, before

Donaghy himself rose high to field, turn and shoot high to the net.

Mayo's first score was a Kevin O'Neill goal in the sixteenth minute, but Kerry hit back with a third goal after 26 minutes, when Colm Cooper squeezed the ball in from a tight angle after goalkeeper David Clarke had pushed his initial effort on to a post. Mayo finished the half with two goals. Kevin O'Neill created the opening for midfielder Pat Harte to blast home, then O'Neill grabbed his second after Ciaran McDonald's shot had come back off a post. Brosnan clipped home Kerry's fourth goal in stoppage time, after a poor second half disrupted by a series of scuffles.

16 SEPTEMBER 2007. KERRY 3-13, CORK 1-9, CROKE PARK

> 'It wasn't going to be a derby. It was an All-Ireland final. And it was going to be tough. We tackled a lot. Our half backs and our half forwards were exceptional. It was our tackling and our working—that's really where games are gone and lost.'
>
> DARRAGH Ó SÉ after the 2007 All-Ireland final

Louth needed three attempts to beat Wicklow in the 2007 Leinster championship, then John O'Brien netted in the fourth minute after a slick move. Incredibly, Mark Stanfield's penalty shot for Louth bounced back off both uprights before J. P. Rooney landed it in the net.

Meath substitute Cian Ward scored the quarter-final equaliser against Dublin from a line ball at the Cusack Stand side. Dublin's goal before half-time was controversial. With Brendan Murphy under pressure from Alan Brogan, the goalkeeper fumbled and the ball dropped into the net. Graham Geraghty had a goal controversially disallowed for a push on full back Ross McConnell. Free-taker Mark Vaughan scored eight points to give Dublin victory in the replay. Graham Geraghty fired a shot off the post and missed another goal chance when put through one-on-one with Dublin goalkeeper Stephen Cluxton.

Michael Tierney scored seven points as Laois came from behind to beat Wexford in the semi-final. They equalised through Paul Lawlor's 47th-minute goal, having fallen 7-2 behind at one stage in the first half, and hitting nine wides in the process.

Dublin beat Laois comfortably 3-14 to 1-14 in the Leinster semi-final, with two first half goals within a minute of each other from Mark Vaughan and Bernard Brogan after Ross Munnelly's goal helped Laois into an early lead, and a third from Alan Brogan.

Kerry beat Cork by two points in the Munster final with injury-time points from Kieran Donaghy and Seán O'Sullivan, as Cork missed out on a late goal and had a penalty claim turned down. After Colm 'Gooch' Cooper scored 1-2 at the start of the second half, Donnacha O'Connor responded with a Cork goal.

Brendan Devenney gave Donegal a 1-9 to 1-8 victory over Armagh in the Ulster championship and revenge for five defeats in five years, his high ball going straight to the net after Oisín McConville had given Armagh the edge with a first half goal. 'That was a cross,' Devenney said afterwards. Reflecting one of the wettest summers on record, the quarter-final between Antrim and Derry was postponed due to a waterlogged pitch at Casement Park.

Tyrone won a third Ulster title in seven years, urged on by Philip Jordan's early goal. Monaghan came back after Thomas Freeman's 51st-minute goal, but were left to mourn two late goal chances for Vincent Corey, one brilliantly saved by Tyrone goalkeeper John Devine, the other blasted over the bar. They went the first eight minutes without a score, as Tyrone scored 1-3.

Sligo outscored Roscommon by 0-9 to 0-1 in the final half-hour of the Connacht semi-final, cancelling out goals from Karol Mannion and Cathal Cregg. Galway blew away Mayo with two well-timed goals from Cormac Bane, a former pupil of Galway manager Peter Ford. Donal Brennan's goal gave Leitrim a 1-9 to 1-2 lead over London at half-time, only for London to finish with thirteen men. Gary McCloskey scored Leitrim's goal in the semi-final against Galway.

Sligo captured their first Connacht title since 1975, and their third overall, Eamon O'Hara finishing the best phase of football in the match with a stunning goal after 24 minutes, before he was forced to retire and watch the finish from the sideline. Twice in the second half Galway edged back to within one point, before Michael McNamara scored the winning point in the 70th minute.

To reduce fixture congestion, Antrim, Carlow, Clare, London, Offaly, Tipperary, Waterford and Wicklow were removed from the 2007 championship qualifiers and placed in the Tommy Murphy Cup instead. Monaghan's was the story of the 2007 qualifying series. Defender Tomas Ó Sé fisted over the match-winning point in Kerry's quarter-final against Monaghan. Monaghan started with a Tommy Freeman goal to go 1-2 to 0-1 ahead. Monaghan had gone three points ahead once more when the ball broke off a defender for a crucial Declan O'Sullivan goal after 57 minutes. Two Stephen Bray goals in the space of four minutes helped Meath come back against Galway, as Graham Geraghty made an inspiring comeback, weeks after his training ground bust-up with a fellow panellist. He then scored the goal that beat Tyrone in the quarter-final. Seán Cavanagh and Eoin Mulligan scored Tyrone's goals, as Meath failed to score for the last sixteen minutes, and yet held their lead.

Kerry started the second half of their semi-final against Dublin with a goal from Declan O'Sullivan, following a lovely pass from Killian Young. Dublin whittled the margin back from six points to one, before Declan O'Sullivan's reassurance point in the fifth minute of injury time.

Kerry won the 2007 All-Ireland final less easily than the 3-13 to 1-9 margin suggests. Disaster befell Cork 27 seconds into the second half, when Kieran Donaghy goaled after dispossessing Ger Spillane, possibly fouling him in the process, to kick into an empty net. Donaghy scored a third goal twelve minutes later. The goals were the result of a change of strategy by Kerry, to get the ball into inside players faster, and it paid off. The scores were level three times up to the fifteenth minute, and Kerry did not have matters all their own way even after man of the match Colm Cooper scored an opportunist goal for Kerry to lead 1-6 to 0-6 at half-time.

'Was Cork's utter collapse triggered by calamitous individual mistakes,' *Examiner* sports editor Tony Leen asked, 'or were those howlers a result of the Rebels' fragile state of mind?' Within months Cork's football squad were in open rebellion against their team manager, sparking a three-year revolution in the appropriately nicknamed Rebel county.

21 SEPTEMBER 2008. TYRONE 1-15, KERRY 0-14, CROKE PARK

> 'Do we want to be the team that let Kerry win the three in a row or do we want to be the team that stopped them doing it?'
>
> MICKEY HARTE's dressing room speech prior to the 2008 All-Ireland final

Cork completed three in a row in the Munster championships, but found they were now losing out to their rivals when the more serious business commenced in August. In the 2008 Munster semi-final, Cork left it late, trailing Limerick by three points with less than two minutes remaining, before Daniel Goulding and Graham Canty pounced on defensive and goalkeeping errors to score two late goals. Cork then trailed by eight points at half-time in the Munster final, thanks to a thirteenth-minute goal from Kerry's Donnacha Walsh, before turning the match round to win by five. Substitute Michael Cussen scored Cork's second half goal. Kerry finished with thirteen players following the dismissals of Darragh and Tomás Ó Sé in the second half.

Kerry then avenged their Munster final defeat against Cork at the second attempt in the All-Ireland semi-final after Cork had come back from eight points down entering injury time of the semi-final, James Masters fisting a goal through Diarmuid Murphy's legs, followed by a controversial 71st-minute penalty goal by John Hayes.

In Leinster, Laois kicked fifteen points from play and also fifteen wides in beating Wicklow, who had knocked out Kildare with ten points between them from Tony Hannon and Seanie Furlong while Kildare hit eleven wides. Goals from Alan Mangan and Denis Glennon helped Westmeath beat Longford.

Wexford came back from eleven points down to beat Meath, under rookie manager Jason Ryan. Goals from Stephen Bray and Graham Geraghty gave Meath a 2-8 to 0-4 half-time lead. Wexford clawed their way back into the tie with goals from Redmond Barry and P. J. Banville and, in a dramatic finish, two late points from Matty Forde. Meath had midfielder Mark Ward sent off and also had a disallowed goal from Joe Sheridan. In the semi-final, Wexford wiped out an early two-point deficit against Laois by the twelfth minute, and never fell behind for the rest of the game.

Wexford's form came unstuck in the Leinster final. Dublin's second half goals from Diarmuid Connolly, Alan Brogan and substitute Mark Vaughan gave them an easy title. In the semi-final Dermot Bannon fisted Westmeath's goal after seven minutes, but Dublin came from behind to win with points from substitute Diarmuid Connolly and defender Colin Moran.

Referee Paraic Hughes booked nine New York players in a Connacht championship first round match in Gaelic Park and sent off Dermot Keane in the dying minutes.

Galway beat Mayo in the Connacht final by a point, thanks to first half goals from Pádraic Joyce and Fiachra Breathnach, and late points from Cormac Bane and substitutes Seán Armstrong and Paul Conroy. After Aidan Kilcoyne's 55th-minute goal gave Mayo the lead, Billy Joe Padden added two big second half points and Pat Harte a third to give Mayo a three-point lead before Pádraic Joyce steadied Galway's nerves.

Fermanagh came the closest they ever had to winning an Ulster title, losing to Armagh in a replay, having waited 26 years for an Ulster final and then played two in eight days. They came back from seven points down. A goal from Eamonn Maguire and points from Mark Little and Mark Murphy set up a dramatic late equalising point for Shaun Doherty. Armagh's Stevie McDonnell scored the goal that secured a six-point victory in the replay.

Tyrone raced into a four-point lead in extra time of their replay against Down. Down roared back and Benny Coulter fisted a goal for a lead they never subsequently lost. Tyrone then began a successful All-Ireland campaign through the qualifier series.

Limerick dispatched Meath for the surprise of the qualifier series with an Ian Ryan hat-trick and what the *Irish Examiner* described as near perfect displays from full back Johnny McCarthy, centre back Stephen Lavin, midfielder John Galvin and centre forward James Ryan. Graham Geraghty retired from inter-county football after the match. Other surprises included

Wexford's quarter-final win over Armagh.

Tyrone's virtuoso victory over Dublin in the quarter-final was the highlight of the qualifier series, one of the best displays of the year, and indeed the decade. They were contesting dominance with an increasingly jumpy Kerry. 'There's an arrogance to northern football which rubs Kerry people up the wrong way,' Kerry manager Jack O'Connor complained. 'They're flash and *nouveau riche* and full of it.' He also said that losing to Tyrone was worse than losing to almost anybody else.

Tyrone's All-Ireland final-winning goal against Kerry came just 22 seconds into the second half, kicked to the net by Tommy McGuigan, after Kevin Hughes, with his first touch of the ball after coming on as a sub, exchanged passes with Stephen O'Neill, and the ball dribbled across the goalmouth, Pádraig Reidy falling on his back as he desperately attempted to kick it clear.

Tyrone goalkeeper John Devine's father died the day before the final, and his replacement O'Connell made two decisive saves, the second with his feet in the 66th minute from Declan O'Sullivan.

Kieran Donaghy had put Kerry ahead after 57 minutes, but Kerry failed to score again as Tyrone tacked on five points, three in the last two minutes, to give the scoreline a more decisive look. 'The team of the decade is Tyrone,' Tyrone forward Brian McGuigan asserted in the dressing room after the match. 'There is no doubt about it.'

Former Kerry star Jack O'Shea wasn't so sure. 'They have won three to Kerry's four. Tyrone have shown that they are a great team. To be considered the best team of the era they will have to avoid their usual trend of disappearing for a year.'

It was the first All-Ireland final between two teams which had been beaten in the championship, the most traditional of champions, with their 35 titles, and the last of the nineteen counties to have won the championship, both squaring up to assert their dominance of the new age.

20 SEPTEMBER 2009. KERRY 0-16, CORK 1-9. CROKE PARK

> 'Pearse O'Neill was like a runaway train. He'll be going through Mallow around 6.15.'
>
> Television analyst COLM O'ROURKE after Cork beat Tyrone in the All-Ireland football semi-final, 23 August 2009

The much-anticipated showdown for team of the decade never took place. Instead, the championship threw up its second all-Munster final in three years.

While it was Kerry who struggled most in the early stages of the 2009 championship, losing a replayed Munster semi-final to Cork and stuttering against Longford and Sligo in the qualifiers, they won the title. Tyrone lost to the under-performers of the decade, Cork, in a semi-final that attracted a poor attendance of 52,492 but a record 622,000 television viewers. This was a surprise considering Tyrone's impressive run through Ulster, and a two-point victory over an emerging Kildare team.

The unpredictability and tactical innovation that was the theme of the championship came at some cost to the spectator. Kerry abandoned what one of their greatest players, Pat Spillane, now a television analyst, described as the 'twin towers' approach of 2008, utilising long ball into a slimmed down full-forward line. Instead, they adopted a variety of approaches that occasionally seemed to confuse themselves as often as their opponents.

Against Longford, Sligo and Antrim, Kerry narrowly won matches they might have lost. They then switched tactics again and crushed Dublin by seventeen points, a margin last seen in the Mikey Sheehy and Bomber Liston final of 1978. Nostalgia helped swell the attendance to 81,892.

The under-achievers of the noughties, Cork, outplayed Kerry twice in the Munster semi-final. They lost a five-point lead with eleven minutes to go, a Bryan Sheehan free earning Kerry a replay in the third minute of injury time. Donncha O'Connor scored the goal as they then won the replay by seven points.

Niall McKeever emerged as the new star of the year as Antrim defeated Donegal and Cavan to reach their first Ulster final since 1970, but they were then outmanoeuvred by the wily Tyrone manager Mickey Harte. A nineteenth-minute Tony Scullion goal fired them up in the qualifiers against Kerry, before they succumbed to Kerry's big finish, scoring four of the last five points.

Mickey Ned O'Sullivan's Limerick came within a point of Cork in the Munster final, only to rue a dubious penalty award and a missed goal chance by wing-back Stephen Lavin nearing half-time. Sligo took Kerry to one point in the third round of the qualifiers.

Cork brushed aside Donegal with astonishing ease before rocking Tyrone in the All-Ireland semi-final. Each of the six forwards scored, and Daniel Goulding landed a rebound goal in the first 20 minutes of the match. They survived a late siege, down to fourteen men, and scored just five points in the last 20 minutes, attributing their victory to the fact tht it was their sixth match against Ulster opponents that season.

Dublin and Kildare both overcame their opponents in Leinster, only for both to lose their quarter-finals. Instead, it was Meath—losers in one of the most disappointing of their serial encounters with Dublin—who went furthest of the Leinster teams. Their semi-final against Kerry was dictated by a goal from a farcical penalty by Darran O'Sullivan in the second minute, another from Tommy Walsh 45 seconds into the second half; and although Meath's high-ball approach yielded a consolation goal in injury time, it was Kerry who emerged from the scrap. Meath utilised a predictable long high ball into attack. Kerry chose to break the ball to loose team-mates. The result was the poorest semi-final in six years, a bench mark for unattractive football with 31 wides and poor underfoot conditions on a pitch which had just been relaid after a U2 concert five weeks earlier.

Connacht provided the best of the provincial finals. Mayo lost a seven-point lead with ten minutes to go when Michael Meehan scored a late equaliser. Galway then missed a free to go ahead, and Mayo's Peadar Gardiner scored the winning point in added time.

Cork raced into an early lead as a tenth-minute goal from Colm O'Neill put the Munster men 1-3 to 0-1 in front, but Kerry moved ahead 0-8 to 1-4, led 0-11 to 1-6 and controlled a low-scoring second half, with 0-5 to Cork's 0-3.

A pattern was emerging. Over the eight years after the introduction of the qualifier series in 2001, an average of two provincial champions each year were destined to lose the quarter-finals. The casualty rate was just one in 2002 and 2006, and three in 2008.

Of the first 32 quarter-finals, seventeen were won by provincial champions and fifteen by qualifier teams. The geographical spread was surprisingly even. Sixteen different counties featured among the 64 quarter-final qualifiers, with 20 appearances by five Ulster counties (out of a possible nine), eighteen by five Leinster counties (out of twelve), and thirteen each by two Munster (out of six) and four Connacht counties (out of five). Tellingly, Munster had served up both All-Ireland finalists twice and Ulster once.

It seemed the innovators of the second biggest change in championship history had achieved their ambition without diminishing the provincial structures that had served the GAA so well.

12 OCTOBER 1997. MONAGHAN 2-15, WATERFORD 1-16, CROKE PARK

> 'In an extraordinary climax to a thrilling game Monaghan equalised six minutes into injury time, before adding two more points, in the next six, to retain the title.'
>
> MARY HANNIGAN, *The Irish Times*, 13 October 1997

It was not just the All-Ireland finals that were drawing bigger crowds. Women's football, nursed into life in the 1960s, began to enjoy bigger live and television audiences as the 1990s progressed.

The revolution, as had so many others in Irish history, started in west

Clare. Tom Garry from Clonreddin started a women's GAA league in Cooraclare parish in 1926. The idea petered out, but interestingly, Cooraclare was one of the first clubs to reorganise when women's football restarted 50 years later.

Representatives from Galway, Kerry, Offaly and Tipperary created Cumann Peile Gael na mBan at a consciously footstepped foundation meeting at Hayes's Hotel in Thurles in 1974.

Offaly, south Tipperary, north Cork and west Waterford were the early strongholds of the game. As well as the four founders, Cork, Laois, Roscommon and Waterford also entered the first championship.

Tournaments in Ballycommon, Tullamore, Clonmel and Dungarvan in 1968 led to the new game's biggest innovation, when women were permitted to lift the ball directly off the ground. Unlike camogie, a full-sized pitch was used. A well-organised Tipperary team, trained at Rockwell College by John O'Donovan, won the first two All-Irelands in 1974 and 1975.

But it was football powerhouse Kerry which dominated women's football in the 1980s, winning nine consecutive All-Ireland championships, with star players such as nine-times All-Star Mary Jo Curran, the unrelated goalkeeper Kathleen Curran, and Annette Walsh.

It claimed to be Ireland's fastest growing participation sport from the early 1990s on, when membership rose to 27,000. Croke Park staged the finals from 1986 on. Thousands of girls began to play in primary school leagues organised by Cumann na mBunscoil throughout the country and games are played in Britain, mainland Europe, Australia, Canada, and the US, where it has a wider following among non-Irish American players than men's football.

Interest was, in the manner of these things, boosted by the controversy over the All-Ireland final of 1997, when twelve minutes of injury time were allowed. The unwanted publicity boosted the profile of the game enormously. An experimental clock was introduced in 1998, just as the rivalry between Monaghan and Waterford, which had captivated the nation, was coming to an end.

Inspired by the Monaghan-Waterford sparring matches, attendances sneaked up to rank among the highest for any female only team sports event in the world, from 2,000 in 1990 to 13,964 in 1996, 15,051 in 1997, 16,421 in 1998, 14,915 in 2000, 21,207 in 2001, 22,783 in 2002, 20,706 in 2004, 23,358 in 2005, 25,665 in 2006, 21,237 in 2007 and 20,015 in 2008. It gave a higher profile to new stars like Cora Staunton of Mayo and helped boost the game in new counties.

The new popularity had its own epic, the All-Ireland semi-final of 2004, which went to four matches before Galway won in extra time by a single point, thanks to a Niamh Duggan goal. Galway completed their remarkable advance from junior to senior champions, beating the Dublin 'Jackies' in the final.

Crucially, the women's football final was televised live after 1997, bringing stars like Jenny Greenan of Monaghan, Sue Ramsbottom of Laois and Diane O'Hora of Mayo to national prominence. TV achieved audiences of 300,000 and began to exceed the viewing figures for three of Ireland's Six Nations rugby internationals.

17 MARCH 2000. CROSSMAGLEN 1-14, NA FIANNA 0-12, CROKE PARK

> 'Carrick-on-Shannon on a wet, blustery afternoon in November is far removed from the new image which the GAA likes to portray for itself. No corporate boxes here, even fewer prawn sandwiches. No, this was the GAA in the raw, the organisation that has a grip on rural Ireland at least that no other sport can come near. About 1,000 people came out to watch the Connacht club semi-final between Corofin of Galway and Aughavas from Leitrim and if you ever wanted a definition of a GAA die-hard then these 1,000 people were living proof of the existence of the species.'
>
> EUGENE MCGEE writing about a Connacht club championship match between Corofin and Aughavas, *Irish Independent*, 13 November 2001

The potential of the club championship, which had been introduced almost unnoticed and in the face of official apathy, or even opposition, was slowly being realised. What was to become arguably the GAA's most important competition had come into existence and grew out of unofficial club championships in Connacht and Munster. The official ambivalence was similar to that which ensured that a motion to set up a club championship was rejected by the 1948 congress: the calendar was too overcrowded.

The first All-Ireland finals were played in 1971. East Kerry footballers defeated Bryansford of Down before a handful of supporters on a Friday evening in Croke Park. Roscrea beat St Rynagh's of Offaly in the hurling final in Birr, the venue for the first inter-county hurling final, on the Sunday before Christmas.

After a truly heroic performance by the small trouble-scarred village of Bellaghy in defeating UCC on another Friday night in 1972, the competition was dominated by big city clubs and large towns. Cork club Nemo Rangers won the first of four titles in 1973. Eugene McGee's UCD won two in succession.

When they didn't field in the 1975 Dublin championship, they were succeeded by St Vincent's, whose semi-final in the Mardyke against Nemo in 1976 was described as being as good as any inter-county game.

The 1979 final was the first to be played on St Patrick's Day, when Nemo defeated Scotstown of Monaghan in front of 4,443 frozen spectators in a snowstorm. The idea was a success. The 1990 final, in which a Baltinglass team led by Kevin O'Brien brought Wicklow its first national success by beating Roscommon's Clan na Gael 2-7 to 0-7, attracted an attendance of 15,708. The 1993 final, in which Skibbereen club O'Donovan Rossa controversially defeated Eire Og from Carlow in a replay, was watched by 21,714 as part of a double header with the hurling final in Croke Park, and 25,000 for the replay in Limerick. The first All-Ireland victory by one of the dominant club teams in 1997, Crossmaglen Rangers, was watched by 34,852 spectators. When they beat Na Fianna by five points to win their second All-Ireland championship three years later, a record 40,106 showed up. Big urban clubs such as Kilmacud and Killarney Crokes, Nemo Rangers and St Finbarrs, shared the podium with small clubs like Ballinderry, Burren, Caltra, Corofin and Lavey. Knockmore, who competed against Crossmaglen in the 1997 final, don't even have a village to call their own.

28 OCTOBER 1984. AUSTRALIA 76, IRELAND 71, CROKE PARK

> 'This international rules series was a bit like the Vietnam War. Nobody at home cared about it, but everyone involved sure did.'
>
> LEIGH MATTHEWS, the Australian coach

The dream of full international competition between Ireland and Australia, born in Adelaide in March 1970, had not been forgotten.

Another team of Galahs came to Ireland in 1978, heavily beat Dublin before a 12,206 crowd in Croke Park, and lost to Kerry in Pairc Uí Chaoimh, with goalkeeper Charlie Nelligan playing the game of his life. But like its 1960s predecessors, the tour was a financial failure.

An Australian tour by Kerry in 1981 was confined to two GAA teams and a poorly attended Gaelic game in Adelaide. Nobody was interested in watching international Gaelic football.

So, it was to a sense of apathy that the Australians arrived in October 1984 to revive the international contacts between Gaelic football and its Australian cousin.

How close a cousin is a matter of controversy. In Canberra in 1984, Australian sports historians Bill Mandle, Rob Hess and Geoffrey Blainey claimed that the games were unrelated, as undue Irish influence would have led to the new game being shunned by English immigrants in Melbourne. The debate continues.

The Canberra trio argue that the four men who drew up the rules in 1857 were English public schoolboy types, including a graduate of Trinity College in Dublin, not caid-playing gold miners, and there are few Irish names among the early team lists.

The point went largely unanswered, but similarities with Gaelic football persist. Unlike the English public school codes, the founding father of Aussie Rules did not introduce an off-side law, and ruled that a player running with the ball must bounce it along the way. The scoring posts closely resembled Gaelic football, which was not codified until 27 years later.

Vast numbers of Irish who arrived in Victoria during the gold rush in the 1850s were already playing football, and the earliest recorded football match in Australia was between two Irish regiments in Sydney in 1829.

When the first international got under way before a paltry 8,000 attendance in wet windy Pairc Uí Chaoimh, the point of the whole series seemed lost—until a free-for-all erupted in the third quarter. Players, substitutes and management joined in. Australia won 70 points to 57, and their newspapers accused the Irish of being 'Fancy Dans'. National pride was hurt. The crowds swelled.

The second match in Croke Park drew a crowd of 18,000 (12,470 paying, with 6,000 students coming in free). This time there was no bad temper, but a fast-moving dramatic game that the spectators loved. Australia levelled the score at 78 points each with two minutes to go. Chants of 'Ireland, Ireland' rang around the ground as Colm O'Rourke and Clare man Noel Roche kicked the two winning points. It appeared that the international dream had at last been realised. The crowd of 32,318 the third day saw a fist-fight as well as fast dramatic football. Australia took the test series by 76 points to 71.

That was the start that the international series needed. But strangely enough, subsequent tours by Ireland to Australia in 1985 and by the Australians in 1986 did not reach the same level of interest. The experiment was parked from 1986 to 1990. The Australians concentrated instead on turning the Victorian football league into a national competition, with the addition of Sydney Swans, Brisbane and Western Australia (Perth) to the Melbourne clubs.

When an Irish team travelled to Perth, Melbourne and Adelaide in 1986, the series was re-established on an annual basis. Canberra was added to the venues in 1990. In 1998 the number of matches was reduced to two. A pattern emerged that the visiting team usually won the series. Public interest remained high, driving attendances past the 60,000 mark in both countries.

The series had an unexpected impact. Several Irish players were signed by Australian clubs. Two made it to the big time, 1983 Kerry minor Seán Wight (a Scot who lived briefly in Ireland and whose life ambition had been to play in goal for Glasgow Celtic), and 1983 Dublin minor Jimmy Stynes. Stynes was the success story of the Australian connection, a high-earning, highly regarded Melbourne Demons player, winner of the Brownlow medal and later president of the club. Tadhg Fennelly, son of Kerry 1970s star Tim, and Setanta Ó hAilpín followed in the 2000s.

The international rules fixtures, as they were redesignated in 1996, were still sought after by the players, so the revival of the series proved much more popular until, predictably, it ran into more controversy over rule interpretations and a free-for-all which turned the second match in 2006 into a farce.

> 'It is to be hoped that Gaelic football will always remain as natural a game as it is today, and accordingly we trust that, while it will ever be developing on the scientific side, it will never become the possession of the professional player.'
>
> DICK FITZGERALD, *How to Play Gaelic Football* (1914)

By the turn of the twenty-first century, the GAA could claim to be the largest and most successful amateur sports body in an increasingly professionalised world.

Among the visiting sportspeople astonished by this was Austrian skiing team manager Hans Pum, when he stopped by at a Meath training session in 2000. He was enthralled by the fact that this huge organisation retained such an amateur and community ethos. 'I am amazed they play for their region, that they are all in college or at work, and meet a few evenings after work and then at weekends, that they play against each other and that there are no transfers. No money passes hands. You have this extraordinary loyalty to your club, to your home and to your county. It is an ethic you cannot buy. If the game goes professional, you could lose that ethic.'

Even as Pum came to visit, that ethic was coming under threat. Gaelic players were asking themselves why they should not be compensated for their efforts, like their highly paid October opponents from the Australian Rules code.

> 'Look after their expense and look after them well, but that's all. It's an amateur game. It is run by professionals, but every business is. I know if I was getting paid, I wouldn't do the job I'm doing. I tell you that up front. Because there is a different onus on it then. Somebody owns you if they are paying you. Nobody owns me as it is. I'm a Gaelic man and that's it.'
>
> SEÁN BOYLAN, *The Will to Win* (2006)

Dessie Farrell of Dublin became the spokesman for the new 'me' generation. His core argument was that higher standards led to higher demands on players, which were unsustainable without higher rewards. 'There is little doubt that the game as a spectacle is more thrilling now,' he said in his 2005 autobiography, *Tangled Up in Blue*. 'It's certainly faster and more intense. But you have to be almost anal to endure the sacrifices required, and the approach is airbrushing much of the character out of the game.'

In October 1999, Farrell became the first chairman of the new Gaelic Players Association, which drew up a series of demands for financial compensation, and a full-time CEO after 2003.

The structure of the new body was like nothing before seen in Gaelic football circles. Initially, it concentrated on getting higher earnings for commercial endorsements for players. Donal O'Neill, formerly from Mark McCormack's international sports agency IMG, organised a sponsorship deal with drinks manufacturer C&C in 2003.

It was their demand for a compensation scheme that caused most concern, technically not pay for play, but a government-funded grant for all inter-county players. An agreement was reached in November 2007 that the Irish government should fund the operation, and was passed was by GAA congress in April 2008. After nine years of lobbying, within eighteen months the worst financial crisis in decades was casting doubt on the ground-breaking measure.

> 'I don't like the direction football is taking at the moment. People going on about what their diet is and how serious they are about their football. They are almost giving the impression that it is a chore to play for their county. What used to piss me off was players, young fellas, telling you how to play the game, telling you the sacrifices they made. Telling you that there should be a government grant at the end of it. How they felt their image rights were being infringed and all that. You're playing for your county like. There are kids out there who would love to do it.'
>
> DARA Ó CINNÉIDE, interview with Joe Ó Muircheartaigh in *Princes of Pigskin* (2008)

The surprise was that when the GAA decided to defend their amateur ethos, they discovered they hadn't got one.

The debate about amateurism had never been fought in the 1880s when English sporting bodies organising in Ireland were tearing themselves apart over the subject. Michael Cusack's vision for the GAA included a rejection of the farcical rules that banned artisans and policemen from competing under athletics rules. Cash prizes were offered at early GAA athletics meetings. Maurice Davin's observations on the subject in a February 1885 letter, rejecting cash prizes, seems to be a personal view. He had no objection to amateur GAA athletes competing alongside professionals, a view that was to prove pragmatic in future years when full-time soccer players like Kevin

Moran were allowed to play on GAA championship teams.

The GAA had not bothered subsequently to have an amateur code. Only in 1954 did the GAA finally adopt a position on its own amateur status, or as it increasingly liked to refer to it 'the amateur ethos'.

In its earliest days, prize money was offered to its athletes. The first mention of amateur status was a lone voice, J. Down of Cork, protesting over the formation of a separate company to manage the Jones's Road grounds in 1914. A 1920s conflict over control of handball suggested that amateurism, if not yet on the rule book, was at least a core GAA value. The expulsion of Belfast Celtic in 1925 that led to the bifurcation of athletics on the island was initially for a breach of rules on professionalism.

In 1926 the GAA queried that Tipperary's Chicago opponents on a hurling tour of the US would all be amateur. Kerry players travelling to America in 1927 were asked to sign declarations promising to conform to amateur status and to return within four months.

Ironically, the GAA came closest to professionalism when it was most steadfastly amateur. The idea of gathering a group of players together for full-time training for a few weeks in advance of an All-Ireland final became an accepted part of GAA culture between 1913 and 1954.

By the early 1950s training payments had risen to up to £18 per man per week, and training camp bills to £1,200. Mick Higgins recalls that the Cavan players were paid £4 in training for the 1952 final. That year Kerry introduced collective training for an All-Ireland semi-final for the first time (they did so again in 1953), adjourning to Lawlor's Hotel in Ballyheigue under the care of Roundy Landers, instead of the absent Eamonn O'Sullivan, to prepare for a replay against Mayo which they lost.

The idea had spread down the grades. Donegal and Leitrim introduced paid training for its junior football teams in preparation for the 1952 All-Ireland semi-final and final.

Eventually, it was at the 1954 congress that a rule on amateurism was introduced as part of a move to curtail paid collective training. The ban had been briefly tried as a result of an Antrim motion to congress, banning expenses for collective training in 1927 amidst a previous scare about professionalism in the GAA, but was overturned by Kerry and other strong rural counties. The issue of collective training had been condemned by GAA secretary Pádraig Ó Caoimh in his reports to congress for several years.

A committee which included Dermot Bourke of Kildare and Patsy Devlin of Cavan found that the 'players brought together for a period or periods of full-time training receive payment in cash or kind and, consequently the committee are satisfied [*sic*] that full-time training is inconsistent with the amateur status of the members of the Gaelic Athletic Association, and recommend to the Central Council that such full-time training should be prohibited.'

The debate which ensued pitted hurling counties against football counties. Kerry, Cavan and Roscommon were proponents of full-time training; hurling counties Cork, Kilkenny and Tipperary were against, as were Galway, Waterford and the 1954 motion sponsors Kildare. Kerry claimed the geography of the county made evening training impossible, and even blamed their 1927 defeat against Kildare on the temporary ban on full-time training at the time.

But by the time it was banned, motor cars were freely available in even the smallest communities, so the problem was looking after itself. One anonymous ex-footballer pleaded in the *Irish Independent* of 31 January 1954, that unless paid training was stopped, 'Commercialism will expand and idealism die, and with it that splendid selfless service on which the GAA has rightly prided itself.'

John D. Hickey opined: 'It all boils down to the fact there has been too much pampering of players. Most followers of our national games are agreed that there would be fewer trouble makers were the game, rather than victory, the main consideration.' The motion banning full-time training passed by 95–56 and the GAA declared for the first time: 'The Association is an amateur association. Payment or other material rewards (officially approved trophies excepted) for participation in games and pastimes under the control of the Association is expressly forbidden.'

> 'You can't wash this lot.'
>
> Bendix washing machine ad featuring the 1985 Kerry team

That was that, until the debate re-emerged unexpectedly in 1971 in relation to GAA members playing professional sport after the removal of the ban, even as the debate over amateurism in sports like tennis, soccer and show jumping had been resolved, and that in Rugby Union was gathering pace.

The issue was parked, although a Thurles juvenile club, St Patrick's, was banned in 1977 for paying players to score goals. The practice had started in its soccer section and was extended to Gaelic football in mid-Tipp Bord na nÓg competitions.

Under the radar, a system of payment for play had already been practised by clubs who used illegal players. Kerry player James Mixie Palmer recalled that he played for fifteen clubs when he was studying in Cork in the 1940s, and 'if your team won and you played well, you'd get a fiver'.

As had happened with tennis and rugby, the next battleground was a series of endorsement controversies, starting with the suspension of Cork footballers for six months for wearing branded Adidas gear in 1976. The ban was subsequently lifted, but it predicated years of disharmony in the south.

Adidas moved in aggressively on the Irish market by supplying, for free, football boots to key county players, equipment that most players had been asked to purchase from their own pocket only a few years earlier. Mick Holden, most famously, played in the 1983 All-Ireland final with a Puma boot on one foot and an Adidas boot on the other, claiming that he had fulfilled the terms of his contract, and adding that he wasn't known for his accurate kicking anyway.

Kerry received £10,000 towards an Australian tour fund in 1981 for posing for a team picture with Adidas logos. Another promotion by the Kerry team for a Bendix washing machine in 1985 went uncensored, as the negotiations had been previously cleared by Croke Park.

In December 1985, the GAA made another doomed attempt to protect its endorsement policy. A special congress forbade members becoming involved in any endorsements or wearing any branded gear.

This coincided with a period of flagrant abuse of the amateur ethos in another area. Barely hidden pay for play deals were being made available for weekending footballers from well-funded émigré clubs in New York. From the mid-1970s the New York GAA, outside the control of the Central Council, was offering players increasingly lucrative incentives to travel to play in Gaelic Park. In 1988 and 89 over 200 players travelled for match fees and occasionally were facilitated for longer stays.

It soon became apparent that managers too were being paid—what a 1985 investigating subcommittee called 'excessive fees and travelling expenses'—to bring success to clubs and county teams.

Soon, players were able to demand hefty signing on fees to move clubs. Much of the largesse was in the form of perks. One Dublin footballer publicly thanked his new club for the provision of his car at a victory ceremony in Parnell Park. In reaction to this, a newly thought out amateur ethos allowing standardised expenses, paid squad holidays, free training gear, increased food allowances, medical and dental cover, and legalising endorsements, but not pay for play, was re-inserted in the rule book in 1997, with little effect.

By 2000 the Gaelic Players Association had adopted a more combative attitude towards Croke Park than any of their predecessors, and began to organise the first threats of industrial action in GAA history. A threat to delay the throw-in of all National Football League matches on 9 April 2006 by fifteen minutes and a threat of all-out strike on 11 November 2007 were signs of the increased militancy of Farrell's organisation. Neither action caused disruption, but there were other areas where the players were demanding more say in their own affairs.

In Carlow, a brief strike followed an argument between the county board and the supporters' association, which funded the increasing number of perks available to players.

In Cork, a series of disputes over the appointment of team managers led to the county missing the start of the 2008 National League season and an arbitration process by which trade union veteran Kieran Mulvey recommended that the players have two positions on a seven-member committee that would decide future managerial appointments.

The decision had an immediate impact on every county and club team in the country. Managers in Donegal and Waterford were forced to resign on the unique grounds that they had lost the confidence of the players. Players were being given a control over their own destiny which was unprecedented in the sporting world.

It was the biggest change in the culture that Hans Pum admired so much since the emergence of the managerial system in the 1970s.

At 125 years of age, Gaelic football was experimenting once more. Tinkering with the playing rules has long been a GAA characteristic. Down the years they have ruled on the tackle, the hand pass, the toe to hand. They have toyed with disciplinary codes and bans. They have tied themselves in knots with demands for Irish language teamsheets and watermarked paper. They have divided matches into quarters and offered up different lengths of time for different stages of a competition.

Throughout it all, Gaelic football has retained its own characteristics. After 125 years, the game that had such an uncertain beginning has a most secure and certain future.

INDEX